Early Medieval Munster

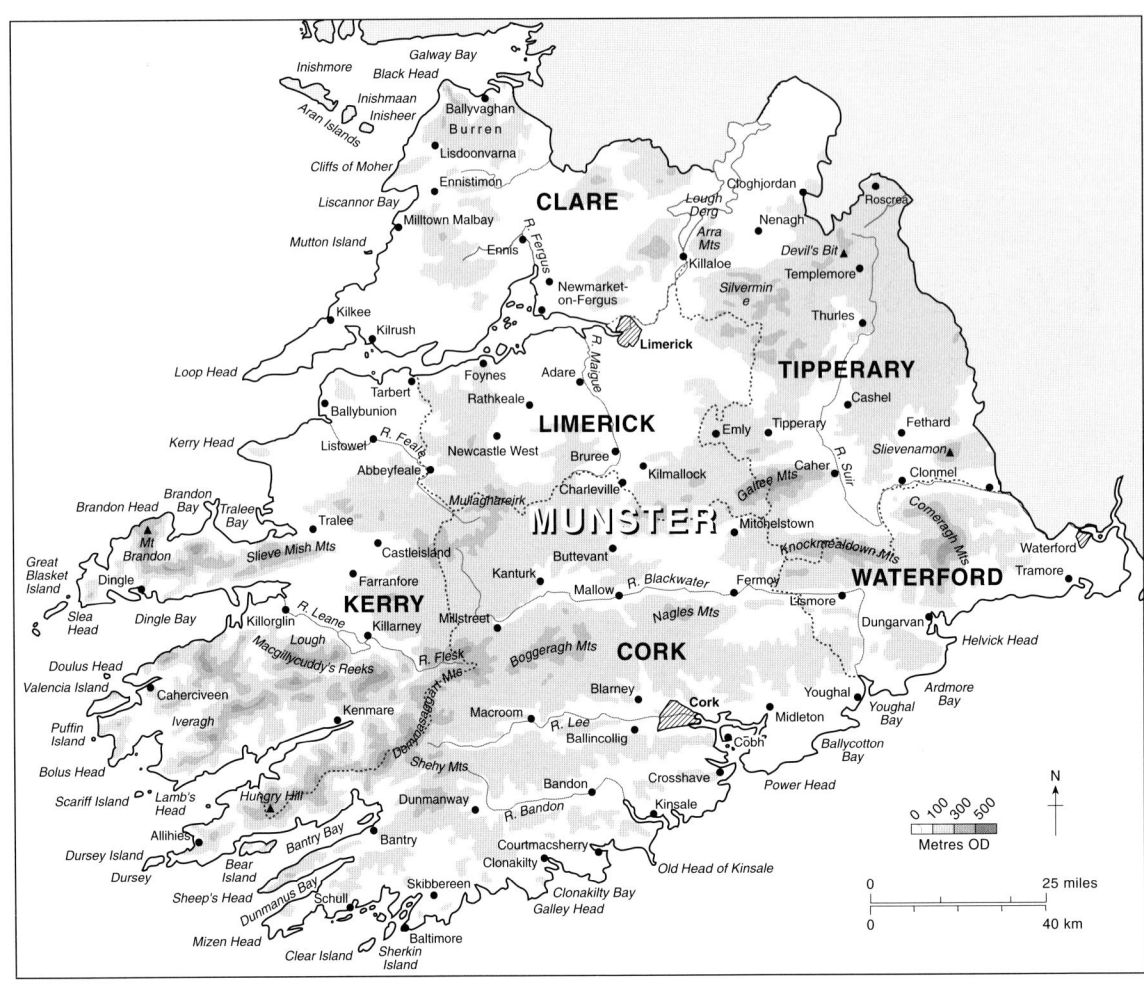

EARLY MEDIEVAL MUNSTER
Archaeology, History and Society

edited by
Michael A. Monk and John Sheehan

Cork University Press

First published in 1998 by
Cork University Press
Cork
Ireland

© Cork University Press 1998

All rights reserved. No part of this book may be reprinted or reproduced or utilized in any electronic, mechanical or other means, now known or hereafter invented, including photocopying and recording or otherwise, without either the prior written permission of the Publishers or a licence permitting restricted copying in Ireland issued by the Irish Copyright Licensing Agency Ltd, The Irish Writers' Centre, 19 Parnell Square, Dublin 1.

British Library Cataloguing in Publication Data
A CIP catalogue record for this book is available from the British Library.

ISBN 1 85918 107 4

Typeset by Phototype-Set Ltd, Glasnevin, Dublin 11
Printed by ColourBooks, Baldoyle, Dublin 13

*In recognition of the contribution to
Early Medieval Munster studies by M. J. O'Kelly,
Professor of Archaeology, University College, Cork, 1946–1982*

Contents

Preface   ix

1. Research and Early Medieval Munster: Agenda or Vacuum?   1
   MICHAEL A. MONK and JOHN SHEEHAN

2. Early Medieval Munster: Thoughts upon its Primary Christian Phase   9
   CHARLES THOMAS

3. The Question of the 'Pre-Patrician' Saints of Munster   17
   DAGMAR Ó RIAIN-RAEDEL

4. Munster Ogham Stones: Siting, Context and Function   23
   FIONNBARR MOORE

5. Early Medieval Secular and Ecclesiastical Settlement in Munster   33
   MICHAEL A. MONK

6. Wood and Woodlands in Early Medieval Munster   53
   JOHN TIERNEY

7. Archaeozoological Studies and Early Medieval Munster   59
   MARGARET McCARTHY

8. Archaeobotanical Studies and Early Medieval Munster   65
   MICHAEL A. MONK, JOHN TIERNEY and MARTHA HANNON

9. Porridges, Gruels and Breads: The Cereal Foodstuffs of Early Medieval Ireland   76
   REGINA SEXTON

10. The Craft of the Millwright in Early Medieval Munster   87
    COLIN RYNNE

11. Illaunloughan, Co. Kerry: An Island Hermitage   102
    JENNY WHITE MARSHALL and CLAIRE WALSH

12. Architectural Traditions of the Early Medieval Church in Munster   112
    TADHG O'KEEFFE

13. Ireland's Earliest 'Celtic' High Crosses: The Ossory and Related Crosses   125
ETIENNE RYNNE

14. Late High Crosses in Munster: Tradition and Novelty in Twelfth-Century Irish Art   138
RHODA CRONIN

15. Viking Age Hoards from Munster: A Regional Tradition?   147
JOHN SHEEHAN

16. Viking Age Towns: Archaeological Evidence from Waterford and Cork   164
MAURICE F. HURLEY

17. Nationalists, Archaeologists and the Myth of the Golden Age   178
JERRY O'SULLIVAN

18. Theory and Politics in Early Medieval Irish Archaeology   190
MICHAEL TIERNEY

19. Early Medieval Munster: Summary and Prospect   200
NANCY EDWARDS

List of Illustrations   206
Contributors   208
Index   209

Preface

This book is the result of a conference held at University College, Cork, in May 1995. It was a UCC150 event and was dedicated to the scholarship of the late Professor M.J. O'Kelly; its organisers were assisted by members of the Student Archaeological Society under the Auditor, Marion Dowd. The conference was a success and it was decided to publish its proceedings. Most of the speakers contributed papers to the volume and several other scholars agreed to contribute to it as well. We hope that the intention of this book – to prompt debate on issues relating to Early Medieval studies, with particular reference to Munster – will be fulfilled.

We should like to take this opportunity to thank the conference sponsors, the UCC150 Organising Committee, the Arts Faculty Research Fund Committee, the Student Societies' Guild and UCC's Archaeology Department, who granted funds towards both the conference and the publication.

The organisers would like to thank Mrs Claire O'Kelly and her family for their encouragement and support. They also wish to thank Dr Nancy Edwards, University College of North Wales, for her major contribution to both the conference and this volume; Professor Peter Woodman, Department of Archaeology, UCC, for his support; Angela Desmond, Department of Archaeology, UCC, for her assistance; Geraldine Murphy for her invaluable help in organising the typescript for publication; Rhoda Cronin and Matthew Stout for their work on the illustrations; and, finally, Judith Monk and Denise Maher-Sheehan for their admirable qualities of patience and forebearance.

MICHAEL A. MONK and JOHN SHEEHAN
January 1998

Digging

Remembering from the beginning
that digging will discover nothing
unless the ground has first
been probed in the imagination,

sink yourself deep into it,
absorbing seed and pollen,
the insinuations of clay.
Below the tangle of roots,

be alert for voices,
a hint of ashes or smoke,
the stench of midden
and always, the hammering of stone.

Follow the incense of ceremony,
a strain of bone flutes.
Be yourself companion to
bodysmells of fear, and love.

Only then open your eyes
and mark out your site
with appropriate measurements
methodically, square by square.

Extract and piece together
the random shards you had sensed.
There will be a tentative, half-glimpsed
outline of bowl or amphora

whose fragments and splinters,
aching for vanished completeness,
can fuse into something
discovering the shape of itself.

Paddy Bushe
from *To Make The Stones Sing* (Wolfhound, 1996)

1. Research and Early Medieval Munster: Agenda or Vacuum?

MICHAEL A. MONK and JOHN SHEEHAN

To date no individual or institution has developed and implemented an overall research strategy for the Early Medieval period in Ireland. This is also true for the period in Munster which, as is pointed out by several of the contributors to this volume, should be regarded as a region of primary importance. It is premature, however, to expect the development of such a research strategy in the absence of any considered review and analysis of the relevant problems and issues. Nevertheless, it is appropriate to ask who should take the initiative in this task. Should it be a university (University College, Cork, in Munster), a long-standing research body like the Royal Irish Academy or a more recently established organisation like the Discovery Programme?

In the past Irish universities have acted as important centres for academic research in the regions. This fact is amply exemplified by the very significant contribution made towards Early Medieval studies in Munster by the late Professor M.J. O'Kelly, the scholar to whom this volume is dedicated. However, government policy decisions have resulted in a marked shift in emphasis from research activities to teaching within the universities. It should be noted, moreover, that there have seldom been consistent levels of project-based interdisciplinary cooperation between scholars in different university departments, and that such cooperation is undoubtedly necessary for the development of a research strategy for Early Medieval Munster. The trends dictated by current government policy have put the possibility of any such interdisciplinary activities even further out of reach. In any case, project funding for the humanities is difficult to attract because such funding is normally directed towards subjects and areas with commercial potential.

National research bodies like the Royal Irish Academy were originally established with a broad interdisciplinary remit. The subsequent growth of scholarship in all areas has caused a divergence of the disciplines, with fewer scholars now co-operating in their research interests. Nevertheless, the Academy has demonstrated its ability to initiate policies towards developing strategic areas of study, such as the industrial archaeology of Cork (Rynne 1998), and it has also recently formed an advisory committee on genetic anthropology which aims to establish a major interdisciplinary project on the genetic history and geography of Ireland. Potentially, therefore, the Royal Irish Academy could have a role to play in the initiation of an overall research strategy for the Early Medieval period.

In 1991, as a result of an initiative prompted by the then Taoiseach, Charles J. Haughey, the Discovery Programme was established with state funding. The stated aim of this body was 'through archaeological and related research to work towards a coherent and comprehensive picture of human life on this island from earliest times' (Discovery Programme 1992, 6). In its initial *Strategies and Questions* document there was a period-by-period assessment of what the advisory panel considered to be the major research questions in Irish archaeology, and from this a core era – 'the Late Bronze Age/Iron Age, or Celtic period' – was selected as the primary period of focus for research. Apart from the self-professed interests of C.J. Haughey it is hardly surprising, given the academic interests of the Discovery Programme's panel members at that time, that the chosen period was a prehistoric one.

The Discovery Programme has gone through a number of recent changes in its constitution, personnel and funding basis. Its research focus, it seems, is also in the process of change. The theme of 'lacustrine settlement' has been identified as an area for future research and this seems likely to be a multi-period, landscape-based study. This is the first time that the programme will potentially address Early Medieval issues, but it could be argued that the theme is peripheral to the major research issues of the period. It is disappointing that the Programme council did not carry out a broad canvass of Early Medieval researchers – archaeologists and others – in order to identify and prioritise crucial research themes. The necessity for such an approach is illustrated by the concluding words of Charles Thomas's contribution to this volume: 'It gives me no satisfaction . . . to imply that archaeological discoveries seem to be lagging behind those of linguistics, epigraphy and history, but they do seem to be; crudely, we are running out of fresh data.' Some of the key research areas and themes which urgently need to be addressed, and which are far more central to Early Medieval studies than lacustrine settlement would seem to be, are discussed in this volume while others are briefly signposted in the closing section of this chapter.

It is important to recognise the contribution that the Discovery Programme has made to those periods it has already explored, but it is a pity that its advisory panel has not so far regarded the Early Medieval period as being worthy of such focused attention. If the panel had been more representative of all interests in Irish archaeology, some relevant Early Medieval themes might have been addressed. A further point may be made in this regard, concerning the fact that the historic era requires a greater level of interdisciplinary input than the prehistoric period does. The advisory panel is constituted solely of archaeologists, and scholars from cognate disciplines do not therefore get the opportunity to contribute to its deliberations as equals. It is widely accepted that the best way forward in Early Medieval studies is through interdisciplinary projects and it seems reasonable to suggest that researchers with backgrounds in disciplines such as history should be represented on the panel.

Following on the above consideration of the main bodies that could potentially lead and support the development of an overall research strategy for the Early Medieval period, it is obvious that there are some shortcomings in each of them. The reasons for these are various, and attention is drawn to them here in the hope that they may be exorcised so that all concerned may start afresh and think positively about future directions.

While it might seem, especially by cognate disciplines, that a great deal of money is being spent on archaeology by the Discovery Programme, large amounts have also been expended through contract archaeology to facilitate developments that threaten archaeological sites. Under the National Monuments Acts, in advance of such developments the archaeology of these sites has to be 'resolved' before developers can get planning permission. It is also the stated policy of the National Monuments and Historic Properties division of Dúchas that the developer should pay for all archaeological work (including the post-excavation process). This policy has a range of consequences – not least the fact that developers can choose whichever appropriately licensed archaeologist they wish to carry out the work. They are in a position to set the price for the contract and independent archaeological contractors have to compete against one another to get it. This type of situation is, of course, common practice in the commercial world, but the dilemma is whether commercial criteria alone are appropriate in archaeology given the nature of the subject. In a situation where commercial considerations are all-important much can suffer, not least the standards of the excavation and the scholarship applied in assessing the results of the work at the report stage. Many contract archaeologists, unlike their state-employed counterparts, have few fixed resources and facilities and they frequently have little time to produce any more than a report sufficient to satisfy the licensing authorities. There is seldom the opportunity to carry out a post-excavation research assessment of the work in order to place it in its broader context. Many developers cannot see the relevance of funding post-excavation processes, and it is true to say that their concern rarely goes beyond dealing with the archaeological procedures that have to be fulfilled in order to expedite the granting of planning permission.

The situation is compounded by the fact that many contract archaeologists justifiably feel that they are not rewarded for what amounts to an academic – not a legal – responsibility to publish a considered and full report. On the other hand, local authority and state archaeologists are normally in better positions to obtain support for publishing – as is best exemplified in Munster by the recently published report on Viking and Medieval Waterford (Hurley and Scully 1997). However, with a few notable exceptions in the area of urban archaeology, rescue archaeology is not contributing significantly towards research agendas. This is simply because it is driven by developer needs, not research questions. It seems likely that in most cases only local authority and state archaeologists have the potential to pursue research issues through rescue opportunities. Even in this situation, however, their scope to do so is limited within the confines of their terms of employment.

Since 1996 the National Monuments and Historic Properties Service (now part of Dúchas) has been adopting a policy that will result in the reduction of both the number and size of urban excavations. This mitigation approach, copied from Britain and forming a response to management problems rather than research issues, involves preserving archaeological deposits *in situ* by using minimal impact foundation techniques, such as piling. It suits developers because it commits them to less archaeological expenditure. The problem is that it has not been convincingly demonstrated that these engineering techniques will have only a minimal detrimental impact on the unexcavated deposits in the long term (Biddle 1994, 8–14). It may well be demonstrated at some point during the new millennium that more destruction will have been caused to the structural deposits of Viking and Medieval Cork as a result of the implementation of this strategy during the late 1990s than was done during the entire eighteenth century, when the city was extensively redeveloped. In any case, knowledge of the archaeology of Ireland's historic cities is not yet detailed enough for considered mitigation decisions to be arrived at. With the recent publication of a number of important excavation reports on, for instance, Cork and Waterford, we have barely crossed the threshold of knowledge about the origins, development and topography of our Medieval towns (see Hurley, ch. 16). The short-term outcome of the state's mitigation policy, at a time when archaeologists could be defining and exploring research questions on the basis of the major excavation reports currently being published, will be to close this door of opportunity.

There are difficulties with the value of the evidence obtained from some rescue excavations, whether urban or rural. Not only is it sometimes likely to have been hurriedly recovered and, perhaps, poorly recorded, but it is obtained only from those areas of sites which are to be directly affected by development. This problem is compounded by the fact that frequently these areas represent only a partial sample of the site and, in addition, one not chosen on the basis of research questions at all. Some of the reports produced for these sites resemble fragmented pictures that are disconnected from their contexts. It would be very difficult for a researcher analysing the data to draw any conclusions which could justifiably be used in inter-site comparisons. For reasons of time these reports, particularly their specialist contributions on artefacts and environmental remains, are generally highly descriptive and contain minimal interpretation. Many environmental specialists are wary of going beyond such merely descriptive statements because they appreciate that they are dealing with only a few small samples which are frequently recovered without any proper sampling strategy (see McCarthy, ch. 7). Rescue excavation reports tend to be highly variable in content and standard, and some seem to be compiled simply in order to fulfil licensing requirements. No standards have been set for them except in the most general way by the licensing authority, whose archive of such reports has yet to become fully accessible to interested parties. Dúchas, however, is currently addressing both of these issues.

Several of the problems associated with rescue archaeology in the context of research have been outlined above. However, the situation with regard to research excavation is also not without its difficulties. The main problem is that these projects tend to take a considerable time to complete and publish, largely because the fieldwork is normally carried out seasonally – funding is allocated annually, not on a total project basis – by directors who are not involved in the projects full time. It is a chastening thought that none of the major Early Medieval research excavation projects carried out in Munster over the last twenty years has yet been fully published. It must be said, however, that when the reports do appear the advantages of research over rescue projects should become evident. These advantages will primarily derive from the fact that the former are carried out within less pressing time constraints, they have the opportunity to apply better standards of excavation and recording and, most importantly, they are more likely to be driven by well-considered research questions. The questioning process may be prompted by the imagination, bringing to mind the opening lines of the poem contributed to this volume by the Kerry poet Paddy Bushe:

> Remembering from the beginning
> that digging will discover nothing
> unless the ground has first
> been probed in the imagination . . .

As a result of the factors noted above, research projects normally produce high quality information on relevant questions. A prime example of this is the excavation of the early ecclesiastical site at Illaunloughan, Co. Kerry (see White-Marshall and Walsh, ch. 11).

Most recently discovered archaeological evidence now takes the form of bits of largely undigested information of variable quality. There are only a few cases of rescue excavation reports where there is any broad discussion of the relevance of this information. It is probably not an exaggeration to say that development-driven archaeology leads to a vacuum of ideas. This is particularly true for the Early Medieval period because a large proportion of the sites threatened by development, in both urban and rural contexts, comes within its date range. The need for research strategies to broaden our understanding of the period – rather than simply identifying and collecting more data – is obvious.

A valid criticism of archaeologists working in the Early Medieval period generally is their apparent reluctance to use the radiocarbon dating method. This is partly the result of a genuine concern that dates obtained for this period are somewhat meaningless because of the wide standard deviation that should be applied to them and the problems that arise from their calibration (Baillie 1985, 11–23). What is seldom realised is that series-dating of suitable material from good contexts in a well-stratified Early Medieval site can be helpful in narrowing down the likely date-range of that site. Obviously, undisturbed contexts with sufficient dateable material are needed to provide such a series for different phases of activity (Baillie 1995, 70–72).

Undertaking such a series-dating programme may seem expensive, but it is of fundamental importance to do so for a period where it is becoming increasingly obvious that there are major social, economic and political changes taking place. Without obtaining a better angle on chronology it will be difficult to appreciate the dynamics of change within Early Medieval society, dynamics indicated in the historical sources and more than hinted at in the archaeological record even as it stands (see Monk, ch. 5). If the dating evidence was exploited carefully and fully, the latitude available to develop better approaches to the evidence would be broadened. In this regard, the work of Berger on mortar samples from Early Medieval ecclesiastical buildings appears to hold considerable possibilities (1995, 159–74).

A further significant problem with Early Medieval scholarship, which is not necessarily confined to those working in this period, is that there is not general acceptance of the value of theoretical archaeology. This issue is addressed by two of the contributors to this volume (O'Sullivan and Tierney, M.). In taking a theoretical approach the archaeologist is more likely to question the validity of received assumptions and to acknowledge the possibility of one's archaeological interpretations being influenced by contemporary issues and beliefs. A theoretical background can lead to the development of a more critical stance in dealing with the archaeological record, as well as leading to a more inquiring, dialectical approach to it. However, just as archaeological practitioners can be subsumed by their methodology, so too can theoreticians become entranced by their own theories. Theory is interesting and valuable but all archaeologists need to engage with the evidence (fragmentary though it might be).

A holistic approach is needed in dealing with the evidence base itself – the material culture and the site record. The practice in the past has been to develop overviews from a number of fully excavated sites which consequently take on the status of 'type-sites' for the period. Type-sites have had their place in the development of the discipline and still figure centrally in discussions of the period, but many of them were excavated over thirty years ago. Modern archaeologists are keenly aware of the crucial importance of stratigraphy in arriving at an understanding of the sequence of development on an archaeological site, yet many of them continue to refer back to type-sites where stratigraphic sequences were poorly understood. We urgently need new data from more secure sequences of contexts on sites that are selected for excavation on the basis of carefully considered research designs, and to reconsider the validity of the concept of the 'type-site'.

A parallel argument can be made for studies of Early Medieval artefacts, which usually have been carried out either on objects with distinctive diagnostic features or on spectacular metalwork items. These, of course, are not representative of the range of finds from Early Medieval sites. This is not to decry the excellent work carried out on such artefact types, but it is true that Early Medieval artefact studies are frequently focused primarily on the objects' physical attributes and tend to avoid discussion of the dynamics and social contexts that they evidence. Standard corpus publishing is important, but it pales somewhat in significance when compared with the results of broader cross-disciplinary approaches (e.g. Thomas 1990; Scott 1991).

Archaeological surveys constitute another type of corpus publishing. There are more of these published for Munster than for any other region in the country and together they form a very important data-base from which to develop future field research. However, most of these surveys are for areas in Cork and Kerry, though fieldwork has been completed in Waterford and is ongoing in Tipperary, Limerick and Clare. It may be valid to ask why there is this bias towards Cork and Kerry. Certainly, part of the answer lies in the fact that the south-west has long attracted scholarly attention because of the number and range of impressive monuments in its dramatic landscape, though the presence of University College, Cork, in the region is clearly also of relevance.

There is, however, a large part of Munster that has attracted significantly less attention from Early Medieval field-archaeologists, the part comprising counties Limerick, Tipperary and Waterford. This is the 'forgotten Munster', evidence from which might well prove crucial towards our understanding of the period as a whole, not least its initial and concluding phases. Waterford, for instance, with its historical links with the Déisi and pre-Patrician saints, is a crucial area for settlement and ecclesiastical studies, especially in the earlier period when it formed a vibrant interface zone from which many important economic and cultural consequences emanated. In the case of Tipperary, at the latter end of the period, there are many settlement sites – such as the raised rath at Kedrah – which seem to have the potential to present insights into the dynamic nature of the changes that took place both before and during the early stages of the Anglo-Norman invasion. Tipperary and Limerick can also provide more potential sites (such as the unusual hybrid earthwork at Kilfinnane, Co. Limerick) from which artefact sequences – up to and including the twelfth century – could be recovered. The soils of the counties that go to form the 'forgotten Munster' are generally less acidic than those in much of Cork and Kerry (where most excavations of Early Medieval sites have taken place) and are therefore more likely to contain deposits from which well-preserved assemblages of both environmental remains and artefacts may be recovered.

It is to be hoped that the future publication of archaeological surveys for counties Limerick, Waterford and Tipperary will provide the impetus for the development of holistic research strategies which will address issues such as these. It is now possible to do this for counties Cork and Kerry, provided archaeologists appreciate the opportunities presented by these data-bases. For instance, serious attention could now be focused on the extent and importance of unenclosed settlement, as represented by the numerous 'unassociated' souterrains and hut sites which are systematically documented for the first time in these surveys. Another research agenda which it is now possible to explore in this region, on an interdisciplinary basis, is the potential correlation of the early historical evidence for diversity in the purpose and function of ecclesiastical sites (Ó Corráin 1981) with their physical and topographical features. The true value of surveys must be recognised, not as ends in themselves but as a foundation from which further work should develop.

In her contribution to this volume Nancy Edwards makes a plea for the development of Early Medieval interdisciplinary studies in Ireland. There is without doubt a great need for this, as it is clear that many specialists working in this field – historians, linguists, placename scholars and archaeologists – are not sufficiently cognisant of each other's research. The problem is exacerbated by the poor understanding displayed by some scholars of the nature of related disciplines and their respective methodologies. This situation is amply illustrated by the ill-informed and unwarranted criticisms of the present state of Early Medieval archaeology in Ireland recently made by the historian Ó Cróinín (1995, 9–10). The most significant interdisciplinary contributions to Early Medieval studies in recent decades have been made by Thomas (e.g. 1981) and de Paor (e.g. 1993), both of whom, perhaps significantly, developed their careers from an archaeological base. This is not to say, of course, that individuals in other fields of Early Medieval studies have not made important contributions which are recognised as such beyond their own disciplines.

There is an unfortunate lack of interdisciplinary study programmes in universities. However, as is demonstrated in a number of contributions to this volume, it is the interdisciplinary approach which most often significantly advances knowledge of the Early Medieval period. It is true to say, none the less, that some research areas should best be dealt with – at least primarily – within one of the cognate disciplines. Gender studies, for example, can usually only be considered in a hypothetical way by using the archaeological record alone and should, perhaps, best be pursued by focusing on the historical evidence. (Admittedly, for prehistoric times, the archaeological record is the primary evidence base.) In contrast, some settlement studies programmes would more suitably be initiated from an archaeological base. The results of primarily unidisciplinary studies such as these will, of course, have cross-disciplinary relevance.

Given the fact that many Early Medieval scholars bemoan the lack of interdisciplinary studies, the question must be posed as to why this crucial interface area has not developed significantly. While there are many and various reasons for this, much of the problem lies in the inadequacies of the university system. A fundamental problem is over-specialisation within the relevant disciplines at postgraduate level, which inevitably leads to further widening of the gulf within and between cognate disciplines. Attempts to rectify this at the undergraduate level by developing integrated programmes that would promote interdisciplinary skills have run into difficulties. This may be partly due to the departmental, and hence compartmental, structure of university faculties. There is perhaps more opportunity for cross-disciplinary development at the postgraduate level, but here cooperation generally has been on an individual basis. In addition, while there is no shortage of enthusiasm for cooperation amongst research students, they generally lack the relevant experience and do not have the appropriate levels of resource backing.

Conclusion

There is a crucial lack of an overall research strategy in Early Medieval studies. The fault for this rests with various research bodies and institutions, including the universities. In terms of expenditure in archaeological energies and resources the main drain, and increasingly so, is contract archaeology. This is undertaken to facilitate commercial considerations rather than to address research questions; to some extent this is professional archaeology late twentieth-century style. While archaeological sites and monuments of all periods are affected, Early Medieval and Medieval sites seem to be most at risk. The lack of a perceived need for a research agenda in public archaeology needs to be seriously addressed, otherwise the process will represent no more than a data-gathering exercise.

To date archaeological scholarship, with some notable exceptions, has not taken a leading role in the recent developments in Early Medieval studies. It has largely had an inward focus and has concentrated on the recording rather than the analysis of a fast-growing body of information, frequently collected in response to factors other than targeted research considerations, while retaining a framework that is largely based on questionable type-sites. Few scholars have set their sights beyond their individual areas of specialisation to see how their work might interact with that of others to provide a more considered and challenging picture of Early Medieval Ireland.

While the limited extent to which Irish archaeologists have developed and expanded their research focus has been a consideration in this chapter, it is important to recognise the potential value of certain types of data-collecting exercises, such as the survey work in Munster, which is broadly based, non-selective, standardised and conducted primarily for archaeological reasons. Moreover, its real value as a resource base for generating research agendas cannot be fully realised without further analysis. It must be seen to provide a springboard towards a deeper and fuller understanding of the changing patterns in human behaviour in Early Medieval Munster.

A central problem for Early Medieval studies is the lack of an interdisciplinary perspective. It has been suggested that this is basically a problem inherent in the university system. There is an urgent need for a more integrated approach to these studies in undergraduate programmes. Old habits die hard and get fixed early, and consequently it is important to direct our putative scholars towards cross-disciplinary goals at an early stage. However, such an approach in itself will not guarantee the development of scholarship nor will it necessarily drive the research agenda forward. The researchers that may surface from interdisciplinary programmes will need support and this would be best achieved by establishing an Institute of Medieval Studies along the lines of the Dublin School of Celtic Studies. The institute would be staffed by scholars from each of the relevant disciplines who would have demonstrated their ability to integrate and develop cooperative studies. Obviously, it would not be desirable to have historians or archaeologists on the staff, however well-respected, who have little demonstrable appreciation of cognate disciplines. Such an institute would be charged with setting research agendas and developing strategies to achieve them; funding would come from state and other sponsorship. It is essential that there would be an ongoing dialogue between the institute and the regulatory authorities, so that they could make informed decisions together with regard to the research directions that archaeology and related disciplines might take in the future.

We feel that there are a number of areas within Early Medieval studies that require urgent consideration by any organisation, such as the proposed institute, charged with developing research strategies. Charles Thomas and others make reference to several important examples of these in their contributions to this volume, while we have drawn attention to the potential of certain areas in the 'forgotten Munster' to provide answers to key questions which are of relevance to the whole island of Ireland. Thomas's concluding remarks admirably serve to reinforce this view for the period as a whole: 'In this quest, all the provinces of Ireland are important; but I suggest that . . . Munster is more important than the others. For the Early Medieval field, one need look no further to discern a very proper challenge to occupy the next quarter-century.'

ACKNOWLEDGEMENTS
We would like to thank Professor Peter Woodman, Department of Archaeology, University College, Cork, and Maurice Hurley, City Archaeologist, Cork, for their comments on draft sections of this chapter.

BIBLIOGRAPHY
Baillie, M.G.L. (1985) 'Dendrochronology and radiocarbon calibration', *Ulster J. Archaeol.* 48, 11–23
Baillie, M.G.L. (1995) *A Slice Through Time: Dendrochronology and Precision Dating*, London
Berger, R. (1995) 'Radiocarbon dating of early Medieval Irish monuments', *Proc. Roy. Ir. Acad.* 95C, 159–74
Biddle, M. (1994) *What Future for British Archaeology?*, Archaeology in Britain Conference, Oxbow Lecture 1, Oxford
De Paor, L. (1993) *Saint Patrick's World: The Christian Culture of Ireland's Apostolic Age*, Dublin
Discovery Programme (1992) *The Discovery Programme: Strategies and Questions*, Dublin
Hurley, M.F. and Scully, O.M.B. (1997) *Late Viking Age and Medieval Waterford Excavations: 1986–1992*, Waterford
Ó Cróinín, D. (1995) *Early Medieval Ireland 400–1200*, London
Ó Corráin, D. (1981) 'The early Irish churches: some aspects of organisation' in D. Ó Corráin (ed.), *Irish Antiquity*, Cork, 327–41
Rynne, C. (1998) *Industrial Archaeology of Cork City and its Environs*, Dublin
Scott, B.G. (1991) *Early Irish Ironworking*, Belfast
Thomas, C. (1981) *Christianity in Roman Britain to AD 500*, London
Thomas, C. (1990) 'Gallici Nautae de Galliarum Provinciis: a sixth/seventh century trade with Gaul, reconsidered', *Medieval Archaeol.* 34, 1–26

2. Early Medieval Munster: Thoughts Upon Its Primary Christian Phase

CHARLES THOMAS

My short contribution seeks to link three phenomena that are not always discussed together as closely as they should be: literacy, particularly in Latin; *romanitas*, in the sense of the Roman empire's cultural influence upon peripheral peoples inside and outside the frontiers; and the adoption of Christianity. I do this first in the setting of the Insular world, Ireland and Britain together, and then with reference to early Munster, the theme of this volume; lastly, since my subtitle is or ought to be 'Some guidelines for the next quarter-century', I look at a few practical recommendations.

Ptolemy's named locations in Ireland, contained in his mid-second-century AD *Cosmographia*, were explored by T.F. O'Rahilly (1946, ch. 1) and have now been mapped again with some fairly challenging Celtic etymologies by Alan Mac an Bhaird (1993). The latter points out that the uneven distribution of these names, concentrated along the Leinster and Munster coasts with the immediate hinterland, points to merchants trading mainly with south-east Ireland as Ptolemy's ultimate source of information. The implication would be that from the first century AD, if not before then, landfalls were sufficiently frequent and intelligible contacts between traders and natives sufficiently fruitful to allow Irish place-names to pass into that much wider repertoire of sailing-directions and commercial lore. Nor should we think only of ships pulling up on isolated beaches and then trying to find surprised entrepreneurs. Richard Warner reminded us some time ago (1976, especially his map, Fig. 3) that these southern access-points by sea extend far inland. Waterford is some 24 km up the river Barrow, Cork harbour is immense, Bantry Bay is effectively an inland sea about 35 km long, and one can reach the heart of Ireland by sailing up the Shannon and its string of lakes without even setting ashore.

What used to be regarded as a probability (constant maritime traffic between parts of Britannia, let alone Roman Gaul, and Ireland) is now a virtual certainty. The catalogue of acceptably genuine Roman finds in Ireland grows all the time. Given the points of intervisibility with the extremities of Britain, two-way sailings may have been as commonplace in Roman times as they were in the Middle Ages. Direct references for the intervening centuries are largely from chance survivals (cf. Thomas 1990 for dated instances), but the point here of the youthful Patrick's escape from Ireland is not so much precisely when or from where he sailed; it is that he writes as if the availability of a ship was nothing out of the ordinary. When Palladius and his party landed in AD 431, somewhere in Leinster, they had left Auxerre and then (like Germanus and Lupus in 429) crossed the

Channel – possibly sailing down the Seine to Le Havre and over to Dorset – before (at a guess) travelling across the south of Wales and putting out again from Fishguard or Cardigan.

Let us move from this salt-water commercial background straight into an oghamological interlude; the perpetually fascinating topic of the ogham script. We are no longer bound to the idea that this ingenious system arose from Irish analysis of fourth-century Roman grammarians, or to the belief that the ogham may have been invented in Britain by Irish immigrants, or, I hope, to the contention that it can *only* have been invented in a Christian setting to write, among other things, exclusively Christian memorials to the Christian dead. After Damian McManus's recent study (1991) more people may be inclined to share with him a conclusion that ogham existed in the fourth century, and conceivably before 300; some would be prepared (if not yet in hard print) to support an even earlier origin.

There can be little doubt, on general lines, that the visual shape of ogham – four groups, each with five strokes or notches – ought somehow to be linked to the perception of the common Roman incremental-bar numerals (I, II, III, IIII, etc.) and perhaps also to some of the vertical and diagonal multi-line letter forms seen in a Roman script used on wax tablets. There is no need to rehearse McManus's very full arguments. He, and others, show beyond reasonable doubt that the framers of ogham were familiar with the system of sound values, the phonesis, of spoken Latin; the conventional twenty-letter Roman ABC (ABCDEFGHILMNOPQRSTUX; K, Y and Z were known but not included here) used in writing Latin; ways in which this Roman alphabet might be classified and taught; and a workable application of the twenty-symbol ogham system to the sound values of contemporary spoken Irish. One longstanding objection, that we still have absolutely no tangible evidence from Ireland's deep south of third- to fourth-century AD material with Roman writing, strikes me as archaeological, not linguistic. Some waterlogged anaerobic deposit may in the future enlighten us.

Can one contend that, as one outcome of prolonged contact with the Roman world, some element of Latin literacy – an ability to read and to understand written and spoken Latin – was present in Munster and Leinster, perhaps already by the third century? I would do so; and, furthermore, I would invite a realization that this constituted the single most important happening in the course of Ireland's history. It was the advent of literacy; a literary revolution. Ireland was fortunate in that, bypassing the obstacles of ideograms and syllabaries, literacy may have begun with two fully alphabetical systems, the Roman and the ogham. It marks that point in time when Ireland emerged from a delayed prehistory and joined the greater, European world of Late Antiquity. In the West, Christianity was an inevitable concomitant and it was inevitable that Ireland would become Christian.

But why, then, if these smart fellows in long-ago Munster had found out from Roman traders and settlers how to read and write through the medium of the Latin ABC, did they need to invent another twenty-letter script of their own? Bearing momentarily in mind the considerable difference in appearance between Roman *capitalis* and Roman cursive, there is a possible answer given below (p. 15). We have to 'de-mystify' ogham. Fourth-century Irish could have been written, using modifications, in Roman letters; it now looks as if people tried to write Roman-period British in Roman letters (see Tomlin 1987). Gaulish was written in both Greek and Roman letters, too. Though nobody would be mad enough to try it, the whole of Cicero's Orations could be written in ogham, and some might argue that the very existence of ogham in fifth- and possibly fourth- or third-century Ireland implies a parallel co-existence of Latinate literacy.

The first applications of ogham to stone, in the form of simple memorials to individual dead saying no more than *A son of B*; *of A, of a son of the tribe of B*; *A son of B of the tribe C* (and further variations thereof), are not in themselves dateable; only context may sometimes supply a clue. I have argued at length elsewhere (Thomas 1994) that, if the inferred and partly recorded minor settlement of Munster Déisi in south-west Wales began near the end of the fourth century AD, there are a few menhir-like pillars in Pembrokeshire with ogham script (alone) and demonstrably Irish names that are probably for non-Christians and should be assigned to the early fifth century. Further memorials in Wales and, after about 500, Cornwall and Devon, many 'bilingual' (i.e., with both ogham and roman lettering), show ogham used for Irish names, ogham for continuing-Roman names like *Latinus*, the Roman alphabet for British and Roman names of course, and also for Irish names. These happen to be within mainland Britain. But among the several hundred ogham memorials in Munster and Leinster we can find three showing genuine Roman names (numbers from Macalister 1945; 56 *SAGITTARI*, 188 *MARIANI*, 265 *AMADU* (Amatus)), and a further three where the son's name is Irish and the father's is Roman (16 *DUNAIDONAS son of MARIANUS*, 166 *COIMAGNAS son of VITALIN* (*us*) and 20 *MAQIDDECCEDAS son of MARIN* (*us*)). The distribution of these very interesting memorials (Fig. 2.1) is predictable, with three coastal, or by the Blackwater, and two up the valley of the Barrow.

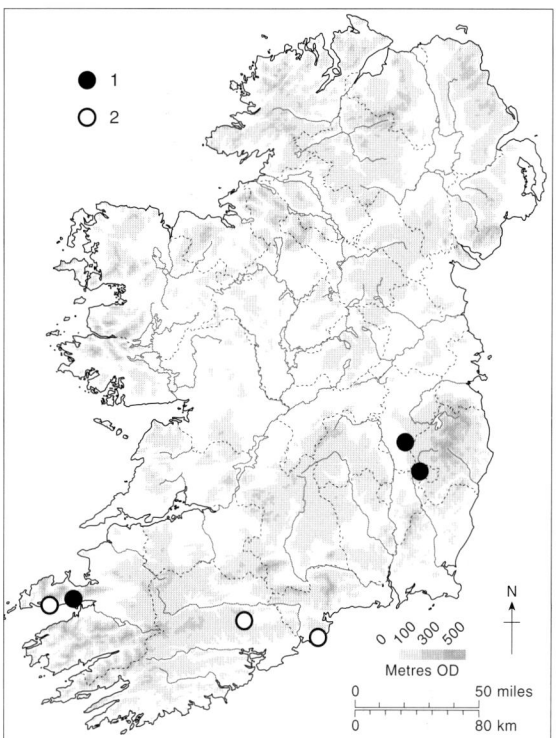

Fig. 2.1 Ogham memorials with Roman personal names: 1, single Roman names; 2, Irish-named sons of Roman-named fathers

I want to present ogham as, to all intents, a parallel to Roman writing; and the latter as an innovation already entrenched in a large part of pre-400 Ireland. Any distribution of literacy is not automatically also a distribution of contemporary Christianity. In Britannia, literacy preceded the triumph of the Faith by several centuries; in Ireland, a literacy derived from secular or commercial Roman contact certainly preceded conversion, though both the pace of the adoption of Christianity in Ireland and much of its development were facilitated by, and spatially influenced by, the initial geography of Ireland's literary revolution. The pattern of surviving oghams on stone is emphatically southern. The map (Fig. 2.2) is an adjusted density-distribution showing total occurrences in the thirty-two counties, with calculated adjustments because certain county areas (Galway with 1.5 million acres; Carlow, Dublin and Louth, each below a quarter of a million) fall above or below a median. For the moment this map can be left to carry its own message.

Ireland's conversion to Christianity was also a revolution, albeit a secondary one. Of Patrick the Briton all that needs to be written now is that, regardless of his real dates, most if not all of his episcopal career took place in Ulster and perhaps northern Connacht. From Patrick's writings we know that he was aware of, and encouraged others in, personal monastic vows in a Late Roman sense, but also that those writings indicate nothing of developed monasticism or of contemporary monasteries elsewhere in Ireland. The arrival of the unconnected Palladius, his standing on the Continent and in papal circles and his likely earlier involvement with an anti-Pelagian mission to Britain, are matters of

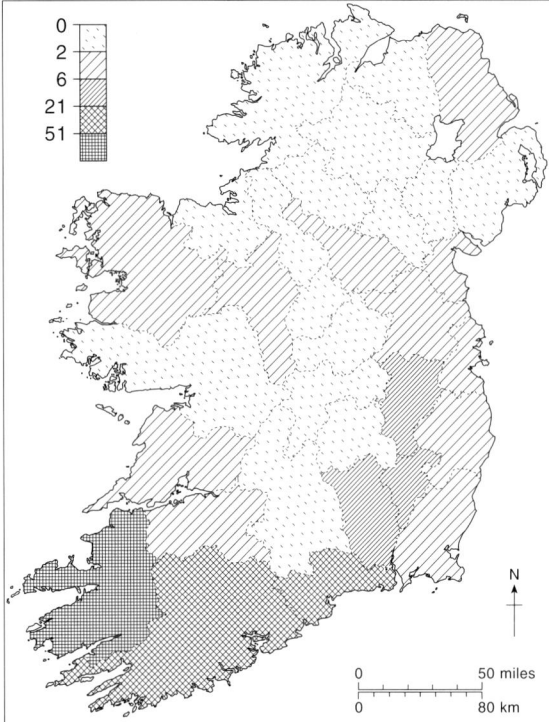

Fig. 2.2 Density-distribution map of ogham-inscribed memorial stones (totals per county adjusted to median area of all counties)

external record (de Paor 1993). To many, it now seems overwhelmingly probable that certain of the names attached to Patrick in the later Armagh writings – Auxilius, Isarninus, Segetius – represent the *familia* with whom an important incoming bishop would have travelled (cf. Dumville 1993, 65 ff., 89 ff.). Prosper of Aquitaine's terse record allows certain inferences. The *Scoti* to whom Palladius was sent may have inhabited Ireland, but they were not necessarily exclusively the ethnic Irish. By 431 there were enough *credentes*, believers, to warrant the papally directed presence of a bishop and there must have been contacts to arrange this. If they were conducting worship and receiving textual guidance, this was in Latin, not British or Irish. To suggest that such *credentes*, perhaps most numerous in Leinster, were all slaves or offspring of slaves from Britain is to extend unduly what Patrick tells us of his own fate, and to ignore many other possible explanations; one such could be no more than literate, Latinate, British Christians settling in Ireland to promote commerce and to evade taxation at home.

There were various words used in fourth-century Britain (other than *ecclesia*, which was still 'a Christian flock, congregation') to denote the nascent idea of a church, in the sense of a privately or communally owned building intended for worship and instruction (Thomas 1981, 147–49); probably the commonest was *dominica*, 'that pertaining to the Lord'. It was among various words transferred to Ireland, either side of AD 400, along with Christianity, initially borrowed as *dominech, then Old Irish *domnach* – on modern maps, often shown by the prefix Donagh (as Donaghmore, Donaghadee). Deirdre Flanagan (1979; 1984) considered that *domnach* relates to the first phase of Irish Christianity, that by the later sixth century it may have no longer been a productive place-name element, and that it might even have been in use (as *dominech) on Irish soil before St Patrick. When her maps are brought together in the density-distribution format (Fig. 2.3) we notice the separate high concentrations in counties Derry and Meath. These may suggest not so much proximity to Christianity in Britain but, in the north, a correspondence to the work of Patrick and, in Leinster, a broad idea of the location of the pre- and post-431 *credentes* who received Palladius as their bishop.

If there were simple churches, '*domnachs*,' of any kind in fifth-century Ireland – and Patrick's *Confessio* might encourage us to think that this was so – they were community provisions, Christian additions to everyday life. When we turn to monasticism with its provisions for another approach for Christian living, a *domnach* map like Fig. 2.3 offers no guidance; there is no evidence that recognizable monasteries existed in Britain until the later fifth century, and no support comes from the oldest Christian Latin loan-words into Irish. Yet all over Ireland we find hundreds of names with Kil- and Kill- elements

Primary Christian Phase 13

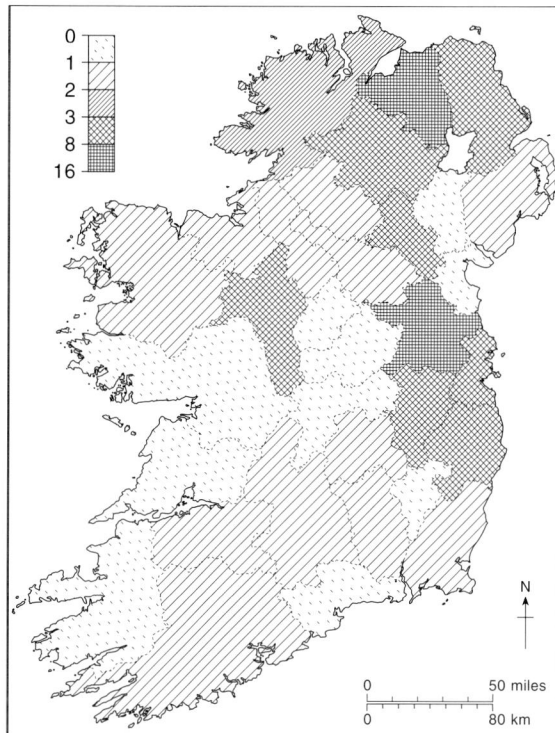

Fig. 2.3 Density-distribution map of ecclesiastical place-names of the type 'Donagh-', etc. (OIr. *domnach*); totals per county adjusted to median area of all counties. Source: selectively from maps in Flanagan (1984)

Parishes and Townlands of Ireland from 17th Century Maps, using the 500-odd parish names. The density-distribution map (Fig. 2.4) shows 336 examples in Leinster and Munster, and less than half that total (147) in Ulster and Connacht. Placed alongside the *domnach* map (Fig. 2.3), it tells us that, even if *domnach* and *cell* both denoted types of Christian sites at much the same early period, the two words cannot have meant the same and that quite separate Christian manifestations are involved.

To some extent the answer to this puzzle lies in the modes of transmission. *Dominech, and at least two other basic terms – Old Irish *Cresen* (Latin *C(h)ristianus*, 'a Christian') and PrIr. **qremiter(as)* (British Latin **pra(e)miter*, priest, presbyter: ogham 145 QRIMITIR, the genitive form) – were carried to Ireland by British speakers of Vulgar Latin, and heard, adopted and

(Kildare, Kilmore, Kilfenora, Killarney) and learn that this prefix is Old Irish *cell*, 'church; monastic settlement or foundation; collection of ecclesiastical buildings; churchyard, graveyard, sanctuary'. Clearly the meaning is wider than that of *domnach;* and linguists know that OIr. *cell* is a borrowing from Latin *cella* (both words are feminine, a-stem nouns), in Classical Latin 'room, chamber, or unit in a complex of rooms; small building, store, outhouse'. Middle Irish *cill*, as in all these place-names, seems to be a fresh nominative re-formed from an older dative-locative *cill*, 'At-the-*cell*'.

To get some idea of the spatial currency, one could look at all the Kil(l)- names in, say, the 1871 Townland Index; but there are more than three thousand of them, many obvious duplications. A better base is *Goblet's Index of*

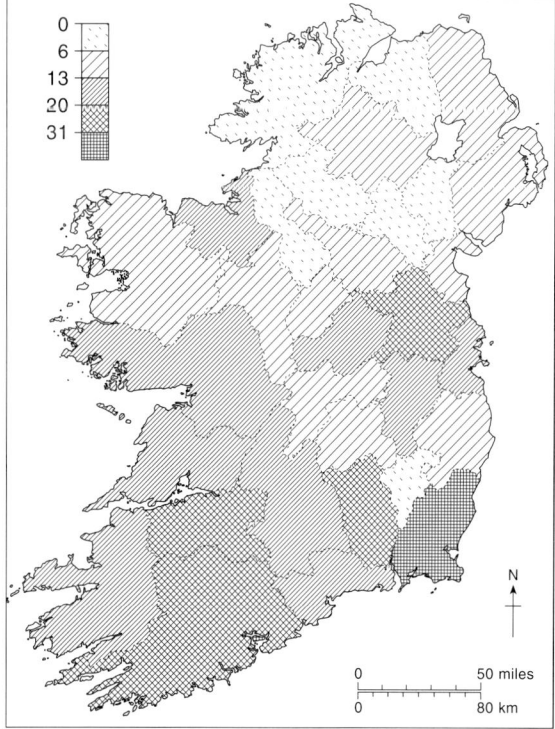

Fig. 2.4 Density-distribution map of ecclesiastical place-names with prefix Kil-, Kill- (OIr. *cell*); totals per county adjusted to median area of all counties. Source: lists in Goblet (1932)

modified in Irish mouths. *Domnach* was a direct loan in everyday life. OIr. *cell* (?PrIr. *cella*) was not; it was literary and indirect. Since I have dealt with its history at some length elsewhere (Thomas 1995), a thumbnail sketch will suffice. Latin *cella* in the senses described earlier was borrowed into the demotic Greek of Egypt as *kella*, with a quasi-diminutive doublet *kellion* (plural *kellia*). When fourth-century (Greek) accounts of the first hermits and monastic founders, the Desert Fathers, appeared, we find Greek *kella*, *kellai*: *kellion*, *kellia* describing the related sites, individual 'cells' and various kinds of monastic settlements. Fairly soon, Latin translations appeared to meet a growing demand for this literature in the (Latin-speaking) western parts of the Empire. *Kella* and *kellion* were, broadly, re-translated back into Latin as *cella* (or *cellula*), but now with these additional, specifically monastic, meanings. At the same time Christian Latin took into use other new words slightly altered from Greek (*monachus*; *monasterium*; *eremus*, 'desert'). Circulation in Italy and southern Gaul of this immensely popular Desert Fathers literature, widespread by the 420s, led to on-the-spot imitation of the Egyptian hermits, coenobitic (communal) monasteries and virtually all aspects of their exciting Christian lives.

I have little doubt myself now that OIr. *cell* was a new word to name a new wave of Christian life in Ireland, at first individual (eremitic) monasticism; that its origin was literary, through the reading aloud, copying and diffusion of relevant Latin writings; and that we can pinpoint the introduction to AD 431 – Palladius and his *familia* landing in Leinster, the relevant *volumina* (obtained mostly in pre-431 Gaul) in their baggage. It is particularly significant that there was no comparable borrowing of Latin *cella* into British. This forms another topic, but similar monastic ideas probably reached south-east Wales first (from Gaul, again with literature) in the later part of the fifth century, were generally realised as forms of sub-Roman coenobitic monasticism and developed an (Archaic) Old Welsh vocabulary in which *lann* (British *land-á*) took on the same set of meanings as did *cell* in Ireland.

If Palladius, AD 431, and the arrival of monastic inspiration in written Latin guise were so important a step in Irish Christianity, why were they seemingly ignored in Ireland's internal records? The short answer is that they were not, and at another time I should hope to expand ideas already put forward by a few percipient colleagues. Palladius was never forgotten, but he awaits further disengagement from all those *acta et dicta Patricii* that not only tell us about him but show him to have been in the right places at the right times to introduce the postulated literature. In Ireland this key word *cella*, summing up all the new and heady Christian teaching, must have spread rapidly through Leinster and Munster; Fig. 2.4 is its partial afterglow. It would take another essay to discuss the relevant archaeology, but one might single out Phase I of O'Kelly's excavated discoveries at Church Island, Co. Kerry (O'Kelly 1958), as typical of a primary cell.

To postulate a *literary* introduction of influential new ideas, carrying their own new vocabulary, is all very well; the corollary is of course that sufficient people could understand what this was about. The further postulation would be that, even as early as the middle of the fifth century, Christian groups in Ireland – notably in the Leinster coastlands, the south-east and all across Munster – were rapidly increasing numerically and spatially and that they contained both priests and laity who worshipped in Latin, read and understood Latin, absorbed Latin words into their own vernacular and at some unascertained phase began to write Latin. Look again at the maps of the place-name elements *domnach* and *cell* as Kil(l)- (Figs 2.3 and 2.4). It is the latter, only, that somehow contains within it a pointer to the concentration of pre-500 literacy (in Latin); and it goes with the map of ogham (Fig. 2.2) because that map relates to the same things. Neither is immediately relevant, before the sixth and seventh centuries, to the Patrician north. This is the point at which we might return to the ogham script. Our growing awareness of the impact of *romanitas* on early Ireland must reinforce the view that the very idea of the inscribed memorial, the stone proclaiming the name and filiation of the deceased for those who could read to read and appreciate, was taken from the pagan Roman empire (and various ways in which this could have happened can be left aside). Is it remotely possible, as Fig. 2.2 seems to hint, that the Irish ogham-memorial fashion actually began in south-west Munster? Why not? Ogham was surely invented by *fili*, the Irish *literati*, before and beyond Christianity and originally for this precise end. It was a realistic gesture; an easy-to-cut, easy-to-read substitute for the Romans' monumental *capitalis* because that may have been the one form of Roman script for which the first Latinate Irish had little use (whereas many other forms, as we know, were adopted as they stood). Related reasons might have been the natural absence of suitable, Roman-quality tabular surfaces; and the obstacles in getting many non-literate cutters to master the intricate curves and planned proportions and layout of the classical Roman style. All in all, one could very well argue that Ireland's literary revolution began in Munster, within the Roman period, and that only such a revolution could have enabled the surprisingly early eremitic monasticism of the fifth century to have taken root.

An appropriately detailed rehabilitation of Palladius must be postponed. What cannot be deferred, however, is a firm reminder that our entire perception of Irish literary and cultural beginnings, both Latin and vernacular (and along with them, those of western Britain), is currently subject to radical modification and modernization. For those still not aware of this, a crash-course in reading should begin with Harvey 1987; Stevenson 1989; Howlett 1994; Howlett 1995, 1–54; and Ó Cróinín 1995, chs. 6–7. And now for the theme of the conference at which this essay formed the opening address, precluded by a personal and professional tribute to Professor M. J. (Brian) O'Kelly, who would most certainly have endorsed my closing message. It gives me no satisfaction (reverting to my role as an archaeologist concerned with Insular Christianity and its remains) to imply that archaeological discoveries seem to be lagging behind those of linguistics, epigraphy and history, but they do seem to be; crudely, we are running out of fresh data. We need, urgently, new material relating to what can now be called 'Roman Ireland', to physical manifestations of all and any forms of early literacy, to firmly dated *primary* Christian sites (particularly the smaller southern and western monastic sites of eremitic character) and to clear evidence of Continental contacts over and above indications already given by imported ceramics. In this quest, all the provinces of Ireland are important; but I suggest that the maps accompanying my words make it obvious that Munster is more important than the others. For the Early Medieval field, one need look no further to discern a very proper challenge to occupy the next quarter-century.

BIBLIOGRAPHY

De Paor, L. (1993) *Saint Patrick's World*, Four Courts Press, Dublin

Dumville, D.N. (1993) *Saint Patrick AD 493–1993*, Boydell Press, Woodbridge

Flanagan, D. (1979) 'Common elements in Irish place-names; ceall, cill', *Bull. Ulster Place-Name Soc.* (2 ser.) 2, 1–8

Flanagan, D. (1984) 'The Christian impact on early Ireland; place-names evidence', in P. Ní Catháin and M. Richter (eds.), *Irland und Europa/Ireland and Europe* (25–51), Klett-Cotta, Stuttgart

Goblet, Y.M. (1932) *Index of Parishes and Townlands of Ireland from 17th Century Maps*, Stationery Office, Dublin

Harvey, A. (1987) 'Early literacy in Ireland: the evidence from ogam', *Cambridge Medieval Celtic Stud.* 14, 1–15

Howlett, D.R. (1994) *The Book of Letters of Saint Patrick the Bishop*, Four Courts Press, Dublin

Howlett, D.R. (1995) *The Celtic Latin Tradition of Biblical Style*, Four Courts Press, Dublin

Macalister, R.A.S. (1945) *Corpus Inscriptionum Insularum Celticarum*, vol. 1, Stationery Office, Dublin

Mac an Bhaird, A. (1993) 'Ptolemy revisited', *Ainm* (*Bull. Ulster Place-Names Soc.*) v, 1–20

McManus, D. (1991) *A Guide to Ogam*, An Sagart, Maynooth

Ó Cróinin, D. (1995) *Early Medieval Ireland 400–1200*, Longman, London and New York

O'Kelly, M.J. (1958) 'Church Island, near Valencia, County Kerry', *Proc. Roy. Ir. Acad.* 59C, 57–136

O'Rahilly, T.F. (1946) *Early Irish History and Mythology*, Dublin Institute for Advanced Studies, Dublin

Stevenson, J. (1989) 'The beginnings of literacy in Ireland', *Proc. Roy. Ir. Acad.* 89C, 127–65

Thomas, C. (1981) *Christianity in Roman Britain to AD 500*, Batsford, London

Thomas, C. (1990) 'Gallici Nautae de Galliarum Provinciis; a sixth/seventh century trade with Gaul, reconsidered', *Medieval Archaeol.* 34, 1–26

Thomas, C. (1994) *And Shall These Mute Stones Speak? Post-Roman Inscriptions in Western Britain*, University of Wales Press, Cardiff

Thomas, C. (1995) 'Cellular meanings, monastic beginnings', *Emania* 13, 51–67

Tomlin, R.O.S. (1987) 'Was Ancient British Celtic ever a Written Language? Two texts from Roman Bath', *Bull. Board Celtic Stud.* 34, 18–2

Warner, R.B. (1976) 'Some observations on the context and importation of exotic material in Ireland, from the first century B.C. to the second century A.D.', *Proc. Roy. Ir. Acad.* 76C, 267–92

3. The Question of the 'Pre-Patrician' Saints of Munster

DAGMAR Ó RIAIN-RAEDEL

This chapter is concerned with the well-known claim that before St Patrick, the national apostle, came to Ireland there were already some saints in the south of the country engaged in spreading the faith. While this claim has engaged the attention of scholars from the seventeenth century onwards, it has usually been treated separately from the other problems associated with the Patrician chronology.[1]

It is now generally accepted that seventh-century Armagh, through propaganda put into writing by the hagiographers Muirchú and Tírechán, promoted the cult of Patrick with a view to furthering its own pursuit of power. By transforming the saint into a national apostle, they set Armagh above all other religious establishments. Simultaneously, by claiming allegiance – and revenue – from all the houses Patrick supposedly founded, Armagh succeeded in turning what had begun as a localised cult into a network of affiliated churches spread over a large area of the country. Furthermore, it would seem that Armagh historians were at pains to accommodate the tradition of Palladius, whose record provides us with the only historically verifiable Irish date in the fifth century. As will become apparent, Palladius was a pivotal figure around whom much of the later record of Patrick was formed.

The chronicler Prosper of Aquitaine records under the year 431: 'Palladius, having been ordained by Pope Celestine, is sent, as their first bishop, to the Irish, who believe in Christ.' Palladius is further mentioned by Prosper in connection with the mission of Germanus, bishop of Auxerre, to Britain to combat the heretical tendencies of Pelagius. The value of Prosper's testimony is enhanced by the fact that he seems to have been at Rome in 431 and would thus have possessed first-hand knowledge (Charles-Edwards in Dumville 1993, 1).

The seventh-century Armagh historians, who were seemingly familiar with the entry for 431 in Prosper's chronicle and thus were very much aware of the threat it posed to Patrick's claim to the title of first bishop of the Irish, resolved the problem by arranging Patrick's career around it. In their writings, as in the Irish annals, Palladius's mission was deemed to have been unsuccessful: either he suffered martyrdom in Ireland or he was dispatched to Britain, where he died subsequently (Dumville 1993, 63–4). To pre-empt any potential claim to the success of Palladius's mission, Patrick's arrival in Ireland was fixed for just one year later in what Dumville calls 'a learned and chronographic reconstruction in the synchronising mode' (1993, 39–43).

The further claim propagated by Armagh, that 'Palladius was Patrick by another name', epitomizes what was later to become the 'question of the two Patricks'. It indicates that another means of reconciling the two records was to merge them. It has been suggested that the details referring to Patrick's sojourn in Gaul were borrowed from Palladius. Indeed, there are indications that the inquiries undertaken on behalf of the Armagh historians extended as far as Auxerre and Rome (Dumville 1993, 77–84). It is interesting to note that some of the sources used for propagating Patrick's cult at the expense of that of Palladius seem to have come from Leinster, for both Tírechán and Muirchú allegedly wrote at the behest of abbots or mentors with Leinster connections. This may not be unrelated to the fact that Palladius's connections with Leinster seem to have been very strong. Thus, having supposedly landed at the port of Arklow, Palladius is brought into association with some other Wicklow churches. Arklow not only stands out as a probable location for Palladius's landing from Britain, it is here also that Muirchú places Patrick's first port of call on his return to Ireland (Bieler 1979, 76, 201). The saints with foreign-sounding names, such as Auxilius, Secundinus and Iserninus, associated with Patrick's mission may also link him to Palladius. If these individuals existed at all, they were much more likely to have been the Gaulish companions of Palladius. The churches connected with them, such as Killeshin, Old Kilcullen and Dunshaughlin, are all located in Leinster (Bieler 1979, 74, 162; de Paor 1993, 41).

While Palladius's mission may have centred on east Leinster, Christianity could well have reached the south of Ireland long before either he or Patrick set foot on the island. Certainly, common sense would suggest this. The settlements of the Déisi and the Uí Liatháin of east Munster in south-west Wales established an important link between Britain and Ireland. The distribution of ogham stones, together with the evidence of names and placenames, show how extensive these settlements were (Richards, 1960). As de Paor has recently suggested, therefore, Christianity may have come to the south coast of Munster as a direct result of raids from there on the Roman provinces of Britain. The booty from such raids would have included slaves, many of whom would have been Christian. De Paor goes on to suggest that Christian communities of some size must have existed in Munster by the beginning of the fifth century, especially in those areas from which the more sustained expeditions emanated, and that the 'first Christian bishops came to minister to these communities, bringing with them the prestige of Rome' (1993, 35). If so, where would these bishops have come from, directly from Gaul or via Britain?

The coast of Munster, of course, faced Gaul so that the most likely ports of call for trading contacts with the Continent would have been located in the south of Ireland. The importance of such contacts, and in particular of the trade in wine, has been confirmed for south Munster by the discovery of sherds of A-, B- and E-ware pottery – dating to the fifth to eighth centuries – at such royal sites as Garranes, Co. Cork, and Cashel, Co. Tipperary.[2] As wine also formed an integral part of the Christian liturgy, we might expect these types of pottery to turn up on ecclesiastical sites as well if Christianity already had a toehold in Munster. It is surely significant, therefore, that similar finds of pottery have been made at sites such as Reask, Co. Kerry, Iniscealtra, Co. Clare, and Derrynaflan, Co. Tipperary (Edwards 1990, 68, 71). However, even if it is possible to conclude on this evidence that Christianity is likely to have been introduced to south Munster through casual trading contacts with the Continent, we still do not know whether (or how) it was formally organised there.

We may recall that the Patrician legend seems to have grown up around the response of seventh-century Armagh historians to the historical record of the arrival of Palladius in Ireland in 431. As we have seen, in trying to merge the two originally separate records, a substantial amount of information concerning Palladius may have been absorbed into the canon of the Patrician biography. If this was the case at Armagh, then why was it not also the case in the south of the country? Is there any good reason to suspect that Munster propagandists would have lagged behind those at Armagh? I suspect not, and considering Kenney's statement that 'some of the chief people of the South, Corcu Loedge, Dési, Eoganacht, Osraige and Lagin, preserved traditions of the introduction of Christianity and its first Irish apostles' (1929, 323), I now propose to examine some of their implications.

As is well known, four saints, the *quatuor sanctissimi episcopi* as they are called since Ussher first drew attention to them in the seventeenth century,[3] St Ailbe of Emly, St Déclán of Ardmore, St Ciarán of Cape Clear and Saigir and St Ibar of Beggery Island, are supposed to have brought Christianity to Munster. As no Life of Ibar survives, his dossier has mainly to be reconstructed from that of his supposed nephew, Abbán of Kilabbán and Moyarney. The other three saints, however, have very full records which, leaving aside the usual miracle stories, agree in maintaining that their subjects converted many people before Patrick ever came to Ireland.

In the course of his recent examination of this tradition, Sharpe identified the conversion at Cashel of King Oengus mac Nadfroích by St Patrick as its central episode (1989, 387–90). Known already from Tírechán's *Life of St Patrick* and its later derivatives, this episode received further elaboration in the Lives of the saints in question. The *Life of Ailbe*, for instance, attaches to the episode the claim that Patrick specifically gave Munster to Ailbe, while the *Life of Déclán* similarly names Ailbe as *secundus Patricius et patronus Mumenie*. Both of these texts also assert that Ailbe was to be the archbishop of Munster, with his seat at Cashel.

Clearly, the composition of these Lives, which, as Sharpe has shown, are all interlinked, must be set in a context involving the need for Munster churches to assert themselves against the predominance of Armagh. Sharpe proposed an eighth-century date for the *Life of Ailbe*, the contents of which in that case reflect the contemporary interests of the Eoganacht church of Emly. Certainly, in 784 a *Law of Ailbe* was promulgated, quite possibly in answer to an earlier *Law of Patrick* which claimed the supremacy of the church in Armagh (Sharpe 1989, 393). Sharpe's dating of the *Life of Ailbe* depends, however, on its place in a group of Lives in the late thirteenth- or early fourteenth-century *Codex Salmanticensis* which exhibit some very conservative features. Full acceptance of the early date must await a thorough examination of the internal evidence of the contents of the Lives.

However, as Sharpe shows, the methods employed by the compiler of the collection preserved in the two fourteenth-century manuscripts now in Marsh's Library and Trinity College Library in Dublin, reveal a more unifying approach. Using the episodes he found in the *Lives* of Ailbe and Déclán, as contained in the *Salmanticensis*, the compiler/collector tried to provide them with a coherent shape. This he achieved by synchronising the events surrounding persons of the same name, thus bringing all the persons concerned together in one big confraternity (Sharpe 1989, 394). According to Sharpe, the compiler of the collection was an antiquarian by nature, motivated by a special interest in the time of the introduction of Christianity into Ireland.

There are, however, certain difficulties in this approach. *The Life of St Ciarán of Saigir*, for instance, which survives in its Latin form only as part of this collection, claims – in what seems to be an independent statement – that its subject founded his church thirty years before the coming of St Patrick. This statement, which seems to rest on the evidence of the Corcu Loigde genealogies, is reflected in the notes on the entry concerning Ciarán in the ninth-century *Martyrology of Óengus*.[4]

As far as Déclán is concerned, Sharpe proposes that his *Life* may have been written in the later twelfth century when Ardmore had aspirations to the status of an episcopal see. Certainly, the text stresses greatly Déclán's role as patron of the Déisi, while at the same time acknowledging the superiority of the archbishop of Munster, St Ailbe, and, above all, St Patrick, who, we are told, converted the kings and nobles of the whole of

Ireland. The *Life* otherwise shares the idiosyncracies Sharpe has identified as the hallmark of the compiler of the collection as a whole (1989, 387–8). Unfortunately, there is no earlier *Life of St Déclán* that might be used for comparison. However, it would seem that the *Life of St Déclán* represents a further link in the chain of textual interconnexions. Thus, while the claim of the Munster hagiographers concerning St Ailbe may originally have been in answer to the propaganda of the Armagh historians, the Ardmore writer went to considerable trouble to establish his patron as second in line in the ecclesiastical hierarchy of Munster.

The discussion so far has shown that, apart from the case of Palladius, the claim of other saints to chronological precedence over St Patrick is mainly found in the Lives of the saints, which, as Sharpe has shown, have been greatly influenced by redactorial policy. In some cases Sharpe was able to illustrate this by comparing the texts with those of the *Codex Salmanticensis* whose 'indiscriminate collecting is one of its most valuable aspects' (Sharpe 1991, 243). However, taking into account the disparate nature of the latter collection, its Lives still have to be looked at singly if one is to recover any historical information from them. And, above all, it will have to be decided first when they were actually written down. As we have seen, the *Life of Déclán*, which seems to have reached the compiler of the collection in the Dublin manuscripts independently of the *Salmanticensis*, seems to belong in a late twelfth-century context. Similarly, the *Life of Abbán*, which provides information on St Ibar, has been attributed to Bishop Albinus of Ferns who flourished at the beginning of the thirteenth century (Ó Riain 1986). In both of these cases the interests of episcopal sees were uppermost in the minds of the composers of the *Lives*, and it must be regarded as very likely that questions of twelfth-century diocesan organisation also underlay the other Lives mentioned here.

This view is strengthened by independent evidence of the assertive character of the southern Irish churches in the late twelfth century. Irish saints' Lives included in the voluminous collection called *Magnum Legendarium Austriacum*, which was commenced at Regensburg in the 1160–70s and which now survives in several Austrian libraries, supply this independent evidence. These texts can be traced back to the activities of the Irish Benedictine monasteries in Germany, called *Schottenklöster*, which from the early twelfth century onwards were governed mainly by Munster abbots who showed great interest in promoting their Irish, and particularly their Munster, connections.[5] Thus, in acknowledgement of benefactions received from the kings of Desmond and Thomond, the *Schottenklöster* produced a variety of documents of Munster interest.[6] Furthermore, besides promoting the cults of Munster saints by including them in calendars and by editing their *Lives*, they can also be shown to be concerned with rewriting the early history of Ireland.[7]

The prologue to a fragmentary *Life of Patrick*, now at Göttweig in Austria, states the by now familiar claim that many years before the advent of St Patrick there were already bishops in Ireland engaged in spreading Christianity. These, we are told, had been the disciples of the Irishman Mansuetus, bishop of Toul in Lorraine, who himself was the disciple of St Peter. Moreover, due to the success of their mission, they had paved the way for St Patrick, who then went on to become the apostle of all Ireland. While no names are mentioned in the fragment, which then breaks off, we may safely assume that the author was attempting to convey the idea of pre-Patrician saints. Furthermore, verbal correspondences suggest that there is a close relationship between this German recession of Patrick's *Life* and the texts in the Dublin manuscripts discussed above.[8]

As Sharpe has pointed out, Cashel was the focal point of most episodes involving pre-Patrician saints. However, Cashel became connected closely with Church affairs only after it was chosen as the site of an archiepiscopal see in 1111. Having no founder saint as such, it understandably came within the ambit of the patron of the neighbouring monastery of Emly, Ailbe. Here too, the Regensburg *Schottenklöster* was instrumental in making the case. About 1150 a monk there composed the *Life of St Albert*, Archbishop of Cashel, who, with his friend, Archbishop Erhard of Armagh, undertook a pilgrimage and ended up in Regensburg, where both found their last resting-place. In the Germanic form of his name, '*Albert*', Ailbe is here firmly connected with the metropolitan see of Cashel.[9]

To put the pre-Patrician claims into context, then, it would seem to be the case that they essentially represent an answer by the southern churches to the political ambitions of Armagh. While no attempt is made to contradict the claim of the successors of St Patrick to the conversion of Ireland, its application to Munster is compromised by the introduction of pre-Patrician saints. The archiepiscopal see of Munster would seem to have been intent on consolidating its position as the second most important ecclesiastical institution on the island. The introduction in 1152, at the synod of Kells, of the two additional archiepiscopal sees of Dublin and Tuam may well have given rise to the need for such consolidation. And, very fortunately for Cashel, the industrious *scriptorium* at Regensburg in Germany was prepared to expend much ink on promoting and defending the interests of Munster.

We have little information on the background to the formation of the various diocesan territories during the twelfth century. However, it may not be a coincidence that nearly all of the churches connected with the so-called pre-Patrician saints were threatened by the interests of other churches at this time. Emly, for instance, had to contend with the encroachments of the O'Brien-sponsored diocese of Killaloe, just as Rosscarbery had to fend off a threat from Cork (Ó Riain 1994, 32, 224–5). Similarly, Ardmore's claim to supremacy over the Déisi flourished for only a short time during the latter half of the twelfth century before losing out to the churches of Lismore/Waterford.

It would thus seem to be the case that the claim for pre-Patrician saints in Munster was first propagated in writing on the Continent in the *Schottenklöster* of Germany, in answer to conditions in Ireland. The establishment and revisions of the Irish diocesan structures by the reforming synods of the twelfth century in effect created the conditions that gave rise to the need for pre-Patrician saints. 'Innovative and forward looking as the reformers undoubtedly were, they were also demonstrably mindful of their inheritance, including, of course, that very substantial part of it which concerned the saints' (Ó Riain 1994, 23). The saints were certainly a godsend when it came to arguing the case for one or other diocesan interest. And whatever accommodation had to be made, whether Palladius had to cede ground to Patrick or Patrick had to contend with the priority claimed for some Munster saints, the argument almost always turned on the position of the patron of Armagh. And that he still has to contend with the notion of a pre-Patrician evangelisation of Munster stems from the inherent plausibility of the claims that it was here that Christianity first took hold in Ireland.

NOTES
1. A survey of the literature on the Munster saints is given by Sharpe (1989, 390–8 and 1991, 115–9). After the spate of Patrician scholarship commemorating the 1500th anniversary of Patrick's death in 1961, the anniversary of the revised year of his death produced some further publications, especially de Paor (1993) and Dumville (1993).
2. See Ó Riordáin 1942. I would like to thank Mr Aidan McDonald for his information on the archaeological aspects of this article.
3. Elrington and Todd 1847–64; see also Sharpe 1989, 389.
4. The *Cenelach Corco Laidhi* was published by O'Donovan 1851, 1–144; 20–23. The notes to the *Martyrology of Óengus* appear in the Rawlinson B 512 manuscript of the fifteenth century. Sharpe argues for the possibility of a lost Latin Life anterior to that contained in the Dublin manuscripts (1989, 393).
5. Ó Riain-Raedel 1984, 1985, 1992.
6. Above all, these are the *Visio Tnugdali*, and the *Libellus de fundacione ecclesie consecrati Petri*, written at Regensburg in the twelfth and thirteenth century respectively. These were edited by Wagner (1882) and Breatnach (1977).

7. These are discussed in Ó Riain-Raedel (1997, 1998).
8. The fragmentary Life from Göttweig has been published by Bieler (1961). In Ó Riain-Raedel (1997), I have identified the author of the Göttweig text with that of the *Vita Mariani* (AA SS Feb II, 365 72) and have discussed the availability at Regensburg of further documents relating to St Patrick.
9. Apart from promoting the claims of Emly and of the McCarthys, one of whom, Christianus (+ before 1158), may have been the abbot at Regensburg when the document was written, the author is also able to accommodate some local concerns. The *Vita Albarti* is published in *MGH rer Merov* VI, 21–3.

BIBLIOGRAPHY

Bieler, L. (1961) 'An Austrian fragment of a Life of St. Patrick', *Ir. Ecc. Rec.* 95, 176–81

Bieler, L. (1979) *The Patrician Texts in the Book of Armagh*, Dublin

Breatnach, P. (1977) *Die Regensburger Schottenlegende – Libellus de fundacione ecclesie Consecrati Petri*, München

De Paor, L. (1993) *Saint Patrick's World: The Christian Culture of Ireland's Apostolic Age*, Dublin

Dumville, D. (1993) *Saint Patrick: A.D. 493–1993*, Woodbridge

Edwards, N. (1990) *The Archaeology of Early Medieval Ireland*, London

Elrington, C., and Todd, J.H. (1847–64) *The Whole Works of J. Ussher*, Dublin

Kenney, J.F. (1929) *The Sources for the Early History of Ireland: An Introduction and Guide*, I (Ecclesiastical), New York

O'Donovan, J. (1851) *Miscellany of the Celtic Society*, Dublin

Ó Riain, P. (1986) 'St Abbán: the genesis of an Irish saint's life', in *Proc. Seventh Int. Cong. of Celtic Stud.*, Oxford, 159–70

Ó Riain, P. (1994) *Beatha Bharra: Saint Finbarr of Cork: The Complete Life*, London

Ó Riain-Raedel, D. (1984), 'Irish kings and bishops in the memoria of the German Schottenklöster', in P. Ní Chatháin and M. Richter, *Irland und Europa*, Stuttgart, 390–404

Ó Riain-Raedel, D. (1985) 'Diarmaid Mc Carthaigh, King of Cork (+1185)', *J. Cork Hist. Archaeol. Soc.* 90, 26–30

Ó Riain-Raedel, D. (1992) 'Das Nekrolog der irischen Schottenklöster. Edition der Handschrift Vat. lat. 10 100 mit einer Untersuchung der hagiographischen und liturgischen Handschriften der Schottenklöster', *Beiträge zur Geschichte des Bistums Regensburg* 26, 1–119

Ó Riain-Raedel, D. (1997) 'Patrician documents in Medieval Germany', *Zeitschrift für Celtische Philologie*, 712–24

Ó Riain-Raedel, D. (1998) 'The travels of Irish manuscripts: from the Continent to Ireland', in T. Barnard, D. Ó Croinín and K. Simms (eds.), *A Miracle of Learning: Studies in Manuscripts and Irish Learning*, Aldershot, 52–67

Ó Riordáin, S.P. (1942) 'The excavation of a large earthen ringfort at Garranes, Co. Cork', *Proc. Roy. Ir. Acad.* 47, 77–150

Richards, M. (1960) 'The Irish settlement in south-west Wales', *J. Roy. Soc. Antiq. Ir.* 90, 133–52

Sharpe, R. (1989) 'Quatuor Sanctissimi Episcopi: Irish Saints before St Patrick', in D. Ó Corráin, L. Breatnach and K. McCone (eds.), *Sages, Saints and Storytellers: Celtic Studies in Honour of Professor James Carney*, Maynooth, 376–99

Sharpe, R. (1991) *Medieval Irish Saints' Lives: An Introduction to Vitae Sanctorum Hiberniae*, Oxford

Wagner, A. (1882) *Visio Tnugdali. Lateinisch und Altdeutsch*, Erlangen

4. Munster Ogham Stones: Siting, Context and Function

FIONNBARR MOORE

The ogham stones of Munster together constitute the largest concentration of this monument type in either Britain or Ireland. Out of the total of 358 ogham stones on record from Ireland, 252 are from Munster, and no fewer than 247 of these are from the counties of Cork, Kerry and Waterford (Macalister 1945 and 1949; Moore 1981; Cuppage et al. 1986; McManus 1991; Power et al. 1992–1997; O'Sullivan and Sheehan 1996; SMR; NMI; NMS). The Munster ogham stones are found in a variety of contexts: one hundred and eight occur in fifty-four ecclesiastical sites, two are associated with ringforts, two with promontory forts, seven with earthen mounds, two with stone cairns, three with small enclosures and eighty-four are derived from souterrains. In addition, one inscription is carved on a rock outcrop which also features prehistoric rock art, one occurs in a stone circle, three in stone rows and twenty-four on standing stones of probable prehistoric date. Other ogham stones have been found in modern contexts, serving, for instance, as drain-covers and lintels.

The comparable figures for the entire country are as follows: one hundred and thirty-three ogham stones occur in sixty-five ecclesiastical sites, one hundred and thirty derive from forty-five souterrains, fourteen are associated with mounds or small enclosures, three are from ringforts, one is from a recently discovered ritual enclosure (Newman pers. comm.), seven occur in stone rows and the remainder, all from Munster, echo the figures given above for that province, i.e., one from a stone circle, two from promontory forts and one from a rock art site. Taken together, these contexts account for all but sixty-six of Ireland's total number of ogham stones (Fig. 4.1).

The existence of such a variety of sites at which ogham stones are found indicates that an inscription's physical and geographical location, rather than the actual stone (or what may have been under it), are important elements to consider in any evaluation of the significance of these monuments. It is clear, none the less, that a large number of the stones served simply as grave-markers, often being cross-inscribed and broadly similar in appearance to cross-slabs of the sixth to eighth centuries. However, when the variety of contexts in which ogham stones occur is considered alongside the topographical evidence, such as their location on geographical and political boundaries and their prominent position within a number of church sites, it can be suggested that in many instances they may have had a broader function than serving as purely memorial monuments.

The siting of ogham stones may provide clues to aid the identification of this broader function. By looking closely at this much neglected area of

24   *Early Medieval Munster*

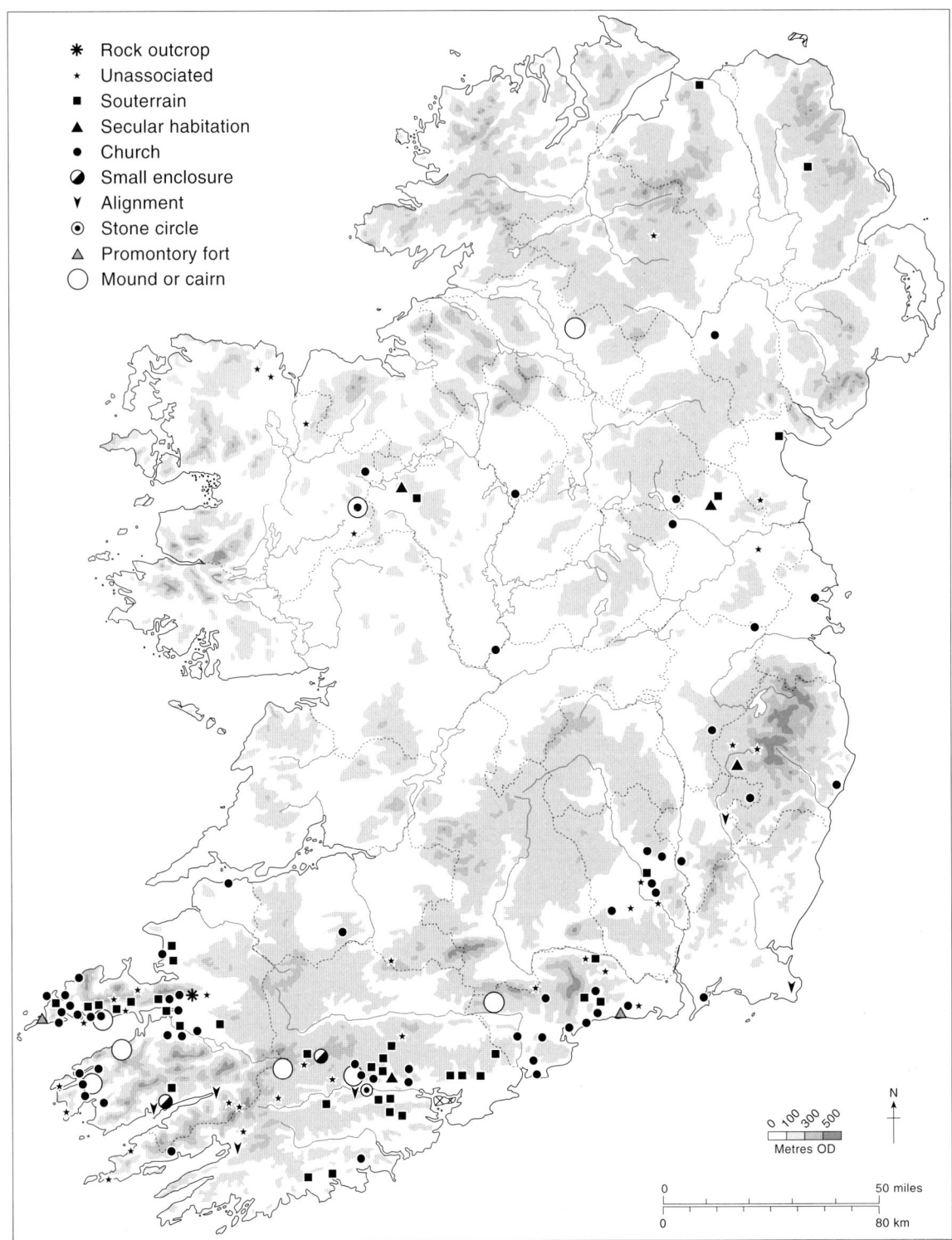

Fig. 4.1   Distribution and contexts of ogham stones in Ireland

ogham studies it may be possible to suggest instances where an ogham stone could have marked a sacred place, burial-ground, grant of or title for land, tribal boundary, church foundation, hermitage or, indeed, a combination of some of these. The presence of ogham inscriptions on what would otherwise be regarded as prehistoric monuments, such as standing stones and stone rows, may imply that there was a continuity of importance from prehistory into the Early Medieval period in relation to these particular sites. Alternatively, it may simply testify to the opportunistic re-use of a prominent feature on the landscape, the original function of which had been forgotten. The archaeological excavation of a few well-chosen sites in the future may resolve some of the questions raised by the variety of ogham locations and site-types in which they occur.

McManus lists a number of references in the Early Irish law tracts which suggest that ogham had a legal function in disputes over land (1991, 163–66). The first of these is from a tract entitled *Berrad Airechta*, in which it is asked: 'How is truth (with regard to land ownership) found in Irish Law when heirs have (only) memories without ogom in stones, without (officially) recognised lot-casting, without *mac* and *rath* sureties?' The answer is given: 'Then it is witnesses who fix truth.' The accompanying gloss states: '*Amal Fíadain he* (it is like a witness) *int oghom isin gallan*' (the ogham on the standing stone). From another law tract comes the phrase '*Comcuimne da crich*', which implies that ogham contained mutual memory of two adjoining lands and could be cited as a form of evidence. In *Gubretha Caratniad* ogham is stated to be among the dead things that overswear the living and, finally, in an archaic legal poem, *Ma be rí rofesser*, ogham stones are portrayed in a contest for land ownership. While McManus is not the first to draw our attention to the relevance of the law tracts for ogham studies (see Plummer 1923), his is the most comprehensive treatment of the topic published to date. It is obviously important to bear this evidence in mind when considering the physical setting of ogham stones.

By the time ogham appears on stone in Ireland it was well established as a script with a consistent alphabet and orthography (McManus 1991, 31). Because of this, McManus considers the possibility of wooden oghams, as referred to in Medieval sagas, to fill in the gaps in the distribution of this monument type and to account for the consistent alphabet and orthography throughout its distribution. He does not, however, consider the sagas to be reliable evidence for ogham prior to the fourth century. The use of wooden pillars for oghams seems unlikely, however, as these would not have had the necessary permanence, or indeed the symbolic power, to invoke ancestral claims. In addition, he holds the view that burial and land claims need not be mutually exclusive (1991, 165), disagreeing with Plummer who saw the two functions as having been quite distinct (1923, 389–90). From the archaeological evidence, however, it seems that there may have been a certain amount of overlap, allowing a dual function to have been served.

McManus demonstrates that the Welsh oghams form a separate group which predates the first forfeda (extra symbols designed to accommodate letters of the Latin and Greek alphabets not already matched by the ogham characters — but see Sims-Williams 1992, 35-36, for an alternative explanation) and the KOI, ANM and CELI formulae (1991, 62–63). While this is undoubtedly the case, the argument can be qualified by recognising that while the script had to evolve, the legal, spiritual and memorial function of ogham was well established by the time of its appearance in western Britain. The earliest application of the script to stone was therefore a broad one which was not confined to any one specific area of function. The British examples, while not surviving in their original locations to the same degree as the Irish ones (Nash-Williams 1950), do provide evidence for the varied functions of ogham having been established from the start of its application to stone. In this context it is worth noting Davies's suggestion that inscribed stones may have been brought into churchyards in Britain from as early as the tenth to eleventh centuries (1982, *passim*). In Ireland, at the same time or earlier, ogham stones were being appropriated for souterrain building.

Thomas has recently presented a typology for the British oghams (1994, 68–85). He proposes a development from simple ogham stones to bilingual and sometimes cross-inscribed ones, with the ogham component of the inscription ultimately receding to a simple name alongside a longer Latin inscription. This typology, however, cannot be applied to the Irish examples. Here, short, one-name inscriptions, such as the example at Lugnagappul, Co. Kerry, are early in form but, by the logic of Thomas's typology for the British examples, they should be late.

On the question of whether ogham stones have a pagan or Christian background it is simply not possible to provide a definite answer. Using the presence or absence of a cross, for instance, as grounds for consigning a monument to a Christian or pagan milieu is an unwise practice. Although certain pointers can be used to indicate the possibility of a Christian context, such as the presence of a cross, the occurrence of a Christian title in the inscription, an ecclesiastical context or a morphological similarity between the shape of the stone and examples from the cross-slab tradition, the absence of such features does not necessarily indicate a monument with a pagan background. For example, the inscription on the stone from Arraglen, Co. Kerry, clearly commemorates the priest Ronann; the stone is cross-inscribed and undoubtedly is Christian. The inscription on the standing stone at Crag, also in Kerry, which commemorates a poet, 'Velitas Luguti', has no Christian connotations, but is it necessarily a pagan monument? The presence of crosses on several stones in clearly secondary positions has often been noted, but this does not necessarily imply that these are Christianised pagan monuments. The crosses might have been added much later than the ogham inscriptions by people who might not have known the religious affiliations of those commemorated in the

Fig. 4.2 Cross-inscribed ogham stone at Ballynahunt, Co. Kerry

inscriptions. Crosses on ogham stones may indicate that these specific stones functioned as grave-markers (e.g. Ballynahunt, Co. Kerry; Fig. 4.2), but until some of these sites are excavated it will not be known if this is indeed the case. Swift has recently argued convincingly for the recognition of Christian groups of stones by reference to those with Maltese Crosses, Christian titles, Latin names, the KOI formula etc. (1996, 11–19; 1997, 125–27), and while these are obvious candidates, the absence of the KOI formula does not necessarily indicate a pagan background. As Thomas suggests, there might well have been pagan Irish imitators of the early memorial traditions of Gaul, who were influencing Britain at the same time (1995, 6). And, he argues, it is not unlikely that Irish people with their own ogham memorial traditions might have provided a major stimulus to the new memorial fashion of the time (ibid., 7).

Hamlin has suggested that ogham stones may represent the earliest archaeologically visible evidence of Christianity in Ireland, referring to Macalister and Lloyd Praeger's excavations at Killeen Cormac, Co. Kildare, to support her argument (1982, 283–85). The excavators of this site suggested a division between a pre-Christian phase, with its pillar stones and ogham-inscribed stones, and a Christian phase, with cross-inscribed stones. Hamlin, on the other hand, has put forward the interpretation that this was a very early ecclesiastical site at which ogham memorials were erected during its earliest phase. She argues that ogham stones are the oldest ecclesiastical monuments but, while the ecclesiastical associations of Killeen Cormac give support to her argument, this does not mean that all such stones were purely memorial in function. Some undoubtedly were, and the archaeological contexts in which they are found may eventually help to identify them, but others may have had a secular or pagan function. In this regard ogham may provide us with a glimpse of a society in transition. It is possible that ogham stones used to roof souterrains were originally from sites, like Killeen Cormac, that were plundered by people who had no memory or regard for the people commemorated on them. In the changing Ireland of the fifth- to seventh-century period such a scenario is not only possible but likely. Smaller religious foundations, specifically single-family proprietary ones, would be very vulnerable in this regard. As Ó Riain has demonstrated, a significant number of early Christian foundations were located on boundaries (1972): ogham stones on boundaries may well mark the sites of such foundations, which in turn may well have been located in the vicinity of, or actually on, ancestral burial sites.

In this context it is worth referring again to ogham stones in souterrains. These are hardly ever cross-inscribed and in the few instances when they are, as in one of the examples from Coolmagort, Co. Kerry (Fig. 4.3), the cross is usually small and often in a clearly secondary position. It is also clear from McManus's work that linguistically early ogham stones are, in the main, not cross-inscribed (1991, 93–97), and when they are it is usually possible to demonstrate the secondary nature of the crosses. These early stones were probably more vulnerable to being appropriated for secondary use in souterrains, and this is what seems to have happened. This would appear to be especially true of the stones in the Cork area, the majority of which seem to have been found in souterrains. Thus, it is possible to detect an early phase in the use of ogham where it could have marked burials, both pagan and Christian, and could also have served to affirm title to land and to delimit territorial boundaries. It may yet be demonstrated through archaeological excavation that the legal and memorial aspects may sometimes have overlapped.

In his publication on ogham McManus has produced a relative chronology of the more legible inscriptions, based on stages of linguistic development. This chronology is used below to see whether any significant trends might emerge between the development in the use of the script and the actual contexts of the ogham stones. By testing the hypothesis that there may be a correlation between the various archaeological

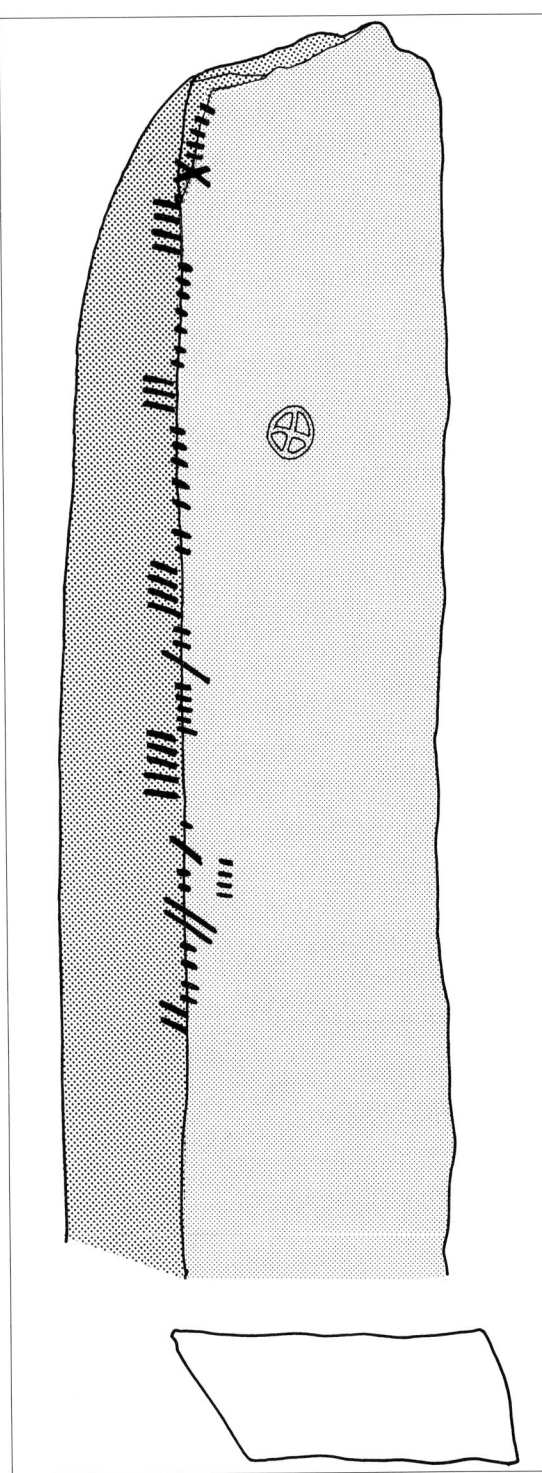

Fig. 4.3 Cross-inscribed ogham stone from souterrain at Coolmagort, Co. Kerry

contexts and the linguistic sequence, it may be possible to demonstrate that linguistically early ogham stones occur in particular locations.

Six early fifth-century stones have ecclesiastical associations (Greenhill, Co. Cork (pers. comm. C. Manning), Old Island, Co. Waterford, and Ballintaggart, Emlagh East, Kinard (Fig. 4.4) and Kilnaughtin, Co. Kerry); four derive from souterrains (Ahaliskey, Burnfort and Monataggart, Co. Cork, and Rockfield, Co. Kerry); three inscriptions occur on standing stones (Faunkill and the Woods, Co. Cork, Crag, Co. Kerry, and Ballingarry, Co. Limerick); and two stones are associated with mounds or small enclosures (Lugnagappul, Co. Kerry, and Seemochuda, Co. Waterford). No ogham inscriptions dating to the end of the fifth century have ecclesiastical associations but three souterrains (Coolmagort (Fig. 4.3) and Rockfield, Co. Kerry, and Ahaliskey, Co. Cork) have stones of this period. The ANM formula occurs as early as this on an unassociated ogham stone (possibly a prehistoric standing stone) at Keenrath, in a souterrain at Ballyknock, and in the church site of Aghabullogue, all in County Cork.

For the period comprising the first half of the sixth century there are ogham stones known from four ecclesiastical sites (Ballintaggart, Ballymoreagh and Kilcoolaght, Co. Kerry, and Dromore, Co. Waterford); nine examples are from souterrains or other locations where they served a secondary purpose (Coolmagort, Gortnagullinagh, Corkaboy and Whitefield, Co. Kerry, and Ballyhank, Ballyknock and Glenawillin, Co. Cork); one stone of this period is located in the promontory fort at Coumeenole, Co. Kerry (Fig. 4.5), and three others have no obvious associations (Ballineesteenig and Ballinvoher, Co. Kerry, and Kealvaugh More, Co. Cork). The stone from Kealvaugh More, however, is located on a possible tribal boundary.

For the period comprising the mid- to second half of the sixth century there are six ogham stones with ecclesiastical associations known from Munster (Coolineagh, Aghabullogue and Deelish, Co. Cork, Curraghmore West and Teermoyle,

Co. Kerry, and Kilbeg, Co. Waterford). The stone from Curraghmore West is cross-inscribed, but it is not located in an ecclesiastical site; it is included here because the cross and inscription appear to be contemporary. Two stones from this period are from souterrains (Tinnahally and Rockfield, Co. Kerry), and there is one unassociated ogham stone, from Camp, Co. Kerry, which may derive from the lintel-grave cemetery recorded near this site (Rowan, 1858).

During the later sixth-century period, but pre-syncope, the pattern of occurrence stays the same with three ecclesiastical associations (Araglen, Letter and Ratass, Co. Kerry), three souterrain associations (Ballyknock, Knockshanwee, and Tinnahally, Co. Cork (Macalister 1945, no. 2)), one unassociated standing stone (Ballyquin, Co. Waterford) and one small enclosure (Derrygarrane South, Co. Kerry). For the late sixth- to early seventh-century post-syncope sequence the breakdown is as follows: three ecclesiastical associations (Kilmalkedar, Dromkeare and Church Island, Co. Kerry); two souterrain associations (Carhoovauler and Monataggart, Co. Cork); one unassociated standing stone (Lomanagh, Co. Cork) and one stone row (Dromlusk, Co. Kerry).

From the above perusal of the variety of contexts in which ogham stones occur and from the linguistic dating as presented by McManus (which is based only on those examples where the inscription is clearly legible), it can be judged that from the first half of the fifth century ogham was well established and was possibly serving a variety of functions, as suggested by the diversity of its locational contexts. The church site at Ballintaggart, Co. Kerry, the cross-inscribed stone at Emlagh East, Co. Kerry, the souterrain at Monataggart, Co. Cork, and the standing stones of Faunkill and the Woods, Co. Cork, and Crag, Co. Kerry, are cases in point.

The presence of ogham stones in souterrains opens up a number of interpretative possibilities. Where there is a large group of stones in a souterrain, at least three or more, it is likely that they were removed from a nearby cemetery. Where there is only one stone, or two at the

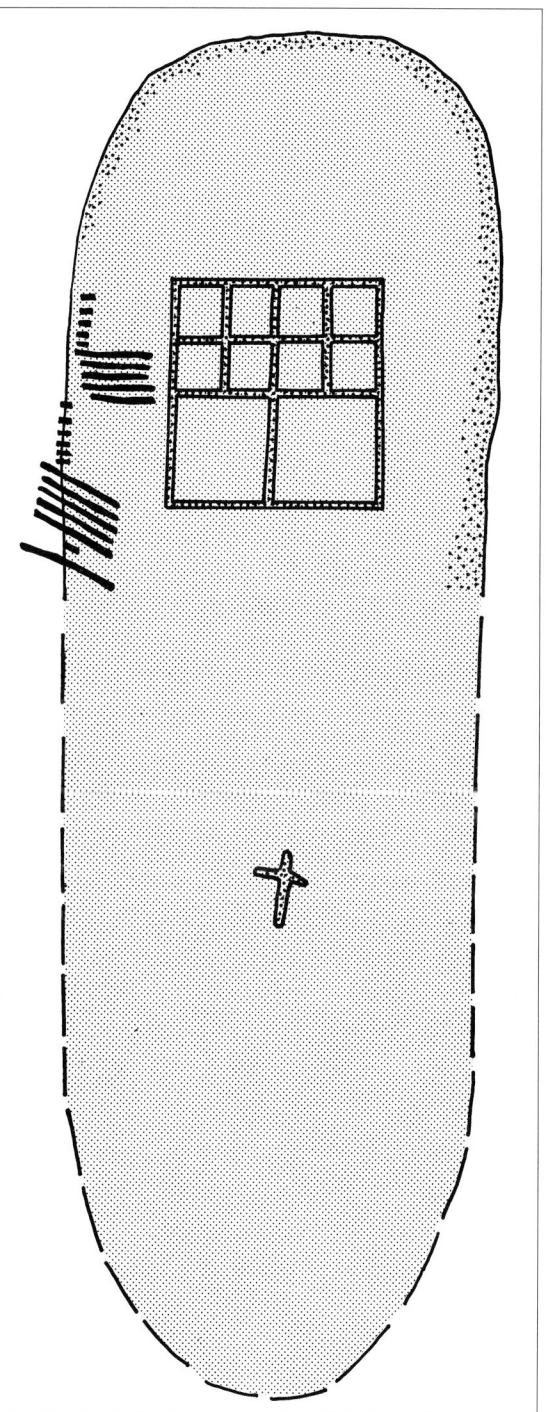

Fig. 4.4 Cross-inscribed ogham stone from Kinard, Dingle, Co. Kerry

30 *Early Medieval Munster*

Fig. 4.5   Ogham stone at Coomeenole, Co. Kerry

most, of standing stone proportions, it is possible that they were taken from the surrounding landscape where they may have marked local boundaries. Cases in point in County Kerry may be Coolmagort (seven) and Rockfield (four), and in County Cork, Ballyknock (fifteen), Ballyhank (five), Monataggart (four) and Ahaliskey (three). From the McManus chronology it can be suggested that these stones were sometimes taken from cemeteries that may have been in existence for over a century. For example, the stones from the souterrain at Rockfield date from the mid-fifth to the mid-sixth centuries, those from Monataggart date from the early fifth to the late sixth or early seventh centuries, and the fifteen stones from the Cork souterrain at Ballyknock range in date from the first half of the sixth to the early seventh century.

It is possible, therefore, that in Munster we have evidence for the first Christian communities adapting to the cultural background of the time when literacy gave rise to the carving of ogham inscriptions to serve different purposes in a variety of contexts. That these inscriptions commemorated Christians as well as pagans is likely, but given that they largely preceded the cross-slab tradition there is very little evidence available to demonstrate this. The possible connection between the use of KOI in some ogham inscriptions and HIC JACET in the fifth-century Gaulish inscriptions is a possible indicator of Christianity, but it is an almost futile exercise to try to demonstrate this as imitation of a formula is not proof of conversion. That there seems to be a definite ogham period, dating to before the development of the recumbent cross-slab and accompanying inscriptions in the Latin alphabet, is clear from both the archaeological contexts and the linguistic evidence. The ogham period overlapped with the cross-slab tradition and was ultimately subsumed into it. While this may appear obvious to some extent, it has not been demonstrated clearly before and is therefore worth emphasising here.

With regard to ogham-inscribed, unassociated standing stones, the three imposing fifth-century examples from Crag and Ballintermon, Co. Kerry, and Faunkill, Co. Cork, may have been carved to exercise territorial claim. There is nothing about these sites to suggest any ecclesiastical association and they are almost definitely reused standing stones of prehistoric date. However, the Ballintermon stone does have a simple cross added to it, which is clearly secondary to the inscription, and the townland name may also hold some relevant significance, as it indicates Church land; this stone is also sited on a parish boundary. While these standing stones probably date to the prehistoric period it is possible that the addition of ogham inscriptions indicates that the sites functioned as burial-grounds in the fourth or fifth centuries. Only excavation will provide the answer to this question and, at present, a territorial function is the most likely explanation. There are other examples of ogham stones on boundaries, including Gleensk, Co. Kerry, and Kealvaugh More, Co. Cork. According to McManus these inscriptions date to the sixth century (1991, 95). It is also probable that ogham stones associated with mounds or cairns, such as the example on Drung Hill, Co. Kerry, may have had dual territorial/memorial functions.

The ecclesiastical associations with ogham stones are strong and if the possibility is allowed that some of the souterrain groups were probably removed from early burial sites this impression is further strengthened. It should also be borne in mind that the survival of ogham stones in ecclesiastical contexts may give a false bias to the picture, as free-standing stones in the open landscape may have been more vulnerable. The archaeological evidence seems to support the legal tracts where they refer to ogham stones as having had a function in relation to title of land. There might have been a parallel tradition of ogham in wood, though this seems doubtful as ogham on stone was permanent – a fixed reminder of title in the face of time, a genealogical affirmation of ancient rights and a useful prop in times of dispute over ownership or control of territories.

The chronology proposed by McManus, when placed alongside the archaeological evidence, indicates that from the start ogham stones were serving a variety of purposes. The most likely place of origin for the application of the script to stone is in the Lee catchment area, between Cork city and the Derrynasaggart mountains, where many large, rough, unadorned and presumably prehistoric standing stones carry ogham inscriptions; these may represent a local response to fashions apparent in the Roman world in the late fourth and early fifth centuries. The evidence for trade between this area and Gaul, as witnessed by the distribution of pottery of fifth- to seventh-century date (Thomas 1994), can provide a context for Latin learning coming into Ireland at this time. The presence of Irish settlements in Britain at the appropriate time (Richards 1960) is undoubtedly also a relevant factor in the development of the ogham alphabet, or at least in its application to stone.

ACKNOWLEDGEMENTS

The author wishes to thank Kevin O'Brien for producing Figs. 4.3 and 4.4, Sharon McMenamin for her assistance in preparing Fig. 4.1, and Caitríona Devane, Damian McManus, Conleth Manning and Séamus Ó Mórdha for their comments on the text.

BIBLIOGRAPHY

Cuppage, J. et al. (1986) *Archaeological Survey of the Dingle Peninsula*, Ballyferriter

Davies, W. (1982) *Wales in the Early Middle Ages*, Leicester

Hamlin, A. (1982) 'Early Irish stone carving: content and context', in S.M. Pearce (ed.), *The Early Church in Western Britain and Ireland*, BAR 102, 283–96, Oxford

Macalister, R.A.S. (1945, 1949) *Corpus Inscriptionum Insularum Celticarum*, Dublin

Macalister, R.A.S. and Lloyd Praeger, R. (1928) 'Report on excavation recently conducted in Killeen Cormac, Co. Kildare', *Proc. Roy. Ir. Acad.* 38C, 247–61

McManus, D. (1991) *A Guide to Ogam*, Maynooth

Moore, F. (1981) 'The distribution and siting of Ogham Stones in selected areas', unpub. MA thesis (NUI), University College, Dublin

Nash-Williams, V.E. (1950) *The Early Christian Monuments of Wales*, Cardiff

NMI *National Museum of Ireland*, topographical files

NMS *National Monuments Service*, topographical files

Ó Riain, P. (1972) 'Boundary associations in early Irish society', *Studia Celtica* 7, 12–29

O'Sullivan, A. and Sheehan, J. (1996) *The Iveragh Peninsula: an archaeological survey of South Kerry*, Cork

Plummer, C. (1923) 'On the meaning of Ogham stones', *Revue Celtique* 40, 387–90

Power, D. et al. (1992, 1994, 1997) *Archaeological Inventory of County Cork*, Vols. 1–3, Dublin

Richards, M. (1960) 'The Irish settlement in south-west Wales', *J. Roy. Soc. Antiq. Ir.* 90, 133–62

Rowan, A.B. (1858) 'On an ogham monument discovered in the county of Kerry', *Proc. Roy. Ir. Acad.* 7, 100–07

Sims-Williams, P. (1992) 'The additional letters of the Ogam alphabet', *Cambridge Med. Celt. Stud.* 23, 29–75

SMR *National Sites and Monuments Record*

Swift, C. (1996) 'Christian communities in fifth and sixth century Ireland', *Trowel* 7, 11–19

Swift, C. (1997) *Ogham Stones and the Earliest Irish Christians*, Maynooth

Thomas, C. (1990) '*Gallici nautae de Galliarum provinciis*, a sixth/seventh century trade with Gaul, reconsidered', *Medieval Archaeol.* 34, 1–26

Thomas, C. (1994) *And Shall These Mute Stones Speak? Post-Roman Inscriptions in Western Britain*, Cardiff

5. Early Medieval Secular and Ecclesiastical Settlement in Munster

MICHAEL A. MONK

It is over twenty-five years since some of the key papers that laid the foundations for research into the settlement and economy of the Early Medieval period were published, in particular those by O'Kelly on ringforts and ecclesiastical sites (1970 and 1973) and by Proudfoot on the economy (1961). This chapter seeks to address aspects of the present research position and, by particular reference to Munster (including preliminary results from two studies within the province), to provide pointers for the direction of future research in this important area.

Ringforts in retrospect
In his 1970 paper O'Kelly, drawing primarily on his own and Ó Ríordáin's work, explored the issues of nomenclature, origins and function of ringforts.[1] Both he and Proudfoot argued that, despite the common acceptance of the name, the sites were not primarily defensive in nature. They pointed out that excavations at these sites seldom produced weapons, most of the items found being of a domestic, craft or agricultural nature. From the results of his excavation of a pair of adjacent ringforts in Garryduff, Co. Cork, O'Kelly proposed that where groupings of enclosures occur it is possible that one or more may have functioned simply as livestock enclosures (1962, 124–25). On the basis of the similarities between ringforts and certain prehistoric enclosures at Lough Gur, O'Kelly argued that the origins of ringforts lay in prehistoric times (1970).[2] He also followed Rynne's proposal (1964) that they continued to be used into Medieval times and beyond, a suggestion which was taken further in a paper by Barrett and Graham (1975, 33–45) but was later challenged by Lynn (1975a and b). This debate on issues of date and origin has continued into recent years, with contributions by Caulfield (1981), Lynn (1983) and Limbert (1996, 282–85).

The issue of function has been less intensively debated, with most commentators being broadly in accordance with the views of O'Kelly and Proudfoot (Edwards 1990, 11, 19; Mytum 1992, 122–23, 181–2). In addition, further sites have been excavated that produced little or no evidence for occupation and this has strengthened O'Kelly's cattle enclosures thesis. These sites include Lisduggan 2 and 3, Co. Cork (Twohig 1990, 24, 27–28), Coolowen, Co. Cork (Twohig 1975, 80), Ballypalady, Co. Antrim (Waterman 1972, 36) and Tullyallen, Co. Armagh. Stout (1997, 33–34) questions whether an enclosure, once built, would not be fully used as a ringfort, given that it represented such an investment in time and energy, and he wonders whether the areas excavated in sites such as those instanced above, which were small in all cases, simply missed the occupied quadrants. Limbert (1991, 152), following Buckley and Sweetman also draws attention to the small sample of excavated sites and to the limited size of their excavated areas (1996, 253, Figs. 6, 8).

Ecclesiastical sites and settlement issues

Very few ecclesiastical sites have been fully excavated in Munster since O'Kelly's work at Church Island, Co. Kerry (1958). Those that have been include Reask and Illaunloughan, both of which are also in Kerry (Fanning 1981a; White Marshall and Walsh, ch. 11). Apart from excavations, work has mostly focused on those sites with highly visible structural remains, where decorative stonework offers the possibility of being dated. Less attention has been paid to the overall layout of the sites, in respect of their structural components, though a number of areas in Munster have had general accounts of their ecclesiastical sites published (Henry 1957; Fanning 1981b, Hurley 1982; Sheehan 1982).

Part of the agenda for the study of these sites seems to have been set by Henry's suggestion that Irish monasticism was primarily eremitical, tending towards remote locations (1957, 154–58).[3] However, Thomas's critical review of them (1971) focused attention on a broader view. A combination of archaeological field-work and historical study has emphasised the physical integration of ecclesiastical sites within secular society. For instance, Hurley has used historical references, place-names and cartographic information to expand the numbers of such sites known from Munster, confirmed by aerial photographs which highlight the distinctive *vallum* (MacDonald, *forthcoming*), and he has shown that they occur in the same general areas as ringforts (Hurley 1982).[4] Aerial photography and field-survey increasingly demonstrate that ecclesiastical sites are located in close proximity to ringforts, such as Kildee and Caheravart, Co. Cork (Power 1992, 268, 271–72), which raises questions concerning their contemporaneity and social interaction. Although Stout, in summarising a number of recent studies, states broadly that ecclesiastical sites are generally located at the margins of ringfort distributions in the midlands (1997, 108), this chapter will attempt to show that the picture is far more complex elsewhere.

Locational studies and field survey

From the late 1970s onwards, under the dual influence of the development of geographically based archaeological studies in America and Britain and the extensive use of aerial photography, various spatial and statistical studies were undertaken in Ireland. Stout's recent book pools the results of this work (1997, 48–106), most of which appears to underline and reinforce previously held views.

Apart from early studies, such as Fahy's in the Skibbereen area (1969), the geographically based approach was developed in Munster by Barrett on the Dingle Peninsula and O'Flaherty in north Kerry (Barrett 1972; O'Flaherty 1982), well before the availability of detailed surveys for these areas. Such early studies derived their ringfort distributions from the sites depicted on various editions of the OS six-inch maps, rather than from the results of any detailed fieldwork, partly because it was felt that large study areas were needed to achieve statistically valid sample sizes. With the publication of inventory surveys – by 1998 two-thirds of south-west Munster had already been covered by published work (Cuppage 1986; Power 1992, 1994, 1997; Toal 1995; O'Sullivan and Sheehan 1996) – there will be, for the first time, a comprehensive platform for the furthering of past settlement studies in this region as a whole. Even without detailed follow-up work, these surveys have added considerably to our knowledge of Early Medieval sites. The Cork Survey team has added a number of previously unrecognised ecclesiastical sites to the record. The variation in size, morphology and location of the sites now documented raises questions, implied in the historical sources (Ó Corráin 1981, 327–41), about the way these sites should now be interpreted.

The more detailed surveys of the Kerry

peninsulas have also led to the identification of numerous hut sites, which can be found both individually and in groups, and this raises issues about unenclosed secular settlement of the Early Medieval period that urgently need to be pursued. It is surprising, given that some of these Munster surveys have been available for years, that more use has not been made of them to date.

Problems with current approaches

Before the study of Early Medieval landscapes can be taken further, flaws in current approaches need to be addressed. In particular, there has been a disproportionate amount of energy spent on typing and classifying sites based on field-observed morphology alone. This can be fraught with difficulties and sometimes leads to unclear definitions (e.g. Buckley and Sweetman 1991, 152). Ringforts, for example, may seem univallate in the field but could have had banks removed without trace in the past. Locational studies of ringforts that result in the creation of a hierarchy of sites based on their morphological characteristics (e.g. Stout 1991, 1997) are founded on massive misassumptions about the unchanging nature of these sites. This chapter will show that this approach is not justifiable.

A second problem stems from the ongoing over-emphasis on debate about the dating of these sites rather than fully focusing on the central fact that two-thirds of all published ringfort excavations date from the seventh to ninth centuries (Stout 1997, Fig. 2). A more important problem arises because many authors of excavation reports have continued to treat these sites in isolation, often with minimal discussion of their context – whether it be historical, environmental or even archaeological. The principal efforts often seem to concentrate on discussing parallels for the artefacts recovered from the excavations – often over some spatial and temporal distance – to fulfil dating priorities. These approaches have led to a unified, self-perpetuating view of Early Medieval culture, the 'ringforts, round-houses, ring-pins and glass beads syndrome'. The crucial question should be whether the material culture of this period is, in fact, so uniform. Are there no subtle variations in time, in area or in social differences?[5] This important issue is raised by Graham in the context of change from a reciprocal society to one based on feudalism at the end of the period (1993, 23).

The growth in developer-funded excavation of sites of this period, beset by time and money constraints, has meant that the subtleties of some sites (especially those on more acidic soils) are often unrecognised or cannot be considered (see Monk and Sheehan, ch. 1). Thus, the cultural stereotype for the period is likely to be reinforced. In the last twenty years there have been only five research excavations of Early Medieval rural sites in Munster. It is high time a research agenda was revived, one based on questions generated by a landscape approach to the data and implemented through excavation as well as detailed field survey in carefully selected areas. The evidence from rescue excavation could then be put into the context of the results of such work. The following discussion centres on two ongoing projects in Munster which explore the possibilities of such an approach to the issue of Early Medieval settlement.

The Caherlehillan project

The potential to explore the association between an ecclesiastical and a secular site could be realised as part of University College, Cork's programme of excavation and research at Caherlehillan, Co. Kerry. At present an early ecclesiastical site, with important cross-slabs and an unusual shrine, is being excavated at this location. Artefactual evidence, in the form of B- and E-ware, confirms that the site dates to the initial and middle phases of the Early Medieval period and that it could have enjoyed relatively high status at that time.

The site, nestled in a small valley ten kilometres east of Cahersiveen, is in an area that is extremely rich in Early Medieval settlement sites. While the ecclesiastical site is situated on the upper edge of the best soils, there are several ringforts elsewhere

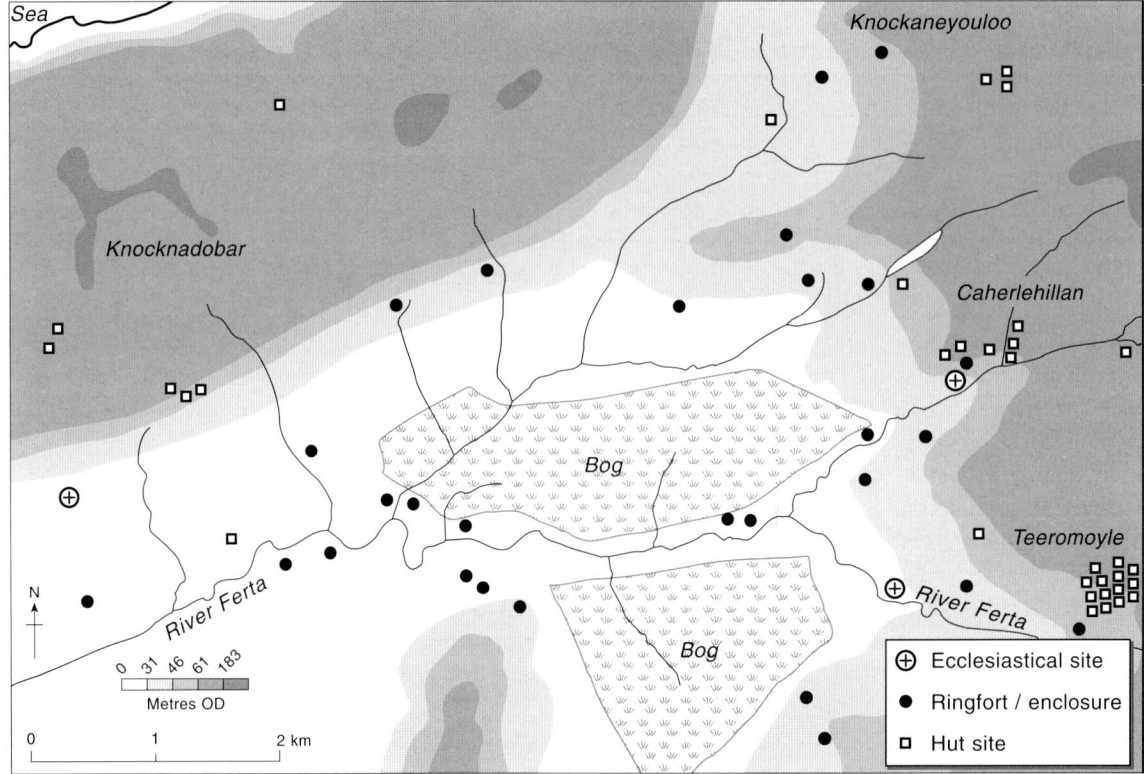

Fig. 5.1   Caherlehillan and other sites of probable Early Medieval date in the Ferta Valley, Co. Kerry

in the valley as well as a large cashel (the second largest in the north-west area of the peninsula) located barely 150 metres upslope from the site. The association of a possibly high-status secular site and an important ecclesiastical site on the edge of the best agricultural land is significant. It reflects similar situations elsewhere in the country where high status ecclesiastical sites sometimes have impressive secular sites associated with them on the edges of marginal areas, indicating that the latter's occupants commanded enough authority to delegate their production to clients located in agriculturally better-favoured areas (O'Meara 1997, 132).

In addition, in the study area around Caherlehillan there are a large number of hut sites. Their distribution is exclusive to that of the ringforts (Fig. 5.1), located above the best areas for year-round grazing, so they may be associated with the practice of booleying (Graham 1953; Aalen 1964a and b). Because this practice continued until relatively recently in the west of Ireland it has often been assumed that all likely 'booley huts' there are post-Medieval in date, but in their circularity and construction the Caherlehillan examples have closer links to structures associated with Early Medieval sites. According to Ó Corráin, some historical sources indicate that booleying dates back to at least Early Medieval times (1972, 54).[6]

Excavated hut sites have yielded various dates: Bennett's excavation of unenclosed *clocháns* at Glin, on the Dingle peninsula, recovered only modern material, none of which was primary to the structures (1994, 44–45); but examples at Beginish Island and, more recently, Coarhabeg, on Valentia Island, have produced Early Medieval dates, the latter producing a radiocarbon date ranging from AD562–748 (Hayden 1995, 44). However, a similar structure elsewhere on Valentia, in spatial association with a fulacht fiadh, has produced a prehistoric date (Hayden 1994, 42–43). Many hut sites are associated with souterrains and in this context it is important to stress that McCarthy noted that 40 per cent of souterrains in Cork are not associated with enclosures (1977), indicating the likely importance of unenclosed settlement during the Early Medieval period.

It is apparent that the unfree tenants or serfs who are mentioned in contemporary texts must have lived somewhere, but rarely, if ever, have their habitation sites been found in potential association with secular or ecclesiastical sites. Our understanding of Early Medieval society would benefit greatly if this matter was investigated further. While the Caherlehillan huts may be specialised in use (booleying) and therefore atypical, it is important to attempt to establish their contemporaneity with the nearby cashel and ecclesiastical site. It is also worthy of note that there are many relict field-boundaries in the general vicinity of the Caherlehillan sites. Although these might be of any date, they are potentially of Early Medieval origin and it is hoped to test this hypothesis.

The Lisleagh project
In 1981 a landscape-based project was initiated in the Lisleagh area of north Cork in order to explore Early Medieval settlement there (Figs. 5.2 and 5.3). The project originally sought to address some of the then-current questions of Early Medieval settlement, not least the exploration of the chronological, functional and social relationships of the clustered ringforts which were becoming increasingly apparent from fieldwork.

As a starting point two ringforts, located just forty metres apart, were chosen for excavation. Preliminary discussions of the results from both sites have been published (Monk 1988, 57–60; 1995, 105–16), but in the present context it is worth repeating that the positioning of their entrances, both of which are upslope from the south-facing common ground between them, implies choices in the organisation and control of space outside as well as inside the ringforts. The disposition of the entrances also suggests that the sites were occupied contemporaneously, though the orientation of the Lisleagh I entrance suggests that it was in place before Lisleagh II was constructed.

Attention must be drawn here to the impressive enclosing bank of Lisleagh I, with its palisade, although it has a relatively simple entrance. In the context of the hit-and-run cattle-raiding style of warfare that was current during the main period of ringfort use (up to the end of the tenth century), such sites could be considered defensive,[7] as was first proposed by de Paor and de Paor (1958, 79). The prospection and subsequent excavation of Lisleagh II demonstrated clearly that this was no mere cattle enclosure. The fact that it too had been an occupation site serves to focus attention on the relationship between it and Lisleagh I. The evidence of an overlapping sequence of occupation between the two sites is of relevance to Mallory and McNeill's caution in accepting clustered ringforts as contemporary, where they suggest that clusters should be seen as a sequence of abandoned sites (1991, 204). For the record, the most conservative estimate shows an occupation range for Lisleagh I of a minimum of 240 years (based on the radiocarbon determinations for the site).

The Lisleagh entrances and their orientation raise other locational issues that have relevance for secular settlement generally. The sites are located on the western end of a ridge that originates in the Kilworth Hills. Any routeway following this ridge, like the 'mass path' marked on the OS map (and used until relatively recently), would pass immediately south of the two sites and swing to the south-west to avoid the boggy ground below them (Fig. 5.3). The two sites have a commanding view to the south and west, overlooking this pathway as it continues westwards in the direction of a ford across the river Funshion, passing en route a possible ecclesiastical site (Killeagh). While the

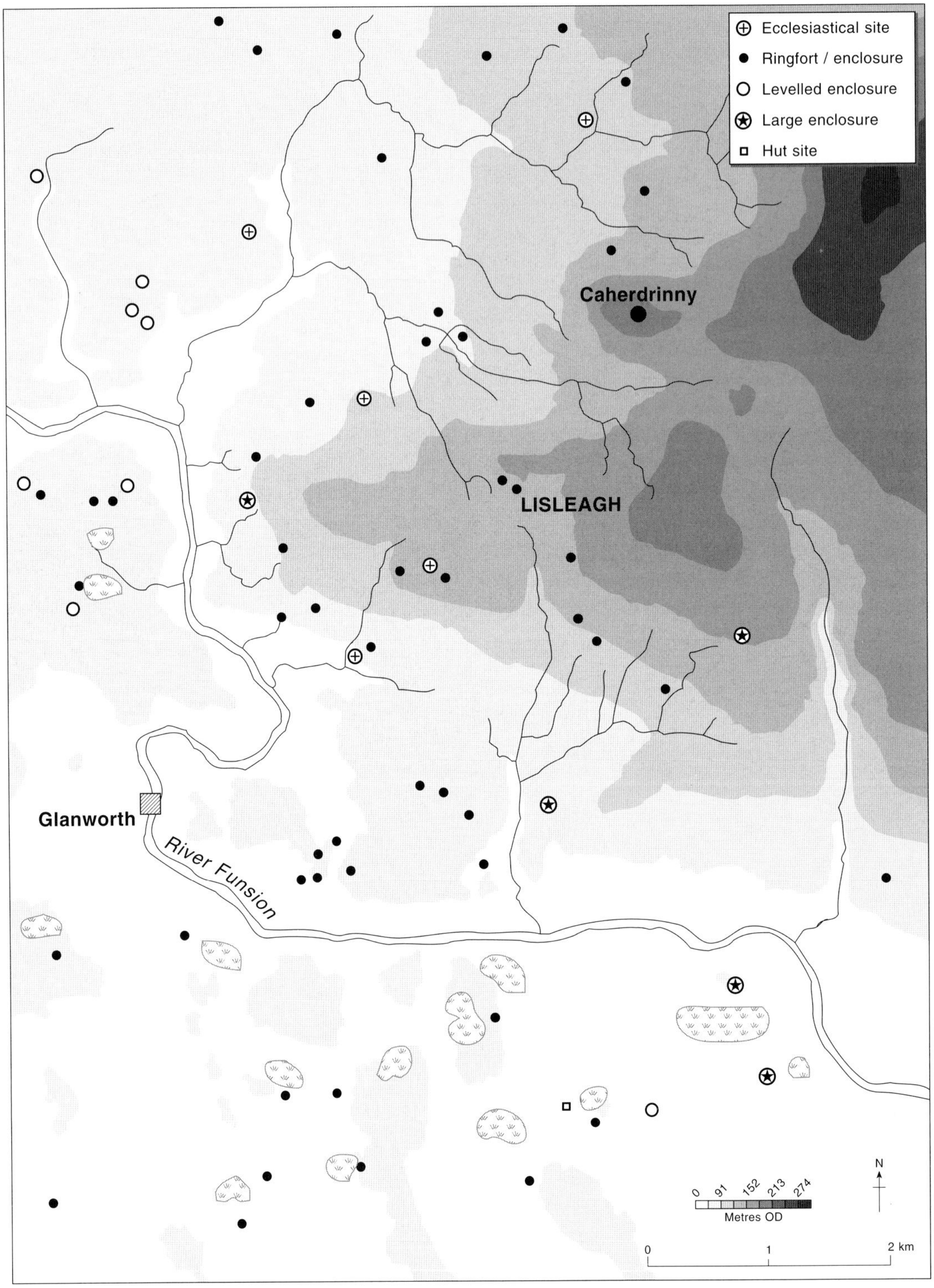

Fig. 5.2 Distribution of sites of probable Early Medieval date in the Lisleagh meso study area

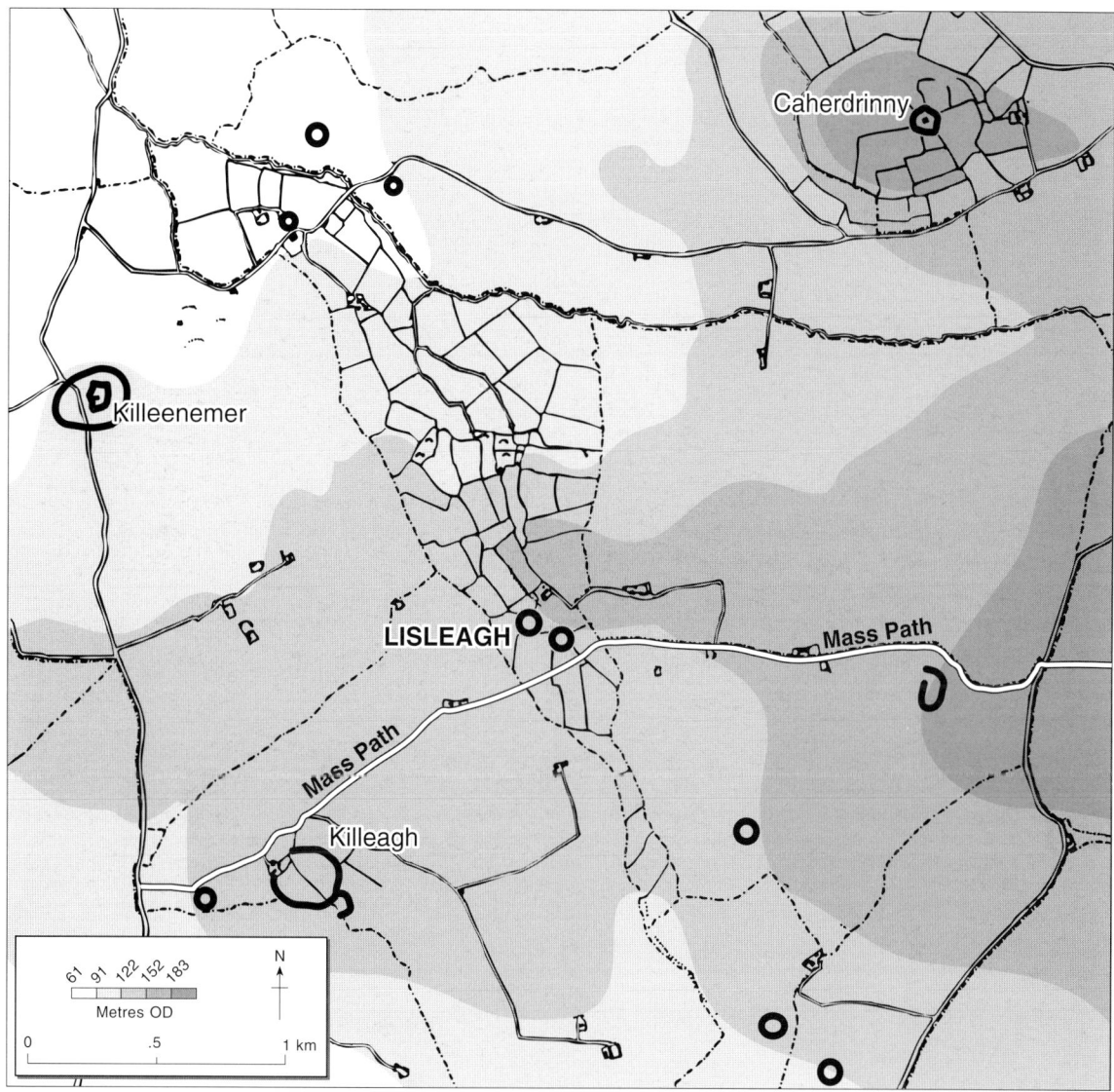

Fig. 5.3 Distribution of sites of probable Early Medieval date in the Lisleagh micro study area

existence of this routeway in Early Medieval times is supposition, its presence – according to Stout (1997, 129) – would have increased the value of land it passed through and, by implication, the status of these sites. (In this regard it is interesting to note that both sites are of above average dimensions for the area.) It has been noted by O'Meara that there appears to be a definite correlation between the location of large bivallate ringforts and the *Sligh Dála*, a major historical routeway, in Laois (1997, 133). Although Stout contends that ringforts avoid major routeways, he notes the presence of high-status ringforts in contentious border areas (1997, 133). Clearly further area-specific studies are needed to look more closely at the potential relationships between routeways, boundaries and the location of ringforts.

Ringforts in isolation?

Most ringforts yield evidence that requires one to look beyond the sites themselves and think of social interaction between their occupants. Two factors will always influence the location of sites: the first, in an agriculturally dependent society, is access to food, land and water, and, the second, social constraints, including those relating to kinship, clientship, hierarchy, ceremony and trade, which may condition or override the need for good land. In the broadest sense, the prime concern of Early Medieval society with agricultural production is reflected in the overall location and distribution of ringforts. Without doubt environmental variables would also have had a strong influence on the choice of sites and economic practice. Locational studies, both within the Lisleagh area and elsewhere in Munster, indicate a preference for siting ringforts in elevated positions, between 200 and 400 ft OD, within 100 m of water and on good well-drained soils (i.e. acid brown earths and brown podzolics). This was the pattern that emerged from the sites studied by Fahy in his pioneering work in the Skibbereen area (1969). It is the degree to which these basic considerations are overridden that points to other preoccupations in contemporary society, preoccupations which can also be glimpsed through the study of artefacts. Indeed, the only occasion in traditional archaeological research when social interaction is normally considered is when obviously traded goods are found – for instance imported pottery. Even then little thought is given to the networks of social interaction that were involved in getting these ceramics inland. The historical evidence, however, makes the importance and complexity of regular interactions at all levels of society very clear – especially through the process of clientship (Patterson 1994).

The notion that there were supporting interactions between groups in Early Medieval times runs counter to the orthodox archaeological mindset that the occupants of ringforts were self-sufficient, independent farmers who had minimal interaction outside the family group or clan. This idea of self-sufficiency seems to have developed from the ideas of Ó Ríordáin (1965, 5) and Proudfoot (1961, 94–122), which were, in turn, the products of the socio-economic attitudes prevalent in Ireland between the 1930s and 1960s (see also O'Sullivan, ch. 17). The implication behind this line of thought was that all ringfort dwellers were equally involved in direct production, particularly in the area of agriculture. This is at odds with the historical evidence for clientship which indicates that the higher status groups (*aire forgill*, *aire ard*) lived in ringforts but may not have farmed their own land at all (Stout 1997, 112).

Ringforts: the socio-cultural context

With the growing availability of inventory-level surveys and evidence from aerial photography it is becoming increasingly obvious that more ringforts occur in clusters than was previously recognised (*contra* Mallory and McNeill 1991, 204; Graham, 1993, 48). Stout also notes this evidence, adding that it is now easier to regard adjacent or nearly adjacent sites as contemporary as the current dating evidence indicates that they may span only a three-hundred-year period (as opposed to the previous belief that they might date to throughout the entire Early Medieval period) (1997, 107). While it may be erroneous to assume that all sites in a cluster were contemporary, even within this shorter chronology, their proximity does raise questions of social interaction within the cluster and, by extension, with other clusters. Indeed, the question of what the social status of such clustered groups was *vis-à-vis* single sites is also raised.

One cluster of ringforts within the Lisleagh study area for which some historical evidence exists is a group of five sites in Manning townland, near Glanworth. Historically, Manning was one of two centres of the O'Duggan chieftancy, which controlled this area until it was taken over by the O'Keeffes towards the end of the Early Medieval period (Power 1932, 16). However, unlike some single royal sites – such as Garranes (a trivallate ringfort which was the seat of a branch of the Eoganachta) – the sites at Manning are not exceptionally large. They are distinctive, however, in the degree of elaboration of their enclosures (three are bivallate and one is cashel-like) and in their location around a steep glen.

The enclosing elements at Lisleagh
Issues relating to the reconstruction of an Early Medieval landscape, or to what degree adjacent Early Medieval sites may have coexisted, have received only selective attention to date. It is obvious that the morphology of ringforts will have changed subsequent to their occupation. But, what has not been questioned, and worryingly so in relation to our abilities to interpret from field-survey evidence alone, is whether the nature of the enclosing element of ringforts remained essentially unchanged throughout their occupation.

Strikingly, at neither of the Lisleagh sites was this the case. Lisleagh I began as a site of average dimensions, but after a short period it was replaced by a more formidable and larger-diameter site with a bank crowned with a palisade. However, this enclosure was not maintained; the palisade rotted and was not replaced and, despite one recut, the ditch was allowed to silt up to half of its depth (and was even used as a dump for iron-working waste). Lisleagh II, by contrast, began as a large ringfort but before the ditch silted up to any significant extent the bank was partially demolished. Occupation, however, continued over the remains of the bank. Subsequent to this a shallow ditch with a substantial external palisade was constructed; this cut across the earlier entrance and reduced the size of the enclosure (Fig. 5.4). In the final phase this ditch was backfilled and occupation continued over it. All of these changes apparently took place within the Early Medieval period – why precisely they occurred may never be known, but it would seem that it was in response to changing social pressures (see Monk 1995).

Evidence such as this serves as a caution against over-reliance on cartographic and survey evidence, which often form the basis for assumptions made by historical geographers. One must be very cautious of the present appearance of earthworks, knowing that one cannot assume that poorly preserved earthworks necessarily result from post-occupation erosion or, conversely, that relatively intact earthworks necessarily indicate that a defensive element was retained throughout a site's history. Mytum's statement that the banks of ringforts were 'insubstantial and only constructed once' (1992, 123) is, at best, naive. It is important to remember that earthworks and stone enclosures (and, indeed, monuments of any type) are no more static than the society that produced them. Their current appearance is the result of many temporal, cultural and natural formation

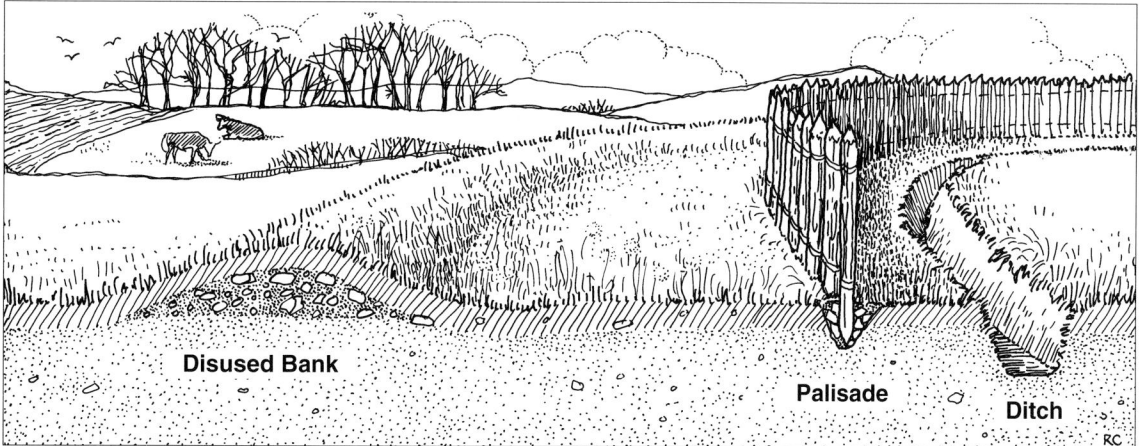

Fig. 5.4 Reconstruction of the penultimate phase of activity at Lisleagh II, Co. Cork

processes about which it is unwise to make superficial assumptions.

The evidence of morphological changes at the Lisleagh sites is not unique. Apart from the raising of ringfort interiors in various sites in the north of Ireland, the site at Lissue, Co. Down, was found on excavation to have had a change in its enclosing element (Bersu 1947, 36–37). Drawing on the lessons from the Lisleagh excavations, morphological changes at other sites in its study area may be suggested, on the basis of aerial photographic evidence, for the ringforts at Curraheen (Fig. 5.5) and Cornhill. However, such speculative interpretations remain to be tested.

Seeing the landscape: a partial record
In order to interpret an Early Medieval landscape it is necessary to incorporate, where possible, the relevant historical data and the recognition of the biases inherent in present-day distributions: the better the soils, the greater the destruction of sites, particularly in lowland areas.

In an area on the north side of the Blackwater valley that could be described as lowland (<300 ft), the Cork Archaeological Survey recorded a 20 per cent increase in probable ringforts from aerial photographs of crop-marks taken in 1989 (pers. comm. D. Power). All of the new ringforts were found in areas that already had a thin scattering of sites, but the greater number of new sites were found on the better soils (Fig. 5.6). An aerial photographic survey outside Munster has also infilled existing distributions, particularly in those areas with better soils (Barrett 1982, 75–95; 1990, 26–28). What these results indicate is that areas with low densities of ringforts and apparent gaps in the distribution patterns need to be tested by aerial

Fig. 5.5 Aerial view of Curraheen I and II

photography before they can be accepted as such.

Mention was made earlier of how apparently well-preserved sites have been shown, on excavation, to have been subject to partial destruction, resulting in a deceptive modern appearance. Field data from ninety-nine possible and actual ringforts on three six-inch OS maps in north Cork (occupying an area from the river Funshion to the Limerick border) revealed that there were sixteen bivallate sites among these sites, while the remainder seemed to be univallate. Aerial photography of some of these sites reveals that partial destruction had already taken place before they were depicted on the first edition maps, with three further sites originally being bivallate and one trivallate (Cork Archaeological Survey archives). These results indicate that conclusions cannot be drawn from site morphology alone without aerial survey or other investigative techniques.

Ecclesiastical settlement

The question of definition is a crucial one both in terms of what distinguishes ecclesiastical sites from those that are primarily secular in function and, developing from this, whether ecclesiastical sites should be expected to be uniform in type. Some excavators, like Fanning (1981a, 159), have followed Thomas (1971) in using the term 'ecclesiastical' in a general, non-interpretative manner. The only ecclesiastical features at the lower levels of Reask were burials and cross-slabs. While ringforts generally do not produce either of these, Fanning was correct to draw attention

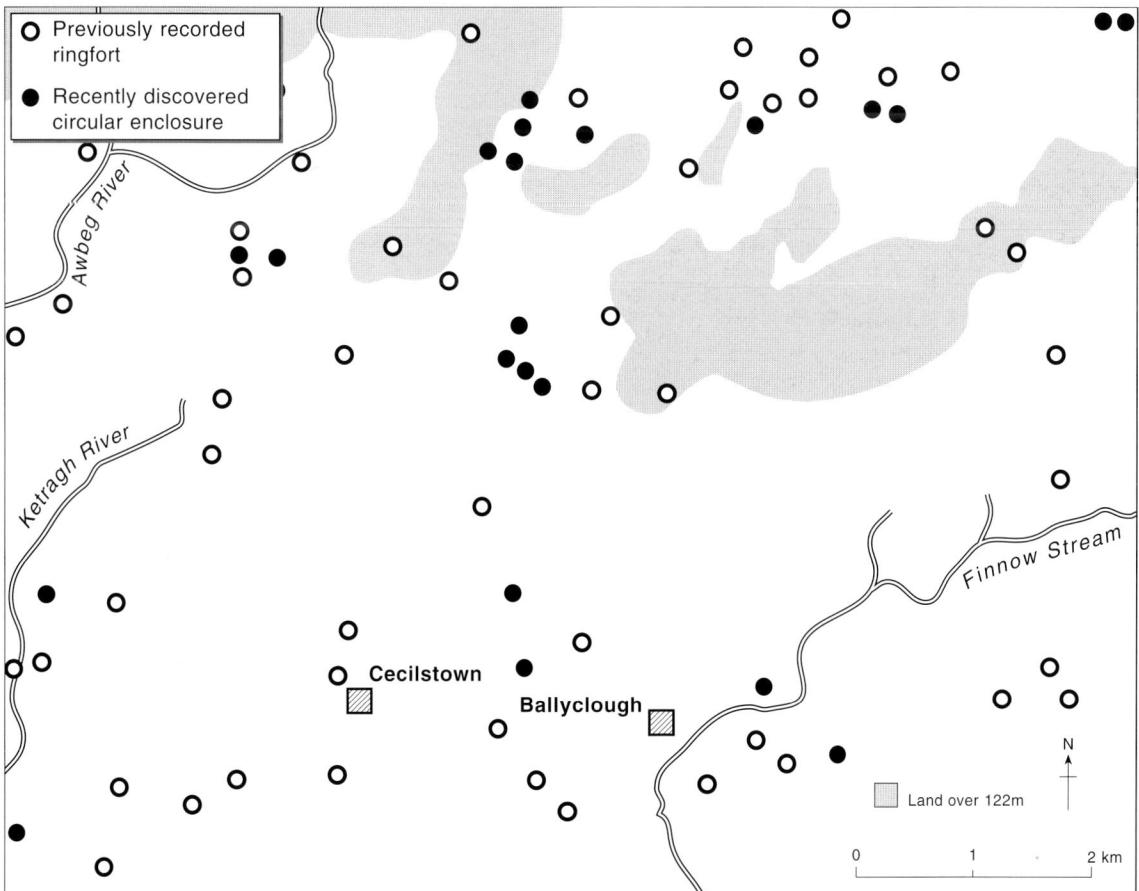

Fig. 5.6 Distribution of known and recently discovered probable ringforts in the north-west Blackwater area

to the inadequacies of definition by using the term 'ecclesiastical' in only the broadest sense to describe the early phase at Reask.[8]

There are a number of sites, not least in south-west Munster, that have secondary Christian elements. These include Knockdrum, Co. Cork, with its cross-slabs, and the hut site at Bray Head, Valentia, with its cross-inscribed stones (Power 1992, 224, 278; O'Sullivan and Sheehan 1996, 388–91).[9] To avoid confusion between this type of context and 'true' ecclesiastical sites, Hamlin has argued that a site should probably not be considered ecclesiastical unless it has clear evidence for a church as well as burials (1992, 144). But there are other indicators which have to be considered, as Hurley points out (1980, 52–65), not least among them the evidence, from maps and aerial photographs, for a large *vallum*, surrounding the site of medieval churches and killeen burial-grounds. Very little work has been done to explore the functional and chronological relationships between churches and their enclosing elements. At best there has been only partial excavation of relevant sites, and many have been no more than test-excavated.

Other evidence for early ecclesiastical sites includes the presence of placenames with ecclesiastical elements (as, for example, Killeagh in the Lisleagh study area). Care should be taken, however, in using this evidence alone. Excavation of at least one site with an apparent '*vallum*' and a 'Kill' placename element did not produce affirmative evidence for its non-secular use. Killederdadrum, Co. Tipperary, excavated by Manning, yielded round houses and souterrains alone (1984, 217–68). Killederdadrum, while extensively excavated in comparison with other sites, was not totally investigated and it is possible that the trenches missed ecclesiastical evidence. There is a strong case to be made for geophysical and geochemical survey of these sites in advance of excavation in order to help identify key areas.

Changes in ecclesiastical status
Once a site has been identified as ecclesiastical (using the indicators outlined above, amongst others, and including the presence of bullaun stones – although see Hamlin 1992, 141), it seems as though the tendency in current archaeological analysis has been to lump it *en masse* with others. The underlying assumption seems to be that most of these sites were permanent monastic settlements. Hurley and Ó Corráin detail the evidence for the existence of a range of sites, from large monasteries to hermitages, some attached to larger monasteries and some linked to particular families (Ó Corráin 1981, 328–29; Hurley 1982, 299). It follows that, within this wide range and hierarchy, the status of a site will affect not only its size and the structures present at it, but also its relations with neighbouring secular sites (Hamlin 1992, 142).

Taking only those few sites in the north Cork area where the *vallum* survives, variations become apparent. Killeenemer, for instance, according to the *Crichad an Chaoilli*, was the chief church of a powerful tuath and later became the site of an episcopal court (Power 1932, 30; MacCotter and Nicholls 1996, 23). It is the largest ecclesiastical enclosure in the area, measuring up to 215 m in diameter (Fig. 5.7). Labbamolaga, chief church of a border tuath, located on a routeway on the periphery of ringfort distribution, has a diameter of 150 m. By comparison, Kilmaculla, probably a subsidiary church (Power, ibid.), is surrounded by an oval enclosure not much bigger than a large ringfort (c. 90 m by c. 60 m). A pattern that emerges clearly in the north Cork area is the pairing of ecclesiastical sites with royal sites or with apparently high-status ringforts. Examples include Rossach (*Rosach na Rí*), thought to be a burial place of kings (Power ibid., 5, 19, 122), which is a large ringfort located within 30 m of an ecclesiastical site, and the O'Duggan centre at Manning, located 900 m from Cromglaise, which Power cites as an early ecclesiastical site with at least one royal burial (ibid., 23, 26, 80).

Historical sources widely document the degree to which the Church and ruling families were intimately associated. The Loichsi genealogies clearly indicate that many ecclesiastical centres were private or proprietary churches of the ruling élite (Ó Corráin 1981, 337). Other sites appear to have fulfilled other roles. Killeenemer, for instance, has no documented royal association and there is no surviving evidence of any high-status sites nearby (Fig. 5.7).

The broad integration of ecclesiastical sites into secular society, whether through the market or craft functions associated with the larger sites or through the liturgical needs which the smaller sites may have fulfilled for surrounding communities, is in urgent need of archaeological exploration (Graham 1993, 23). Fluid association between ecclesiastical and secular sites occurred throughout the Early Medieval period and must, inevitably, have left traces, however subtle, whether as recognised sites, routeways or boundaries in the landscape. As Ó Corráin recognised, the need to search for traces of these shifting and subtle relationships should have been on the archaeological research agenda since the results of O'Kelly's excavation at Church Island were published in 1958.

It should be evident from the points made above, which have been primarily sourced from Munster (the centre for several formative studies relevant to these issues), that the Early Medieval period is not at all as static as it might seem. Confirmation of this is now coming from landscape-based projects, which obviously provide a better basis for reaching understanding than either a focus on single sites or the use of parallels derived from large-scale regional studies. It is likely that the evidence for dynamic change gained from area projects will have a wider relevance that could then be applied and explored in regional projects.

Fig. 5.7   Aerial view of Killeenemer ecclesiastical site

Conclusion

In this chapter I have reviewed some of the acknowledged agendas which have affected the study of Early Medieval settlement in Munster and noted that research in this area is still dominated by typological, terminological, chronological and functional concerns. The application of a geographically based approach, however, despite its limitations, allows for the emergence of questions concerning social interaction between the monuments in the context of the social, physical and economic landscapes in which they are set. It is this strategy, formulated with a view to detailing chronological change in the landscape, that has provided the basis for the new agenda already inherent in the two Munster projects detailed above. This approach has been greatly facilitated by the availability of published surveys. In turn, the sheer mass of the data now available highlights the need to explore more fully the changing socio-economic relationships between secular and ecclesiastical settlement.

Postscript

This chapter began as a relatively straightforward account of the background and present state of knowledge of settlement in Early Medieval Munster. The more the evidence comes together, however, the more difficult it is to regard settlement or society as being in any way static for any time during the period. The changes that gave rise to the dynamic settlement situation in Munster are likely to have been part of an island-wide phenomenon for which there are now, from several different sources, some key pieces of evidence becoming available. It is not possible to go into any detailed arguments at this stage (a more detailed discussion of this evidence and the interpretations that could be made from it will be published at a later date). It is, perhaps, appropriate at this point to make a broad brushstroke summary of some of the main themes that are relevant to changes in Early Medieval settlement.

In the period from the late seventh to the tenth centuries, a time of favourable environmental conditions (Lamb 1977, 437, 440; 1981, 60–61; Baillie 1995, 27), the evidence from pollen, macro-plant remains and animal-bone studies combines to indicate that there was an expansion in agriculture (McCormick 1983, 1995; Monk 1991; O'Connell 1991; Weir 1993; McCarthy, ch. 7; Monk et al., ch. 8). In turn, perhaps, this led to the adoption and proliferation of horizontal water-mills during the period. Whether this expansion was necessitated by a population increase or created one is not clear.[10] Dendrochronological and pollen records indicate that large areas of woodland were cleared for agriculture, but this clearance was presumably also carried out to supply fuel for domestic fires as well as for smithying and smelting[11] (see Tierney, ch. 10). Iron tools, in particular, became very common during this period and are likely to have enabled more effective land clearance and tillage.

Ecclesiastical institutions possibly led the way in this period of agricultural expansion and technological change – particularly in areas such as milling – and they provided patronage for various craftsmen, especially metal-workers. Ecclesiastical sites probably became centres for trade and local agricultural 'marts' (hence, perhaps, their large enclosures), and leading secular families developed close ties with them. Amongst other benefits this enabled donations to be made to the Church while keeping the wealth 'in the family', as it were.

It seems likely, then, that there was a population increase. However this came about, it would certainly have caused a serious strain on the client-based social structure and exchange system. The contemporary codification of the law tracts could be viewed as an attempt to halt some sort of social disintegration resulting from this strain. In this context, these tracts might together be regarded as an aspirational or idealised statement and hence should not be taken to reflect situations which obtained throughout the period. (They have been regarded in this way in the past, not least by Stout in his interpretation of the midlands settlement evidence (1991,

201–43).) Although there was an expansion of agriculture into marginal areas in the west and north of Ireland at this time, the areas with the best agricultural land would have been the most intensively exploited ones. With the increasing density of settlement in such areas individual client groups may have been less able to fulfil their obligations (especially during poor agricultural seasons). Territorial and social unrest may have resulted, and though this probably preceded the main period of Viking activity it may have been exacerbated by their raids. The main attraction, whether the raiders were Vikings or not, was the fact that sites such as monasteries possessed easily portable wealth.

While Ó Corráin, following Lucas (1967, 208), has noted that raiding monasteries was not an uncommon occurrence before the arrival of the Norse, it seems possible that the activities of the Vikings were used as a justification by the more powerful secular hierarchies to increase their power and influence by attacking their neighbours (including their monasteries). In this way they might have used 'the politics of fear' to increase their control of communities within their sphere of influence. The peak of the dispersed-settlement, client-based economy coincided with the beginnings of the Viking raids on Ireland (795–840), when raids were largely coastal and engendered fear rather than widespread social disruption. However, by the beginning of the 840s these raids became more intensive and, as they were penetrating further inland, they probably became more disruptive.

The Early Medieval social structure appears to have been coming under increasing pressure, both internally (from the population increase) and externally (from the Vikings), forcing changes that had an inevitable effect upon settlement patterns. By the end of the ninth and during the early tenth century there was probably an increased shift towards nucleation of settlement. Some of the people who were dislodged from the collapsing clientship system may have attached themselves, as dependants, to the more powerful secular and ecclesiastical élite groups. With larger-scale dynastic conflict many dislodged people may have gravitated to the larger settlements for protection.

However, during the first decades of the tenth century the Vikings had begun to establish towns along the coasts of Leinster and Munster. From this time onwards they were increasingly involved in local dynastic politics. The historical evidence indicates that the larger dynasties were increasingly at variance with one another as well as being affected by internal feuding (Ó Corráin 1972, 111–37). It was also the century when proto-towns developed around monasteries, although their antecedents probably preceded the Scandinavian settlements (Doherty 1985). This seems clear from the historical evidence and is now, in a small way, also being demonstrated in the excavation record.[12] The process probably involved a period of rationalisation whereby the settlements that flourished were well placed in terms of the more important lines of communication throughout the country. From the tenth century, it is likely that trade was further facilitated by the adoption of an easily portable medium of value that could be seen as interchangeable for any goods. This medium was silver and, as noted by Sheehan (ch. 15), the silver hoards datable to this period consist of coins or hack-silver whereas those of the preceding period are composed mainly of ornaments.

The trading activities of the Scandinavian towns offered greater potential for the acquisition of high-status and long-distance goods by the local élites. These items may have been used to enhance and emphasise their power and prestige which had, to an extent, already been growing at the expense of the lower orders. The latter, in their turn, may have been finding it increasingly difficult to meet their social obligations under the clientship system. As wealth and power accrued to a smaller group of people, and to those groups located in nucleated settlements, the dispersed-settlement and economic pattern (based on extensive agricultural practices) may have begun to contract. People may have begun a process of withdrawal from the peripheries to the centres. The latter were most likely located in areas of better agricultural land, and the process would have inevitably necessitated more intensive agriculture in those areas.

Baillie has suggested that the regeneration of oaks from *c.* 930 onwards, for a hundred years or so, corresponds to a possible downturn in the climate following a period of amelioration.[13] Such a deterioration may be reflected in some pollen diagrams, particularly those from the north-east (see Weir 1995, 112). However, not all pollen diagrams reflect this change and, indeed, as O'Connell suggests, the general pattern of an open landscape continues throughout the tenth century (1991, 21–25). While there may have been some climatic cause for them, the changes indicated by the evidence may have resulted more from transformations in society and the concentration of population in the developing centres. These centres were probably being influenced both by an economy that was increasingly leaning towards a dependence on silver as a medium of exchange and by the decline in the clientship system. The decline in the widely dispersed settlement and economic systems that had developed from the sixth century, as well as the increasing power of the controlling élite, may have marked the effective end of the ringfort which had been the main feature of the dispersed socio-economic system based on clientship.

The nature and type of Early Medieval territorial conflict had changed by the later tenth century. The development of larger socio-political units would have resulted in a situation where larger armies could have been sustained. Wars were no longer little more than a series of hit-and-run cattle raids. Even by the beginning of the century the Vikings played an important part in changing the nature of Irish warfare. From the mid-tenth century onwards there was an increased occurrence of pitched battles (Flanagan 1996, 53).[14] The weapons and style of warfare changed and may have rendered the ringfort obsolete as a defensive structure. Only those that were able to raise their ringfort interiors could have afforded themselves some defence. The ability to do this may have rested only with the senior members of the tuath, who had enough retainers or clients to draw on to carry out the large amounts of labour involved in raising the interior of even a standard-sized ringfort. Platform ringforts or rath mounds in this scenario, therefore, probably date to a period from the ninth or tenth centuries (see Lynn 1981, 148–51, 166–69). During the initial period of unrest (from the ninth century) it is likely that ringforts continued to be built, refurbished and furnished with souterrains,[15] although, because of the changes discussed above, they became increasingly redundant.

By the early part of the eleventh century, society would have stabilised to some extent. But it was a very different society to that of a century earlier. To date there is very little archaeological evidence for settlements of this period apart from the Scandinavian towns. Both Doherty and Graham argue that the monastic and perhaps the royal centres functioned primarily as proto-towns by this period (1985; 1993, 26). Some level of dispersed rural settlement must have continued, however, and the areas within some ringforts probably continued to be occupied, though the basis for the use of these sites would have been very different. On balance, and as suggested from the dating evidence, there would have been widespread abandonment of ringforts by this time (Stout 1997, 29). Unfortunately, there is very little evidence for the settlement forms that replaced the ringfort; because they were probably unenclosed such sites have so far eluded the archaeologist. The clientship structure had given way to a semi-feudal society, as Ó Corráin (1972, 72) and Graham (1993, 21) have argued, while the developing medium of exchange with the Norse towns may have been silver and slaves (Sheehan 1998, 173–74).

Much of the above discussion is highly speculative and only loosely based on datable evidence. It also raises the question of whether the issues can be demonstrated at the provincial scale; there are, in any case, likely to be regional variations. The intention here has been to make the point that such speculative frameworks are needed to energise the exploration of the dynamics that are obviously relevant to Early Medieval settlement studies. This has to begin at the local level, through landscape-based survey and research excavation in carefully chosen areas that offer both archaeological potential and the availability of relevant historical sources. Only through the results of such studies will it be possible to develop a picture of the dynamics of socio-economic change that can be used to test such speculative overviews. The evidence is likely to be quite subtle, and simplistic interpretations will not suffice as the exploration of the socio-economic dynamics begins. It is time to embrace an approach that allows the Early Medieval period in Ireland, including Munster, to emerge from its static 'Saints and Scholars'/'Golden Age' stereotype (see O'Sullivan, ch. 17, for an exploration of the basis of this mindset). Elsewhere in Europe the period is seen as one where fundamental changes formed the basis of what ultimately became a pan-European Medieval culture and social order. So why is Ireland different? Is it different?

ACKNOWLEDGEMENTS

In the past I have benefited from discussions with many people on issues related to this chapter, not least among them the late Professor M.J. O'Kelly to whom the volume is dedicated. In addition I wish to thank Chris Lynn, Matthew Stout (whose book marks a major step forward for ringfort studies), Tadhg O'Keeffe and Jerry O'Sullivan. I would also like to acknowledge the work of former postgraduate students Brendan O'Flaherty, T.J. O'Meara and Mark Keegan, whose theses I supervised. I wish to express my thanks to Denis Power for allowing me to refer to his unpublished aerial photographic work in north Cork and for the use of his map, and I would similarly like to acknowledge John Sheehan for information on his ongoing work at Caherlehillan. Daphne Pochin Mould facilitated the taking of aerial photographs by her piloting skills. I would especially like to thank the Cork Archaeological Survey for all their support over the years and for allowing me to reference their unpublished archives. Thanks are also due to Rhoda Cronin, who produced the reconstruction drawing and base map for the north Cork area. Judith Monk and John Sheehan commented on an earlier draft of this chapter: their advice and help is much appreciated. Matthew Stout reproduced the maps and Geraldine Murphy typed the final draft – thanks to them both.

NOTES

1. For the purpose of this chapter the 'generic' term ringfort is used to describe not only circular earthen, banked and ditched enclosures but also those sites defined by a stone wall. Included are hybrids that are part stone and part earthwork.
2. Much later, however, despite his earlier arguments for the prehistoric origin of ringforts based on excavations at Carrigillihy and Aughinish island, O'Kelly states: 'Nevertheless the strict use of the term ringfort, like that of *crannóg*, is perhaps best reserved for structures of the Early Christian period, such as Garranes and Garryduff, both in County Cork, and numerous others in the whole of Ireland' (1989, 307).
3. This may reflect a chronologically definable phase in the development of Christianity in Ireland which postdates the missionary phase, but existed alongside or predates the assimilation of the Church into secular society. For instance, it is the earliest phase at Church Island which Ó Corráin (1981, 339–40) interprets as being either eremitical or relating to the founders and families.
4. Similar work (also in the 1980s), to an extent based on aerial photography as well, has increased our knowledge of ecclesiastical sites in Leinster and Ulster (Swan 1985; Hamlin 1985, 279–85).
5. This uniform view could be taken to pose an hypothesis which needs testing. The uniform approach is reinforced by historians who, in general works, usually take an Ireland-wide framework (e.g. Patterson 1995; Ó Cróinín 1995).
6. The early evidence for transhumance is also discussed by Byrne (1971), Lucas (1989, 58–67) and Kelly (1998).
7. It is worth noting that there are few references to cattle raids which mention the cattle being run into a ringfort for their protection (Lucas 1989). Ringforts were more likely to protect non-combatants during a determined raid possibly involving the capture of slaves (for a discussion of slavery see Ó Cróinín 1995, 250, 268–69). This argument runs contrary to that put forward recently by McCormick (1995, 33–35), who links the rise of the ringfort with the increased value attached to cattle following the more widespread adoption of a dairying economy.
8. Outside the region, the results of the excavation of a site at Millockstown, Co. Louth, raises some issues that may have implications further afield (Manning 1986). The site produced evidence of a lintelled-grave cemetery but no clear evidence for any other ecclesiastical association. While it was only partly sampled through a series of trenches, the site revealed a succession of enclosures, the earliest producing an Iron Age date. The second-phase enclosure was more typical of a ringfort. If the burial evidence is any indication and given the limited area

9. In the case of Knockdrum, Somerville mentions that the cross-marked stone's location in the entranceway of the site indicates that it was not in its original position. There may be a question as to whether it was primary to the site at all. In the few cases in the south-west where cross-inscribed stones are found associated with ringforts, they are usually in a secondary position, as in two examples from the Dingle peninsula – at Gortnagullanagh and Aghacarrible. In the first case, the feature is an ogham stone and forms a lintel over the entrance to the fort while, in the second, it is built into a souterrain (Cuppage 1986, 226, 103–4).

Excavated, it seems that there was not only a possible succession from a secular to a ritual function on this site but also later Iron age antecedence to this activity. Perhaps such evidence, where ritual/ecclesiastical sites may not have developed on virgin ground, needs to be explored further elsewhere – not least in Munster.

10. The question of population expansion in Early Medieval Ireland is raised by Ó Corráin (1972, 48–49) where it is linked to the expansion of monasticism in the sixth to seventh centuries. He discusses the increased use of words from this time which suggest expansion into new areas, for example *Disert* (waste land) and *Cluain* (pasture once under forest). Both Ó Cróinín and Patterson are sceptical of the population-expansion hypothesis; Ó Cróinín (1995, 103, 108), quoting MacNiocaill (1981), feels it is impossible to estimate past populations, while Patterson is critical of Charles-Edwards's (1972) formative position on this issue and the evidence that Ó Corráin uses (1994, 371). She argues that *Disert* is not necessarily totally waste ground, but could have been used at one time for grazing and tillage, and that *Cluain* could refer to the re-clearance of land previously cleared. Depending on the context, the increased usage of these terms would still mean greater agricultural activity – perhaps resulting from the demand of a greater population. Equally, however, the usage could have arisen from an increased demand for surpluses in power struggles between secular and ecclesiastical élites. On balance, despite various plagues, particularly in the mid-seventh century, the population seems to have increased, at least up to the mid-ninth century, as evidenced from the trends suggested by pollen diagrams (O'Connell 1991; Weir 1993).

11. The importance of iron-working in Early Medieval times is attested to by Scott's work (1990, 99–101). O'Kelly noted from his experiments that it takes 4 cwt of oak charcoal, or 2.4 tons of wood, to produce 1 lb of usable iron (O'Kelly, pers. comm.). This would represent a considerable impact on oak woodlands in such areas as County Cork, where there is substantial evidence for iron-working from Early Medieval sites.

12. See, for instance, King 1996 for relevant evidence from Clonmacnoise, Co. Offaly.

13. Lamb has suggested that, following a damp climatic phase from the 500s until 650–700 for Northern Europe, there was a warm drier phase, with temperature extremes, lasting until the tenth century. In the later tenth century, and for a time afterwards, there was moisture stress with oaks putting on narrow rings. A cooler, damper climate followed from c. 1200 onwards (1981, 60–65).

14. This reference to a pitched battle at Sologhead, Co. Tipperary, in 967, is taken from *Cogadh Gaedhel re Gallaibh*. While Flanagan recognises that this source may have been subject to exaggeration, she feels that it could not have been totally exaggerated – otherwise it would not have been accepted at the time it was written in the twelfth century.

15. The increased occurrence of souterrains from the eighth century onwards may indirectly indicate a change in the concept of wealth from bulky agriculturally based produce to portable, interchangeable and more easily convertible items of metalwork for which hiding places were needed.

BIBLIOGRAPHY

Aalen, F.H.A. (1964a) 'Clochans as transhumance dwellings on the Dingle Peninsula, Co. Kerry', *J. Roy. Soc. Antiq. Ir.* 94, 39–45

Aalen, F.H.A. (1964b) 'Transhumance in the Wicklow Mountains', *Ulster Folklife* 10, 65–72

Baillie, M.G.L. (1995) *A Slice Through Time*, London

Barrett G.F. (1972) 'The ringfort: a study in settlement geography with special reference to south Co. Donegal and the Dingle area', unpublished PhD thesis, Queen's University, Belfast

Barrett G.F. (1980) 'A field survey and morphological study of ringforts in south Co. Donegal', *Ulster J. Archaeol.* 43, 39–51

Barrett G.F. (1982) 'Aerial Photography and the study of early settlement structures in Ireland', *Aerial Archaeol.* 6, 27–37

Barrett, G.F. and Graham, B.J. (1975) 'Some considerations concerning the dating and distribution of ringforts in Ireland', *Ulster J. Archaeol.* 38, 33–45

Bennett, I. (1994) 'Excavations at Glin North', in I. Bennett, (ed.), *Excavations 1993*, 44–45, Dublin

Bersu, G. (1947) 'The Rath in Townland Lissue, Co. Antrim; a report on excavations in 1946', *Ulster J. Archaeol.* 10, 30–58

Buckley, V. and Sweetman, D. (1991) *Archaeological Survey of County Louth*, Dublin

Byrne, F.J. (1971) 'Tribes and tribalism in early Ireland', *Ériu* 22, 28–66

Caulfield. S. (1981) 'Some Celtic problems in the Irish Iron Age', in D. Ó Corráin (ed.), *Irish Antiquity*, 205–15, Cork

Charles-Edwards, T.M. (1972) 'Kinship, status and the origins of the hide', *Past and Present* 56, 3–33

Cuppage, J. (1986) *Dingle Peninsula Archaeological Survey*, Ballyferriter

De Paor, M. and de Paor, L. (1958) *Early Christian Ireland*, London

Doherty, C. (1985) 'Monastic towns in Ireland', in H.B. Clarke and A. Simms (eds.), *The Comparative History of Urban Origins in Non-Roman Europe*, 45–76, Oxford

Edwards, N. (1990) *The Archaeology of Early Medieval Ireland*, London

Fahy, E. (1969) 'Early Settlement in the Skibbereen area', *J. Cork Hist. and Archaeol. Soc.* 74, 147–56

Fanning, T. (1981a) 'Excavations of an Early Christian cemetery and settlement at Reask, Co. Kerry', *Proc. Roy. Ir. Acad.* 81C, 67–172

Fanning, T. (1981b) 'Early Christian sites in the barony of Corkaguiney', in D. Ó Corráin (ed.), *Irish Antiquity*, 241–46, Cork

Flannagan, T. (1996) 'Irish and Anglo-Norman warfare in twelfth-century Ireland' in T. Bartlett and K. Jeffery, *A Military History of Ireland*, Cambridge

Graham, B.J. (1993) 'Early Medieval Ireland: settlement as an indicator of economic and social transformation, c. 500–1100 A.D.', in B.J. Graham and L.J. Proudfoot, *An Historical Geography of Ireland*, London

Graham, J.M. (1953) 'Transhumance in Ireland', *Advancement of Sci.* 10, 74–79

Hamlin, A. (1985) 'The archaeology of the early Irish Church in the eighth century', *Peritia* 4, 279–99

Hamlin, A. (1992) 'The early Irish Church: problems of identification', in N. Edwards and A. Lane (eds.), *The Early Church in Wales and the West: Recent work in Early Christian Archaeology, History and Place-Names*, 138–44, Oxford

Hayden, A. (1994) 'Coarha More, Valentia Island. Co. Kerry', in I. Bennett, (ed.), *Excavations 1993*, 42-43, Bray

Hayden, A. (1995) 'Coarhabeg, Valentia Island, Co. Kerry', in I. Bennett (ed.), *Excavations 1994*, 44, Bray

Henry, F. (1957) 'Early monasteries, beehive huts and drystone houses in the neighbourhood of Caherciveen and Waterville, (Co. Kerry)', *Proc. Roy. Ir. Acad.* 58C, 45–166

Hurley, V. (1980) 'Additions to the map of monastic Ireland: the south-west', *J. Cork Hist. and Archaeol. Soc.* 85, 52–65

Hurley, V. (1982) 'The early church in the south west of Ireland: settlement and organisation', in S. Pearce (ed.), *The Early Church in Western Britain and Ireland*, 297–332, Oxford

Kelly, F. (1998) *Early Irish Farming*, Dublin

King, H.A. (1996) 'New graveyard, Clonmacnoise', in I. Bennett (ed.), *Excavations 1995*, 76–77, Bray

Lamb, H.H. (1977) *Climate: present, past and future*, London

Lamb, H.H. (1981) 'Climate from 1000 BC to 1000 AD', in M.K Jones and G. Dimbleby (eds.), *The Environment of Man: the Iron Age to the Anglo-Saxon period*, 53–66, Oxford

Limbert, D. (1996) 'Irish ringforts: a review of their origins', *Archaeol. J.* 153, 243–89

Lucas, A.T. (1967) 'The plundering and burning of churches in Ireland, 7th to 16th century', in E. Rynne (ed.), *North Munster Studies*, 172–229, Limerick

Lucas, A.T. (1989) *Cattle in Ancient Ireland*, Dublin

Lynn, C.J. (1975a) 'The medieval ringfort – an archaeological chimera?', *Ir. Archaeol. Forum* 11 (1), 29–39

Lynn, C.J. (1975b) 'The dating of raths: an orthodox view', *Ulster J. Archaeol.* 38, 45-47

Lynn, C.J. (1981) 'The excavation of Rathmullan, a raised rath and motte in Co. Down', *Ulster J. Archaeol.* 44–5, 65–171

Lynn, C.J. (1983) 'Some early ringforts and crannogs', *J. Ir. Archaeol.* 1, 47–58

McCarthy, J.P. (1977) 'The souterrains of County Cork', unpublished MA thesis (NUI), University College, Cork

McCormick, F. (1983) 'Dairying and beef production in Early Christian Ireland, the faunal evidence', in T. Reeves-Smyth and F. Hamond (eds.), *Landscape Archaeology in Ireland*, 253–67, Oxford

McCormick, F. (1995) 'Cows, ringforts and the origins of Early Christian Ireland', *Emania* 13, 33–37

MacCotter, P. and Nicholls, K. (1996) *The Pipe Roll of Cloyne*, Midleton

MacDonald, A. (forthcoming), 'Aerial Photography and the Early Church in Munster'

Mallory, J.P. and McNeill, T.E. (1991) *The Archaeology of Ulster*, Belfast

Manning, C. (1984) 'The excavations of the early Christian enclosure of Killederdadrum in Lackenavorna, Co. Tipperary', *Proc. Roy. Ir. Acad.* 84C, 237–68

Manning, C. (1986) 'Archaeological excavation of a succession of enclosures at Millockstown, Co. Louth', *Proc. Roy. Ir. Acad.* 86C, 135–81

Monk, M.A. (1988) 'Excavations at Lisleagh ringfort, north Cork', *Archaeol. Ir.* 2:2, 57–60

Monk, M.A. (1991) 'The archaeobotanical evidence for field crop plants in early historic Ireland', in J.M. Renfrew (ed.), *New Light on Early Farming*, 315–28, Edinburgh

Monk M.A. (1995) 'A Tale of Two Ringforts: Lisleagh I and II', *J. Cork Hist. and Archaeol. Soc.* 100, 105–16

Mytum, H. (1992) *The Origins of Early Christian Ireland*, London

O'Connell, M. (1991) 'Vegetational and environmental changes in Ireland during the later Holocene', in M. O'Connell (ed.), *The Post-Glacial Period (10,000–0 B.P.): fresh perspectives*, 21–25, Dublin

Ó Corráin, D. (1972) *Ireland before the Normans*, Dublin

Ó Corráin, D. (1981) 'The Early Irish Churches, some aspects of organisation', in D. Ó Corráin (ed.), *Irish Antiquity*, 327–41, Cork

Ó Cróinín, D. (1995) *Early Ireland 400–1200*, London

O'Flaherty, B.D. (1982) 'A locational analysis of the ringfort settlement of North Kerry', MA thesis, (NUI), University College, Cork

O'Kelly, M.J. (1958) 'Church Island, near Valencia, Co. Kerry', *Proc. Roy. Ir. Acad.* 59C, 57–136

O'Kelly, M.J. (1962) 'Two ringforts at Garryduff, Co. Cork,' *Proc. Roy. Ir. Acad.* 63C, 17–125

O'Kelly, M.J. (1970) 'Problems of Irish ringforts', in D. Moore (ed.), *The Irish Sea Province in Archaeology and History*, 50–54, Cardiff

O'Kelly, M.J. (1973) 'Monastic sites in the west of Ireland', *Scot. Archaeol. Forum* 5, 1–16

O'Kelly, M.J. (1989) *Early Ireland*, Cambridge

O'Meara, T.J. (1997) 'The ringforts of County Laois: some distributional and morphological characteristics', unpublished MA thesis (NUI) University College, Cork

Ó Riordáin, Seán P. (1965) *Antiquities of the Irish Countryside*, London

O'Sullivan, A. and Sheehan, J. (1996) *The Iveragh Peninsula: An Archaeological Survey of South Kerry*, Cork

Patterson, N. (1994) *Cattle Lords and Clansmen: The Social Structure of Early Ireland*, London and Indiana

Power, D. et al (1992, 1994, 1997) *Archaeological Inventory of County Cork*, vols 1–3, Dublin

Power, P. (1932 edition and translation) *Crichad an Chaolli – being the topography of ancient Fermoy*, Cork

Proudfoot, B. (1961) 'The economy of the Irish Rath', *Medieval Archaeol.* 5, 94–122

Rynne, E. (1964) 'Ringforts at Shannon Airport', *Proc. Roy. Ir. Acad.* 63C, 245–77

Scott, B.G (1990) *Early Irish Iron Working*, Belfast

Sheehan, J. (1982) 'The Early Historic church-sites of north Clare', *N. Munster Antiq. J.* 24, 29–47

Sheehan, J. (1998) 'Early Viking age silver hoards from Ireland and their Scandinavian elements', in H. Clarke et al. (eds.), *The Early Viking Age in Ireland and Scandinavia*, 164–200, Dublin

Stout, M. (1991) 'Ringforts in the south-west Midlands', *Proc. Royal Ir. Acad.* 91C, 201–43

Stout, M. (1997) *The Irish Ringfort*, Dublin

Swan, L. (1985) 'Monastic proto-towns in Early Medieval Ireland: the evidence of aerial photography, plan analysis and survey', in H.B. Clarke and A. Simms (eds.), *The Comparative History of Urban Origins in non-Roman Europe*, 77–102, Oxford

Thomas, C. (1971) *The Early Christian Archaeology of North Britain*, London

Toal, C. (1995) *North Kerry Archaeological Survey*, Dingle

Twohig, D. (1975) 'Excavation of a Ringfort at Coolowen, Co. Cork', *J. Cork Hist. Archaeol. Soc.* 80, 74–83

Twohig, D. (1990) 'Excavations of three ringforts at Lisduggan, Co. Cork', *Proc. Roy. Ir. Acad.* 90C, 1–32

Waterman, D. (1972) 'A group of ringforts at Ballypalady, Co. Antrim', *Ulster J. Archaeol.* 35, 29–36

Weir, D. (1993) 'Dark ages and the pollen record', *Emania* 11, 21–30

Weir, D. (1995) 'A Palynological Study in County Louth', *Discovery Programme Reports 2: Project Results 1993*, Dublin

6. Wood and Woodlands in Early Medieval Munster

JOHN TIERNEY

Charcoal and waterlogged wood are the most commonly found ecofacts on archaeological excavations, yet in their abundance they are often neglected. Until recently the investigation and discussion of Early Medieval woodlands has been the sole preserve of palynologists and dendrochronologists. Archaeologists have limited themselves to making assumptions about woodland management issues based on the recovery of large quantities of wood from some excavations. This situation has recently begun to change with the increasing realisation of the importance of environmental remains, and the aim of this chapter is to propose a number of avenues of research for wood studies in the future.

Woodland in Early Medieval Ireland had a relatively high economic value (Mac Niocaill 1971, 85). Enclosed woods had twice the value of those that were unenclosed and the presence of a wood at the end of a 'way' or road conferred extra value on such woods, indicating that accessibility was an important factor. Woods were used as sources for firewood, timber, wood, bark and mosses. People had to plan their time in woods in order to retrieve enough to fence their infields and build their houses, and pastoralists grazed their cattle, sheep and pigs there; they also served as refuges during periods of unrest. If communities mismanaged their woodland resources they could lose their self-sufficiency. It is evident that an archaeological investigation of woods can reveal much about past societies and economies.

Distribution and extent in Munster

Present-day Ireland has little woodland cover (Tomlinson 1997, Fig. 3, 124; Drew 1997, Fig. 18, 295), following extensive deforestation in the late seventeenth and eighteenth centuries. The earliest available figures for woodland coverage, from the mid-seventeenth century, immediately pre-date this deforestation and are worth examining (Fig. 6.1).

McCracken's reconstruction of seventeenth-century woodlands is based on various cartographic and historical sources, mainly the Civil Survey of 1654–56 (Simmington 1931–61) and the Down Survey. The woodlands are mostly located along river valleys and apparently occur over larger areas in the southern half of the country. The rivers Lee, Blackwater and Maigue, as well as the lower reaches of the Suir, Nore and Barrow, all have high amounts of woodland. Rackham also used the Civil Survey records, in association with the OS six-inch maps from the mid-nineteenth century, to determine the causes of the deforestation of Ireland. Using a range of historical sources, McCracken (1971, 39) outlines the main bodies of wood in seventeenth-century Ireland and arrives at a cover of less than 12 per cent; using similar figures, mainly the Civil Survey, Rackham (1986, 113) arrives at a figure of just 3 per cent.

Both McCracken and Rackham have published Civil Survey figures on a county basis. Analysis of the Civil Survey figures for Muskerry barony provides interesting information about the nature and extent of the woodlands in this part of mid-west County Cork (Fig. 6.1). Some 173 (50 per cent) of the 340 townlands recorded had some underwood, while 148 townlands (43 per cent) contained timber woods. Eight of the twenty-seven Civil Parishes contained no wood at all, most of these being very small and in close proximity to Cork City. A simple geographical trend is noticeable – the further west one goes the higher the amount of wood cover is found. This is probably attributable to a number of factors, the dominant one being the relatively poor value of the land in the west which may have led to lower population levels and a less dramatic impact on woodland cover. Secondly, the terrain is composed variously of lowland river flood-plains and rocky uplands; it was difficult to traverse and thus difficult to exploit. To quote the Civil Survey, 'here is a great store of timber wood, which is of little use or commodity by reason of ye roughness of ye ways and ye depth of ye water and bogs and also the long distance of said parish from any place of traffic or navigable rivers'.

The ability to transport timber by water was a key factor in determining the survival of older woods. The Earl of Cork recounts felling timbers southwest of Mallow, sawing them into spars on the spot, floating them down-river for fifty miles to Cappoquin (the point at which the Blackwater River turns abruptly southwards), where they were loaded onto lighters (some up to twenty tons in size) and brought to Youghal for export (McCracken 1971). Timber woods along these rivers could not survive for long; even the 'incommodius' woods of Muskerry fell prey to exploitation following the Civil Survey; fifty-eight

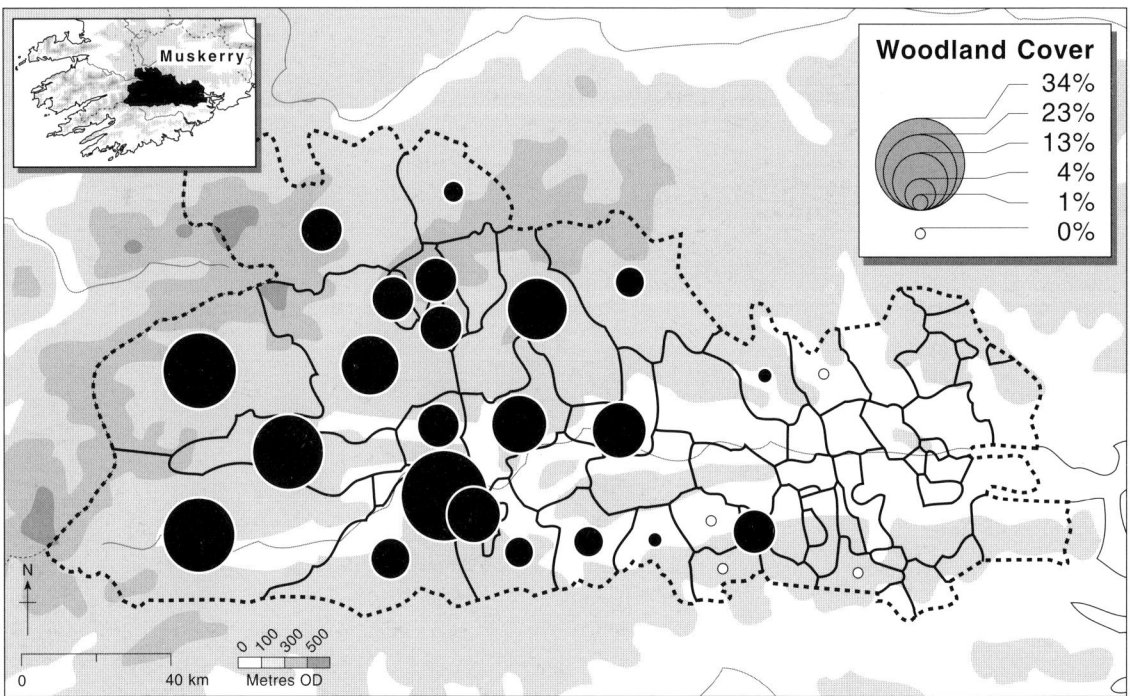

Fig. 6.1 Seventeenth-century woodlands in Muskerry

years after it was completed a note added to the survey stated that all 5,278 Irish acres of timber previously recorded were gone. The author of the note does state, however, that coppices and underwood were still to be found.

Ketch (1992) analyses woodland cover in seventeenth-century Waterford and notes that timber woods were most common on the peripheries of the county while underwood was found mostly in the western half, particularly along the valleys of the rivers Bride, Blackwater and Suir. Woodland resources were extremely rare in the eastern half of the county, especially around the city of Waterford.

Resource management

The craft of woodmanship involves the management of woodlands for the production of timber, firewood and rods for assorted uses. The main result of the craft is the conservation of areas of woodland and the development of a body of knowledge including skills, stories and beliefs. Vestiges of woodmanship survive in Ireland today primarily in the production of rods for basketry and thatching – 'sally gardens' survive in places throughout the countryside but are most obvious on the Aran Islands, where usable trees are a scarce resource. While hazel abounds on the islands it produces rods long enough for basketry or thatching only when it is enclosed in a stone-walled garden to protect it from grazing and wind damage. It is significant that a resource is often best managed when it is rare.

The availability of woods as a resource has been discussed by archaeologists in a number of recent publications. Hurley suggests that 'rigorous regulation of coppiced woodland' was largely unnecessary in Ireland because of the vigorous plant growth resulting from its climatic and environmental conditions (1997, 43). He hypothesises a *laissez-faire* approach to woodland management in the Medieval period. Geraghty estimates that if 900 houses stood in Viking Dublin, enough wood to construct between fifty and seventy houses would be required every year (1996, 63) and that, in addition, an area of 6,750 acres would be needed to meet total fuel requirements (i.e., about 7.5 acres per family).

If Hurley's hypothesis is combined with Geraghty's estimates and these are compared with yield figures for hazel coppice in Britain (no such figures are available for Ireland), a rough estimate of how much woodland would be required to service urban and rural settlements can be arrived at. Analysis of a neglected coppice wood in Essex reveals that when cut in the early 1980s it produced few wood products except for firewood logs (Tabor 1989). However, eight years later, this section of woodland was considered saleable for thatching rods. More significantly, between 5,000 and 12,000 hazel rods can be produced from one acre of managed hazel wood. In this chapter the lower figure is used in order to reflect the productivity of less intensively managed woods.

Assessments of building techniques in the Medieval period show that different amounts of hazel rods are required, depending on the design of the structure (Lynn 1989; Tierney and Hannon 1997). The basket-style of construction encountered at Deer Park Farms, Co. Antrim, would require approximately one acre of managed hazel wood to build one house while the double-walled type 1 houses encountered at Viking Waterford and Dublin require about one-fifth of an acre. It may be inferred from this that the inhabitants of Deer Park Farms had a plentiful supply of hazel woods from which to gather rods.

Therefore, to build fifty to seventy new houses per year in Dublin would require from ten to twenty acres of good hazel coppice each year. If done on a cycle of less than ten years, this would result in approximately one hundred acres of managed woodland. Using the same figures for a ringfort containing one post-and-wattle roundhouse and a number of outhouses (as found at Lisnagun, Co. Cork (O'Sullivan et al., in press), ten acres of managed woodland would meet all wood requirements for structures and firewood. This might amount to one-seventh of a small farmer's landholding in eighth-century Ireland (using Mitchell's (1997, 154) estimate of farm size).

Neither palynology nor history can provide the evidence needed to test these figures; the first detailed figures of woodland acreage in Ireland are found in the Civil Survey. The use of seventeenth-century figures for assessing Early Medieval rates of wood cover is not as inappropriate as it might appear. It is now generally accepted that when the Anglo-Normans colonised Ireland they did not impose a totally new system of land assessment units on the landscape; rather they grafted their parishes and manors onto the older Irish territorial framework based on the *tuath* (Simms 1986, 55). The Civil Parishes and the *tuatha* upon which they may have been based were units of taxation organised to ensure equitable access to resources (the tuath, it seems, was an ideal land unit within which a community could be largely self-sufficient, the purpose of this self-sufficiency being to maintain productivity and population levels and 'to ward off debt and its political danger' (Patterson 1991, 113)).

For this reason we should look at the Civil Survey percentages of woodland cover at the level of the Civil Parish rather than at the county level. By so doing it can be seen that, in west Cork at least, Civil Parishes had an average woodland cover of approximately 6 per cent. This figure tallies roughly with estimates of the amount of wood needed for a community engaged in an economy based on self-sufficiency. Thus a model of woodland management centring on the provision of firewood is offered. The cutting of wide areas of woodland to produce firewood would have resulted in adventitiously generated and managed woodlands. When resources were plentiful the most accessible woods would have been the first to come under pressure resulting from economic changes or a rise in population levels. Unless the woodland management strategy changed from a *laissez-faire* approach to deliberate management, wood and timber resources could be depleted with woods surviving only in places not suited to cultivation, such as steep valley slopes.

Palynology

Palynological research has made a significant contribution to woodland studies in Ireland; a number of investigations have been conducted in the south-west. There is however, a westerly geographical bias in such studies generally, given that the western bogs and lakes are more suited to consistent pollen preservation. It is hoped that recent work by the Discovery Programme in counties Clare and Tipperary will redress some of this imbalance. The analysis of pollen collected from archaeological sediments should be supported by the funding bodies, as this could result in local environmental reconstructions.

Summaries of the results of pollen studies in Ireland are widely available (Mitchell and Ryan 1997; Stout 1997) and this chapter will not address the more general points except to question the model that a fall in tree pollen equals an increase in agricultural activity (and also, probably, a rise in human population levels). Because woodlands are often used as a barometer for the wellbeing of a society, investigation of Early Medieval woodland can lead us to address questions such as changes in population levels, climatic and edaphic deterioration and changes in economic systems. Palynological results are presented as curves of arboreal and non-arboreal pollen fluctuation, and palynologists seek to explain a decline in arboreal pollen by a number of different hypotheses. When such a decline is associated with high charcoal influx rates, a rise in human activity or even population is hypothesised, while a decline without the accompanying charcoal is usually explained by natural phenomena (such as grazing by wild deer (Mitchell 1988)). Weir hypothesises a late Iron Age migration of people with greater involvement in tillage as the cause of the rise in non-arboreal pollen rates (1995). Social upheaval caused by warfare or disease is also occasionally used as an explanation for an observed decrease in these rates.

Palynologists use a range of techniques when interpreting pollen curves. Firstly, they are based on an understanding of the processes of competition and succession within woodlands, secondly, upon the ecological preferences of the plants involved and, thirdly, by drawing on information from adjacent archaeological sites. A fourth tool, involving ethnoarchaeology, can be added to this list. Recent ethnoarchaeological investigations of woodland management strategies (Rasmussen 1990; Halstead et al., forthcoming) indicate that some woodland management practices can result in the opening up of the wood canopy leading to greater mobility of tree pollen and higher deposition rates in the regional sink traps of bogs and lakes.

Charcoal studies

Charcoal is the most commonly found ecofact on most archaeological sites, yet it is also the most neglected. While there are problems of quantification in charcoal studies (five fragments can come from either one branch or five), its identification and analysis can provide valuable information.

A detailed analysis of charcoal from the ringfort at Lisleagh I, Co. Cork (Lennon, pers. comm.) involved species identifications and ring-counts. The type of information that can be gleaned from such a method includes an assessment of whether different trees were preferred for different functions and whether these preferences changed through time. The remains from one post and wattle roundhouse at the site shows that the latter were composed of hazel and the former of oak (results similar to those found in at least one structure at Deer Park Farms and a number of type 1 Viking houses in Waterford). A preliminary analysis of charcoal from the cashel at Ballynavenouragh, Co. Kerry, reveals that oak, hazel/alder and willow-type were represented in most archaeological contexts. It would appear that a different dynamic dictated the wood resource management strategies at these two sites. One can hypothesise that wood was a scarcer resource at Ballynavenouragh, where it was gathered regardless of species for firewood and structural uses. At Lisleagh, on the other hand, wood was carefully selected to meet structural requirements.

Charcoal identification is a relatively easy task, especially in Ireland where there are a limited number of tree species. It can be taught quickly to archaeological workers and, if broader identification categories are allowed for, such as ring-porous (oak, ash, elm) and diffuse porous (willow, hazel, alder), identifications can be conducted on-site and written into context sheets. Low-level identifications can be immediately incorporated into an archaeological stratigraphic report and this will result in a more sophisticated analysis at an early stage of the interpretative process. When sieving for plant remains, a more detailed programme of charcoal analysis can be used to augment on-site identifications.

Woods and society

Finally, the social dimensions of life in a wooded environment should be considered. Certainly ethnoarchaeology and anthropological research can extend our knowledge in a general sense, but the particulars of past ways of life in a large woodland in Ireland are probably unfathomable. An examination of the National Folklore Archive for superstitions or beliefs associated with trees and woods may facilitate some reconstruction of social activities. Woodcrafts are recorded in the National Folklore Archive and many examples can now be viewed in the folklife exhibition at the National Museum of Ireland. Folklore associated with the Gearagh, west Cork, records a phenomenon known as the *Meascán Maraíocht*, whereby strangers to the woods experienced a confusion of the mind and easily became lost (O'Donoghue 1996).

Poems such as *Cill Chais* give us some idea of people's attitudes to trees and woodcrafts. However, a brief survey of the historical records provides only tantalising glimpses of woodland dwellers. Sir John Davys, Irish Attorney General, wrote in 1607 about seeing the inhabitants of extensive woods in the Bann valley: 'The wild inhabitants wondered as much to see the King's Deputy as the ghosts in Virgil wondered to see Aeneas alive in hell.' Here Davys reveals much about his own culture and mythologies, but nothing about that of the woodlanders (McCracken 1971, 40). Arthur Young described the inhabitants of Derrycunnihy Wood in Killarney, Co. Kerry, as a 'sacreligeous tribe, who have turned the Dryades from their ancient habitations' (Young 1780, 293). It is recommended that these sources be pursued in tandem with archaeological researches.

Conclusions

This chapter concludes by calling for archaeologists to work more closely with historians, ecologists and ethnographers in order to develop the nature of our understanding of past woodlands. The techniques and experience of groups such as the Irish Archaeological Wetland Unit should be applied to excavations of urban waterlogged sites. Excavation directors need to put in place sampling strategies for the recovery of charcoal and all archaeologists should acquaint themselves with historical evidence for how Medieval farmers organised their annual tasks. We must determine the nature of how woodland management was practised in the past; it is no longer sufficient just to presume that it must have been going on.

ACKNOWLEDGEMENTS
The volume editors are to be thanked for their patience. Anne-Marie Lennon and Erin Gibbons are also acknowledged for providing information about their sites.

BIBLIOGRAPHY
Drew, D. (1997) 'The Burren, County Clare', in F.H.A. Aalen, K. Whelan and M. Stout, *Atlas of the Irish Rural Landscape*, Cork
Geraghty, S. (1996) *Viking Dublin: Botanical evidence from Fishamble Street*, Dublin
Halstead, P., Tierney, J. et al. (forthcoming) *Leafy Hay: an ethnoarchaeological study in Northwest Greece*
Hurley, M., Scully, O. and McCutcheon, S. (eds.) (1997) *Late Viking Age and Medieval Waterford, Excavations 1986–1992*, Waterford
Ketch, C. (1992) 'Landownership in County Waterford c. 1640: the evidence from the Civil Survey,' in W. Nolan and T. Power, (eds.), *Waterford, History and Society*, Dublin
Lynn, C. (1989) 'Deer Park Farms,' *Current Archaeology* 113, 193–98
McCracken, E. (1971) *Irish Woods Since Tudor Times: their distribution and exploitation*, London
McKeown, S. (1994) 'Wood remains', in W. O'Brien, *Mount Gabriel: Bronze Age Mining in Ireland*, Galway
Mac Niocaill, G. (1971) 'Tír Cumaile,' *Eriú* 22, 81–86
Mitchell, F. (1986) *The Shell Guide to Reading the Irish Landscape*, Dublin
O'Donoghue, S. (1996) *The flooding of the Lee Valley*, Cork
O'Flanagan, P. (1986) 'Placenames and change in the Irish Landscape', in W. Nolan (ed.), *The Shaping of Ireland: The Geographical Perspective*, Cork
O'Sullivan, J., Hannon, M. and Tierney, J. (in press), 'Excavation of Lisnagun ringfort, Darrara, Co. Cork (1987–89)' *J. Cork Hist. Archaeol. Soc.*
Patterson, N. (1991) *Cattle-Lords and Clansmen: Kinship and Rank in Early Ireland*, Indiana
Rackham, O. (1986) *The History of the Countryside*, London
Rasmussen, P. (1990) 'Pollarding of trees in the Neolithic: often presumed difficult to prove', in D. Robinson (ed.), *Experiment and Reconstruction in Environmental Archaeology*, Oxford
Simmington, R.C. (ed.) (1931–61) *The Civil Survey AD 1654–1656*, Dublin
Simms, A. (1986) 'Continuity and change: settlement and society in Medieval Ireland c. 500-1500,' in W. Nolan (ed.), *The Shaping of Ireland: The Geographical Perspective*, Cork
Stout, M. (1997) *The Irish Ringfort*, Dublin
Tabor, R.C.C. (1989) 'A role for hazel woodland in conservation', *Quarterly Journal of Forestry* 83, 177–82
Tierney, J. and Hannon, M. (1997) 'Plant Remains', in M. Hurley, *Late Viking Age and Medieval Waterford, Excavations 1986-1992*, Waterford
Tomlinson, R. (1997) 'Forests and woodlands', in F.H.A. Aalen, K. Whelan and M. Stout, *Atlas of the Irish Rural Landscape*, Cork
Weir, D. (1995) 'A palynological study of landscape and agricultural development in County Louth from the second millenium BC to the first millenium AD', *Discovery Programme Reports: 2, Project results 1993*, Dublin
Young, A. (1780) *Tour in Ireland 1776–9*, London

7. Archaeozoological Studies and Early Medieval Munster

MARGARET McCARTHY

Introduction

This chapter provides an outline of the archaeozoological work undertaken by the author on Early Medieval assemblages with particular reference to Munster. The unrepresentative nature of much of the material and the small size of many of the samples have, unfortunately, rendered the data of somewhat limited interpretative value. It will be pointed out that archaeozoological research on Early Medieval Ireland to date has concentrated mostly on mammal bones, with little or no attention being paid to birds, fish and molluscs. Emphasis will be placed on the effects of taphonomy and it will be suggested that much of the observed patterning for Early Medieval Munster may be the result of a combination of poor preservation and the problems caused by inadequate recovery strategies. The chapter is, therefore, mostly concerned with drawing attention to the limitations of the existing database and suggesting priorities for the future. It concludes by commenting that there has been an over-reliance on the abundant documentary sources of the period in interpreting animal bones found on Early Medieval archaeological sites.

Data and problems

The most comprehensive survey of early Irish faunal material to date has been produced by

TABLE 7.1
Distribution of minimum number of individuals (MNI) from Early Medieval rural sites where N>20

	MNI N	Cattle %	Pig %	Sheep/Goat %
Ballyfounder	25	60	28	12
Knowth, phase 1	60	52	33	15
Knowth, phase 2	84	33	32	35
Lagore, phase 1A	88	61	13	26
Lagore, phase 1B	146	71	14	15
Lagore, phase 2	112	46	34	20
Larrybane	39	52	8	41
Lough Faughan	25	70	21	9
Marshes Upper, Site 3	40	45	35	20
Moynagh, sample D	258	40	37	22
Moynagh, sample A1	59	19	27	51
Rathmullen, phase 1	25	36	16	48
Rathmullen, phase 2	65	31	52	17
Rathmullen, phase 3-4	28	29	57	15
Deer Park Farms	78	47	31	22

(after McCormick 1991, 43)

McCormick (1991, 40–52) and the bulk of this evidence comes from Leinster and Ulster. Most of the collections from elsewhere in Ireland are too small to represent any more than a partial species list and consequently the information they provide is neither of the detail nor the quality to allow any real assessment of the economy of the period. The largest and best-preserved Early Medieval collections, such as those from Lagore, Co. Meath (Hencken, 1950), were excavated during the early part of this century when the techniques used were not as rigorous as those of today. The sample of bones recovered during excavations at Kiltiernan, Co. Galway, in the early 1950s was relatively large (McCarthy 1995, 192–97) but most of it was too mixed to be of any value in reconstructing the economy of the site. There are few detailed modern reports of large assemblages of Early Medieval bones from this country; the most notable form part of McCormick's study of the material from Knowth, Moynagh Lough and other Leinster sites (1987). His work has set a standard for current and future research on Early Medieval animal husbandry, and the data produced by him for the three main domestic animals are presented in tabular form in Table 7.1. On most of the sites listed cattle are the most frequently represented animal (40–71 per cent), with pigs usually occupying second place and sheep/goat third. The archaeological evidence suggests that goats were of little importance, indicating that 'sheep/goat' can be taken to mean 'sheep' with a high degree of certainty.

In the rural assemblages McCormick has interpreted the high mortality rate amongst young calves, together with a predominance of adult cows, as evidence that dairying was an important element of stockrearing in Ireland. An increased incidence of sub-adult individuals from tenth- and eleventh-century Fishamble Street indicates that part of the herd was deliberately fattened for slaughter outside the city to provide meat, hides and horns, which were profitably traded with the Hiberno-Norse occupants of Dublin. For sheep, McCormick concludes that the combined ageing evidence indicates that they were exploited principally for their wool in the Early Medieval period, referring to documentary sources which indicate that the early Irish disliked mutton (Mac Niocaill 1982, 8). He links the larger numbers of sheep bones in the later phases at Moynagh Lough and Knowth to an overall increase in the importance of wool production in Europe at this period. As the Hiberno-Norse traded extensively in wool and cloth, farmers living in the vicinity of Dublin probably began to

TABLE 7.2
Numbers of identified mammalian bones (NISP) from some Early Medieval sites in Munster

	Cattle	Pig	Sheep/Goat	Horse	Dog	Deer
Ballyegan	272	60	275	9	8	1
Croom 1	32	5	13	2	45	–
Lisnagun	2	2	5	–	–	–
Raheens 1	20	–	1	–	–	–
Raheens 2	11	–	14	–	–	–
Sluggary	264	113	74	3	6	1

keep larger herds of sheep to supply the demand.

The number of identified fragments and relative percentages for bone collections from Munster which have been recently examined by the author are presented in Table 7.2. The numbers total less than a thousand fragments per site and are therefore considered to be too small for further quantification. As sites from which to reconstruct the Early Medieval animal economy of Munster, the samples listed in Table 7.2 are far from ideal and much of the patterning is influenced by the quality of the quantitative data. In many instances the areas excavated in these sites – all of which are ringforts – were not very extensive and most bones originated from types of surface deposits that are the least favourable for preservation. However, the data do suggest that not all Early Medieval collections are dominated by cattle and pig remains. Despite the small sample sizes, sheep seem to have played a greater role in the subsistence economy of Ballyegan[1] and Raheens (McCarthy 1994, 62–65). The lower incidence of pig bones at Ballyegan and their complete absence from Raheens suggest that there may have been little tree cover in the immediate vicinity. The variability of the data presented in Table 7.2 could be the result of a combination of factors and it would be unwise to suggest significant differences in animal husbandry between different regions and sites on the basis of the existing data. The remainder of this chapter, therefore, is concerned with the limitations of the evidence we currently have for the Early Medieval animal economy of Munster.

There is a growing awareness amongst Irish archaeozoologists of the biases that can be introduced into animal bone samples by post-depositional taphonomic processes. The reconstruction of past diet and economy can only be interpreted when biasing factors such as poor preservation and inefficient retrieval have been taken into consideration.

Very little archaeological evidence for Early Medieval animal husbandry in Munster exists, as all of the relevant excavated sites – including the more recent excavations at Lisleagh and Caherlehillan (see Monk, ch. 5) – are located on acidic soils where bone survival is extremely poor. The limited bone collections from these excavations are of little value, despite sieving strategies being specifically designed for them to ensure a more scientific attitude to on-site retrieval methods. The highly acidic nature of the soils at all of the relevant sites excavated in Munster has led to the destruction of many bones, and one therefore has to doubt the reliability of the relative frequency of the species. Archaeozoologists need to examine large, well-preserved, representative samples in order to determine the relative frequency of the species present as well as the age of slaughter of the animals and their original stature. No attempt can be made to analyse the herd structures of cattle and sheep from any of the Early Medieval settlement sites from Munster because the faunal samples have produced virtually no ageing and sexing data. While one must make use of what evidence there is, the paucity of data means that it is currently impossible to compare animal husbandry and economy between the various sites or to compare it with results from other regions of the country. Research designs for investigation on Early Medieval sites in Munster should take soil chemistry into consideration; it would increase the possibilities of archaeozoological studies significantly if only those sites where the potential for organic preservation is known to be favourable were selected for research excavation in the future.

While the analysis of animal bone assemblages in Ireland has a considerable history, the importance of sampling and sieving a broad range of archaeological deposits is only beginning to be appreciated. To ensure the retrieval of a representative sample of all archaeozoological data it is essential that proper sampling and sieving techniques should become a normal part of excavation. Archaeological excavation by its very nature is biased, but the use of a careful retrieval strategy should control this bias to some extent. The major bias caused by manual excavation, and one that has undoubtedly influenced the current state of knowledge of Early Medieval diet and economy, is the relative under-representation of fish and bird remains.

Many of the written sources refer to the importance of fish in Early Medieval Ireland (Kelly 1998, 285–98), yet their bones are extremely rare items in the recorded archaeological samples. This is most likely a result of preservation and recovery factors alone, as fish bones are very susceptible to decay in acidic soils and are subject to loss during manual excavation. While this chapter is concerned mainly with the evidence from rural sites, a good picture of fishing activities has recently been obtained by examining assemblages from Early Medieval Dublin[2] and Wexford.[3] An important development in the Wexford excavations was the operation of an on-site bulk sieving programme, which resulted in the recovery of large quantities of fish bones and allowed comparisons to be made with the results from normal manual excavation. Written sources stress that the demand for fish was supplied almost entirely by inland freshwater fisheries, but most archaeological evidence is of common marine species including hake *(Merluccius merluccius)*, cod *(Gadus morhua)*, ling *(Molva molva)*, plaice *(Pleuronectes platessa)*, and herring *(Clupea harengus)*. While there may be cultural reasons for this discrepancy between the written and the archaeological evidence, given, for instance, that the Hiberno-Norse were engaged in the European fish trade, it is clear that marine species of fish fulfilled a vital dietary role in early Dublin and Wexford.

In a rural context, fishing must have been necessary in order to provide people in coastal areas with additional sources of protein. The written sources refer occasionally to seafishing from boats (Kelly 1998, 296), and excavations at Church Ireland (O'Kelly 1958, 133–34) provided evidence for marine fish such as cod and ballan wrasse *(Labrus bergylta)*. More recently, the writer has identified a relatively large collection of fish bones from an ecclesiastical site at Drumcliffe, Co. Sligo, including scad *(Trachurus trachurus)*, herring and salmon *(Salmo salar)*, which were recovered during routine sampling and sieving of pit deposits.[4] Future research design should focus on coastal sites, including shell middens, with known potential for organic preservation. One particular site in Munster which deserves attention is the extensive shell midden at Fahamore, on the Maharees peninsula, Co. Kerry (Cuppage 1986, 15), which has produced a radiocarbon date of AD 1185. Inland sites located near rivers and lakes where preservation conditions are known to be good should also be deliberately chosen for excavation. These sites should yield larger quantities of fish bone, given the abundant references to inland fisheries exploiting salmon, eel and trout in the written sources (Kelly 1998, 295–96).

Marine mammals were regarded as a valuable source of food in the Early Medieval period and their remains are found in small quantities on many archaeological sites. A variety of different species of seal were recovered from Church Island (O'Kelly 1958, 133), and the written sources record the slaughter of a school of porpoises by the Vikings in 828 off the coast of Dublin (Kelly 1998, 283). The recovery of a butchered whale vertebra from Raheens, a ringfort near Ringaskiddy, Co. Cork (McCarthy 1994, 65), demonstrates further this exploitation of marine resources. Given the poor soil conditions prevailing at this site, the occurrence of only a small amount of fish bones does not provide a meaningful indication of the importance of marine resources in the diet of its occupants.

The study of the role of birds in the economy of Early Medieval Ireland has been much neglected compared with that for stockrearing. Bird bones are quite common finds on excavated sites in Leinster, where preservation conditions are favourable. Identifications by Stelfox from Lagore, for instance (1938, 37–43), indicated that bones from wild birds were more frequent than those from domestic species. Ireland's Early Medieval inhabitants seem to have been keen hunters of wildfowl and the written sources contain many references to gamebirds, including woodcock *(Scolopax rusticola)*, snipe *(Gallinago gallinago)*, mallard *(Anas platyrhynchos)*, and red grouse *(Lagopus lagopus scoticus)* (Kelly 1998, 298). Domestic species of fowl and goose were also of economic importance, both as food and as providers of eggs, down and feathers. Domestic fowl were introduced into Britain by the Romans and presumably were brought to Ireland shortly afterwards. Hens are frequently mentioned in the law tracts and, together with cattle and sheep, formed part of the Irish currency system (Kelly 1998, 102). Many types of bird bones are easily retrieved during trowelling, but the remains of smaller species are frequently underrepresented because of the lack of sieving strategies on excavations.

An additional problem associated with the study of Early Medieval bone assemblages in Munster is the difficulty of accurately phasing and dating the archaeological deposits from which bone samples are generated. Archaeozoologists need to know how the bones were excavated and what attempts were made at phasing material from a period with a temporal framework of almost eight hundred years. Without detailed phasing it is impossible to see what changes in animal exploitation occurred through time, changes demonstrated by McCormick at Knowth, Moynagh Lough and Rathmullen (1987).

The Early Medieval period is the earliest phase of Ireland's history in which human interaction with animals can be studied from documentary evidence, not just from the archaeological bones themselves. We are fortunate that this period generated abundant historical sources to illustrate its economy, and faunal analysts should be aware of their content. Our knowledge of the Early Medieval animal economy, particularly for Munster, is still very much dependent on the these texts, however. While they can undoubtedly provide a rich source of data, their validity should be scientifically tested by using other categories of information. Most archaeologists agree that animal bones are a vital category of economic information but, at present, we have neither the amount nor the quality of archaeozoological data to carry out valid comparisons with the information contained in the documentary sources. More significant quantities of material must be collected, particularly from Munster and Connaught, before animal bones can yield the same wealth of information that has already been gained from the written texts. However, it is important to point out that the written sources are often generalised and may be idealised statements of animal husbandry and diet in Early Medieval Ireland. Both temporal and regional variations are likely to have existed and these can be best detected via the evidence of the bones of the animals themselves.

Conclusions

Munster has yet to produce a collection of bones in sufficient quantity to be reasonably representative of the local subsistence economy. To date there has been a tendency to generalise from small samples excavated using poor retrieval methods. The problems of preservation, excavation and site choice have been discussed and there are many areas of Munster where no bones of any kind are likely to survive. There are sites, however, such as the raised raths in counties Limerick and Tipperary, where the survival rate of bone is likely to be much better (Monk and Sheehan, ch. 1) and future research excavations should focus on them. The extent to which fish and birds contributed to the nutritional requirements of Early Medieval population groups is difficult to interpret at present, and the number of biases influencing our understanding of their relative role has been discussed above. The importance of sieving to understand the role of fish and birds has been outlined and recent results from Early Medieval urban sites have demonstrated the value of this method. Precise identification of bird remains has the potential to yield invaluable information on the environment in the vicinity of a site.

Although the collections from Munster are broadly informative in terms of the animals present in this region during the Early Medieval period, they are too small for a realistic interpretation of past economic strategies to be based on them. The percentages of bones of the main species excavated from Early Medieval sites provide general information about the value of these animals as the meat supply for the inhabitants. However, the selection of sites with poor bone-preservation potential, together with the absence of proper sampling strategies on most sites, has probably contributed to an imprecise reconstruction of the economy. There is a great need to study larger collections of bones from sites which should be selected for excavation following consultation with bone specialists.

The picture of animal exploitation in Early Medieval Munster is still extremely general and there can be no meaningful attempt to compare the data from this area with the larger samples obtained from Ireland's east coast sites. There is a pressing need to study clearly stratified and securely dated groups of bones in order to extend our knowledge of the period. There has been insufficient archaeozoological input into site choice and advice should be sought from bone analysts on sieving strategies, including the sieving of bulk samples for the retrieval of birds, fish and microfauna. A thorough archaeozoological analysis of the subsequently excavated bones, combined with an integrated study of the plant and macrofossil remains as well as the documentary evidence, should provide much more valid information and enable us to reconstruct diet and animal husbandry practices in Early Medieval Munster more accurately. This, in turn, will lead to a greater understanding of wider cultural issues, such as inter-site and inter-regional comparisons.

ACKNOWLEDGEMENTS

This chapter is dedicated to the memory of my good friend and colleague, Liz Anderson.

NOTES

1. McCarthy, M., 'The faunal remains from Ballyegan, Co. Kerry', unpublished report lodged in site archive.
2. McCarthy, M., 'Dublin Castle – The faunal report', unpublished report lodged in site archive.
3. McCarthy, M., 'A report on the faunal remains from Viking and Medieval levels at Wexford', unpublished report lodged in site archive.
4. McCarthy, M., 'Fish bone evidence from Drumcliffe, Co. Sligo', unpublished report lodged in site archive.

BIBLIOGRAPHY

Cuppage, J. (1986) *Archaeological Survey of the Dingle Peninsula*, Ballyferriter

Hencken, H. O'N. (1950) 'Lagore Crannog: an Irish royal residence of the seventh to the tenth centuries AD', *Proc. Roy. Ir. Acad.* 53C, 1–247

Kelly, F. (1998) *Early Irish Farming*, Dublin

McCarthy, M. (1994) 'Animal bone report', 62–65, in A.M. Lennon, 'Summary report on excavation of ringfort, Raheens No. 2, near Carrigaline, Co. Cork', *J. Cork Hist. Archaeol. Soc.* 99, 47–65

McCarthy, M. (1995) 'Faunal report', 192–97, in J. Waddell and M. Clyne, 'M.V. Duignan's excavations at Kiltiernan, Co. Galway, 1950–1953', *J. Galway Archaeol. Hist. Soc.* 47, 150–203

McCormick, F. (1987) 'Stockrearing in Early Christian Ireland' unpublished PhD thesis, Queens University, Belfast

McCormick, F. (1991) 'The effect of the Anglo-Norman settlement on Ireland's wild and domesticated fauna', in P.J. Crabtree and K. Ryan (eds.), *Animal Use and Cultural Change*, 40–52, Pennsylvania

Mac Niocaill, G. (1982) 'Investment in Early Irish Agriculture', in B.J. Scott (ed.), *Studies in Early Ireland in Honour of M.V. Duignan*, 7–9, Belfast

O'Kelly, M.J. (1958) 'Church Island, near Valentia, Co. Kerry', *Proc. Roy. Ir. Acad.* 59C, 57–136

Stelfox, A.W. (1938) 'The birds of Lagore of about one thousand years ago', *Irish Naturalists Jour.* 7, 37–43

8. Archaeobotanical Studies and Early Medieval Munster

MICHAEL A. MONK, JOHN TIERNEY and MARTHA HANNON

Introduction

Some years ago one of the authors published an overview of the archaeobotanical evidence for cereal husbandry in the Early Medieval period in Ireland (Monk 1991). This chapter is intended to lay the foundations for a research strategy to be followed up by work on a regional basis, with the ultimate aim of addressing the question of regional as well as temporal variability. Now, with the availability of evidence from six recently excavated sites in Munster, it is possible to begin to address these issues and to make some suggestions concerning future research.

Various authors have stressed the importance of arable agriculture in Ireland's past economy (Jessen and Helbaek 1944; Duignan 1944; Evans 1946; O'Loan 1965; Brady 1994). Apart from Jessen and Helbaek's work the factual basis for these assertions was not fully discussed and the prevalent mindset of agriculture in Ireland being primarily pastoral still surfaces in general works on the Early Medieval period (e.g. Patterson 1994; Ó Croinín 1995). Ó Croinín makes an erroneous association between the small numbers of quern stones and ploughshares found on excavations and the relative importance of the cereal economy, equating high archaeological visibility with importance. In recent years there have been several publications dealing with the factual basis for various aspects of tillage agriculture and their consequences (e.g. Brady 1987; Rynne 1990). While pollen, particularly in the upper horizons of deposits, is subject to a range of taphonomic processes, there appears to be a steep upsurge in cereal and weed types in diagrams that cover this period. Plant remains, which because of their small size have low visibility, are more commonly present than is generally appreciated. Macro plant remains themselves, which usually survive in the form of seeds and grains, are the most incontrovertible evidence for Early Medieval tillage agriculture.

Relatively few regional surveys and discussions of archaeobotanical work have been published. This is also the case in Britain, even though considerably more work has been carried out in recent years (exceptions would include the work of van der Veen in the northwest (1992) and Green in Wessex (1981)). Usually such work is published on either a general or a pan-regional basis and the approach has been either essentially palaeoeconomic or palaeoenvironmental; seldom have social issues been tackled. In addition, only limited attention has been paid to integrating the results with other information about people/plant interaction in the past. In the Irish case, some priority has been given to addressing social issues and, by so doing, integrating the results of archaeobotanical studies with the evidence from the documentary sources for the period. More sophisticated analyses of subsistence farming need to be undertaken for Early Medieval Ireland, viewing arable and pastoral practices not as rival activities but as equally valid agricultural strategies.

Sites and contexts

Four of the six sites chosen for this study (Fig. 8.1) are located in county Cork – Killanully (Mount 1995), Lisnagun (O'Sullivan et al., forthcoming) and Lisleagh I and II (Monk 1995) – while the remaining two, both cashels, are in Kerry – Loher and Ballyegan (Byrne 1991). All are situated in topography typical of ringforts, on local eminences or on the mid to upper slopes of ridges, and while having good drainage, all are usually situated reasonably close to a water source. The major soil series on which the ringforts are located tend to be acid brown earths or brown podzolics; soils that have reasonable to good potential for pastoralism or tillage, or both (Gardiner and Radford 1980).

The sites selected have produced a number of samples of macro plant remains from a wide range of contexts (such as areas around hearths, post-holes, pits, wall-trenches, etc.). Of these the most prolific came from areas of burnt debris around hearths or from destruction deposits. Some dump deposits, particularly the infills of souterrains, have produced a reasonably high incidence of remains. Since souterrains appear to be a mid to late phenomenon in the Early Medieval period, these deposits could generally be considered late. A working model might compare the remains extracted from them with those from stratified material associated with earlier buildings. There are surprisingly few samples from primary use/disuse contexts, for example hearths, kilns or ovens; most come from at least secondary locations. There are also very few from what might be called catastrophe deposits, like the remains associated with the burning down of Structure V at Lisleagh I. Hence, in most samples, several taphonomic processes have intervened between the carbonisation (itself a major taphonomic process – Boardman and Jones 1990), the primary deposition of these remains and their extraction and identification.

Preservation sampling : recovery and analysis

None of the six sites being considered produced any anaerobic deposits. Therefore the preservation of all the plant remains extracted was entirely the result of carbonisation (the plants having been exposed indirectly to some kind of fire – domestic, industrial, or catastrophic). As is common on most sites of this kind, the remains which are recovered intact have a bias towards cereal grains. The distribution of such evidence within individual sites is also uneven, with a clustering of remains in or close to the sources of heat that preserved them. The remains were separated from the mineral elements of the samples by manual flotation and washover or a combination of both techniques (Greig 1989). Once dried, the samples were sorted under a low- to medium-powered binocular microscope and identifications were made in University College, Cork's Archaeobotany Laboratory with the aid of the Department of Archaeology's comparative collection. The work on three of the sites was undertaken by two of the authors (Hannon and Tierney) as part of their work with the Archaeological Services Unit, while the samples from the remaining three sites were carried out as part of a research programme by the third (Monk).

Comparison of selected evidence

The samples selected for this study produced, with some exceptions, a low frequency of remains per unit of deposit. The exceptions included those from an early fire-pit deposit at Lisleagh I (C 2819) and the upper fill of the souterrain at Ballyegan (C 33). In many samples the frequency of non-charcoal remains was far less than the charcoal present and, as might be expected, the highest incidence of remains was from the larger fill contexts. (However, this was partly because these contexts produced larger amounts of sediment for sampling.) Although the higher

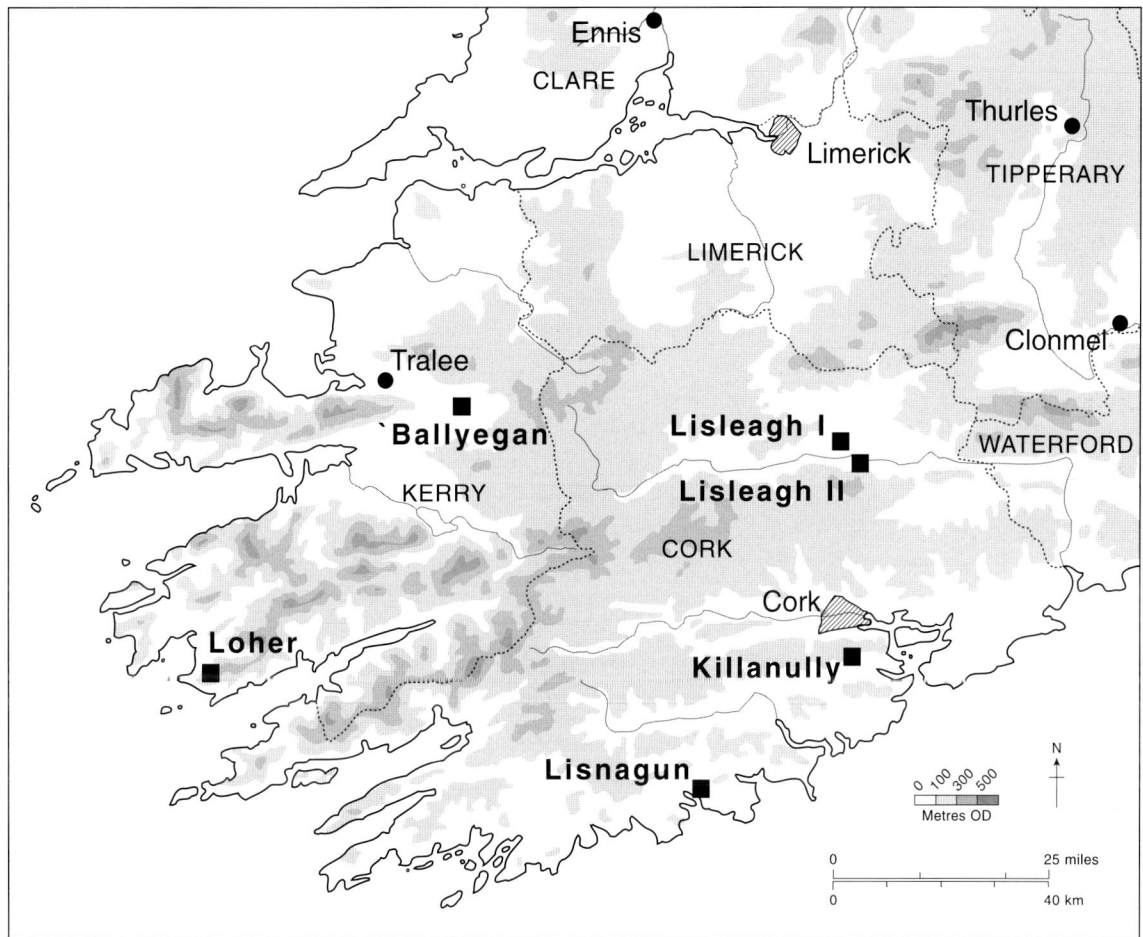

Fig. 8.1 Sites discussed in this chapter

frequency of remains was partly reflected in the number of items per unit of deposit, there was not a significant difference between the density of these remains and those from the other types of contexts sampled.

While there was some indication of intra-site variation in the date of contexts on two sites, for the most part there is little specific dating or stratigraphic evidence available for the sites included in this study. In several cases the excavation records are currently being worked on and so in time it may be possible to explore more fully any degrees of temporal variation in the plant-remains evidence. It is possible, however, to indicate some within-site chronological differences at both Lisleagh I and Lisnagun.

The contexts from which the evidence derives on the six selected sites can be organised into several common groups: souterrain fills; other large fill deposits (e.g. non-structural pit fills); structural features (post-hole fills and building foundations); layers and spreads; and, finally, deposits derived from hearths. Taking all the sites and the contexts within them together, while there is variation from context to context the most common plant remains evident, other than charcoal, are cereal grains. These are mostly barley (*Hordeum* sp.) and oats (*Avena* sp.) but also present, in lesser numbers, are grains of rye (*Secale cereale*), wheat (*Triticum* sp.) and seeds of flax (*Linum* sp.). In addition, at generally a low incidence, there are sometimes seeds of large-seeded weed-type plants, such as the docks and the persicarias (*Rumex* sp., *Polygonum* sp.), fat hen (*Chenopodium album*), mustard (*Sinapis* sp.), radish (*Raphanus* sp.) and buttercup (*Ranunculus* sp.). In some samples there are remains of gathered plants, especially hazel nut fragments (*Corylus avellana*), but also blackberry drubes (*Rubus* sp.) and, very occasionally, sloe stones (*Prunus spinosa*) and elder pips (*Sambucus nigra*).

In most instances the carbonised remains are not well enough preserved to identify them to species level. However, in the case of the cereals, some samples yielded better-preserved remains and it is possible to suggest the presence of, for example, six-row hulled barley (*Hordeum vulgare/hexastichum*). Several species of oats are likely to be present, including the cultivated oat (*Avena sativa*) and bristle oat (*Avena strigosa*), with constricted lemma bases and small grains, as well as the wild oat (*Avena fatua*). In none of the samples selected for this study could a species distinction of oats be definitively suggested in the absence of such features as rachillas, the presence of hairs on grains and unbroken lemma bases. The few wheat grains present are probably of the compact bread-wheat group (*Triticum aestivo-compactum*), but with only a few rachis fragments present this cannot be clearly ascertained.

Some variation in the cereal remains can be noted even when the sites they come from are located close together. At Lisleagh I, for example, barley and oats appear in almost equal amounts, with perhaps slightly more barley, and there is a low representation of wheat and rye. At Lisleagh II, on the presence basis, barley and oats are almost equal, with oats having the edge in dominance terms (i.e. sheer numbers) (Fig. 8.2). This site also produced a low incidence of rye and wheat as is the case on two of the other sites, Loher and Lisnagun (Fig. 8.4). As regards barley and oats at these latter sites the picture is similar to Lisleagh; Lisnagun has an overall dominance of oats but a significant presence of barley while, at Loher, barley and oats are about equally present, although the former is more dominant. Flax occurs in very low numbers in the Lisnagun, Loher and Ballyegan samples and is not present at the other sites. Although preservation was very poor at Killanully, barley dominates and has the highest presence; at Ballyegan, oats and barley have an equally high presence but oats clearly dominate in individual samples (Fig. 8.3).

Contextual comparisons
Souterrain fills
Samples from souterrain fills come from Lisnagun, Lisleagh II, Ballyegan and Killanully. At Lisnagun and Lisleagh II these deposits produced the most remains, and there are few other contexts as intact because of subsequent surface erosion. In these two cases the souterrain fills produced not only the highest incidence of remains but also the greatest range, suggesting a mixed dump of material. In the case of Lisleagh II the remains are somewhat eroded, possibly because they were on the surface for some time before being backfilled into the souterrain. In neither case did the primary deposits yield many remains, indicating that in their primary use, souterrains did not contain plant remains (certainly not in a form in which they might have been preserved); the remains are from the later backfill when the souterrains were being used as dumps for waste occupation material. In terms of the actual remains oat grains dominate in both cases, although there is also a reasonable presence of barley (almost equal in the case of Lisleagh II). At

Archaeobotanical Studies 69

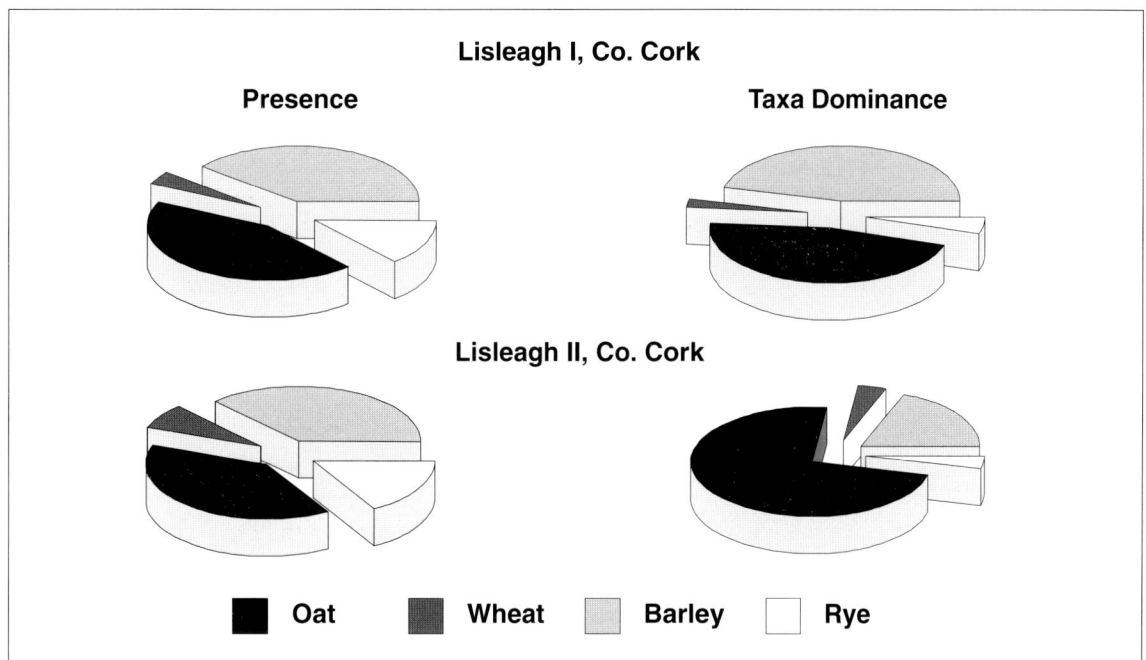

Fig. 8.2   Pie charts showing the relative proportion of different plant species at Lisleagh I and II, Co. Cork

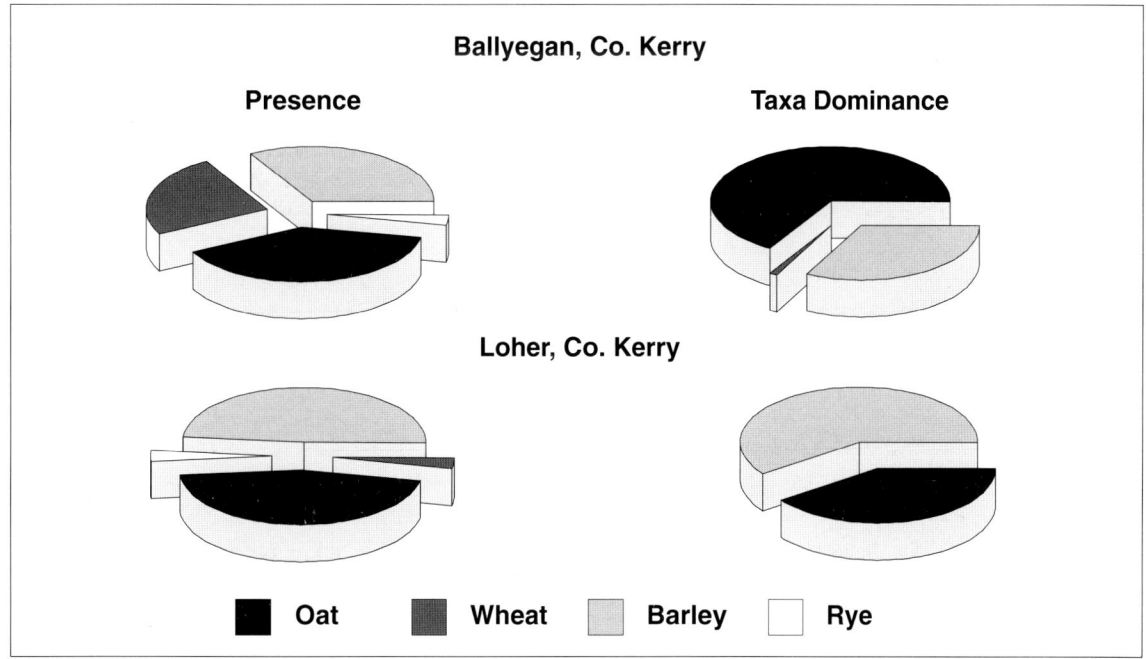

Fig. 8.3   Pie charts showing the relative proportion of different plant species at Loher and Ballyegan, Co. Kerry

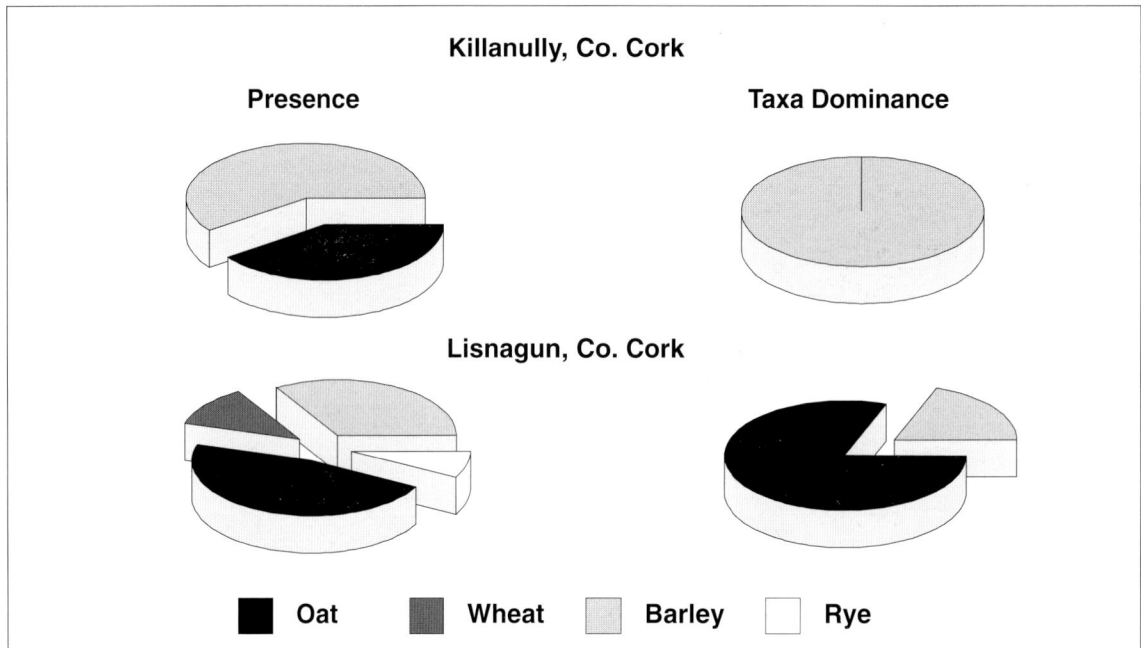

Fig. 8.4 Pie charts showing the relative proportion of plant species at Kilanully and Lisnagun, Co. Cork

this site there is also a significant presence of rye, hazelnut fragments, weed seeds, bracken frond tips and straw node fragments.

There are fewer samples from the souterrains at Killanully and Ballyegan, only three and four respectively. The Killanully samples are either poorly preserved (in two cases seeds cannot be identified beyond saying that they are cereals) or contain few remains. Two of the three samples produced some non-cereal remains; in one case seeds of fat hen and dock (representing either arable weeds or colonisers of waste-rich nitrogen ground at the site) and in the other some hazelnut fragments. In both cases the other non-plant remains – marine mollusca, animal bone and charcoal – indicate that a mixture of various waste materials had been dumped into the souterrain after use.

Other large fill contexts
These contexts, as with the souterrain fills at Lisleagh II and Lisnagun, produced both a relatively high incidence and a wide range of remains – including seeds of large seeded weeds, as at Lisnagun where the group produced brome (*Bromus* sp.), plantain (*Plantago* sp.), radish (*Raphanus raphanistrum*) and docks (*Rumex* sp.). The cereals most frequently present on all sites are oats and barley. At Lisnagun and Lisleagh II a dominance of oats is indicated, although there is a more significant presence of barley in this context group than in the structural deposits at Lisleagh II.

By contrast to Lisleagh II and Lisnagun, the fill features at Loher and Lisleagh I produced a higher presence as well as a dominance of barley. The barley remains from Loher are well preserved and may be mostly of the six-row hulled variety. The other crop plants present include rye, wheat and flax: indeed they are not only present but dominant in at least one sample from Lisleagh I. Large fill samples from several of the sites produced straw nodes and rachis fragments as well as grains, and at Lisnagun and Lisleagh I these samples offer the possibility of chronological separation. At Lisnagun a couple of the pit features (e.g. 1150) are interpreted as being early in the history of the site (in fact pre-bank construction) and these yielded a higher than background incidence of wheat including, in one instance, a wheat rachis fragment. In the case of Lisleagh I all of these fill features are stratigraphically late in the history of the site and it is interesting that, by contrast to the remains from the more definite structural features on the site, these features produced a dominance of barley.

While the site at Killanully produced a number of samples from large fill-type contexts, one context was particularly significant. It was a large circular pit, interpreted as a furnace, which contained non-charcoal plant remains as well as charcoal, animal bone and teeth. All four fill contexts from within this feature produced varying quantities of remains. The two samples from the uppermost fills, samples 27 and 39, had contrasting complements of items. The former produced a moderate quantity of highly fragmented, unidentifiable cereal grains, while the latter produced a predominance of seeds of fat hen. Of the four samples, that from context 41 produced the highest frequency of remains, along with other material like charcoal and charred animal bone. While the preservation was not particularly good, grains of barley and wheat were present along with charred seeds of fat hen; this deposit may have derived from a hearth or kiln rake-out operation. At the base of the pit was a fire-reddened oxidised sediment which produced charred grains of barley and wheat as well as fat hen seeds, suggesting that these remains had derived from context 41 above it. It is not possible from the plant remains or the other archaeological evidence to make a definitive interpretation of this pit's function. However, it had clearly been backfilled with burnt debris of various types and some of this material may have derived from its final use, a fire having oxidised its base.

One other fill feature from Killanully, an irregular slot of unknown function, is worth noting because it is the only feature from the site that has a presence of oats, albeit few in quantity and poorly preserved. This lack of oats, and the relatively greater significance of wheat, contrasts markedly with the other sites included in this study.

Structural features

Most of the contexts sampled from the sites were structural ones – post-holes, stake-holes and linear features; they were generally low in volume and consequently the number of remains from them is low. However, sometimes there was a localised concentration of remains, as at Lisleagh I where structural features around the hearths of structures I and V produced a high incidence of remains.

The most common cereals in this context type again are barley and oats, with the latter usually dominant in numbers and the former having a variable presence. At Lisleagh I there is a higher presence as well as a dominance of oats, while at Lisnagun, although there was an overall dominance of oats, barley was more equal in presence terms. At Lisleagh II the incidence of remains was low, except for the linear features in which barley was dominant. Generally, however, while on a presence basis barley was more significant in the samples in terms of frequency, oats were dominant. The same situation occurs in the Loher samples, but here the post-holes produced a dominance of barley while oats dominated in the stake-hole samples. At Ballyegan, five post-pipe samples produced very low quantities of remains, containing both barley and oats; oats, however, were more dominant. In all the structural samples other species and plant remains other than charcoal occurred at a low incidence, though there is only a minor occurrence of cereals like rye in the samples from Lisleagh I and Lisnagun. In the case of wheat, no finds were made in the structural contexts at either Lisleagh I or Lisleagh II, while it occurred very occasionally at Lisnagun. However, at Loher, one post-hole that produced a high frequency of remains also produced flax seeds and, possibly, those of strigosa oats, but it was not possible to confirm this. Seeds of weed plants, while they occur in some of the samples from Lisleagh I and Lisnagun, were generally infrequent in this sample grouping.

Spreads and layers

Apart from Ballyegan, this grouping of contexts had the smallest number of samples included in the study and so any generalisation would be even less secure than that from the other groupings. Nevertheless, on all of the sites, this grouping of contexts yielded a similar occurrence and range of remains to the other contexts discussed. While the incidence of remains is generally low, in all cases barley and oat grains were most frequently represented. For Lisleagh I and Lisnagun, which after Ballyegan have the largest number of samples within this category, barley and oats are almost equal in presence terms but in both cases there is a dominance of the former. Also present in the Lisnagun and Lisleagh I samples are some grains of wheat, while in the Lisleagh II samples there are possibly *strigosa* oats. Ballyegan produced eleven samples, with remains ranging in incidence from a couple of items to several hundred. In the latter cases oats are the most dominant cereal. At Loher only a couple of samples fall within this group and these produced an equal representation of oats and barley. The only relevant sample from Lisleagh II has a presence of wheat equal to barley and an equal dominance of all three species, including oats. The sample from Lisnagun with the greatest range of remains and, indeed, greatest frequency, was a buried sod horizon which produced seeds of the usual weeds – *Polygonum convolvulus, Polygonum lapathifolium* and *Rumex* sp. The one sample from Lisleagh II also yielded a mixture of remains – plantain, buttercup and hazelnut fragments – probably indicating a mixed derivation.

Hearth deposits

The five groupings of samples included are those derived from the hearths at Lisleagh I and Lisnagun. The most significant Lisleagh I sample comes from packing around a hearth and yielded mainly rye grains. The other sample from this site was a stakehole from close to the Structure I/V hearth area and, like the hearth samples, it produced a high incidence of charred grain – especially of barley but also of rye. The two hearth-derived samples at Lisnagun present a contrast in their complement of remains, one producing oats, wheat and barley (the latter having the highest frequency of remains), the other producing no cereal remains but instead some hazelnut fragments along with blackberry drubes and elder seeds.

Concluding remarks and future research

Generally the incidence of remains from all of these Munster sites was low. They came mainly from secondary, if not tertiary, reworked deposits. This fact alone mitigated against high incidence and good preservation (fragmentation counts were high in most samples). The best preserved and widest range of remains came from the larger fill deposits.

While there was some variation in the evidence from site to site and between context groupings within sites, barley and oats were overall the most frequent cereal remains present in these samples. Wheat and rye grains were also present in some cases but, while wheat grains were noted from most sites, their incidence was extremely low. Rye, however, was present on only a few of the sites (especially Lisnagun and Lisleagh I). For the most part, there was a low incidence of weed seeds in the samples and these were mainly of the large seeded varieties. Notwithstanding taphonomic factors, which would have had an influence, the generally low incidence of rachis and straw fragments (by comparison with the higher incidence of grain) would suggest that the remains derived from domestic or structural contexts and resulted from accidents in food preparation or the burning of residues from stored products.

Only one sample examined – from C2819 on Lisleagh I – produced convincing carbonised waste from pre-storage crop processing. This sample was not only carbonised *in situ* but, being sealed at the base of a backfilled pit, it had not been subject to later reworking. Because the stratigraphy on this site was thoroughly recorded and has already been analysed, it is known that the context and the 'fire pit' in which it was contained were an early feature on the site. For most of the other sites there is either little clear stratigraphic evidence to suggest a sequence or the stratigraphic sequence has yet to be finalised by the excavators. This is unfortunate, because there is little that can be concluded about temporal changes in the exploitation of the plants at these sites. There is, however, some hint of chronological variation in the exploitation of the different cereals from Lisleagh I and Lisnagun; at Lisleagh I the later features on the site produced a greater prevalence of barley in their fills, while at Lisnagun the earlier features, including pits beneath the bank, produced a greater incidence of wheat. It is unfortunate that little more can be concluded about changes in the patterns of the exploitation of cereals in the region. A future research policy towards the excavation of settlement sites of all dates, but particularly from the seventh to twelfth century, would do well to target those sites where some finely tuned chronological variation could be explored.

Comparison with documentary sources

Some extremely important works on the documentary sources for agriculture, including the crops grown and the uses to which they were put have recently been published (Sexton 1993 and ch. 9; Kelly 1998). In each there is some discussion of a key law tract *Bretha Déin Chécht* – a medical treatise that, in its preamble, compares different levels of society with various crops. Perhaps the most interesting point that arises when a comparison is made between the status level of the different cereals mentioned in this early document and the archaeobotanical evidence, is that there is an almost inverse relationship between the two sources of evidence. Wheat and rye have the highest status in the law tract, being compared with the highest levels in society, but their occurrence in the samples from the Munster sites dealt with here is very low. By comparison, oats and barley have a low status in the documentary record but have the highest incidence of remains. Should we be surprised? Another problem is that the *Bretha Déin Chécht* lists other crops (*suillech*, *ibdach* and *rúadán*) for which, if linguistically interpreted correctly by Sexton and Kelly, we have either questionable evidence or none at all so far in the archaeobotanical record.

In part answer to the first issue, one has to remember that the jurists compiling the law tract, by associating the higher classes of society with wheat and rye, were indicating that these crops – like the social classes with which they were equated – were uncommon. It can perhaps be suggested that from an ecological point of view wheat, certainly in the west (and possibly the south-west), was rarely grown because of the dampness of the climate and the relative lack of deep mineral-rich soils and sunshine. This is not to say that it could not have been grown in some quantity in the east and south-east of the country. (Indeed, it has been found more frequently in Later Medieval samples from these areas (Monk 1986, 34).) There are fewer ecological reasons why rye should not be found more frequently in Early Medieval samples, even from the west where it is currently the main cereal component of the low-technology, fallow-based agricultural system which survives on the Aran Islands (Curtis, McGough and Wymer 1986). There are good ecological reasons for the high incidence of oat-growing indicated by the archaeobotanical evidence, and barley is also a relatively versatile crop. Another factor necessary to consider in the case of barley, and to a lesser extent oats, is the broader use to which these crops can be put by comparison with wheat and, up to a point, rye. The latter are principally grown for human food whereas barley and oats are also used for animal fodder. In addition, there are numerous references in the documentary sources to the use of barley for malting purposes (Kelly 1998, 245). It is suggested, therefore, that the evidence for oats and barley in the archaeobotanical record, while possibly indicating something about the status of the occupants of the sites sampled as well as local growing conditions, represents the wider usage of these cereals for both people and animals. This would be a fundamental consideration in the subsistence-based economy that existed prior to the structured market economy, when different settlements may have been able to afford to specialise and orientate themselves more towards a particular cash crop (as happened under the Anglo-Normans).

Before one gets carried away by such speculation it is important to stress that only six sites from Munster form the basis of this discussion; this represents a very small sample in comparison to the potential number of sites of Early Medieval date in the province. There is another problem: in all cases the evidence dealt with here comes from partially excavated sites and in only four of these was there an intensive collection and recovery strategy in place. A further problem is that none of the sites included, with the exception of Lisleagh I and, to an extent, Lisnagun, produced a clear stratigraphic record that could provide some basis for considering temporal variations in crop use and disuse. The sites sampled, despite variation in location, were all of a particular type – ringforts. It might be expected that as well as intra-site variation in the presence and incidence of non-charcoal plant remains, there would be variations from site to site and from one site type to another.

Samples from ecclesiastical sites, for example, would perhaps present a different view of the evidence. Kelly (1998) makes the point that, as many of the Irish terms relating to crop processing are derived from Latin, the Church may have had a major role to play in introducing new technologies into Ireland for tillage agriculture. We eagerly await the processing of the samples from the ecclesiastical sites at Caherlehillan and Illaunloughan, both in County Kerry, to see if they will alter the general picture that has emerged from the Munster ringforts of a barley/oat cereal-based economy. The way forward, indeed the only way the tantalising evidence offered here can be put into perspective, is by more systematic and intensive sampling programmes on all excavated sites. Such programmes should cover not only all site types dated to the period but as wide a contextual variation on those sites as possible. It is no longer sufficient to produce a plant-remains report that consists simply of a list of the remains.

Unenclosed early medieval settlements must also be investigated and recent survey work by Michael Connolly (pers. comm.) in the Lee valley, Co. Kerry, may provide suitable assemblages. While this survey is identifying new sites from a range of archaeological periods, current palaeoeconomic analysis of samples from the Early Medieval levels of a multi-period unenclosed site at Ballycarty, Co. Kerry (quite close to the cashel at Ballyegan) reveals a wide range of different cereal and weed species in relatively large amounts (Tierney and Hannon 1997a).

It is also necessary to compare urban and rural sites dated to the late tenth to twelfth centuries. The basis for such a comparison is now possible with the recent publication of two large Early Medieval plant-remains assemblages from urban contexts (Geraghty 1996; Tierney and Hannon 1997b). However, as yet there are few contexts from rural sites that may confidently be dated to these centuries. At Killanully, Lisnagun and perhaps Ballyegan, occupation continued into the tenth century. These sites have few contexts with plant remains actually dating to this period and are well outside the catchment areas of Dublin and Waterford. At this stage a comparison between the latter early urban sites and the ringforts would be purely hypothetical. Clearly evidence is needed for sites dated to this period within the catchment areas of the Viking Age settlements, as well as from the urban sites themselves. More targeted systematic programmes of plant-remains recovery are needed overall, not only within the Munster region but also elsewhere in Ireland. Only then will it be possible to see how the Munster evidence compares or contrasts with that from other socio-political and ecologically different regions within Ireland.

ACKNOWLEDGEMENTS
We would like to acknowledge Fergus Kelly who allowed us access to the unpublished manuscript of his book 'Early Irish Farming'. We are grateful to the excavators for allowing us free access to their contextual data and for permission to publish the results in this chapter.

BIBLIOGRAPHY

Boardman, S. and Jones, G. (1990) 'Experiments on the effects of charring on cereal plant components', *J. Archaeol. Sci.* 17, 1–11

Brady, N. (1987) 'A late ploughshare type from Ireland', *Tools and Tillage* 5. 4, 1987, 228–42

Brady, N. (1994) 'Fifty years a-ploughing', *Archaeol. Ir.* 8. 3, 15–17

Byrne, M. (1991) 'A report on the excavation of a cashel at Ballyegan, near Castleisland, Co. Kerry', *J. Kerry Arch. and Hist. Soc.* 24, 5–31

Curtis, T.G.F., McGough, H.N. and Wymer, E.D. (1988) 'The discovery and identification of rare and threatened arable weeds, previously considered extinct in Ireland, on the Aran Islands, Co. Galway', *Ir. Naturalist J.* 22, 505–12

Davies, O. (1942) 'The Twomile Stone, a prehistoric community in County Donegal', *J. Roy. Soc. Antiq. Ir.* 72, 98–105

Duignan, M. (1944) 'Irish agriculture in historic times', *J. Roy. Soc. Antiq. Ir.*, 74, 124–45

Evans, E.E. (1946) 'The origins of Irish Agriculture', *Ulster J. Archaeol.* 9, 87–90

Gardiner, M.J. and Radford, T. (1980) *Soil Associations of Ireland and their Land Use Potential*, Dublin

Geraghty, S. (1996) *Viking Dublin: botanical evidence from Fishamble Street, Dublin*, Dublin

Green, F.J. (1981) 'Iron Age, Roman and Saxon crops: the archaeological evidence from Wessex', in M. Jones and G. Dimbleby (eds.), *The Environment of Man: the Iron Age to the Anglo Saxon Period*, 129–53, Oxford

Greig, J. (1989) *Handbooks for Archaeologists No. 4. Archaeobotany*, Strasbourg

Jessen, K. and Helbaek, H. (1944) *Cereals in Great Britain and Ireland in prehistoric and early historic times: Det Kongelige Danske Viden Skabemes Selskab*, 3 (2)

Kelly, F. (1998) *Early Irish Farming*, Dublin

Monk, M.A. (1986) 'Evidence from macroscopic plant remains for crop husbandry in prehistoric and early historic Ireland', *J. Ir. Archaeol.* 3, 31–36

Monk, M.A. (1991) 'The archaeobotanical evidence for field crop plants in early historic Ireland', in J.M. Renfrew (ed.), *New Light on Early Farming*, Edinburgh

Monk, M.A. (1995) 'A tale of two ringforts: Lisleagh I and II', *J. Cork. Hist. and Archaeol. Soc.* 100, 105–16

Mount, C. (1995) 'Excavations at Killanully, County Cork', *Proc. Roy. Ir. Acad.* 95C, 119–57

Ó Croinín, D. (1995) *Early Medieval Ireland 400–1200*, London

O'Loan, J. (1965) 'A history of early Irish farming' (3rd Instalment), *Depart of Ag. and Fish. J.* 62, 31–197

O'Sullivan, J., Hannon, M., and Tierney, J. (forthcoming) 'Excavations at Lisnagun Ringfort, Darrara, Co. Cork', *J. Cork Hist. Archaeol. Soc.*

Patterson, N. (1994) *Cattle Lords and Clansmen: The Social Structure of Ireland*, London

Rynne, C. (1990) 'Some observations on the production of flour and meal in the early historic period', *J. Cork Hist. Archaeol. Soc.* 95, 20–29

Sexton, R. (1993) 'Cereals and cereal foodstuffs in Early Historic Ireland', unpublished MA thesis (NUI), University College, Cork

Tierney, J., and Hannon, M. (1997) 'Archaeobotanical Assessment Report for Ballycarty, Tralee, Co. Kerry' (unpublished report for Eachtra Archaeological Projects)

Tierney, J. and Hannon M. (1997) 'Plant Remains', in M.F. Hurley and O.M.B. Scully, *Later Viking Age and Medieval Waterford: Excavations 1986–1992*, 854–93, Waterford

9. Porridges, Gruels and Breads: The Cereal Foodstuffs of Early Medieval Ireland

REGINA SEXTON

It is almost forty years since the publication of Lucas's (1960) pioneering survey of Medieval Irish food. While many subsequent studies have addressed the subject in a general fashion (cf. Ó Corráin 1972; Ó Cróinín 1995; Kelly 1998), this work remains a standard reference in the field of food studies. The expansive documentary material of Early Medieval Ireland represents one of the most useful, though most underutilised, sources of information for the food historian. However, its potential has yet to be fully recognised before any satisfactory understanding of food, and ultimately of the overall economy, can be achieved. This chapter sets out to demonstrate the wealth of source material relating to one aspect of the Early Medieval diet, the cereal foodstuffs,[1] which can be categorised into two broad groups, pot-based preparations and breads. However, an unfortunate aspect of such a survey is the inevitable allocation of space to enumerate what is present in the period at the expense of any detailed discussion of the material.

Porridges and gruels

Four varieties of porridge are documented in the sources, each differing slightly in ingredients and methods of preparation. *Littiu* is described in the legal text *Cáin Íarraith* as porridge made variously with oaten, barley or wheaten meal combined with water, buttermilk or new milk (CIH 1759.36–1760.2). In the comic tale *Aislinge meic Conglinne* (hereinafter AMC) the same dish is made with sheep's milk (Jackson 1990, 13 § 31). Elsewhere in the same text (39 § 69) porridge is described as the smoothest and sweetest of all foods (*is míne 7 is millse da cach biúd*), which suggests that equal quantities of meal and liquid were boiled together until the required smooth and palatable consistency was attained. A similar procedure is described in *Cath Maige Tuired* (Gray 1982, 46). The accompanying condiments for *littiu* include heavily salted preserved butter (*gruiten*), fresh butter (*imb*) and honey (*mil*) (CIH 1759.36–1760.2).

The reference in *Cáin Íarraith* to wheaten porridge being prepared with new milk and taken with honey is an important one (CIH 1760.1–2). From the list of ingredients this could equally be interpreted as a basic frumenty recipe. Frumenty (clean crushed wheat, milk and optional extras) was considered a delicacy and was a standard dish of the great European lords and senior clerics until well into Later Medieval times (Barber 1973, 83; Black 1992, 24). The only difference between this dish and porridge is the use of cracked wheat instead of coarse wheaten meal in the former. The method of preparation is the same as that for porridge: the lightly crushed wheat is soaked in hot milk or water at the side of the fire until the mixture swells and gelatinises into a spangled white aspic (ibid., 23–24). It can be eaten hot or cold, with honey, and is sometimes enriched with egg yolks to make a thick and well-balanced meal. The legal text *Bretha Cróligé* (Binchy 1938, 42 § 52), in outlining the feeding instructions for young children during sick-maintenance, stipulates that they should be given 'a soft fare of fosterage: the yolks of eggs, butter, curds and gruel' (*maotbiad altruma .i. in buidecan 7 im 7 maotla 7 lictiu*). The association of egg yolks and gruel in *Bretha Cróligé* suggests that rich frumenty may well have been a nourishing dish of the period.

The remaining three pot-based preparations are best interpreted as types of watery gruels and most are associated with the stringent dietary rules of penitential monks. *Brothchán* is referred to throughout the body of penitential literature. *The Rule of Tallaght* (Gwynn 1927a, 26 § 43) describes it as a mixture of meal and water, the amount of meal added being only a quarter of a *cingit* (i.e., an ounce).[2] The small quantity of meal in this instance must be a reflection of the severity of the diet of Máel Ruain and may not refer to the standard preparation procedure. In *An Irish Penitential*, however, *brothchán* is made with good milk and, if there is no milk, it may be taken with a portion of rich condiment (Gwynn 1914, 140 § 3).

The use of milk in the preparation of *brothchán* is supported in the legal texts where, in Heptad 41, the phrase *bó brothcain* is used to describe a cow that produces milk for fine boiling (CIH 38.21). Nonetheless, for fasting monks, it seems that milk was used in the preparation of the dish only on festive occasions in order to mark a relaxation in their otherwise severe dietary regime. On such occasions good milk (*as maith*), which may be interpreted as undiluted or unadulterated full-fat milk, was employed in the preparation of *brothchán*. But, whether made with milk or water, *brothchán* was an overwhelmingly wet preparation. An indication of its watery consistency is evident from Máel Ruain's ruling that the dish may be taken when whey-water and ale were unavailable, which seems to imply that it was a drink substitute. Additionally, he orders his monks to sip the mixture instead of drinking it at a full draught, as 'a man finds less sensual pleasure and satisfaction in sips than in draught, when he is thirsty (*acht bolgama dol, oir coisgid sin an ítaidh 7 as luga an sians 7 an t-aiteas bhios ag neach a n-aimsir tharta isna bolgamaibh ina san digh*)' (Gwynn 1927a, 26 § 43–28 § 44).

Despite its watery consistency, *brothchán* was considered a luxury to be consumed on Sundays and great festivals (ibid., 32 § 52). Máel Ruain also permitted his monks to occasionally partake of the dish on Saturday nights as an indulgence (ibid., 2 § 1), and for those who had taken a vow of perpetual celibacy it came as a welcome break from the usual penitential diet of bread and water (Gwynn 1914, 140 § 3). In the *Rule of the Céli Dé* (Gwynn 1927b, 78 § 50) the implication is that *brothchán* is valued for its nutritional and sustaining properties: 'During the monthly sickness of the daughters of the Church they are excused from vigils, morning and evening, so long as it lasts, and *brothchán* is made for them at tierce, at whatever time this happens, because it is right that this sickness would have attention. (*Galar mistai bís for ingenaib eclaise, saire a figle doib oiret bis foraib, maiten 7 fescor, 7 brochán do denam doib am theirt, secip aimser, fobith dlegar airmitiu in galair sin.*)'

According to *An Irish Penitential*, *brothchán* is to be made with good milk and served with additional relishes on Sundays and festivals (Gwynn 1914, 140 § 3).[3] The relishes mentioned are the fruits of all seasons and honey (Gwynn 1927a, 28 § 45), suggesting that the dish in this instance could well have been an early example of muesli. Indeed, the ingredients for muesli were widely available in the period. The basic constituents of *brothchán* were meal and milk, with a combination of some of the following: honey (*mil*), apples (*ubla*), wild (*uball fiadhan*) or cultivated sloes (*áirne*), blackberries (*sméra*), mulberries (*sméra grianáin*) and hazelnuts (*cnó cuill*), all of which are listed as foodstuffs in the documentary material. It is a feasible suggestion that the simple concoction of any of the above could have featured in the diet of all classes.

In addition, a straightforward *brothchán* mixture of meal and water or milk, once heated, will form a good base that can be readily transformed into a soup or broth by the simple expedient of adding vegetables, meat scraps, fat or whatever ingredients were to hand. This hotch-potch of ingredients was standard Medieval fare, especially when the open cooking pot dictated cooking methods. Therefore, broths, soups and gruels enjoyed a close culinary relationship and the modern-day distinctions between such dishes were as yet blurred and undefined.

The third porridge variety, *tiuglagin*, is described in *The Monastery of Tallaght*. The ingredients are the same as for *brothchán*, the distinguishing feature being the use of butter in its preparation. The method of preparation is outlined in the text (Gwynn and Purton 1911, 147 § 52): 'he added one-third of water to the daily allowance and boiled the water. When this third had boiled away, he put a lump of butter on each man's allowance, and boiled it on the water, and then put meal over it (*dobert trian forcridi de usci ar chuid cach lae sin 7 roberbi ind usce am dechaid a trian sin la bruith 7 doratt cnoc de imbim ar chuid cach ae 7 roberbi ar usci 7 is iarum dorad min aire*).'

It is clear that *tiuglagan* was prescribed only for sickly penitents who needed the extra nourishment of the butter which was secretly incorporated in to their diet, lest their 'perpetual confinement should cause their death' (*fochand báis dóib in sircharcrad*) (ibid., 146 § 52).

The fourth dish, *menadach*, which has been interpreted as a type of watery gruel, is referred to widely. The exact nature of this dish is elusive and accounts of its form are contradictory. O'Curry (cf. DIL entry *garbán*) maintains that *menadach* is simply a dish of coarse meal: *menadach, .i. garbán*. In *An Irish Penitential* the term is used to describe a gruel dish of meal and whey-water (Gwynn 1914, 140 § 3). Similarly, the ninth-century *Cáin Adamnáin* mentions it within the context of the penalty for a woman who kills another or digs under a church for treasure; she is to be set adrift in a boat with one paddle and a vessel of meal and water (*long menathcha do breith lee*) (Meyer 1905, 30 § 45). A more detailed description of the dish is found in *The Monastery of Tallaght*, in which it is stated that, since many of the penitents who fasted on a diet of bread and water died, a more sustaining dish was devised by mixing some meal with butter (Gwynn and Purton 1911, 157 § 73). It is clear that the ingredients are identical with those of *tiuglagin*, but there are fundamental differences in the methods of preparation. The references cited from *The Monastery of Tallaght* can be used to suggest that *menadach* is first and foremost a type of paste of kneaded butter and coarse meal – the Irish equivalent of the Greek *maza* and Roman *puls*. Such a paste-like mixture is referred to in the twelfth-century Icelandic saga *Landnámabók*, where the preparation of *menadach* by Irish slaves is described as follows (Mahon 1991, 63): 'The Irish thralls found the expedient of kneading meal and butter and said it would quench the thirst. They called it *minapak*.' The paste-like quality of this dish is also borne out by the fact that sickly monks were permitted to spread *menadach* on their bread on Sundays and holy days (Gwynn 1914, 140 § 3).

In culinary terms *menadach* can be interpreted as an early and rudimentary form of *roux* or *beurre manié*, used in the preparation of enriched, fatty, soup-like gruels. *The Monastery of Tallaght* indicates that the consistency of the gruel varied in accordance with the proportions of butter to meal or in the texture of the meal used in the preparation of the paste. This text refers to three types of gruel: 'gruel upon water (*menadach uas usce*)', presumably a mixture of *menadach* rich enough in butter to be buoyant; 'gruel between two waters (while it does not sink right down to the bottom of the vessel, it does not float above on top of the water) (*menadach eter da usci sech ni teit sis arrec co dommain lestir ni theit súas huas usci*)', which is perhaps richer in meal than butter, but has enough butter to remain semi-buoyant; and 'gruel under water . . .

it reaches the bottom of the vessel; the grain carries it downwards (*menadach usci. Rosaigi immurco dommain lestair berthus arbar sis*)', a mixture composed mostly of coarse meal (Gwynn and Purton 1911, 158 § 74).

It is reasonable to suggest that *menadach*, as a basic thickener, could have been used in the preparation of various soup or pottage dishes. Brassica/kale or nettle pottage (*braisech*), meat pottage (*scaiblín*) and branchy/sproutty (? vegetable) pottage (*cráibechán cráebaig*) are all listed in AMC. It is probable that the consistency of these broths and soups was improved at times by the addition of *menadach* or raw meal. It is likely that *menadach* was popular because the mixture was a long-established method of preserving and storing butter and meal, and could be used instantly in several different ways. Tannahill indicates that the paste remains palatable over a long period and refers to Pliny, who recommends packing such pastes into a container for long storage and covering them with a layer of flour or bran (Tannahill 1973, 65).

Breads

The AMC speaks of seven bread varieties, each made with a different cereal type (Jackson 1990, 38 § 68).[4] More usually the sources refer simply to wheaten, barley, oaten and rye breads in a generic sense, without elaborating on the specific cereals used in their preparation. It is possible, by reference to the gluten content of each of the cereals, to distinguish further between the types of bread current during the period. The percentage of gluten-forming proteins present in cereals largely determines the quality of the flour, the baking potential of the dough and the texture of the finished product (Dickson 1990, 37). The low gluten content of oaten and barley flours produces characteristically flat breads. Even with the addition of a leavening agent, thick oatcakes rarely rise above a centimetre (Irwin 1937, 57; Murray 1974, 52; Danaher 1978, 47–48). Though barley is a little more responsive to leavening, it has a distinctly inferior status as a bread type and the finished loaf is heavy with a characteristic grey colour and an earthy tang. In contrast, the high gluten content of wheat renders a good-quality, light loaf with more volume and a better colour. Rye's high gluten content also makes it responsive to leavening, although leavened rye loaves are notoriously heavy and dark, making rye flour more suitable for the production of maslin (mixed cereal) breads. Given these considerations, it is possible to divide the breads mentioned in the sources into two categories: flat, heavy, unleavened cakes of oats and barley and lighter, aerated wheaten loaves or maslin breads.

Keeping these observations in mind, some indication of the size and dimension of various types of breads can be gleaned from the sources. The legal text *Cáin Aicillne* outlines the dimensions of loaves rendered as part of food-rents (*bés tige*) in clientship (CIH 483.33–34): 'twenty four cakes/loafs of woman's baking two fists in width and a fist in thickness (*ceitheor bairgena .xx. do banfuine 7 imb da dorn a leithet 7 dorn a tighet*).'

The bread, in accordance with the fist measurement (cf. DIL entry), is eight to twelve inches (200–300 mm) in diameter and four to six inches (100–150 mm) in thickness. The Old Irish text *The Rule of Ailbe of Emly* mentions a cake of twelve inches (300 mm) which weighed thirty ounces (850 gr) (O'Neill 1907, 102 v. 31a). This indication of size and weight is confirmed from an independent reference in *Cáin Íarraith*, which indicates that a milk vessel of twelve inches (300 mm) diameter is equal in volume to the ingredients of six cakes of woman's baking (CIH 1766.12–14). O'Loan, with a note of caution, estimates that a cow in full milk would yield about eighteen pints (10.2 litres) per milking (1965, 170–71). The calculation, therefore, involves the weighing of a piece of dough equivalent in volume to three pints, which surprisingly weighs almost exactly thirty ounces.[5] This dough, when shaped into a round of twelve inches diameter, is rather thin and measures between half an inch (13 mm) and three-quarters of an inch (19 mm) in thickness. *Cáin Aicillne*, in reference to flat bread, supports this measurement of thickness, stating (CIH 1781. 29): 'A man's little finger measures it in thickness (*Lútu laime fir dodomidightur dia tigut*).' It is clear that two categories of bread are being referred to in these sources: firstly, a flat cake, as described in *The Rule of Ailbe of Emly*, and, secondly, a loaf of raised bread, *bairgen banfuine* (a loaf of woman's baking). The difference in height between the two varies from three-quarters of an inch (19 mm) to four inches (102 mm), or more.

A variation of the raised *bairgen banfuine* is the closely related *bairgen ferfuine* (a loaf of man's baking), which the legal text *Bretha Comaithchesa* states was twice the size of the former and which was considered to represent a properly made loaf (Binchy 1938, 22 § 27). The existence of two raised loaf types, each fixed in terms of size and weight, presupposes that these were the standard forms that were routinely produced in the period. The labels, women's and man's baking, may, therefore, distinguish between a standard small and large loaf. Since baking was a female-dominated activity, it is difficult to assign the epithet *ferfuine* to any social context other than that of the male-dominated ecclesiastical sites. Therefore, *bairgen ferfuine* might use as its standard the type of loaf that was produced on a professional and large-scale basis within monastic contexts. It is possible that this standard type of loaf originated, as Lucas suggests, 'in the early monastic communities where a woman would not have been tolerated and the cook was a man' (Lucas 1960, 4).

The size and thickness of the standard loaves (*banfuine* and *ferfuine*) are comparable to modern-day Irish soda breads. Such dimensions strongly suggest the use of wheat and a leavening agent in their preparation. However, doubt has been cast on the existence of leavened bread in the period because of the lack of evidence for the built-up oven, but the absence of an oven is easily overcome. The griddle or baking flag can readily be transformed into a small-scale domestic oven by placing an inverted clay pot over the prepared dough (Frayn 1978, 29; Danaher 1981, 62; Cubberley 1995, 55–68). A refinement of the 'baking-under system' is the pot oven with a close-fitting lid. Both the inverted and pot ovens can be surrounded with hot embers, thus ensuring the uniform baking of the overall surface of the loaf. In addition, the widespread availability of both grain ferments (barm, wort, sourdough) and acid ferments (sour milk, buttermilk) presents a strong case for their use as leavens in bread-making. Indeed, given the extent of the ale-making industry in the period, it is reasonable to assume a relationship between ale and bread-making. Joyce was of the opinion that barm yeast (*descad*) was successfully employed in the production of leavened wheat bread and draws attention to two texts which he claimed refer to the leavening of dough in such a manner as to show that the writer was quite familiar with the process (Joyce 1903, 119, 143).

In summary, it is possible to distinguish three broad categories of bread from the literary sources: flat breads of either oats, wheat, barley or rye and the standardised *bairgen banfuine* and *bairgen ferfuine*, prepared with wheat and possibly leavened.

Ingredients of bread

One of the shortcomings of the documentary evidence is the lack of information detailing the ingredients used in bread-making. In more recent times oaten, barley and wheaten cakes were mixed to a dough using flour or meal, hot water, milk or buttermilk and salt (Stokes 1868, 107; Danaher 1978, 47). Butter or lard was often used as an additional ingredient (ibid., 48; Irwin 1937, 57). The fact that salt was often taken as a relish with bread during the Early Medieval period suggests that the bread itself did not always contain this ingredient. Bread served with salt (*pane et sale*) is referred to in the *Penitential of Finnian* (Bieler 1975, 80–82 § 23) and in the legal text *Crith Gablach* (Binchy 1979, 6.149–50), where salt and heavily salted condiments such as dulse are mentioned. In addition, the popularity of serving salted bacon (*tinne*) and highly salted preserved butter (*gruiten*) as condiments would have satisfied the desire for flavouring. Honey, used as a sweetener in the preparation of wheaten cakes (*cóic fichit bargen cruithnechta and iarna fuine tría mil*), is referred to in *Fled Bricrend* (Best and Bergin 1992, 248.8124–25). Indeed, buns found during the excavation of the Iron Age site at Glastonbury, England, were found on examination by Clement Reid to be composed of unbroken wheat grains that seem to have been mixed with honey (Renfrew 1973, 193). Ó Sé maintains that *breacan* was a type of griddle cake made with curds (1948, 87), and this may correspond with the Roman *athletae* bread which was mixed with soft curd cheese. Pea, bean and acorn meals may also have been used as flour substitutes, particularly in times of bad harvests and famine (Lucas 1960, 5; Renfrew 1973, 193). The unintentional incorporation of ingredients into the bread must also be considered. Archaeobotanical analyses of samples from Early Medieval sites reveal that the cereal crops were contaminated by certain weed species (see Monk, Tierney and Hannon, ch. 8). Consequently, many of the weeds and their seeds, in particular those of fat hen (*chenopodium album*) and red shank (*polygonum persicaria*), would have been ground, either unintentionally or as flavour enhancers, into the flour (Brothwell 1986, 92). Perhaps, then, it is more accurate to envisage bread made by using a combination of cereals, with optional additional ingredients, rather than the single cereal varieties which are emphasised in the documentary material.

Baking utensils and methods of preparation

An array of baking utensils is listed in the legal text *Bretha im Fhuillema Gell* (CIH 472.3–4). The text states that the griddle (*lann*), the griddle slice (*lainnín*), the wooden vessel for measuring grain (*airmed*), the bucket (*síthal*), the kneading trough (*losat*), and the sieve (*criathar*) all formed part of the *batterie de cuisine* and were essential items for baking. That these were commonplace household utensils is clear from the legal text *Di Chetharshlicht Athgabála*, in which they were legally protected against misappropriation or damage. Such crimes entailed the imposition of distress with a stay of one day (*athgabál óine*), since these items were considered essential to every household (CIH 368.26–30; 376.6–9). The dough mixture was prepared in a kneading trough, though the sources do not specify whether the trough was of wood or stone. It might be suggested that the prehistoric saddle-querns found on a number of Early Medieval sites may, in fact, have been reused as kneading troughs.

The consistency of the dough mixture will, to a large extent, determine the shape and texture of the baked bread. Flat breads, particularly oaten bread, can be prepared from either a runny batter-like dough or a thick paste-like mixture. Indeed, the griddle or baking flag is conducive to the production of pancake-like flat breads that are quickly and easily prepared and resemble modern-day drop-griddle scones. However, the thickness of the loaves described in the documentary material indicates that bread was more commonly prepared from a thick, stiff dough.

In the apparent absence of the built-up oven, the open hearth dictated baking methods. The griddle and the baking flag were employed, though the flag is reputed to produce a lighter loaf. Once set on the griddle, the cake was turned and portioned into farls with the aid of the griddle knife or slice (CIH 472.3–4). The *Senchas Már* states that the cakes were divided into eight thin farls (*srubán*) (CIH 370. 23–24) which must allude to the large twelve-inch cakes referred to in *Cáin Aicillne* and *The Rule of Ailbe of Emly*. A more rudimentary baking method, which demands no baking utensils, is the resting of the dough on glowing embers or on a suitable leaf to bake. It is probable that this method was frequently employed in less prosperous households where items like a griddle did not exist. The antiquity and commonalty of the practice is evident from the fact that Cato, Pliny, Columella and Apicius all mention it as normal procedure (Frayn 1978, 29). In addition, Mahon states that this method was employed in Ireland as late as the 1920s, when cakes wrapped in cabbage leaves were cooked on a bed of hot ashes with other hot ashes piled on top (1991, 72).

Working with the above listed utensils was a female-dominated activity within a domestic setting. *Cáin Íarraith*, for example, states that the skills of bread-making should be taught to young girls of inferior social grades during fosterage (CIH 1760.22), while in more prosperous households such culinary operations were the task of female slaves (CIH 285.36–286.4). Equally, the allusion to the legendary *Cíannacht* in *Din Techtugad* symbolically affirms that bread-making was regarded as woman's work. In the text she makes her legal entry (*bantellach*) and repossession of a disputed land-holding while carrying the tools of the trade – her sieve and kneading trough (CIH 208.17–18).

Monastic and penitential bread

The normal daily bread of the monks, as recommended by strict disciplinarians like John Cassianus and sources such as the *Regula Sancti Benedicti*, comprised coarse loaves (*secundarius*) prepared from inferior-grade sifted flours of barley, oats or pulses that could be baked on ashes (*panis subcinerarius*) or fashioned into dried biscuits (*biscoctum, panis paximatius*) (Dembinska 1986, 153–55). Breads of similar grades of unsifted flours were made up especially for penitent monks, for those who had failed to keep enough of their bread ration until supper and for alms-giving (ibid., 155). The continental sources stipulate that these breads could be softened with water or added to green soups or other such dishes, like *alica* soup – a watery gruel of flour, salt and a few drops of oil (ibid., 153–4).

The Irish sources do not specify the type of flour used in the production of monastic bread, but evidence from the hagiographical sources indicates that heavy cakes of barley meal were the usual penitential fare (Stokes 1890, 81.2734; Plummer 1922, I, 233 § 149). In line with the continental evidence, they do specify that bread may be taken with water, whey or milk drinks, hard-boiled eggs, curds or a little slice of fish and could also be added to dishes of kale cooked in milk (Gwynn 1927a; 1927b). On Sundays bread was served with a ladleful of honey, a little portion of condiment and a measure of ale to celebrate the Lord's Day (ibid., 1927a, 28 § 45). However, the fact that fresh bread was not baked on Sundays (Gwynn and Purton 1911, 132 § 13) may have provided an additional reason for the serving of such moist condiments. In addition, *Canones Hibernenses* provides evidence for the production of small biscuit-like cakes. It states that, in commutation for a year's penance, the penitent could spend twelve days and twelve nights on a diet of twelve biscuits that amounted to the size of three loaves (Bieler 1975, 164 § 5). If the standard monastic loaf is twelve inches (300 mm) in diameter (O'Neill 1907, 102 v. 31a), then the biscuits described above would roughly equate with farls measuring six inches (150 mm) along their perpendicular sides or a quarter of a round of a cake.

The Rule of Ailbe of Emly states that the daily ration of monastic bread was a loaf of thirty ounces (850 gr), an allowance substantially more generous than the Benedictine ration which was one pound (506 gr) (Dembiska 1986, 155). When doing penance, however, the daily ration in Ireland for a non-labouring penitent was reduced to six ounces (170 gr) of bread, which, according to *An Irish Penitential*, was enriched with a *menadach* spread and supplemented with additional nourishing foods, including kitchen herbs and hard-boiled eggs. Furthermore, the text states that if the man was in poor health he was also entitled to a jug of good milk along with buttermilk or curds (Gwynn 1914, 142 § 7; Binchy 1975, 263 § 7).

There can be no doubt that bread was staple monastic fare. However, it is evident that concentration on a bread- rather than a gruel-based diet was particularly pronounced during periods of penance and fasting. Indeed, the extremes of fasting relied almost exclusively on a diet of bread and water. *The Teaching of Máel Ruain* outlines the diet as follows (Gwynn 1927a, 16 § 28): 'The fasting diet which he appointed in his Rule is as follows: the measure of bread called a mouthful and a *buigén* (pannikin) of whey-water, for persons in sound health. If a man were sickly, he received two mouthfuls and two pannikins of whey-water (*Ase sasadh troisgthi do ordaigh se san Riaghail .i. an tomhas arain da ngoirthi boim, 7 buigheun medg-uisgi do lucht fuis. Mas duine tinn é do gheibheadh se da bhoim 7 uisge*).' St Ciarán of Saigher also exemplifies the ideal of the monastic rule by partaking only of bread and water, while St Finnian of Clonard, St Molaise of Devenish and St Maedóc of Ferns condemn themselves to a sparse and harsh diet of heavy barley bread (Lucas 1960, 4). Similarly, the penitential literature demands that the fasting diet constitute bread and water, enhanced at times with morsels of non-meat or animal fat foods. No doubt such a diet was designed to alleviate hunger without arousing any sense of taste or sensuality and still allow the monks to work and pray hard, thus satisfying the principles of the monastic rule (Dembinska 1986, 153). In summary, therefore, reliance on a diet of poor-quality breads became a means of self-mortification and an expression of religious fervour.

The condiments and relishes associated with bread

The coarse texture and insipid taste of flat breads, aptly compared to horses' hoofs in AMC (Jackson 1990, 35; 1072–74), necessitated that they be served with a palatable relish (*annland*) or condiment (*tarsand*). The terms *annland* and *tarsand* are used interchangeably in the documentary material. This confusion is reasonably explained by Thurneysen's suggestion that *annland* represents a relish eaten specifically with bread, such as butter or cheese, while *tarsand* is a term used for condiments in general (salted or fresh meats, garden herbs and sweet fruit) (Binchy 1938, 62). This interpretation does not agree with Triad 184 (Meyer 1906, 24), which describes *tarsand* as honey, salt food or *echmuir* (an unspecified plant). Thurneysen's point can be modified further, however, and it is reasonable to suggest that *tarsand* represents any relish spreadable on bread. Butter (*imb*),[6] cheese (*cáise*),[7] curds/biestings (*maethal*)[8] and butter and meal paste (*menadach*)[9] are all listed as spreadable relishes for bread. Indeed the moist and soft nature of these relishes served to improve the taste and texture of bland coarse breads, thus ensuring their position as popular accompaniments. However, butter is certainly the most common; one is reminded of Evans' observation that 'the staple was butter and oatcake rather than oatcake and butter, the gritty stoneground flour demanding a lubricant to assist the swallowing process' (1988, 82). The taste for butter is well illustrated in *Betha Colmáin maic Lúacháin*, where Colmán butters his bread on both sides during his Lenten fast (Meyer 1911, 84 § 82). But, apart from the question of taste, the serving of butter with bread was also an effective means of demonstrating social standing. Butter stands out as a superior relish in the legal text *Críth Gablach*, where it is offered as part of the food provision (*bíathad*) only to the strong farmers and noble grades in place of less fatty items such as curds and corn (cf. Binchy 1938).

After butter, other moist, fat-based relishes include cow suet rendered as dripping (*annlantus*) (Thurneysen 1923, 355 § 13). In AMC, juicy pudding dripping is considered a delicacy for a priest to spread on his bread (Jackson 1990, 35.1084–87), while the prevalence of serving fat or lard (*blonoc*) is also evident in both the legal texts (CIH 1605.26–27) and the penitential literature (Gwynn 1927a, 6 § 8; 1927b, 66 § 6). Other condiments and beverages frequently served with bread include ale (*linn*),[10] apples (*ubla*),[11] brassica/kale (*braisech*) dressed with milk,[12] buttermilk (*bláthach*),[13] celery or parsley (*imus*),[14] dulse (*duilesc*),[15] fish (*iasc*),[16] fresh garlic/Welsh onions (*cainnenn*),[17] garden herbs (*lus lubgoirt*),[18] hard-boiled eggs (*ubh thirm*),[19] honey (*mil*),[20] milk (*as*),[21] sorrel (*samad*),[22] sour or skimmed milk mixed with new milk (*draumcu ar lemlacht*),[23] sweet fruits (*cumrai*),[24] watercress (*biror*)[25] and whey (*medg*).[26]

Conclusion

A number of conclusions and general observations can be drawn from the documentary data on the cereal foodstuffs of Early Medieval Ireland. Firstly, on the subject of porridge/gruel, the comprehensive nature of the evidence testifies to the existence not only of a generalised and non-specific porridge dish but to a diverse number of pot-based dishes using different ingredients and preparation techniques. While there may not be a bank of individual porridge/gruel/broth recipes, the evidence does suggest an ability to work with available ingredients to produce a variety of different cereal-based dishes.

As mentioned above, outside monastic circles the pot-based preparation most frequently alluded to is *littiu*, the thick-textured porridge that could be enriched and sweetened with the addition of honey, butter, milk or eggs. No doubt its nourishing qualities and the ease of its digestibility ensured its reputation as sustaining childhood fare. The three other gruel variants all display a close relationship with the monastic and penitential diet and appear to have been taken on holy days as a break from the usual diet of bread and water. At first glance, the differences between these dishes seem trivial and insubstantial, but the ability to negotiate the subtle differences in ingredients and preparation techniques may be taken as evidence of the monastic familiarity with, and reliance on, a cereal-based diet. Such a diet is summarised in *Indarda Mochuda a rRaithin*, where a monk's basic refection is given as pottage/gruel, milk, and corn (*brothcán 7 ass 7 arbhar*) (Plummer 1922, 300 § 3). Indeed, porridge and, more importantly, bread emerge as indispensable monastic foods, thereby suggesting a strong relationship between the Church and the cereal economy.

The detailed descriptions of porridge/gruel in the documentary sources should not be taken as suggesting that the cereal crop was used predominantly for such preparations. A commonly held myth, comparable to the self-perpetuating myth of a pastorally based economy (Monk 1986, 31), is the one which maintains that most cereals were consumed in the form of porridge or watery gruels rather than bread (Lucas 1960, 5–6). Both misconceptions tend to bolster each other, promoting a sense of poor economic and culinary evolution within the period. This inherited, yet flawed reasoning can be summarised as follows: in a pastorally dominated economy an essentially moist, milk-based diet is indicative of a society of primitive culinary evolution, characterised by a limited range of cooking utensils, of which the open cooking pot holds pride of place; when cereals are used, in the preparation of simple dishes such as meal mashes, pastes and porridges, they assume a secondary role in stretching dairy produce stocks; in all, therefore, milk, cereals and the cooking pot render an overwhelmingly wet diet – effectively one which has failed to make the transition from wet to solid cereal foodstuffs (unleavened and leavened bread). What results is the impression of an overall backward culinary culture, limited to a hotchpotch and single-pot cuisine.

Such lines of argument have been supported by using often suspect sixteenth- and seventeenth-century social commentaries which note the infrequent use of bread in the Irish diet. However, these commentaries are often limited in their understanding of the term bread. It is likely, as Lucas points out, that their definition was limited to wheaten loaves, or more specifically, to professionally produced oven-baked leavened wheaten loaves, and thus they pay no heed to the widespread domestic production of oaten, barley, wheaten, and rye cakes. The numerous references to such breads in economic, social and religious contexts in the Early Medieval texts affirm the existence of a well-established baking tradition within the period (cf. Sexton 1993). It was bread, for instance, and not porridge that was demanded during sick-maintenance and hospitality and in the payment of food rents and *smachta* (penalty) fines. Consequently, any general theory which argues that porridge was the predominant cereal dish of the period ignores the broader cultural complexities of the cereal diet.

It seems appropriate in the light of the evidence to assign the consumption of specific cereal dishes to particular social groupings. It has already been stated that porridge/gruel had a particular association with the young, the sick and those following a rigid religious dietary regime. But, apart from special needs and religious orientation, diet is conditioned by several other factors, not least being the status of the consumer. A cereal diet, depending on whether it is consumed in wet or dry form, is an excellent means of demonstrating socio-economic status. Porridge, for example, is a quickly prepared dish which requires few cooking utensils and little culinary expertise, making it appropriate to the lower social grades whose economic means limited their access to the necessary utensils required for successful baking. In contrast, the choice or at least the technological ability to resort to a bread-based diet is an excellent means of manifesting economic affluence and social standing. In this context the possibility of producing palatable and superior quality leavened wheaten loaves deserves further consideration. The consumption of porridge/gruels and bread, be it flat or leavened, is imbued with social significance. Finally, it is necessary to point out that any comprehensive understanding of the diet can only be achieved by combining the resources of the literary and archaeological records. Each can be of service to the other in understanding the subtleties and nuances that are essential to the advancement of food studies.

ACKNOWLEDGEMENT

I am grateful to Dr Fergus Kelly, Dublin Institute of Advanced Studies, for permission to consult his *Early Irish Farming* before its publication.

NOTES

1. This chapter draws on a variety of Old Irish (seventh to ninth century) and Middle Irish (tenth to twelfth century) texts in an attempt to piece together a comprehensive overview of the Early Medieval cereal diet. Most of the material presented here is based on the Old Irish law-texts, the corpus of Irish penitential literature and the middle Irish epic tale *Aislinge meic Conglinne* (AMC). Linguistic evidence shows that the majority of the law-texts originate in the seventh and eighth centuries; most survive in fourteenth- to sixteenth-century manuscripts and thus have been subject to much suspect rewriting and reinterpretation. The surviving legal material has been collected and edited by D.A. Binchy (1978) and presented in his six-volume *Corpus Iuris Hibernici* (CIH). He has also produced editions of the legal texts *Bretha Crólige* (1938), *Bretha Déin Chécht* (1966) and *Críth Gablach* (1979). Much of the Old Irish penitential literature of the Irish church reformists, the *Céli Dé*, has been edited and translated by Gwynn and Purton (1911), Gwynn (1914; 1927a; 1927b) and Binchy (1975), and these eighth- to ninth-century sources have provided detailed, though possibly idealised, descriptions of the monastic and, in particular, the fasting regime. The AMC has been variously dated to the eleventh or twelfth century. The text, for the most part, is an exhaustive, though possibly fanciful, litany of medieval Irish foods and is one of the most important extant sources available to the Irish food historian. It has been edited and translated by Kuno Meyer (1892), though many of his interpretations of individual foodstuffs remain unsatisfactory and at times incorrect. Kenneth Jackson (1990) has produced a more recent edition of the text.
2. Binchy (1975) 275, n. 6, comments that the *cingit* (goblet) corresponds to *hemina* (a half-pint) in the Latin Penitentials. The meal ration of a quarter of a *cingit* or one-eighth of a pint, when weighed (by the author), equals one ounce.
3. Binchy (1975) reads *bochtán* (a small liquid measure) for MS. *brothchán* (cf. Binchy 1975, 275 n. 6). This revised reading, therefore, disagrees with Gwynn's (1914) interpretation of the MS. The author agrees with Gwynn's original reading of the MS. *brothchán*, which means porridge or gruel.
4. For a full discussion and possible identification of the seven cereal varieties listed in AMC, see Sexton (1993).
5. The author, in experimentation, mixed a dough of wholemeal wheat flour and water to a regular and workable consistency which occupied a space of three pints in volume.
6. Binchy (1938) 24 § 28, 38 § 46 and 48; (1979) 3 § 9, 11 § 19, 12 § 20, 14 § 24, 15 § 26, 16 § 27, 17 § 28.
7. Gwynn (1927a) 2 § 2; (1927b) 64 § 4; Binchy (1938) 24 § 28.
8. Gwynn (1927a) 2 § 2; (1927b) 64 § 4.
9. Gwynn (1914) 140 § 3, 142 § 7.
10. Gwynn (1927a) 28 § 45; (1927b) 66 § 9, 68 § 19; Binchy (1938) 38 § 49.
11. Gwynn (1927a) 2-4 § 2; (1927b) 64 § 4.
12. Gwynn (1927a) 2 § 2; (1927b) 64 § 4.
13. Gwynn (1914) 142 § 7; Binchy (1975) 263 § 7.
14. Binchy (1938) 22 § 27, 36 § 45, 40 § 49.
15. Binchy (1979) 6 § 12.
16. Gwynn (1927a) 2 § 2, 30 § 48; (1927b) 64 § 4.
17. Binchy (1938) 20 § 24, 22 § 27, 38 § 49; (1979) 6 § 12.
18. Binchy (1938) 22 § 27, 40 § 49.
19. Gwynn (1914) 142 § 7; (1927a) 2 § 2; (1927b) 64 § 4; Binchy (1975), 263 § 7.
20. Binchy (1938) 20 § 24, 36 § 45.
21. Gwynn (1914) 140 § 3 and 6, 142 § 7; Binchy (1975) 262 § 3, 263 § 6 and 7.
22. Plummer (1922) I, 29 § 35.

23. Binchy (1979) 5 § 10.
24. Binchy (1938) 40 § 49.
25. O'Neill (1907) 104 v. 35.
26. Gwynn (1914) 140 § 3 and 6; Binchy (1975) 262 § 3, 263 § 6; Gwynn (1927a) 16 § 25 and 28; (1927b) 68 § 19.

BIBLIOGRAPHY

Barber, R. (1973) *Cooking and Recipes from Rome to the Renaissance*, London
Best, R.I. and Bergin, O. (eds.) (1929, 3rd repr. 1992) *Lebor na hUidre: The Book of the Dun Cow*, Dublin
Bieler, L. (ed.) (1963, repr. 1975) *The Irish Penitentials: Scriptores Latini Hiberniae*, vol. 5, Dublin
Binchy, D.A. (ed.) (1936) *Studies in Early Irish Law*, Dublin
Binchy, D.A. (ed.) (1938) 'Bretha Crólige', *Ériu* 12, 1–77
Binchy, D.A. (ed.) (1941, 2nd repr. 1979) *Críth Gablach*, Medieval and Modern Series, II, Dublin
Binchy, D.A. (ed.) (1966) 'Bretha Déin Chécht', *Ériu* 20, 1–66
Binchy, D.A. (ed.) (1975) 'The old Irish Penitential', in L. Bieler (ed.), *The Irish Penitentials: Scriptores Latini Hiberniae*, vol. 5, Dublin
Binchy, D.A. (ed.) (1978) *Corpus Iuris Hibernici*, 6 vols., Dublin
Black, M. (1992) *The Medieval Cookbook*, London
Brothwell, D. (1986) *The Bog Man and the Archaeology of People*, London
CIH See Binchy (1978)
Cubberley, A. (1995) 'Bread-baking in ancient Italy: *clibanus* and *sub testu* in the Roman world', in J. Wilkins, D. Harvey, and M. Dodson (eds.), *Food in Antiquity*, Exeter, 55–68
Danaher, K. (1978) *In Ireland Long Ago*, Cork
Danaher, K. (1981) 'Bread in Ireland', in A. Fenton and T.M. Owen (eds.), *Food in Perspective: Proceedings of the 3rd International Conference on Ethnological Food Research*, Cardiff, 1977
Dembinska, M. (1986) 'Fasting and working monks: regulations of the fifth to eleventh centuries', in A. Fenton and E. Kisbán (eds.), *Food in Change: Eating Habits from the Middle Ages to the Present Day*, Edinburgh, 152–59
Dickson, C. (1990) 'Experimental processing and cooking of emmer and spelt wheats and the Roman army diet', in D. Robinson (ed.), *Experimentation and Reconstruction in Environmental Archaeology: Symposia of the Association for Environmental Archaeology no. 9 Roskilde, Denmark, 1988*, Oxford, 33–39
DIL = (1983, repr. 1990) *Dictionary of the Irish Language based mainly on Old and Middle Irish materials*, Royal Irish Academy, Dublin
Evans, E.E. (1957, repr. 1988) *Irish Folkways*, London
Frayn, J.M. (1978) 'Home-baking in Roman Italy', *Antiquity* 52, 28–33

Gray, E.A. (ed.) (1982) *Cath Maige Tuired: The second battle of Mag Tuired*, London
Gwynn, E.J. (1914) 'An Irish penitential', *Ériu* 7, 121–95
Gwynn, E.J. (1927a) 'The teaching of Máel-Ruain', *Hermathena* 44, 2nd suppl., vols. 2–63
Gwynn, E.J. (1927b) 'Rule of the Céli Dé', *Hermathena* 44, 2nd suppl., vols. 64–87
Gwynn, E.J. and Purton, W.J. (1911) 'The monastery of Tallaght', *Proc. Roy. Ir. Acad.* 29C, 115–80
Irwin, F. (1937) *Irish Country Recipes*, Belfast
Jackson, K.H. (ed.) (1990) *Aislinge Meic Con Glinne*, Dublin
Joyce, P.W. (1903) *A Social History of Ancient Ireland*, London
Kelly, F. (1998) *Early Irish Farming*, Dublin
Lucas A.T. (1960) 'Irish food before the potato', *Gwerin* 3, 1–36
Mahon, B. (1991) *Land of Milk and Honey*, Dublin
Meyer, Kuno (1892) *Aislinge Meic Congline*, London
Meyer, Kuno (1905) *Cáin Adamnáin: An Old-Irish Treatise on the Law of Adamnan: Anecdota Oxoniensia*, Medieval and Modern Series 12, Oxford
Meyer, Kuno (1906) *The Triads of Ireland*: RIA *Todd Lecture Series* 13, Dublin
Miller, A.W.K. (1880–81) 'O'Clerys Irish Glossary', *Revue Celtique* 4, 349–428; v, 1–69
Monk, M.A. (1986) 'Evidence from macroscopic plant remains for crop husbandry in prehistoric and early historic Ireland: a review', *J. Ir. Archaeol.* 3, 31–36
Murray, P. (1974) 'Oatbread in North Staffordshire', *Folklife* 12, 48–54
Ó Corráin, D. (1972) *Ireland before the Normans*, Dublin
Ó Cróinín, D. (1995) *Early Medieval Ireland 400–1200*, London
O'Curry, Eugene (1873) *On the Manners and Customs of the Ancient Irish*, London
O'Loan, J. (1965) 'A history of early Irish farming' (3rd instalment), *Dept. of Ag. and Fish. J.* 62, 131–97
O'Neill, Joseph (1907) 'The rule of Ailbe of Emly', *Ériu* 3, 92–115
Ó Sé, M. (1948) 'Old Irish cheeses and other milk products', *J. Cork Hist. Archaeol. Soc.* S 53, 82–87
Plummer, C. (1922) *Bethada Náem nÉrenn: Lives of the Irish Saints*, 2 vols., Oxford
Renfrew, J.M. (1973) *Palaeoethnobotany*, London
Sexton, R. (1993) 'Cereals and cereal foodstuffs in the Early Historic Period', unpublished MA thesis (NUI), University College, Cork
Stokes, W. (1868) *Sanas Chormaic: Cormacs Glossary, translated and annotated by the late John O'Donovan, LLD*, Calcutta
Stokes, W. (1890) *Lives of the Saints from the Book of Lismore: Anecdota Oxoniensia*, Oxford
Tannahill, Reay (1973) *Food in History*, London
Thurneysen, R. (1923) 'Aus dem irischen Recht I', *Zeitschrift für Celtische Philologie* 14, 335–94

10. The Craft of the Millwright in Early Medieval Munster

COLIN RYNNE

Water-powered mills and their associated features – mill dams, races and ponds – were a common feature of the Early Medieval Irish cultural landscape, a circumstance which tells us quite a lot about the developed state of agriculture in the same period. There can be little doubt that only a relatively prosperous and productive agrarian economy would have had the resources necessary both to construct and maintain them. Indeed, there are more scientifically dated mill sites of the first millenium AD in the province of Munster alone than there are from the rest of Europe, and these include the earliest-known tide mills (Rynne 1992a), the earliest close association of vertical- and horizontal-wheeled mills in post-Roman Europe (Rynne 1989) and the earliest European twin-flume horizontal-wheeled mills (Rynne 1992b). Early Irish law makes ample provision for potential legal difficulties associated with mill use, whilst the earliest known vernacular technical terms in any European language for the component parts of the horizontal-wheeled mill are in Old Irish. As in all crafts, the skill of the artisan can best be judged from examples of an individual's work. But apart from the huge corpus of Early Medieval Irish watermill components, the earliest indications that a specialised trade of millwrighting existed anywhere in Early Medieval Europe are to be found in contemporary Irish documentary sources. Moreover, as will be argued below, only in Ireland, with its wealth of archaeological remains, has it thus far been possible to point to the evolution of regional millwrighting styles in the Early Medieval period.

The existence of a specialized craft of millwrighting in Early Medieval Ireland is made explicit in the early Irish documentary sources. In the law tracts ample recognition is given to the *saer muilinn*, or millwright, who is accorded the status of an *Aire Désa*, the lowest grade of nobility. In a story of the mythical *ard rí*, Cormac MacAirt, related by the poet Cuán ua Lothcáin (d. 1024), Cormac was said to have brought a millwright over from England to construct a watermill in order to relieve his mistress, Ciarnait, from the labour of the hand mill (Stokes 1890, 861; Gwynn 1903, 22–23). Indeed, according to *Uraicecht Becc*, millwrights were accorded the same status as other master carpenters such as wood carvers, shipwrights and those capable of making an oratory (a *durthech* or 'oak house'). Furthermore, in Triad 106 the construction of a watermill is included in 'three payments' (*dulchinni*) in which assistance to a craftsman is apportioned a share, as the craftsman cannot complete the work by himself and is obliged to employ another worker (*gniae*).

From the archaeological evidence it is clear that two varieties of horizontal-wheeled mill,

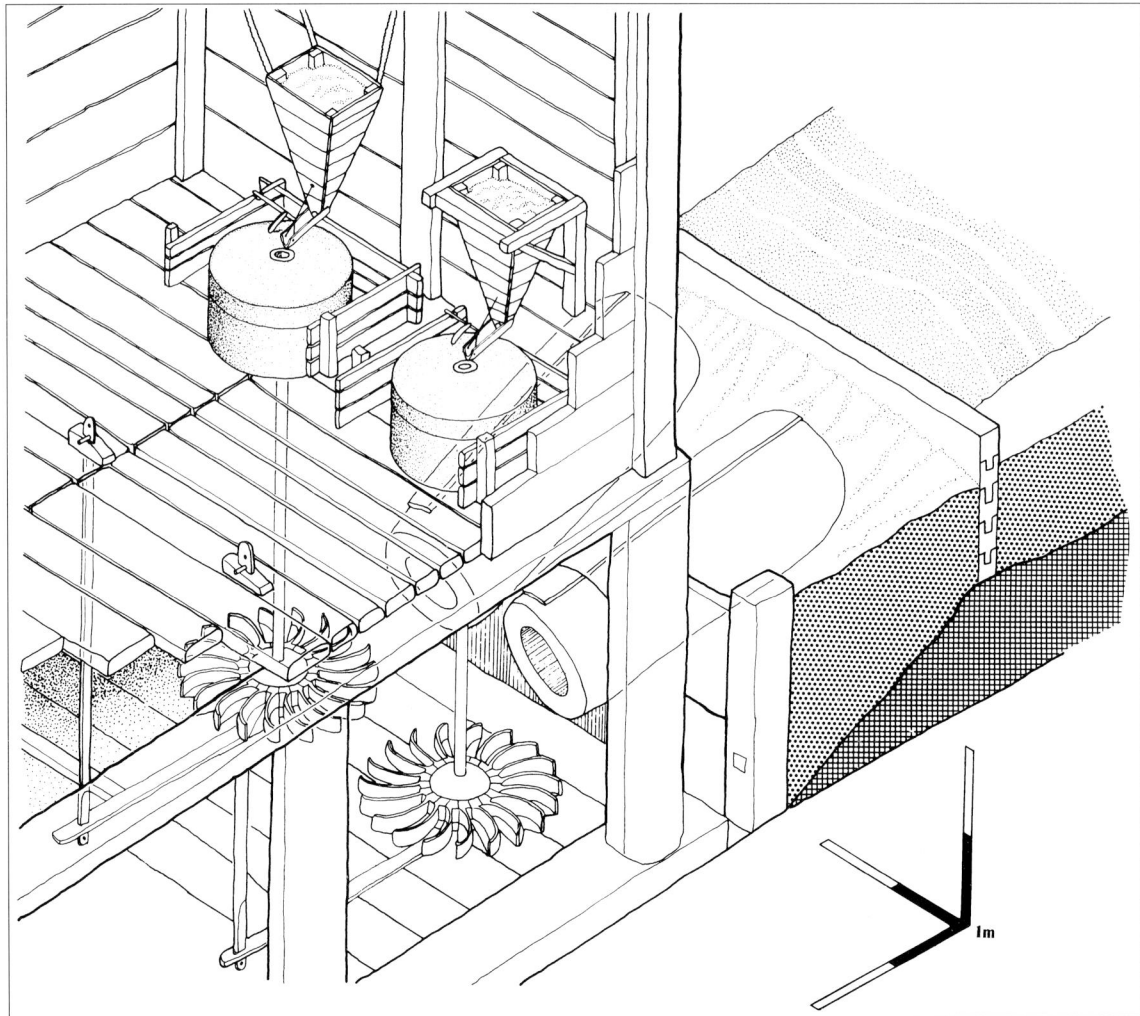

Fig. 10.1 Conjectural reconstruction of twin-flume horizontal-wheeled mill at Little Island, Co. Cork (*c.* AD 630)

employing either single or double flumes, were in use during the Early Medieval period in Ireland. The vast majority operated with a single flume or water delivery chute, but there are at least six recorded examples of mills, including the earliest known Irish horizontal-wheeled mill at Little Island, Co. Cork, that employed two delivery chutes (Fig. 10.1; Rynne 1992a). The existence of multi-flume mills is referred to in passing in *Fled Briciu*, an Ulster cycle text which was written down in the twelfth century but describes an Early Medieval milieu. The description in *De Ceithri Slichtaib Athgábala*, a late sixth- or early seventh-century legal text on distraint *'muilend dec foircel'* or 'mill of ten *oircel*' uses OIr. *oircel*, literally 'a trough', to refer to a mill flume (Mac Eoin 1982). While the description indulges in hyperbole 'to convey an impression of enormous speed and power' (Lucas 1953, 31), it clearly refers to the existence of mills utilising more than one delivery chute. The vertical-wheeled mill in Ireland (Fig. 10.2) is at least as early as the two varieties of horizontal-wheeled mill (Rynne 1989), and so the work of the early Irish

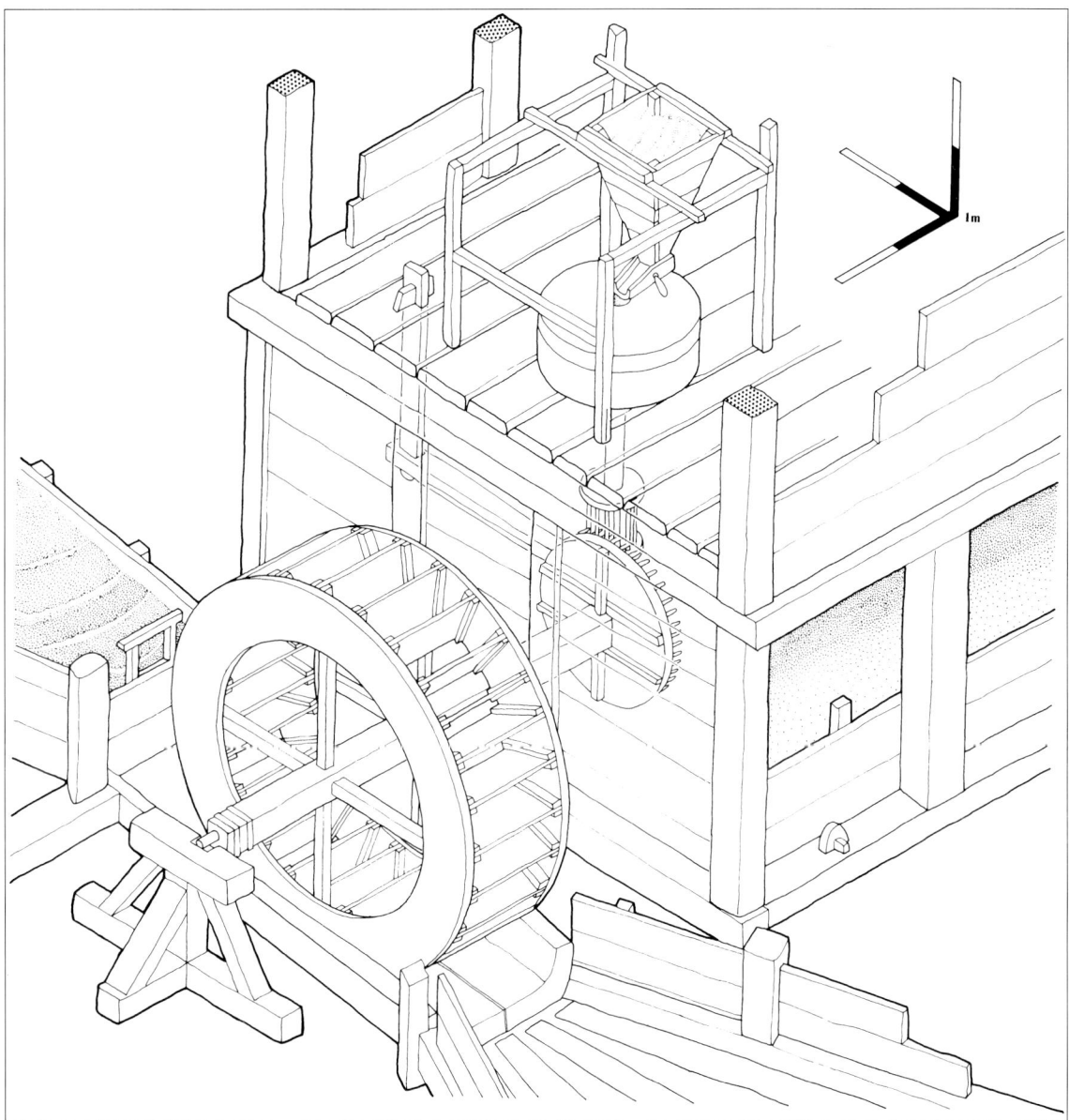

Fig. 10.2   Conjectural reconstruction of vertical-wheeled mill at Little Island, Co. Cork (*c.* AD 630)

millwright can be said to have encompassed at least three basic mill types. But what basic functions did the early Irish millwright actually perform? For the most part the rather overwhelming nature of the Irish evidence for early water-powered mills has tended to deflect attention away from this important group of highly skilled craftsmen. So let us now examine the work of these individuals in the light of the documentary and archaeological evidence

Laying out the site

The first priority of the millwright when entrusted with the construction of any variety of

Early Medieval water-powered mill would have been to identify a suitable water supply. The suitability and ultimate utility of any supply of water would have been governed by a number of factors: its accessibility relative to the site chosen for the millworks, the degree of seasonality and the fall from the source to the proposed mill site. On present evidence, fast flowing upland streams were the most common water source for watermills in Early Medieval Ireland (Rynne 1988, I). However, even the most copious waterflow could run at greatly reduced levels during crucial periods, particularly during the summer months. Indeed, the vast majority of the water-powered mill sites established in Ireland during the last century suffered from the seasonality of their watercourses. But whereas millwrights in more recent times could partially compensate for this by being able to calculate rates of flow available to them, relative to the power input and output of the waterwheel, their Early Medieval counterparts would have been almost wholly reliant on local observation of a watercourse or water supply over a long period of time. None the less, Early Medieval millwrights must surely have possessed some basic survey skills to ensure a steady fall from the bed of the millpond, through the millrace or leat to the millworks themselves. In the Later Medieval Latin and Irish lives of St Féchin of Fore, the saint miraculously draws water to a dry millpond, drowning the millwright who had fallen asleep in the area set out for the pond (Stokes 1892, 347–49; Plummer 1968, 1, 81–82; Wikander 1985, 151, n. 21). The requisite survey knowledge for establishing relative levels for watercourses would have been commonplace in Medieval Europe. In many parts of Europe, from the Roman period onwards, agriculture was possible only through the construction of complex irrigation networks. The engineering structures associated with European, North African and south west Asian irrigation societies – artificial watercourses, dams and storage reservoirs – began to be widely used in Ireland with the advent of water-powered mills. And it is by no means unreasonable to assume that the survey skills necessary for their construction formed part of the craft of the early Irish millwright.

To date, there is only one excavated example of an Early Medieval mill dam in Ireland, from Mashanaglass, Co. Cork (Rynne 1990, 25), although the remains of what appears to be a further example, associated with the remains of an Early Medieval monastic watermill on High Island, off the Galway coast, have recently been investigated (Rynne et al., 1996). However, at least two further examples have been noted in association with Irish horizontal-wheeled mill sites at Milverton. Co. Dublin (O'Donovan 1858–59, 252) and at a early ninth-century site at Crushyriree, Co. Cork (Cotter, forthcoming). Yet although mill dams, ponds and channels would have been common features of the Early Medieval Irish landscape, as the law tract *Coibnes Uisci Thairidne* and the large corpus of mill sites which have thus far come to light clearly attest, very few Irish examples have been identified, let alone excavated. The OIr. term *lind* or *tir linde* (literally 'the land of the pond'), which is used in *De Ceithri Slichtaib Athgábala*, is the earliest-known non-Latin term for this feature in post-Roman Europe. Occurrences of related terms in other vernacular languages are, curiously enough, somewhat later.

In many instances, considerable effort was expended on the provision of a water supply for these mills. An ingenious system of feeder ponds and leats was constructed on High Island to power a small horizontal-wheeled mill for the adjacent monastery (Rynne et al., 1996). A further island mill site on Little Island in Cork Harbour, dating to *c.* AD 630, exploited tidal changes to power a large double horizontal-wheeled mill and a small vertical-wheeled mill (Rynne 1992a; 1993). The structural arrangements of the Little Island mills have no parallel in the existing corpus of Early Medieval mill sites in either Ireland or Europe as a whole. None the less, whether a relatively large milling complex such as Little Island or more ordinary sites such as Cloontycarthy (Rynne 1989) and Mashanaglass (Fahy 1956; Rynne 1990) were involved, all of the construction work would have required close supervision from the individual responsible for laying out the site. In at least one later hagiography of St Fechín of Fore, the work of the millwright is miraculously executed by the saint (see above), whilst St Moling is said to have dug his own millrace as a penance (Plummer 1968, I, lxxxii; II, 193–94; Mac Eoin 1982, 15).

The mill buildings and mechanism
The setting of the waterwheel assembly, of the tentering gear, of the intermediate 'cog and rung' transmission in vertical-wheeled mills and of the millstones – all highly specialised tasks – would have been undertaken by the millwright, who is also likely to have dressed the millstones. It has recently been suggested that a 'mason would have been needed for the manufacture of its "anvil" [i.e., the stationary bedstone] and grinding stone [i.e the runner stone]' (Ó Cróinín 1995, 97). Indeed, the episode in the seventh-century life of St Brigid, which provides a detailed account of the cutting and fitting of a millstone to the watermill of the monastery at Kildare (Thomas 1971, 210–11; Connolly 1987, 24–25), would also appear to confirm this. However, it appears much more likely that while skilled stone cutters may have been involved in freeing the millstone rough-outs from the quarry face and transporting them to the mill site (as described by Cogitosus), the actual manufacture of the millstones would have been a specialist task. Apart from the dressing of the working surfaces of the millstones, which itself requires specialist skills (Rynne 1990), the execution of other features such as the rynd (or power-take-off sockets) and the distinctive bushing sockets would also require specialist knowledge. In more recent traditional watermills, both vertical- and horizontal-wheeled, the dressing of the millstones was undertaken by the miller. However, all of the evidence relating to customs and usages of water-powered mills from both Ireland and Europe as a whole during the Early Medieval period suggests that the actual operation of watermills was not generally regarded as a specialist craft. The OIr. term *tairbert*, which designates the act of using a mill (Mac Eoin 1982, 18), clearly indicates that the operation of early Irish mills was generally performed by those wishing to use them (i.e., non-specialists), a practice also suggested in *Coibnes Uisci Thairidne*. The term *muilleoir* (miller) would appear to be a Latin borrowing, its earliest-known usage appearing in the ninth-century *Immram Maele Dúin* (Stokes 1888, 483). In this source it is used in connection with the supernatural miller at *Inber Tre Canand*, which is one of the two known uses of this term up to the late MIr. period (Mac Eoin 1982, 18). Indeed, references to a specialised craft of milling are quite rare in Early Medieval European written sources. The earliest indications of the existence of specialist millers on the Continent are the *farinarii* or *mulinarii*, who are carefully distinguished from other monastic serfs in the *Consuetudines Corbinienses* of AD 822, written by Adalhard, abbot of the Benedictine monastery of Corbie (Horn 1975, 249). However, while the earliest Irish and Continental references to millers appear to be broadly contemporary, millers (*custos molini* or *molinarii*) are rarely mentioned in the eleventh-century Domesday survey (Lennard 1966, 278) or in southern Italy around the same time (Skinner 1992, 41). The actual operation of water-powered mills, therefore, may well have been a casual occupation during the Early Medieval period, and the manufacture and maintenance of the millstones is much more likely to have been executed by millwrights until such time as milling *per se* became a craft in its own right.

The Early Medieval Irish millwright was also a highly skilled woodworker. Many fine examples of this work, some arguably the finest of any wood-worker's craft, have come to light throughout Ireland. All of the known millhouses of Early Medieval Irish horizontal-wheeled mills are rectangular in outline, with retaining walls of planks, masonry or both (Rynne 1988, I, 54). Three main types may be distinguished:
(a) Where the sole plates (i.e. the main foundation

beams) defining the mill undercroft are jointed to a transverse beam supporting the front end of the flume or water-delivery chute (e.g. Ballykilleen, Co. Offaly, AD 635; Lucas 1955);

(b) Where the side walls are of rubble masonry with the flume-support beam abutting them at right angles (e.g. Mashanaglass and Knockrour, Co. Cork; Fahy 1956; Rynne 1988, I, 56; for the probable Early Medieval date of Mashanaglass see Rynne 1990);

(c) A combination of (a) and (b) with the foundations of the side walls built over the sole plates (e.g. Cloontycarthy, Co. Cork, AD 833; Rynne 1990, Fig. 1).

The early Irish horizontal-wheeled mill was a split-level building, the lower level of which housed the waterwheel and the tentering arms and the upper (usually at ground level) the grinding machinery. Unlike the arrangements made at many sites for water-jet delivery onto the waterwheel, the plans of many mill undercrofts, apart from the essential rectangular outline, appear to differ in many respects. None the less, as far as the archaeological record is concerned, mill undercrofts with masonry retaining walls are clearly less common than those with timber frameworks. The two known Irish examples of vertical-wheeled mills dating to the same period were also entirely constructed from timber (Rynne 1989). For the most part this is likely to have been a function of individual site conditions and the availability of particular building materials. But with regard to key mill components, such as the waterwheel, where design characteristics are entirely independent of site location, there is good evidence to suggest that regional millwrighting techniques were already evolving during the Early Medieval period in Ireland.

To date some ten Irish horizontal-wheeled mill sites have produced water wheel hubs, four of which, Rasharkin (*c.* AD 822), Moycraig (8th century) and Deer Parks Farm (8th century), all in Co. Antrim, and Cloontycarthy (*c.* AD 833) have been dated (Baillie 1982; Rahtz and Bullough 1977; Chris Lynn, pers. comm.); in many cases dished paddles have accompanied such finds. Such paddles have been recovered from two further dated sites: Ballykilleen, Co. Offaly (*c.* AD 635, the earliest known examples of their type from anywhere in Europe) and Drumard, Co. Derry (*c.* AD 732) (Lucas 1955; Baillie 1975). The Early Medieval Irish horizontal waterwheel has a distinctive set of design characteristics (Fig. 10.3); the proportions of the surviving examples are remarkably similar and in the case of the Mashanaglass and Moycraig wheelhubs, strikingly so (Fahy 1956). I have dealt with the function of these design characteristics elsewhere (Rynne 1988, I, 66–75). However, while almost all of these waterwheels utilised essentially the same set of design features, no two waterwheel paddles or wheelhubs are exactly the same. The widespread variations on a basic design can best be explained in terms of regional millwrighting traditions. By reference to Fig. 10.5 it will be seen that in the traditional *rodizio* mills of Portugal individual horizontal waterwheel types have developed in the different regions where separate millwrighting traditions had evolved. The *rodizios* are also remarkable in having very close analogues in Early Medieval Ireland (compare Figs. 10.4 and 10.5), but if one looks closely at the various horizontal waterwheel types found throughout Mediterranean Europe it becomes clear that the *rodizios* and their analogues in Spain and Italy have Medieval origins. The Italian term for this distinctive type of waterwheel (*ritrecine*) is etymologically related to the Spanish term *rodezno*, from which *rodizio* is derived. *Rodezno*, indeed, is attested from at least the twelfth century (Rynne 1992c, 24). It is hardly surprising, therefore, given the widespread use of horizontal-wheeled mills in Early Medieval Ireland that regional waterwheel types (albeit closely derived from a basic design) should have developed at an early stage. Early Irish millwrights may have originally plied their trade over the entire island. As and when the numbers of operational mills increased it may well have been possible for individual millwrights to become established in particular areas, to service existing mills and to construct new ones.

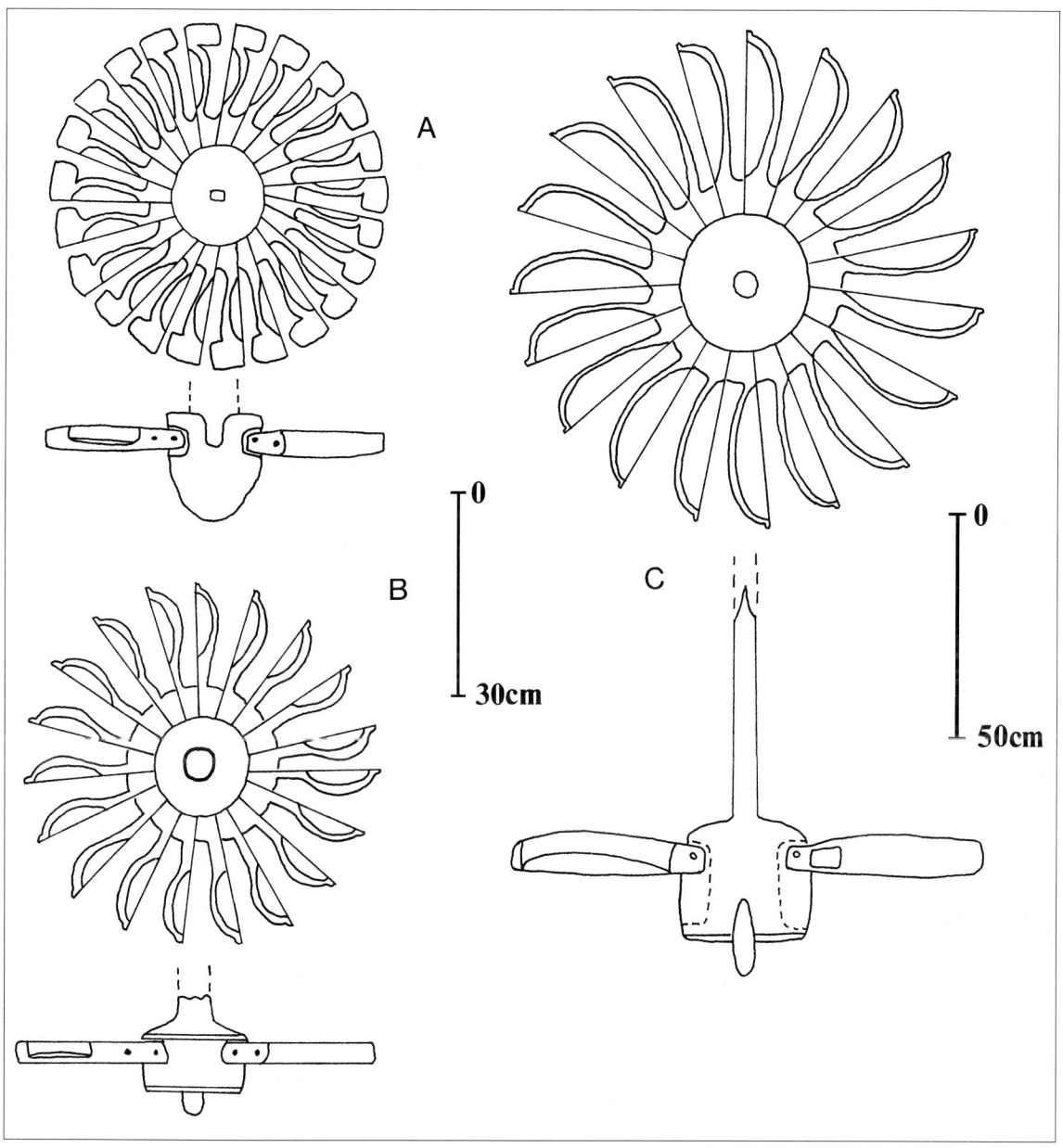

Fig. 10.3 Horizontal waterwheels from (a) Mashanaglass, Co. Cork, Early Medieval; (b) Cloontycarthy, Co. Cork, *c.* AD 833; (c) Moycraig, Co. Antrim, 9th century AD

Woodworking technology

The woodworking techniques associated with the early Irish mills owe much to Roman woodworking technology. Indeed, most of the early Irish millwright's woodworking repertoire is similar to that of the Roman woodworker, both in the finishing of the wood and in the choice of joints for specific tasks. Scarf joints, for example, seem to have been rarely used in the construction of the early Irish mills (Wallace, 1982, 265;

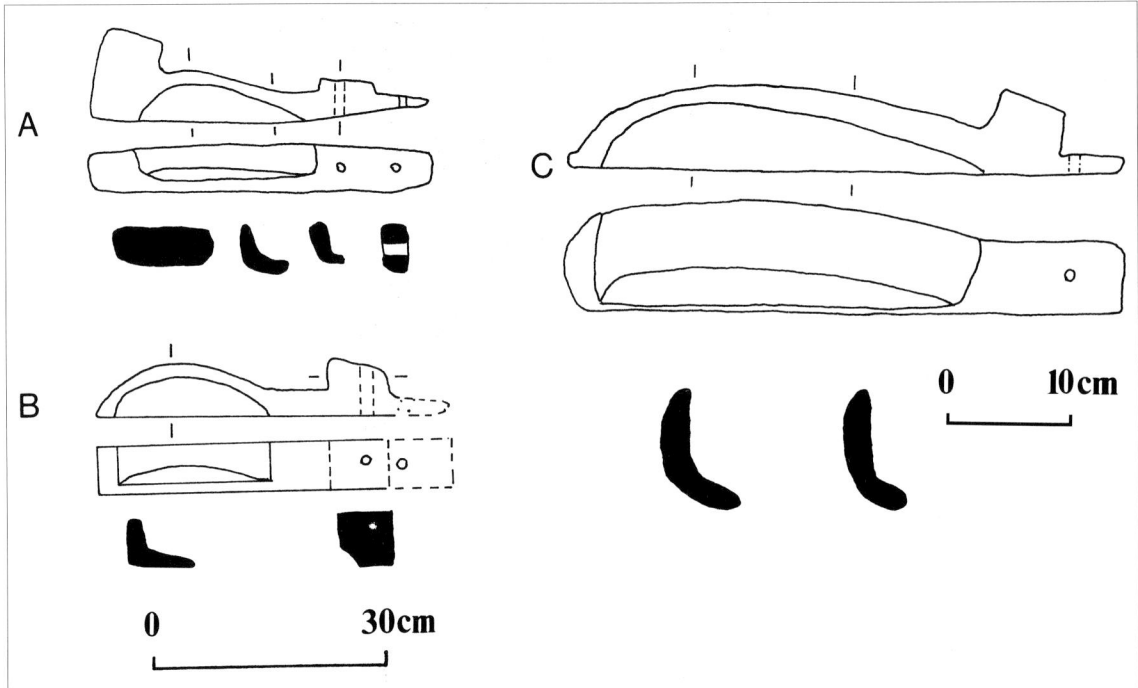

Fig. 10.4   Waterwheel paddles from a) Mashanaglass; b) Moycraig; c) Cloontycarthy

Rynne 1988, I, 99), but when they are found they are rudimentary affairs as in Roman carpentry (Weeks 1982, 166). The large piles used at the early seventh-century Little Island watermills (Rynne 1988, II), which are similar to those used in the construction of the timber bridge across the Cashen River in Co. Kerry (O'Kelly 1961), most probably (on the basis of the Little Island evidence) in the Early Medieval period, can thus far only be paralleled with those used in Roman-period timber bridges. The latter often spanned wide, fast-flowing rivers, such as the Rhine (Schmidt 1981) and the Mosel (Cuppers 1969), where piles between 10 and 15 metres in length were employed. Less imposing Roman bridges, such as the Romano-British example investigated at Aldwincle (Jackson and Ambrose 1976, 44), have piles which can be paralleled with the early Irish examples. The use to which certain carpentry joints have been put in the early Irish mills, such as the dovetail cleat on one of the Cloontycarthy sole plates, can thus far only be paralleled with a joint employed in a Roman 'pump house' at St Malo (Langouet and Meury 1976, 115).

Vertical-wheeled mills
With regard to Romano-British influences on the woodworking technology associated with early Irish mills, recent work on the second- to third-century AD vertical-wheeled mills at Ickham in Kent, has highlighted remarkable similarities between their wooden mill channels and those of the earliest-known Irish horizontal and vertical-wheeled mills at Little Island. Apart from the sheer scale of operations involved at Little Island, the site differs from all other Irish ones in terms of location, water supply, close association of a horizontal and a vertical-wheeled watermill, and the finishing of the mill timbers. Were it not for the existence of a near-contemporary site at Ballykilleen, Co. Offaly (Lucas 1955; Baillie

1982), one could argue that the Little Island remains represent a putative early phase of Irish millwrighting. The carpentry and general wood-finishing at Ballykilleen are very similar to that found at many other Irish sites of the Early Medieval period. The generally poor quality of the timber finishing at Little Island, however, contrasts sharply with that of the other early Irish sites. A similar contrast is evident between the Ickham mills' carpentry and Romano-British carpentry in general. At both Ickham and Little Island the mill timbers appear to have been improvised and, with the exception of the use of nails to fasten flooring timbers to the mill channels at Ickham, the timber-lined inlet and outlet channels at both of these sites are very similar (Rynne, forthcoming). The ultimate place of origin of the skills required in constructing the early Irish vertical-wheeled mills may well have been Britain, where such mills were by no means a rarity during the Roman period (Wikander 1986). There is, however, no evidence for the use of the horizontal-wheeled mill in Roman Britain and while these were used in the Roman world the variety of mill involved was very different to those used in Early Medieval Ireland (Wilson 1995, 499–510). Moreover, there is as yet no evidence to suggest that any variety of watermill was used in Britain in the immediate post-Roman period and, with the exception of the seventh-century vertical-wheeled mill site at Old Windsor, the English evidence for the widespread use of water-powered mills suggests that this was a later development than in Ireland.

In view of more recent archaeological evidence for the use of vertical-wheeled mills in Roman Britain and Europe (Wikander 1986), it would seem that the vertical-wheeled mill in Ireland was introduced no later than the end of the sixth century. The horizontal-wheeled mill was most likely introduced around the same period, most probably from a European source (Rynne 1992c), and presumably the requisite skills involved in millwrighting came directly from Europe as well. The close similarity between early Irish horizontal waterwheels and those used up

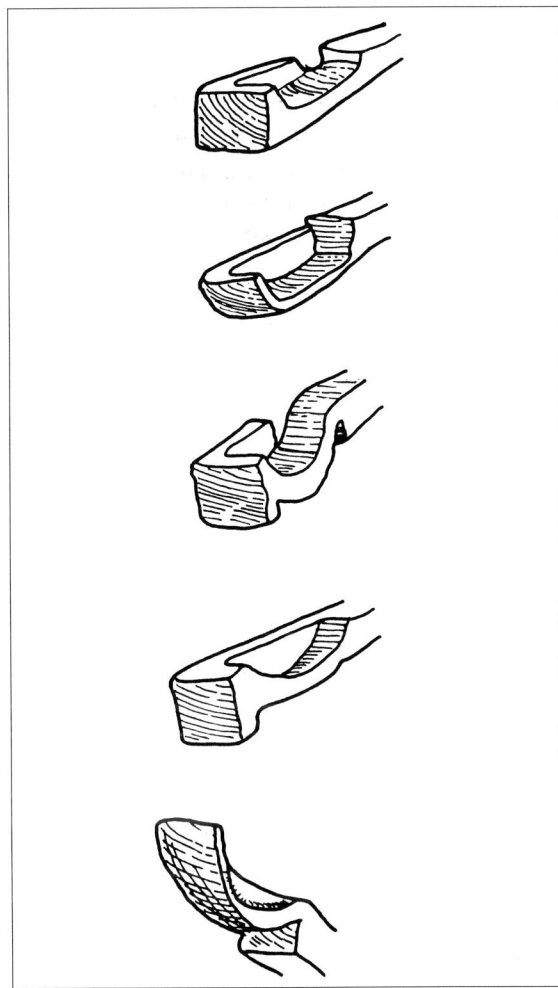

Fig. 10.5   Regional variation of horizontal waterwheel paddles in Portugal (after J. Galhano, *Moinhos e Azenhas de Portugal*, Lisbon, 1978)

until very recent times in Mediterranean Europe would suggest close ties with this general region, although some aspects of the early Irish mills can only be paralleled with traditional Balkan watermills. Indeed, the existence in Ireland of the two main varieties of watermill, along with twin-penstock horizontal-wheeled mills and tide mills during the first millenium, places Ireland – and particularly Munster – firmly in the mainstream of the millwrighting technology of the period (Rynne 1992c).

A declining craft?

As various commentators have pointed out (Rynne 1988; Mytum 1992; Powell 1995), there is an apparent gap in the evidence for horizontal-wheeled mills from about the end of the first millenium AD. More recent attempts to explain this phenomenon have centered on a perceived shortage of large oaks in Ireland towards the end of the tenth century which, as some have suggested (Edwards 1990, 52; Mytum 1992, 195), directly affected the construction of water-powered mills. The argument is based on the available dates for both horizontal- and vertical-wheeled mills, the vast majority of which (from dendrochronological and carbon 14 determinations) lie between the seventh and tenth centuries (Baillie 1982; 1995, 126–27). A number of fundamental questions are raised by this clustering of dates, not least of which concerns the fate of the craft of millwrighting. To begin with, most of the arguments for the alleged decrease in mill construction are based almost exclusively on a perception that this date range is somehow immutable, that the archaeological record for early Irish mills is a fixed entity in terms of chronology. Those arguments which are not based on this perception develop from a fundamental misunderstanding of the archaeology and technology of early Irish horizontal-wheeled mills and, ultimately, of the development of the early Irish landscape.

If, as has been argued by some, mill building went into decline or ended completely towards the end of the tenth century, the most obvious question that arises must surely concern the technology which replaced it. Apart from the alleged scarcity of good building timber there is no evidence to suggest that there was any decrease in population which might further have influenced a decline in mill construction. Indeed, Medieval Irish society appears to have been a relatively prosperous one (Ó Cróinín 1995, 108). Nor is there any evidence that cereal crops were in decline during the same period. On the contrary, all indications are that, if anything, agriculture was expanding. If horizontal-wheeled mills were no longer being built after the tenth century (Mytum 1992, 195), or even if their construction was curtailed owing to a scarcity of suitable building timber (Edwards 1990, 52), how were cereal crops being milled? As I have argued elsewhere (Rynne 1990), water-powered mills were an essential part of the expansion of tillage in Ireland during the Early Medieval period and their appearance then corresponds to an increased demand for cereal foodstuffs.

With regard to chronology, it is now clear that there is at least one twelfth-century horizontal-wheeled mill site at Clonlonan, Co. Westmeath (*c*. 1145, Victor Buckley, pers. comm) and a thirteenth-century example from Corcannon, Co. Wexford (*c*. 1228, Moore 1996, 45). There can be little doubt that further sites of a similar date range will eventually come to light. Thus far, of the twenty-seven watermill sites dated to the period AD 630–1228, just over half (56 per cent) were built with timbers felled in the period 770–850 (Baillie 1995, 126). For every dated site there is at least one further mill site recorded in the nineteenth or early twentieth century which has not been dated. Were all of these sites also built before the end of the first millenium AD? The existence of the Clonlonan and Corcannon sites alone suffice to throw considerable doubt on this and should serve as a cautionary tale for those who would view the Irish archaeological record for water-powered mills as a fixed entity.

A number of years ago I pointed out that the horizontal-wheeled mill in Ireland received no mention in Irish or English sources between the tenth and the seventeenth centuries (1988, I, 227). Given that unambiguous references to horizontal-wheeled mills in the early Irish documentary sources, while significant, are quite rare, their absence is only surprising given the enormous corpus of archaeological material. There can be little doubt that the 'eight parts of the mill' listed in the law tract *De Ceithri Slichtaib Athgábala* are those of the horizontal-wheeled mill variety (Mac Eoin 1982; Rynne 1988, I, 17–22). Then there is a gap of some five centuries before we find our next unambiguous reference, which occurs in *Togail Bruidne Da Derga* (an eleventh-century text which may well have been first written down in the ninth century), which refers to a *sciatha* or horizontal waterwheel paddle (Knott 1936, 734; Mac Eoin 1982, 16). The use of the OIr. term *oircel* (which forms part of the 'eight parts of the mill' in *De Ceithri Slichtaib Athgábala*) in *Fled Briciu* has already been noted above. That this term should survive into the twelfth century is a fair indication that the audience of the copyist would have been familiar with its meaning, and there can be little doubt that such mills were in existence at this time. Thus while unambiguous references to horizontal-wheeled mills are rare for the greater part of the Early Medieval period, they certainly do occur in the eleventh and twelfth centuries. On the basis of the enormous corpus of Irish archaeological evidence for Early Medieval watermills, the scarcity of references to specific varieties of watermill is clearly a matter of lacunae rather than the abandonment of certain types of mill.

Despite the rarity of cut and dried references to horizontal-wheeled mills in the early Irish sources, these references are all the more remarkable if one considers that it has hitherto not been possible to identify similar mills in European sources before the twelfth century. Vernacular terms such as *rodezno* in twelfth-century Spanish sources (Glick 1979, 233), *molin terragno* in Dante's *Inferno* or *ritricene* in fourteenth-century Italian sources (Muendel 1974, 200), all of which refer specifically to horizontal-wheeled mills, are the earliest unambiguous continental European references to their existence. Of course, no one has suggested that such mills did not exist in Europe before this period, even though archaeological evidence for water-powered mills of the Early Medieval period in regions other than Ireland has only come to light in very recent times. Yet on the basis of the alleged *absence* of the horizontal-wheeled mill from the Irish archaeological record after the tenth century AD, and its recorded *presence* in the early post-Medieval period, Mytum and others have suggested that the later mills had to be re-introduced. In other words, given the documented introduction of the horizontal-wheeled mill into Ireland during the Early Medieval period, the perceived difficulty of finding sites which dated to after the tenth century necessarily implied that they had 'disappeared'. From the foregoing it is all too obvious that this is not the case, whilst the horizontal-wheeled mills documented in the seventeenth century in Ulster and Connaught (Rynne 1988, I, 228–36) are clearly survivals of a long-established tradition. As late as 1934 the OIr. term for a horizontal-wheeled mill sluice gate, *comla*, was still being used in Connemara (Lucas 1953, 28), whilst the Scots-Gaelic term for horizontal waterwheel paddles, *sgiathain*, is obviously derived from the OIr. term *sciath* (see above, Curwen 1944, 141).

All the recent commentators on the lack of archaeological evidence for water-powered mills in Ireland after the tenth century (e.g. Edwards 1990) have cited increased deforestation in the Early Medieval period as the principal cause. To begin with, there can be little doubt that native forests began to be cleared during the Early Medieval period to facilitate arable farming and this is borne out by palynological studies as well as by dendrochronological, documentary and archaeological sources. This is, of course, the exact milieu in which water-powered mills would be needed most, but is it realistic to suggest that forest clearance could affect their distribution and frequency by creating a scarcity of building timber? One recent commentator has argued that with the relative abundance of wood in the first millenium 'there was no great need to salvage wood from abandoned or derelict structures' (Powell 1995, 221).

Powell's argument is based on a series of grave misconceptions, which involve not only the archaeology of the early Irish mills but also the contemporary Irish documentary sources in general. While he readily concedes that there is no real evidence for a critical timber shortage in Ireland during the Medieval period, he thinks it is the decline of oak, which he believes was the principal wood used in building construction in Ireland at that time, that directly affects the occurrence of timber buildings in the archaeological record. Unfortunately, this assertion is totally contradicted by the archaeological and documentary records. The overwhelming majority of buildings erected in Ireland during the period as a whole were post-and-wattle constructions, of which hazel was probably the most commonly used wood for wattling rods. Oak, it is clear, was also a very important timber. However, a scarcity of woods suitable for wattling rods would have had far more serious consequences, and the extent to which wattling was used in early Irish building construction can only suggest that some elementary form of woodland management was practised (see Tierney, ch. 16). Early Irish law specifies strict penalties and fines for damage caused in private woods, and whilst 'immunities of the forest' (*dílsi cailli*), such as the gathering of kindling wood, are recognised (Binchy 1971; Ó Cróinín 1995, 86), the importance of woodland to the early Irish is fully acknowledged. Powell also notes that while Giraldis Cambrensis, in the *Topographia*, refers to Ireland as well-wooded, his reference to the profusion of yew trees could be an indication that the available woodland was not necessarily suited for building purposes. According to Powell, yew was a 'wood of little use for building' (1995, 221). Giraldis only observes that the yew was more common in Ireland than in other territories he had seen; however, he can hardly be considered a reliable source on Medieval Irish forestry. In any case, early Irish carpenters and woodworkers in general clearly did not concur with Powell's assessment of yew as a building timber. Apart from furniture and wood-turning crafts, it was extensively used for shingles and door frames.

The scarcity of large oaks clearly concerns most recent commentators, but according to Powell this did not necessarily discourage mill construction. The shortage of oak, he has suggested, would have increased the value of timber in derelict structures and thus the tendency for it to be salvaged from abandoned mills. However, the archaeological record completely contradicts this argument. To begin with, while he is entirely correct in his belief that horizontal-wheeled mills did not 'disappear' during the later Medieval period in Ireland, his assertion that after the tenth century people were less disposed to leave unused mill timbers lying around is entirely erroneous. There is an overwhelming body of archaeological evidence which demonstrates that pre-tenth-century horizontal-wheeled mills were often dismantled, whilst there is no evidence that Early Medieval Irish carpenters in general were profligate with used timbers. The Little Island watermills are a case in point. These were built at the beginning of the seventh century, at a time when no one would argue that timber was in short supply. None the less, the millwrights responsible for their construction clearly chose to reuse existing mill timbers or timbers brought from other wooden structures for repairs. The site was abandoned owing to severe tidal flooding, a circumstance which would have discouraged further salvage (Rynne 1992a). At other sites in Munster, and throughout Ireland, there is widespread evidence for the reuse of mill timbers. One of the foundation beams for the Cloontycarthy millhouse (*c.* AD 833), for example, was a clearly a reused beam brought from another site (Rynne 1988, II, 322). This obviously has nothing to do with timber shortages, although it is perhaps too readily assumed that mature trees were always to hand. The cutting and transportation of large trees in the forest was a laborious task, as contemporary documentary sources readily attest. As in the case of the Cloontycarthy mill, the reuse of timber from a nearby site would have been a much more practical expedient if circumstances allowed.

With regard to the preservation of timbers from Early Medieval Irish mill sites, it is noticeable that the uprights which supported the mill's grinding room rarely survive, even as decayed stubs. Were it not for the fact that the chute or penstock very often does survive in excellent condition in such circumstances (even though it was located nearer the surface than the lower mill timbers), one could assume that the uprights had totally decayed. But if the foundation beams and the flooring boards could survive at the same level as the lower extremities of the upright beams and the flume can often remain intact at a much higher level, how does one explain their absence? The simple and most obvious answer is that the upper mill building may often have been dismantled after abandonment, probably for reuse in another building. Clearly this was a common practice in the Early Medieval period.

Another factor that has not been taken into account is that although mature oak trees are likely to have been more abundant in the first millenium AD, they may not always have been easily accessible to, for example, millwrights operating in the west of Ireland. There is a shortage of dated sites from the west, most probably because the main material used for the mill buildings there was stone. The eighth- to ninth-century mill on High Island, off the Galway coast, is a good example of this (Rynne et al. 1996), although the Mashanaglass mill, which is likely to date to the first millenium AD (Rynne 1990) and which was situated upwards of ten miles from the Cloontycarthy mill, was also almost wholly a stone structure. In such cases mature oaks would be required only for the mill penstock – an item on which the Early Medieval Irish millwright appears to have never compromised – as they were not needed for other wooden components such as the waterwheel or the tentering arms. However, we cannot rule out the possibility that composite mill penstocks, made from planks, were also used in the Early Medieval period, particularly in areas removed from oak woodland.

Conclusion

There can be little doubt that the craft of millwrighting was so highly developed in Munster by the beginning of the seventh century that watermills could be constructed in the most demanding locations, such as on an island on the estuary of the River Lee. Archaeological evidence for millwrighting in the Munster region, in the period *c.* AD 630–1000, clearly points to the existence of regional variations in waterwheel design at a remarkably early period. Similar developments in Europe, including the recognition of millwrighting as a specialist craft are, on present evidence, somewhat later. That early Irish millwrights were also using the earliest-known vernacular technical terms from any European region for the machinery of these mills suggests that they were amongst the earliest and most accomplished practitioners of their craft in post-Roman Europe.

Most of the speculation based on the date cluster for early Irish watermills has been premature; there is clearly no evidence that the craft of millwrighting went into decline towards the end of the tenth century. It has taken twenty years or so to establish the present chronology for them, and only recently has the appearance of twelfth- and thirteenth-century horizontal-wheeled mill sites underlined the need for caution. On average at least one new Early Medieval mill site is discovered every year in Ireland, and other sites of post-tenth-century date will doubtless come to light. In this regard the Irish archaeological record has not yet lost its ability to surprise. The discovery of an urban Anglo-Norman watermill at Patrick Street in Dublin, built in the thirteenth century and almost entirely rebuilt in the fourteenth (Rynne 1997), should also serve as a cautionary tale for archaeologists and historians of technology. There may well have been increased deforestation at the end of the tenth century, but on present evidence there is no sound basis for the conclusion that the extent of this activity in any way affected the construction of water-powered mills or the absence of later sites in the archaeological record.

ACKNOWLEDGEMENTS

Special thanks to Ms Stella Cherry, Cork Public Museum, for her comments on earlier drafts of this chapter and to Mr John Sheehan, Department of Archaeology, UCC, and to Mr Victor Buckley, National Monuments and Historic Properties Service, for information on recent dendro dates for Irish mills.

BIBLIOGRAPHY

Baillie, M.G.L. (1975) 'A horizontal mill of the 8th century A.D. at Drumard, Co. Derry', *Ulster J. Archaeol.* 38, 25–32

Baillie, M.G.L. (1982) *Tree-Ring Dating and Archaeology*, London

Baillie, M.G.L. (1995) *A Slice Through Time: Dendrochronology and Precision Dating*, London

Binchy, D.A. (ed.) (1955) 'Irish Law tracts re-edited: *Coibnes Uisci Thairidne*', *Ériu* 17, 52–84

Binchy, D.A. (1971) 'An archaic legal poem', *Celtica* 9, 152–68

Connolly, S. (1987) 'Cogitosus's Life of St. Brigit: content and value', *J. Roy. Soc. Antiq. Ir.* 117, 5–27

Cotter, E. (forthcoming) 'An early medieval horizontal mill at Crushyriree, Co. Cork'

Cuppers, H. (1969) *Die Trier Römerbrücken*, Koblenz

Curwen, E.C. (1944) 'The problem of early watermills', *Antiquity* 17, 130–46

Edwards, N. (1990) *The Archaeology of Early Medieval Ireland*, London

Fahy, E.M. (1956) 'A horizontal mill at Mashanaglass, Co. Cork', *J. Cork Hist. Archaeol. Soc.* 61, 13–57

Glick, T.F. (1979) *Islamic and Christian Spain in the Early Middle Ages*, Princeton

Gwynn, E. (1903) *The Metrical Dindsenchas*, Dublin

Horn, W. (1975) 'Waterpower and the plan of St. Gall', *J. Medieval History* 1, 219–58

Jackson, D.A. and Ambrose, T.M. (1976) 'A Roman timber bridge at Adwincle, Northamptonshire', *Brittania* 7, 39–72

Knott, E. (ed.) (1936) *Togail Bruidne Da Derga*, Dublin

Langouet, L. and Meury, J.L. (1976) 'Les éléments de la machinerie gallo-romaine d'Atlet', *Les Dossiers du Centre Regional Archaeologique d'Atlet*, 113–25

Lennard, R. (1966) *Rural England, 1086–1135: A Study of Social and Agrarian Conditions*, Oxford

Lucas, A.T. (1953) 'The horizontal mill in Ireland', *J. Roy. Soc. Antiq. Ir.* 83, 1–36

Lucas, A.T. (1955) 'A horizontal mill at Ballykilleen, Co. Offaly', *J. Roy. Soc. Antiq. Ir.* 85, 100–13

Mac Eoin, G. (1982) 'The early Irish vocabulary of mills and milling', in B.G. Scott (ed.), *Studies on Early Ireland: Essays in Honour of M.V. Duignan*, 13–19, Belfast

Moore, M. J. (1996) *An Archaeological Inventory of County Wexford*, Dublin

Muendel, J. (1974) 'The horizontal mills of medieval Pistoia', *Technology and Culture* 15, 194–225

Mytum, H. (1992) *The Origins of Early Christian Ireland*, London

Ó Cróinín, D. (1995) *Early Medieval Ireland: 400–1200*, Harlow

O'Donovan, W.J. (1858–59) 'Note on Milverton, Co. Dublin', *J. Roy. Soc. Antiq. Ir.* 2, 252

O'Kelly, M.J. (1961) 'A wooden bridge on the Cashen River, Co. Kerry', *J. Roy. Soc. Antiq. Ir.* 91, 135–52

Plummer, C. (1968) *Vitae Sanctorum Hiberniae*, 2 vols., Oxford

Powell, T.E. (1995) 'The disappearance of horizontal mills from Mediaeval Ireland', *Trans. Newcomen Soc.* 66, 219–24

Rahtz, P. and Bullough, D. (1977) 'The parts of the Anglo Saxon mill', *Anglo Saxon England*, 6, 15–39

Rynne, C. (1988) 'The archaeology and technology of the horizontal-wheeled watermill, with special reference to Ireland', unpublished PhD thesis (NUI), University College, Cork

Rynne, C. (1989) 'The introduction of the vertical waterwheel into Ireland: some recent archaeological evidence', *Medieval Archaeol.* 33, 21–31

Rynne, C. (1990) 'Some observations on the production of flour and meal in the Early Historic period', *J. Cork Hist. Archaeol. Soc.* 95, 20–29

Rynne, C. (1992a) 'Milling in the 7th-century – Europe's earliest tide mills', *Archaeol. Ireland* 6.2, 22–24

Rynne, C. (1992b) 'Early Medieval mill penstocks from County Cork', *J. Cork Hist. Archaeol. Soc.* 97, 54–68

Rynne, C. (1992c) 'The early Irish watermill and its continental affinities', in *Medieval Europe 1992: Technology and Innovation*, vol. 3, 21–25, York

Rynne, C. (1993) *The Archaeology of Cork City and Harbour: from the earliest times to industrialisation*, Cork

Rynne, C. (1997) 'The Patrick Street watermills: their technological context and a note on the reconstruction', in C. Walsh, *Archaeological Excavations at Patrick, Nicholas and Winetavern Streets, Dublin*, Dingle, 81–89

Rynne, C., Rourke, G. and White Marshall, J. (1996) 'An early medieval monastic watermill on High Island', *Archaeol. Ireland* 10.3, 24–27

Schmidt, B. (1981) 'Dendrochronologische untersuchungen an Pfahlresten einer römerzeitlichen Rheinbrücke in Koblenz', *Bonner Jahrbücher* 181, 301–11

Skinner, P. (1992) 'Mill ownership and social status in Southern Italy, c. 800–1200 AD', in *Medieval Europe 1992: Technology and Innovation*, vol. 3, 37–42, York

Stokes, W. (1888) 'The Voyage of Mael Duin', *Revue Celtique* 9, 417–95

Stokes, W. (1890) *Lives of the Saints from the Book of Lismore*, Oxford

Stokes, W. (1892) 'Life of St Féchin of Fore', *Revue Celtique* 12, 344–47

Thomas, C. (1971) *The Early Christian Archaeology of North Britai n*, Oxford

Wallace, P.F. (1982) 'Carpentry in Ireland A.D. 900–1300', in S. McGrail (ed.), *Woodworking Techniques before 1500, BAR Brit. Ser.* 129, 263–99

Weeks, J. (1982) 'Roman carpentry joints: adoption and adaptation', in S. McGrail (ed.), *Woodworking Techniques Before AD 1500, BAR Brit. Ser.* 129, 157–68

Wikander, Ö. (1985) 'Mill-channels, weirs and ponds: the environment of ancient watermills', *Opuscula Romana* 13.7, 93–104

Wikander, Ö. (1986) 'Archaeological evidence for early water-mills – an interim report', *History of Technology* 11, 151–79

11. Illaunloughan, Co. Kerry: An Island Hermitage

JENNY WHITE MARSHALL and CLAIRE WALSH

Introduction

Many of the small islands off the western coast of Ireland still have the remains of small monastic foundations which owe their preservation to their isolated locations and their construction in stone. There is a particular concentration of such sites in south-west Munster, nine of them located on the offshore islands of the Dingle and Iveragh peninsulas (Cuppage 1986; O'Sullivan and Sheehan 1996). Several of these sites have been the subject of intensive archaeological work, in particular Church Island, Valencia Harbour (O'Kelly 1958) and the monastic site and hermitage on Skellig Michael (Horn, Marshall and Rourke 1990; O'Sullivan and Sheehan 1996). The smallest of these islands and the one closest to shore is Illaunloughan, sited in Portmagee Channel which runs between Valencia Island and the south Kerry mainland (Fig. 11.1). The tiny island, measuring 0.1 hectares in area at high tide, is low-lying. Most of it is only a few metres above sea level, except for a narrow ridge across its western end. Although sheltered by its position in the channel, the island is occasionally swept by gales and storms. It has consequently been subjected to severe erosion, and a minimum of 4 m of land has vanished from the northern, southern and eastern shores. The island is accessible from the mainland on foot for a brief period at certain low tides, but it is otherwise cut off by the strong currents which run in the channel.

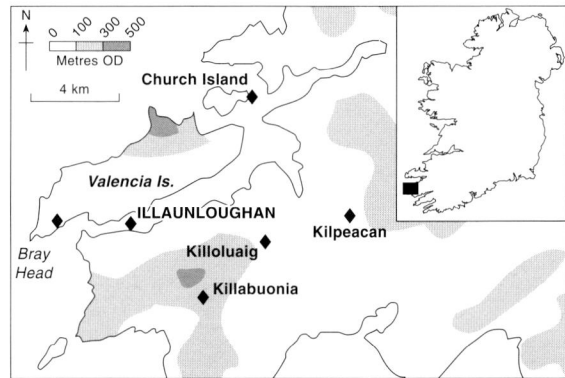

Fig. 11.1   Location map of south-west Kerry, showing Illaunloughan

There is no historical documentation for the island, and the origin of its name is uncertain. *Lochán* may be the name of a saint associated with the island, a theory supported by the mention of two Lochans in the *Martyrology of Oengus*, written *c.* AD 800 (Stokes 1984, 255, 263) and by the inland location of Killoughane (*Cill Lócháin*) ecclesiastical site at the eastern end of the Iveragh peninsula (O'Sullivan and Sheehan 1996, 357). The origin may be more mundane, however, for Dineen defines *lochán* as 'chaff, light over-dried or withered grass' and further notes

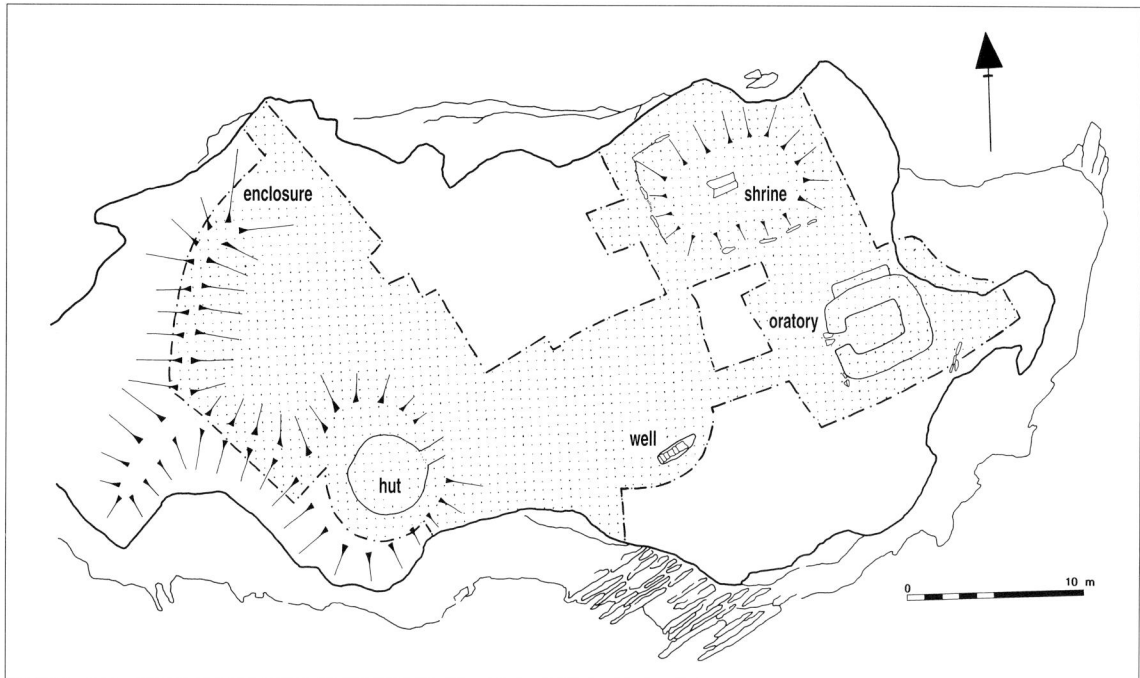

Fig. 11.2 Plan of Illaunloughan, showing excavated areas

'*Oileán an Locháin* – the island of broken seaweed, a small island at the southern side of Valencia' (1927, 669).[1] Apart from a brief description by Henry (1957, 96–98), details of which were reproduced by Thomas (1971, 142–43; 1973, 11), and a pre-excavation survey by O'Sullivan and Sheehan (1996, 307–8), the island has enjoyed relative obscurity and is seldom visited.

A detailed survey of the remains on the island was carried out by Grellan D. Rourke and Jenny White Marshall in 1987. The visible structures consisted of a circular drystone cell at the south-western end of the island, a rectangular drystone oratory on the eastern side, a stone-lined well and a gable- or house-shaped shrine located on top of a large mound defined by large orthostats. All of the structures, apart from the stones of the gable-shrine (which are of slate), were built from the sandstone indigenous to the island. The raised ridge at the western side of the island appeared to be the remains of an enclosing wall. An extensive midden was exposed on the eroded southern shore, adjacent to the cell. Numerous uninscribed gravemarkers testified to its later use as a cemetery and *ceallúnach*, which local tradition ascribes to famine burials and unbaptized infants. The mid-nineteenth-century Ordnance Survey name-books (1841) note the island as 'a burial place for children and adult strangers' (Killemlagh, 55).

Four seasons of archaeological work, carried out from 1992 to 1995, have completed the excavation of about 70 per cent of the island (Fig. 11.2). The working hypothesis was that the remains were those of a small eremitical settlement whose important components were encompassed within a relatively small area. Despite the large-scale excavation of comparable sites, such as Church Island (O'Kelly 1958) and Reask (Fanning 1981), the excavation evidence from sites of this type is sketchy and their chronology remains problematic. Neither of the above-mentioned sites has provided the

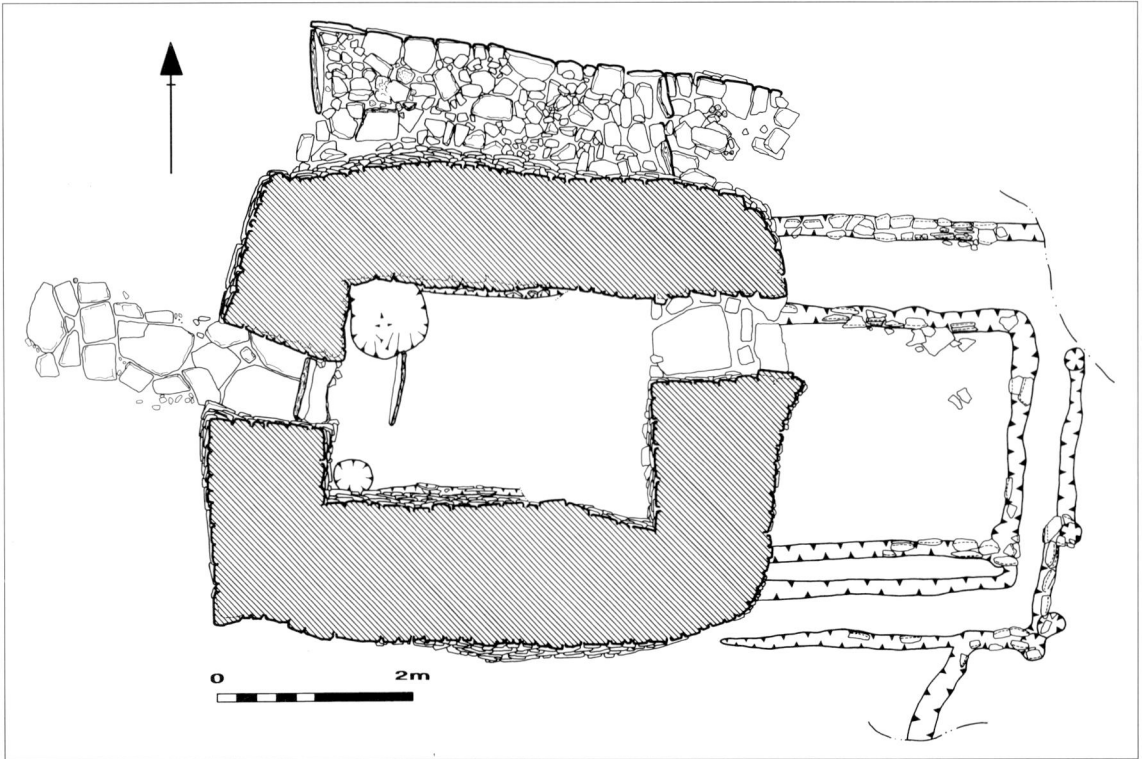

Fig. 11.3   Plan of oratory area, Illaunloughan

framework necessary for a full understanding of the chronological, social and economic development of such small monastic establishments. At Illaunloughan, however, the excavation of a sequence of relatively well-stratified structures within a localised area, combined with the extensive use of C14 dating, will provide such a framework. Much of the work is ongoing, and this chapter serves only as a preliminary report on work in progress. The excavation of three main areas, namely those containing the oratory, the gable-shrine and the domestic quarters and midden, are described in sequence.

The oratory area

The remains of an earthen- or sod-walled structure were uncovered at the earliest level in this area (Fig. 11.3). This structure was considerably larger than the later drystone one, measuring over 6 m from east to west by 2 m from north to south internally. The main evidence for it was the foundations and base of its walls. These were each composed of two narrow earth-cut trenches, running parallel to each other, giving an overall wall-width of from 0.8 m to 1.1 m. Much of the sides of these trenches was lined with thin sandstone slabs. A well-defined deposit of grey silt, interpreted as the decayed sod walling of the structure, occurred between the lines of the trenches. The inner trenches of the side-walls were detected continuing beneath the walls of the later stone-built oratory to the west. The entrance to the earlier structure, indicated by a sill-stone flanked by two postholes, was at its western end. A number of postholes also occurred on the outer line of the eastern end-wall.

The trenches probably functioned as sockets for the kerbstones which retained the core of the wall structure. The postholes at the east end of the building and at its entrance indicate that the roof-support mechanism was largely independent of the wall structure. A basic four-post roof-support system is envisaged, with two longitudinal pairs of tie-beams linking the inner posts of the east wall with the doorjambs and oversailing the walls; auxiliary roof supports are indicated by a sole remaining posthole at the south side of the east wall. No evidence for the roofing material remained, although this is likely to have been of sod and thatch, and no flooring levels of the building survived. Five burials, located directly east of the structure, are associated with it and confirm its function as an oratory. A series of C14 dates for the sod-walled structure are awaited.

Few convincing examples of clay or sod-walled structures have been excavated to date and in only one example, that at Dunsilly Rath, Co. Antrim, were the remains of turfs found (Lynn 1986, vol. 2, 88). This structure was interpreted as an animal shelter by the excavator. The best parallels for the style of wall-construction of the Illaunloughan building are found in Hut A at the west side of the island and in a series of huts excavated at nearby Bray Head, Valencia, from 1995 to 1997 (Hayden 1997). The walling evidence at these huts comprised parallel trenches, which in many cases had orthostatic kerbs. These kerbs retained a wall of sods, earth and small stones. While churches built largely of timber were probably the norm in seventh-century Ireland, Tírechán's account of the construction of 'a square earthen church of clay' by Patrick (Bieler 1979, 159) does indicate an alternative building method of the time. Dating of both the rectangular structure and the round huts at Illaunloughan may indicate the longevity of this building method.

The drystone oratory

The drystone oratory was built directly over the foundations of the earlier sod structure, but a short distance further to the west. Its well-built walls survive to a maximum height of 1.28 m and it measures 3.2 m from east to west by 2.2 m from north to south internally. It is of average size for drystone oratories in the region, and is comparable to the large oratory at Skellig Michael and the one at Kildreelig. There is, however, considerable variation in size among the sixteen similar oratories which occur in the immediate locality between Waterville and Cahersiveen, a factor which is difficult to relate to the size of the ecclesiastical community. Clearly other factors such as prestige – particularly in the case of the Church Island oratory, which was built from imported Valencia slate – are significant determinants. Whether the Illaunloughan site is truly a hermitage or whether it also served as a community church (Hurley 1982, 299) could have some bearing on the size and nature of the oratory structure there. However, as all of the adult burials from the island's Early Medieval levels that could be sexed proved to be those of males, it seems unlikely that Illaunloughan served as a community church.[2]

Another feature which the Illaunloughan oratory shares with the large one at Skellig Michael is the presence of a low *leacht*, with its borders defined by vertically set stones, on its north side. Although it is generally difficult to relate the construction of a *leacht* to that of other structures on the ecclesiastical sites where they are found, the *leacht* at Illaunloughan (like that at Skellig Michael) is clearly in a primary position as the wall of the oratory overlies it. The occurrence of white quartz on the *leacht* at Illaunloughan, which was sealed by up to 0.5 m of stone collapse and sod, is also a primary feature. The *leacht* was carefully built and was clearly an important structure, but its function remains obscure. *Leachta* are generally believed to have been used to mark the burial place of a saint (Thomas 1971, 144) or as reliquaries, but they may also have served as outdoor altars and pilgrimage prayer stations (Herity 1989, 56). The Illaunloughan *leacht* does not fit satisfactorily into any of these categories. It is far too low to have served as an altar and, while it overlies two burials, these were both intersected by its construction so that only part of each skeleton is covered by the structure.

Consequently, the relationship appears fortuitous rather than deliberate.

No window or altar survives in the Illaunloughan oratory and of its architectural features only the west doorway, with its sill stone, paved threshold and part of a paved path leading west from it, remains. It appears simpler in general style than the oratory at Skellig Michael, and its rounded external eastern corners and lack of plinths are more reminiscent of that at Reask.

A deposit of ash and charcoal on the clay floor of the oratory was overlain by rubble and silting; a radiocarbon date from carbonised material overlying the clay floor gave a provisionally calibrated date of AD 640-790 (UCLA 2873C), providing a *terminus post quem* for the usage of the structure. The building was subsequently modified later in the Medieval period when the west doorway was blocked and a breach was made in the east wall. Two large stone-lined and stone-lidded pits, of uncertain function, which were cut through the floor at the east side of the oratory, also date to this late phase.

The graveyard
Ranks of extended adult burials were uncovered to the west, north and south of the oratory. There was no physical boundary to this graveyard at its western limit. Several poorly preserved burials underlay both the drystone oratory and the *leacht*. Some of the graves were lintelled, while most of the others had the remains of stone lining along the sides with smaller stones protecting the burial. These latter graves could be termed long cists (O'Brien 1992, 132). All of the graves were aligned from east to west, with their heads to the west. Many of the burials had quartz pebbles placed with the body, and two (of a lintel grave variant) had small regularly sized quartz pebbles placed neatly around the edges of their slab bases. No grave finds were placed with the bodies.

Lintelled graves and long cists were used for a long period in Ireland. The date of their introduction is uncertain, but they were in regular use in Britain from the fourth century onwards (ibid., 132). The lintel grave cemetery at Whithorn dates from the first half of the sixth century, and there the form was replaced by interments in log coffins (Hill 1992, 8). Many of the lintel graves at Reask predate the construction of the stone oratory, and a date range from the fifth to the seventh century is suggested for this burial practice at that site (Fanning 1981, 79). Only two of the thirty-three inhumations excavated at Church Island were protected by stone, and there was no evidence for coffins (O'Kelly 1958, 92). The lintel graves excavated on Omey Island, Co. Galway, were earlier than a group of burials in unlined graves (T. O'Keeffe, pers. comm). While several skeletons from Illaunloughan have been selected for C14 dating, comparative evidence suggests that the bulk of the burials from the site date from the Early Medieval period. The graveyard did, however, continue in use into the Later Medieval period; six silver pennies of Edward I and Edward III, deposited sometime after AD 1351, were placed with a burial at the west side of the oratory.[3] In contrast to the Early Medieval period, many of the adult burials of the Medieval period were of women.

The island was utilised as a *ceallúnach* in more recent times. In contrast to the earlier adult burials, the infant skeletons were well preserved. These burials usually had simple uninscribed headstones, and many were placed in small boxes made from Scots Pine.[4] Most of these later burials were placed towards the western side of the island.

The gable-shrine
The gable-shrine (Fig. 11.4) is one of a small group of reliquary shrines that occurs at the western end of the Iveragh Peninsula: similar examples are found at Killoluaig, Kilpeacan and Killabuonia (Fig. 11.1). These shrines or specially marked graves are generally ascribed to the founder, as was the case with St Cuthbert, who in the seventh century requested burial on his hermitage, Farne Island, rather than at Lindisfarne, because 'the presence of my remains

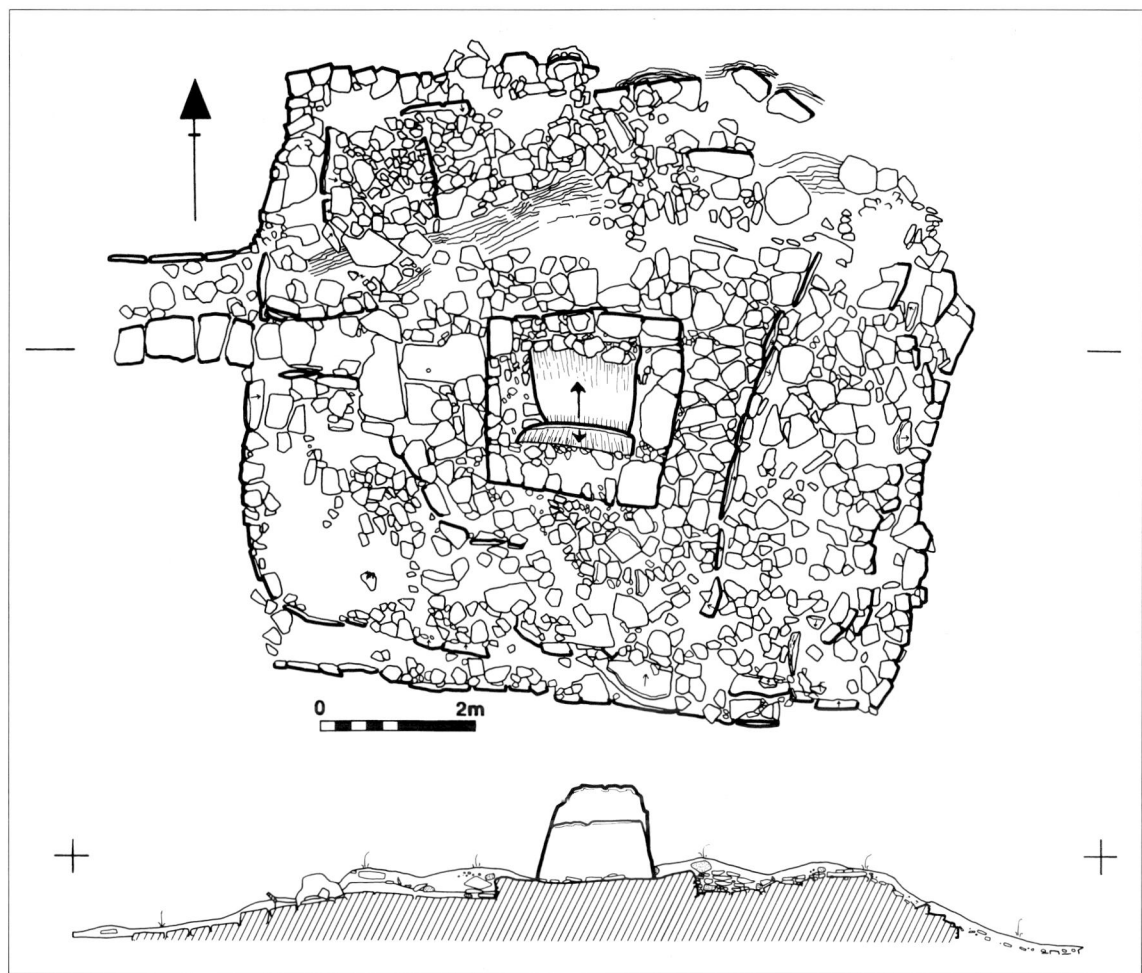

Fig. 11.4 Plan and section of the gable shrine and terraced mound, Illaunloughan

will prove very irksome due to the influx of fugitives and every other kind of malefactor. They will flee for refuge to my body' (Colgrave 1940, 37). A variety of forms of tomb-shrine are found in Ireland (Herity 1993, 188–95), of which the earliest is considered to be the gable-shrine (Thomas 1971, 141).

The base of the gable-shrine at Illaunloughan consists of a large terraced mound, 9 m by 7.6 m, which rises to a height of 1.5 m. The mound is partly built on an area of rock outcrop which was levelled off on its southern side with soil, stone and pea-gravel. Vertically set kerb-stones and masonry walling were placed along the edges to retain this fill; the mound has been eroded on the northern side by the action of the sea. White quartz stones of varying sizes were liberally scattered over the mound. At its western edge stone steps lead up to an area of rough paving that surrounds a rectangular drystone structure on which stands the slab-shrine. The end-slabs are missing. When the side-slabs were removed an underlying core of pea-gravel and white quartz was exposed. This sealed two small, irregularly shaped, stone-lined cists, each of which contained neatly stacked exhumed human bones. A minimum of three individuals, all male, is represented in this skeletal assemblage which comprised fragments of the skulls of two individuals, a single mandible, and several long bones. Large numbers of scallop shells and white quartz pebbles were placed both within and around the cists.

The eastern quadrant of the gravel mound was evidently planned as a cemetery for monks who wished to be buried close to their saints, for at least five bodies were interred here. These were laid side by side, and were extended inhumations oriented from east to west, with the heads to the west.

Following excavation, much of the shrine platform was dismantled. This revealed three rock-cut graves, all oriented from east to west, sealed beneath the mound material. The graves, located on the north-eastern, the southern and the western sides of the shrine, clearly predate the construction of the mound and shrine. Fragments of human bone were recovered from two of them, including a sizeable part of a shattered femur, found at the western end of the grave. No bone was recovered from the third grave. It is hoped to determine, through trace element analysis, whether the bones in the earlier graves represent parts of the individuals translated into the cists beneath the gable-shrine.

The evidence so far collated on the Illaunloughan shrine indicates that it is a multi-period structure. The presence of a sacred focus (an earlier shrine?) is strongly suggested by the earlier graves, though no trace of any such structure survives. C14 (AMS analysis) dating of bone from the cists beneath the gable-shrine has yielded a date in the early seventh century for one individual and the middle of the eighth century for a second. It is intended to obtain further dates. A silver penny of Irish Viking type, with a circulation period of AD 1020–35, was recovered from the gravel bedding of the paving at the east side of the shrine. This does not in itself imply a late date for the shrine structure, for although the coin was recovered from gravel sealed by the paving around the central reliquary, it could have been deposited some considerable time after the interment of the bones in the shrine. Rather, it is important evidence for the continued veneration at and refurbishment of the shrine in this period. Half-scallop shells, present in the fill of the cists and on their stone lids, were clearly of some significance to those who interred the translated bones. *Pecten maximus* (great scallop) shells occur abundantly throughout the midden outside the drystone hut (see below), but they have not been recovered from other graves on the island. Some of the scallop shells from the shrine have been perforated and they may have been suspended from cords. The scallop is, of course, the emblem of St James, whose remains were 'discovered' in a field of shells in Compostela, north-western Spain, in AD 813. The shrine at Compostela rose to prominence as a place of pilgrimage in the eleventh century (Harbison 1991, 22). This may be further evidence of refurbishment of the shrine at a late period and C14 dating of some of the shell (results awaited) may yield the answer. It is unlikely that a lapse of several hundred years would have separated the original burials of the holy men and their subsequent translation into the shrine (O'Brien 1992, 136). Rather, it would seem that the construction of the gable-shrine dates to a period soon after the death of these individuals, possibly to be identified with those whose bones were found in the cists beneath the gable-shrine.

In Ireland and Britain house-shaped shrines made of stone, wood or metal were common in the Early Medieval period and varied in size from the small and portable to that of actual churches (Waterman 1960; Ryan 1989). A contemporary account by the Venerable Bede in the seventh century described the shrine of Chad, in St Peter's Cathedral, Lichfield, Mercia, thus: 'Moreover the place of his burial is covered with a wooden coffin made in the shape of a little house, having a hole in one side through which those who go thither out of devotion may insert their hands and take some of the dust' (Thomas 1971, 147).

One of the end-slabs of the Illaunloughan shrine may have had an opening similar to that at Killabuonia, but there was no access to the bones for the pilgrims. The evidence suggests that the shrine on Illaunloughan continued as a focus of activity in the Medieval period long after the oratory had fallen into disuse, and that the island was an important pilgrimage site during the Early Medieval period. The shrine is regarded locally as having a cure for sore eyes.

The domestic quarters

A large trench was excavated around the drystone hut and over the raised ridge at the west side of the island, which was revealed as part of an enclosure. Towards the area of the drystone hut it was represented by an outcrop of bedrock, contained to the north by a well-built drystone wall standing to a height of over 0.5 m. The enclosure wall is a primary feature, but it is not known if it continued around the island as the shore has been considerably eroded elsewhere.

Three round huts predate the construction of the drystone hut at the west side of the island; two of them, A and B, are conjoined, and hut A is built up against the enclosure wall (Fig. 11.5). The construction of hut A is interesting: the well-preserved wall structure of the north-west side is similar to that of the sod-walled structure found beneath the drystone oratory. Thin slabs remained *in situ* in the narrow trenches which kerbed a core of grey silt, a construction which can readily be interpreted as an earth-walled hut. The hut utilised the enclosure wall as the outer component of walling: on the inside the earth core was revetted with horizontally laid drystone walling. There were no internal roof supports, and the internal diameter of the hut was 3.8 m.

Hut B measured 6.7 m in overall diameter and was set into a semicircular arc cut vertically through the bedrock outcrop on its west side. Its walls were on average 1.5 m thick, and were defined by two shallow parallel trenches. Several postholes, spaced between 1.5 m and 2 m apart, occurred around the line of the inner trench. A paved pathway led to the doorway at the east side of the hut which was defined by two postholes set 1.3 m apart. Both hut A and B had substantial rectangular stone-kerbed hearths.

The partial remains of a timber round house (Hut C) were uncovered on the southern shore of the island, sealed beneath the midden. Most of this structure had vanished due to erosion, but a well-defined semicircular trench with postholes suggested that it took the form of a post and

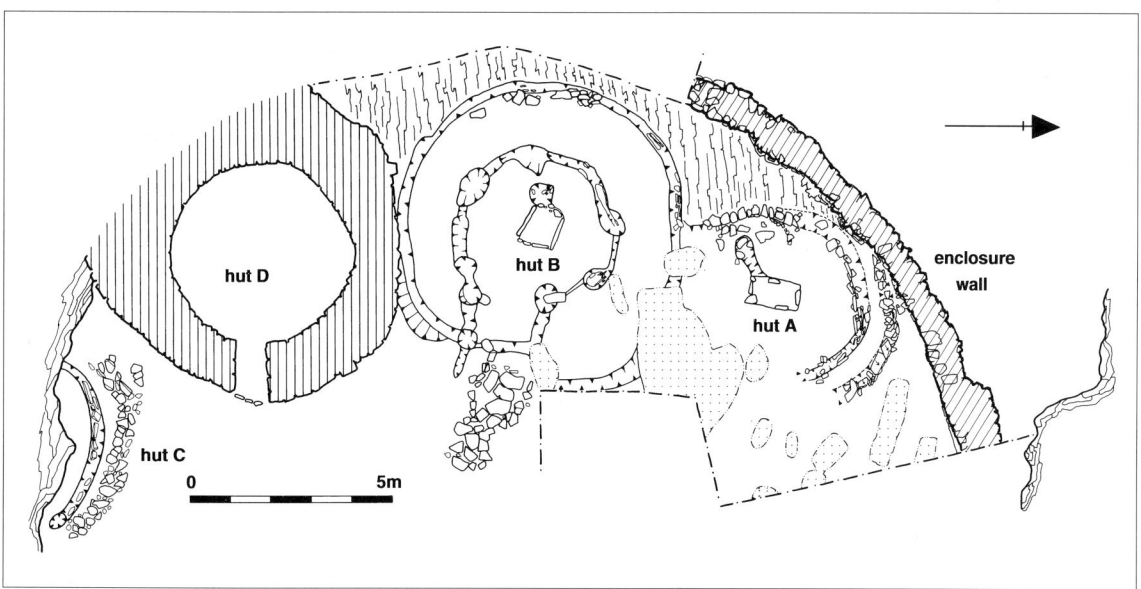

Fig. 11.5   Plan of excavated huts, Illaunloughan

wattle structure approximately 4.8 m in diameter. This structure also had a doorway on the eastern side. A rough arrangement of sandstone blocks aligned outside the arc of the trench may have supported the base of an insulating wall of sods or turfs. Bronze-working debris – consisting of over eighty ceramic mould, crucible and *tuyère* fragments – was recovered from associated soil levels, as was a bone motif-piece. The assemblage provides evidence for the manufacture of a minimum of four objects: a penannular brooch; a circular brooch or mount with fret-pattern ornamentation; a pin, possibly for the penannular brooch; and a smaller pin with a square, decorated head. The bone motif-piece, carrying panels of interlace and triquetra knots with bands of diagonally hatched motifs, has parallels in a motif-piece from Lagore which dates to the eighth or early ninth century (Ó Floinn 1989, 176).

The well-built drystone cell, with its thick walls of tightly packed sandstone, was corbel-roofed. The walls stood to a maximum internal height of 2.3 m. While its large size (4.3 m in diameter) indicates that the cell might have housed from one to three men, plus their supplies and equipment, in reasonable comfort, no evidence for internal features or fittings was recovered as its interior had been considerably disturbed by late burials. The cell was cut below external ground level on its western side, a feature that provides maximum protection from the prevailing westerly winds. It was constructed over the remains of huts A and B, and postdates the abandonment of hut C. C14 dating of animal bone incorporated in levelling dumps beneath its wall yielded a date of AD 775 to 961, calibrated to two standard deviations (UB 3860).

A sizeable deposit of midden, up to 0.9 m deep, had accumulated outside the cell. This comprised abundant marine shell, butchered animal bone and shattered sandstone. An examination of the faunal assemblage identified sheep, pig, cattle (including a significantly high number of calves), horse and cetacean; bird and fish bone was also present in considerable quantity.[5] The evidence suggests that many of the animals were butchered on the island. Sealed layers of the midden soil have been analysed for botanical remains and charred grains of wheat, oats and barley were identified.[6] The crops were imported to the site in a highly processed state, and their origin may lie in the farm complex of Early Medieval date on the south slopes of Bray Head, Valencia (Fig. 9.1), where a well-preserved kiln is associated with a group of stone houses in this area (Henry 1957, 93–95; Mitchell 1989, 45–46; O'Sullivan and Sheehan 1996, 388–92). Ongoing work on Bray Head has uncovered the remains of a further corn-drying kiln of similar form, which dates to the Early Medieval period (Hayden 1993). The environmental evidence indicates that the occupants of Illaunloughan were generously supported by neighbouring farming communities.

Several artefacts were found in the midden, among which were the head of a decorated bronze ring-brooch, a simple bronze ring-brooch, a shale or lignite bracelet, fragments of antler comb, and twenty-five bone disc beads. More mundane objects such as knives and whetstones, along with part of a rotary quern, were also recovered.

Excavation of the small island of Illaunloughan has yielded a wealth of evidence about small ecclesiastical sites of the Early Medieval period. It is apparent that the site underwent a number of transitions over time, which indicates changes in the size and probably the function of the settlement. When completed the results of the excavation will contribute significant new information about the chronology, development and evolution of small monastic sites and offer new information about the economy of such small island sites.

NOTES
1. We are grateful to Prionsias Ní Cathain for supplying us with this reference.
2. A study of the human skeletal remains from Illaunloughan has been carried out by Laureen Buckley.
3. The coins were kindly identified by Michael Kenny.

4. Wood identification by Aidan O'Sullivan and Mary Deevy.
5. Analysis of the faunal bone remains from the site has been carried out by Finbar McCormick.
6. Analysis carried out by Brian Bentley.

BIBLIOGRAPHY

Bieler, L. (ed.) (1979) *The Patrician Texts in the Book of Armagh*, Dublin

Colgrave, B. (1940) *Two Lives of St Cuthbert*, Cambridge

Dineen, P.S. (ed.) (1927, repr. 1934) *Focloir Gaedhilge agus Bearla*, Baile Atha Cliath

Fanning, T. (1981) 'Excavation of an Early Christian cemetery and settlement at Reask, County Kerry', *Proc. Roy. Ir. Acad.* 81C, 3–172

Harbison, P. (1991) *Pilgrimage in Ireland: The Monuments and the People*, London

Hayden, A. (1993) 'Excavation of a grain drying kiln at Bray Head, Valentia Island', unpublished report lodged with the National Monuments Service, Department of Arts, Heritage, Gaeltacht and the Islands

Henry, F. (1957) 'Early monasteries, beehive huts, and drystone houses in the neighbourhood of Cahersiveen and Waterville (Co. Kerry)', *Proc. Roy. Ir. Acad.* 58C, 45–166

Herity, M. (1989) 'Early Irish hermitages in the light of the *Lives* of Cuthbert', in G. Bonner, D. Rollason and C. Stancliffe (eds.), *St Cuthbert, his Cult and his Community to AD 1200*, 45–63

Herity, M. (1993) 'The forms of the tomb-shrine of the founder saint in Ireland', in R.M. Spearman, and J. Higgit (eds.), *The Age of Migrating Ideas, Early Medieval Art in Northern Britain and Ireland*, Edinburgh, 188–95

Hill, P. (1992) *Whithorn 4: Excavations 1990–1991*, Whithorn

Hurley, V. (1982) 'The early church in the southwest of Ireland: settlement and organisation', in S.M. Pearce (ed.), *The Early Church in Western Britain and Ireland*, *Brit. Archaeol. Rep.* 102, 297–332

Lynn, C. (1986) 'Houses and related outbuildings in Early Christian Ireland', 3 vols., unpublished PhD Thesis (NUI), University College, Dublin

Mitchell, F. (1989) *Man and Environment in Valencia Island*, Dublin

O'Brien, E. (1992) 'Pagan and Christian burial in Ireland during the first millenium A.D.: continuity and change', in N. Edwards and A. Lane (eds.), *The Early Church in Wales and the West*, 130–37

Ó Floinn, R. (1989) in S. Youngs (ed.), *The Work of Angels*, London

O'Kelly, M.J. (1958) 'Church Island near Valencia, Co. Kerry', *Proc. Roy. Ir. Acad.* 59C, 57–136

Ordnance Survey Name Books (1841), MSS at Ordnance Survey Office, Dublin

O'Sullivan, A. and Sheehan, J. (1996) *The Iveragh Peninsula: an Archaeological Survey of South Kerry*, Cork

Ryan, M. (1989) 'Church metalwork in the eighth and ninth centuries', in S. Youngs (ed.), *The Work of Angels*, London, 125–50

Stokes, W. (ed.) (1905, repr. 1984) *The Martyrology of Oengus the Culdee (Felire Oengusso Ceile De)*, Dublin

Thomas, C. (1971) *The Early Christian Archaeology of North Britain*, London

Thomas, C. (1973) *Bede, Archaeology and the Cult of Relics*, Jarrow Lecture 1973

Waterman, D.M. (1960) 'An Early Christian mortuary house at Saul, Co. Down', *Ulster J. Archaeol.* 23, 89–96

12. Architectural Traditions of the Early Medieval Church in Munster

TADHG O'KEEFFE

This chapter is an exploration of church architecture in Munster in the period leading to the mid-twelfth century *floruit* of the Romanesque style. Combining the evidence of the form, function and iconography of buildings both in and beyond the boundaries of the modern province (Fig. 12.1), it attempts to disentangle the converging and diverging building traditions of which the corpus of Early Medieval ecclesiastical architecture in Munster is the product.

Mos Scottorum
The appearance in 1958 of the late Professor O'Kelly's report on his excavation of Church Island, County Kerry, is a key event in the historiography of medieval architectural history in Ireland. A mere three years after the publication of the first volume of Harold Leask's celebrated trilogy on Irish ecclesiastical architecture, O'Kelly's revelation that a stone oratory was built above an earlier timber structure and its associated cemetery (Fig. 12.2a) added a new dimension to the study of the built environment of early Irish Christianity. The building of stone churches above wooden structures was a widespread phenomenon in the Early Middle Ages north of the Alps (Oswald et al. 1966), and the Church Island community revealed itself in O'Kelly's investigations to have belonged within this mainstream.

Clearly a lack of suitable wood at Church Island did not, *contra* Leask (1955, 17), deter the founders of this small monastery from building in the *mos* which Bede and other early commentators (Radford 1977; Murray 1979) might have us expect of them. Of course, Bede's distinction between the Irish and Roman 'manners' of building was as much an expression of differences in the politics and practices between the two churches as it was an expression of different technologies (Gem 1983, 2). Roger of Howden, five centuries later, described how Irish kings built a palace of wattle for Henry II, *ad morem patriae illius* and *ad modum patriae illius constructum*, and the term *mos* here is used to convey a similar political reality (Flanagan 1989, 203). None the less, the Church Island excavation provided the first archaeological validation of the observations of contemporary writers about Ireland's building industry.

The excavated structure at Church Island was small, with a width of about 2 m and an estimated length of about 3 m, and upright posts formed its principal structural element. Other excavated timber churches are comparable (Edwards 1990, 123). Finely carpentered timber structures may have been comparatively rare: in a telling coda to his description of a wooden oratory, the author of *Hisperica Famina*, a seventh-century poem, does not bother to 'unroll

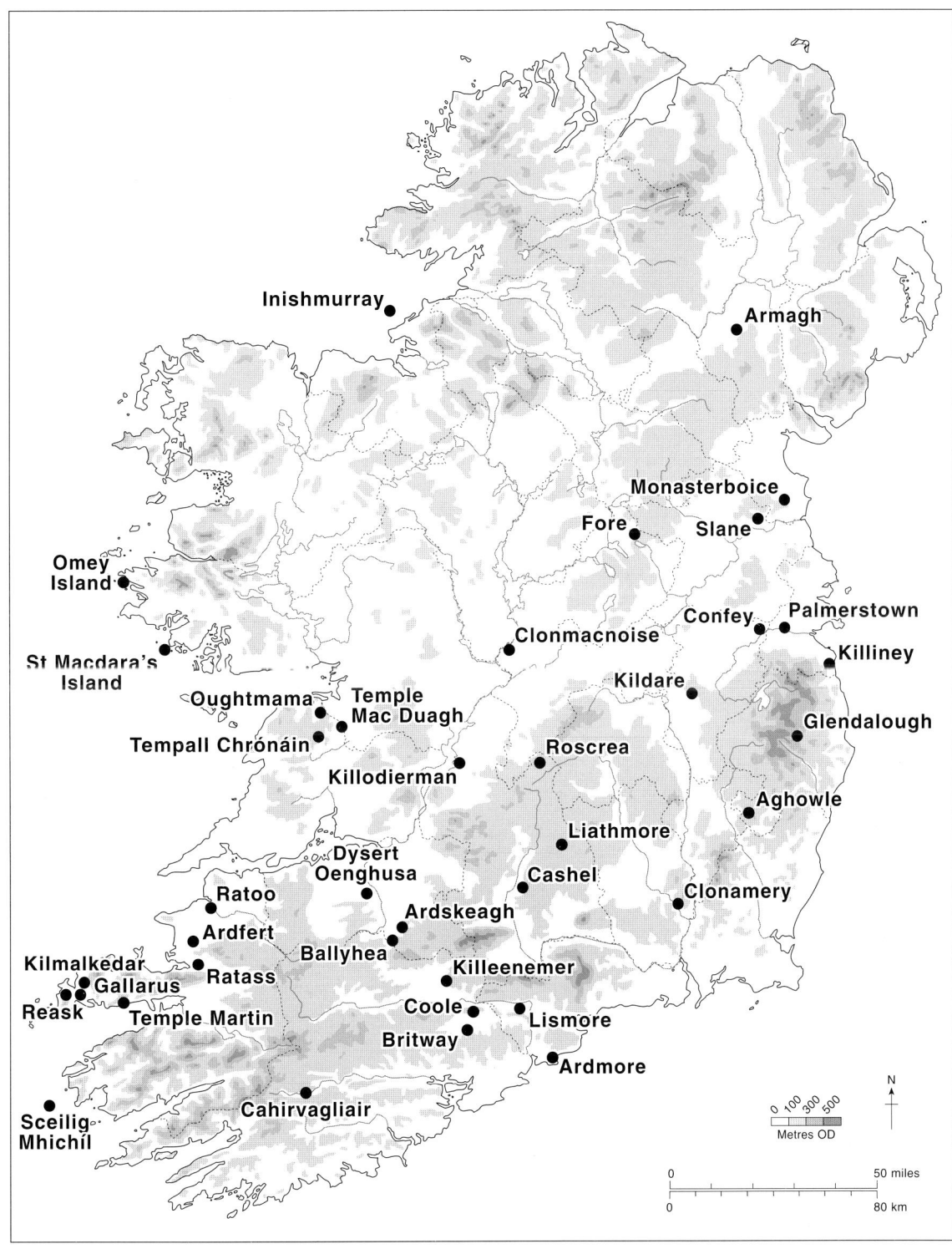

Fig. 12.1: Location map of sites mentioned in this chapter

from his wheel of words' a description of the oratory's contents (Herren 1974, 109), presumably because what was contained within was less unusual than the building itself.

How old is Gallarus Oratory?

The small oratory which replaced the even smaller timber structure at Church Island is of the same family as Gallarus Oratory, located further to the north on the Dingle Peninsula. Gallarus itself measures a mere 4.65 m by 3.10 m internally (a ratio of 1:1.5), is entered through a battered and lintelled west doorway with long-and-short jamb stones, and is lit by a small monolithic-arched east window (Fig. 12.2b). Its simple form disguises the considerable skill required to create it: not only do all the walls simultaneously begin their convergence towards the crest of the roof at ground level, but the exact correspondence of their curvature is ensured by discrete dressing of the stones. Buildings of this type are confined to the western littoral, with a particular concentration in Kerry.

While the sequence revealed at Church Island indicates that these so-called oratories are not the earliest Christian churches in the peninsular southwest (see White Marshall and Walsh, ch. 11), it does prompt the suggestion that they are the earliest churches built in stone in the region. The buildings themselves offer little evidence that may be used in elucidating their chronology: the dressing on the stones at Gallarus, for example, can be paralleled with that on the stone-walled entrance passage at Cahirvagliair ringfort, County Cork, and also at Temple Martin, County Kerry, which has a lintelled west doorway no older than the tenth century and possibly as late as the twelfth. However, Gallarus undoubtedly has its pedigree in the *clochán* tradition; it reflects, as Herity puts it (1995, 176–7), the cross-fertilisation of the *clochán*, with its square interior and round exterior, with the rectilinear exterior requirement of Christian practice. Even more significantly, perhaps, the recurring association of oratories of the Gallarus type with cross-slabs of various forms, and with *leachta*, suggests that they belong within the same, early, religious-cultural horizon. A calibrated radiocarbon determination of AD 690–880 from the mortar of Phase I of St Michael's Church on Sceilg Mhichíl, County Kerry (Berger 1995, 172), a building which lies off the oratory-cell axis and which can therefore be considered later than either (Fig. 12.2c), may provide a *terminus ante quem* for the oratory at this particular site.

The documentation of stone churches begins in the annals only at the end of the eighth century (Hamlin 1984, 118), suggesting that the process of replacing or supplementing wooden churches with stone churches began in earnest around 800, and it is not inconceivable that many remote west-coast communities made the change from wood to stone around the same time. The term *doimliacc* (DIL, 333–4; Macdonald 1981, 306–7), first recorded in the early eighth century (*AU sub anno* 724) but used more frequently in the ninth century, was possibly intended to convey a church built in a style approximating to that found within the Romanised world; a church, in other words, with vertical walls which were bonded with mortar and carried a gabled roof. The main line of architectural evolution in Early Medieval Ireland probably springs from within this concept of *doimliacc*.

The Christian communities of Ireland's west coast were not beyond the influence of the Roman world, as the imported pottery indicates (Thomas 1976), but with its clear ancestry in the pre-Christian Iron Age, Gallarus, like oratories of its type, qualifies as a *doimliacc* only in the most literal sense of the word. Notwithstanding the examples of dry-stone, corbel-roofed huts noted by Henry over a wide geographical area (1948) and the building of *clocháns* into recent centuries, the building tradition which Gallarus represents so nobly seems to have had no significant impact on later architectural developments; claims that Gallarus is related in one way or another to stone-roofed and barrel-vaulted churches (Leask 1955, 27; Harbison 1970, 45–47) can be dismissed on aesthetic or technological grounds. Gallarus was an architectural cul-de-sac.

Church Architectural Traditions 115

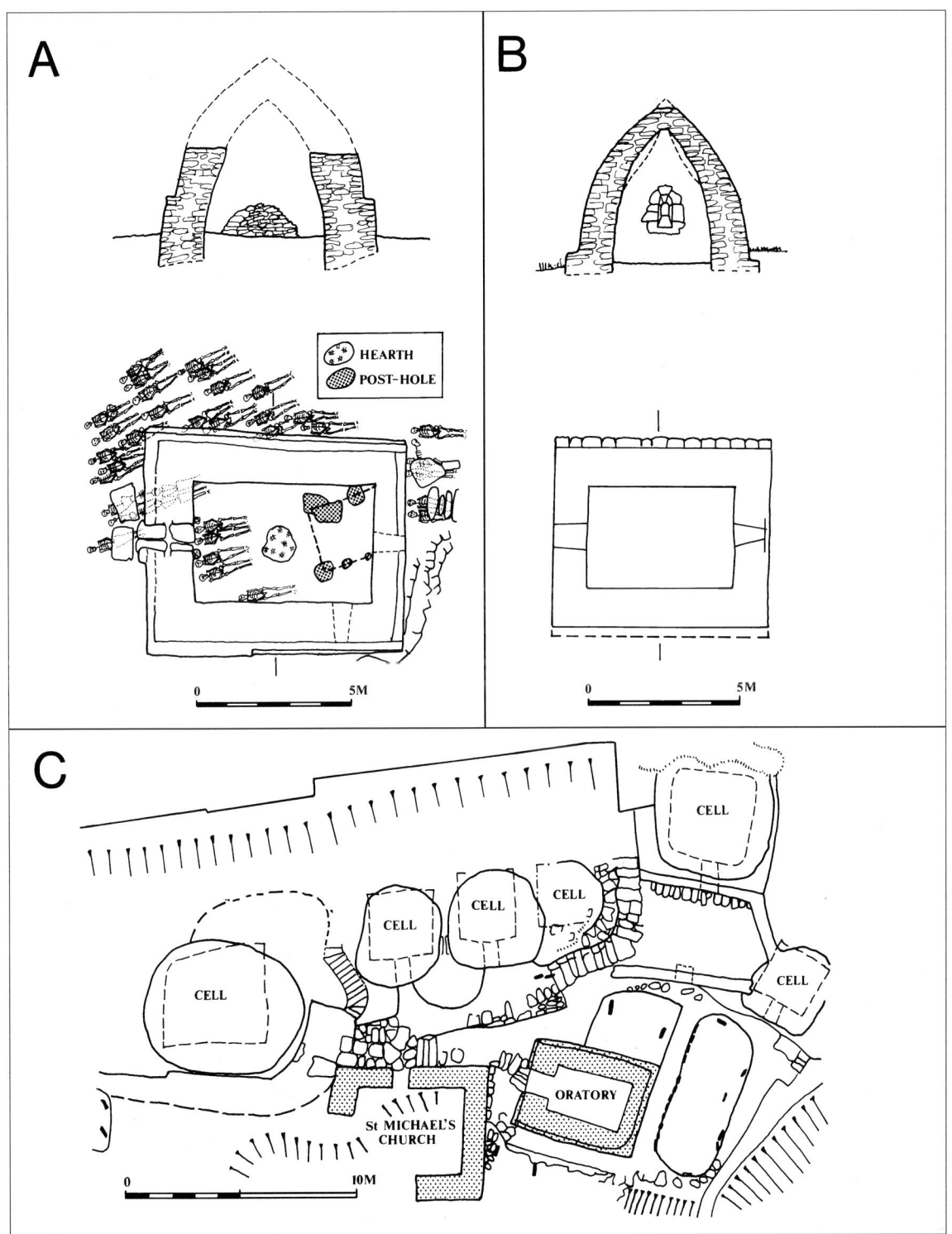

Fig. 12.2 a) Church Island (Valencia, Co. Kerry; b) Gallarus Oratory, Co. Kerry; c) Sceilig Mhichíl, Co. Kerry

The architecture of the Memoria

The technique of dating mortar by radiocarbon analysis offers the prospect of reconstructing a chronology of buildings about which history is silent and for which stylistic analysis is too imprecise. Dates published by Berger (1995) from Teampall Chiaráin at Clonmacnois, County Offaly (AD 660–980), Teach Molaise on Inismurray, County Sligo (AD 690–980), and St Michael's Church, Sceilg Mhichíl, mentioned above, confirm the impression garnered from the annals that stone churches became common around 800. Early dates (AD 540–1020; AD 610–980) have also been obtained for the lower parts of St Columba's 'House' in Kells, County Meath, a building with a later superstructure of probable eleventh- or twelfth-century date (Hamlin 1984, 120; O'Keeffe 1994b, 139).

The Clonmacnois and Inismurray buildings referred to here were not conventional churches but tomb-shrines (Herity 1995, 290–91). Comparable Munster buildings which lie within the broadly defined family of *memoriae*, funerary monuments which may contain relics or corporeal remains (Colvin 1991, 109; Duval 1992, 552), are the south 'church' at Labbamolaga, County Cork (Fig. 11.3a) and St Declan's 'House' at Ardmore, County Waterford (Fig. 11.3b).

The status of martyr could be achieved by voluntarily following a demanding lifestyle – Green and White martyrdoms as distinct from the blood-letting Red martyrdom (Ryan 1931, 197–99; Herity 1995, 277, 280) – so technically it may be correct to describe these *memoriae* as *martyria*, mausolea containing the corporeal remains of those who had acquired martyr status (Grabar 1946; Colvin 1991, 105). The concept of the free-standing *memoria* or *martyrium* building had emerged by the early fourth century (Duval and Picard 1986, *passim*; Colvin 1991, 105), but it is tempting to view the radiocarbon dates as evidence that it did not actually enter Ireland until around 800. Prior to this, the *inhumation privilégiée* in Ireland, not least in Munster, seems to have been marked by a free-standing commemorative monument inscribed with a cross or with an ogham inscription, or by an A-roofed shrine (White Marshall and Walsh ch. 11), a box shrine, or a corner-post shrine (Herity 1995, 280–87). These latter shrines all reveal a certain architectural consciousness which probably reflects the derivation of their forms from structural exemplars elsewhere; the stone-lined surrounds of the A-shaped shrines have, for example, been compared by Thomas to *cellae memoriae* in the Mediterranean lands (1971, 144). The *leacht*, an open-air altar-like construction of solid stone often associated with ancient pilgrimage rounds of demonstrable antiquity (Herity 1995, 91–143), may represent another type of *memoria*. The etymology of the word – *lectus* (Latin) and *lecht* (Old Irish) both mean 'bed' – suggests a grave, as does the ancient practice among pilgrims of depositing quartz pebbles on them as they would on graves. The phenomenon of the *leacht* may well have begun life as an actual marker of a high status grave, but *leachta* are dedicated to persons who were clearly buried elsewhere, as is the case on Inismurray (Wakeman 1893), which suggests that these are essentially surrogate graves. Examples of *leachta* inside cemeteries might not always be grave-markers in any conventional sense; the example investigated on Omey Island, County Galway, for example, had graves beneath it, but it covered no specific grave (O'Keeffe 1994a). The building of *leachta* seems to have continued well into the post-1000 period: at Temple MacDuagh in the Burren, County Clare, a *leacht* stands on the ruined foundations of a church which is possibly no older than the twelfth century.

The new *memoria* buildings may have been built to incorporate the exact place of original burial. North of the Alps, no less than in the Mediterranean lands, Early Medieval churches can often be shown to have been located in pre-existing cemeteries (Mertens 1976, 46–47), cemeteries which might be characterised as 'undeveloped' (Thomas 1971, 50–51). The evidence of Church Island shows that the likelihood of cutting through earlier burials did not discourage the erection of new buildings

Church Architectural Traditions 117

Fig. 12.3   a. South 'church', Labbamolaga, Co. Cork (top); b. St Declan's 'house', Ardmore, Co. Waterford (above)

(O'Kelly 1958, Fig. 2). Indeed, Grabar offered the thesis that the cult of martyrs developed within the cemeteries in which the martyrial remains were first interred, and that the great basilicas erected directly above the burial-places of the martyrs from the time of Constantine meant that the architecture of church and shrine developed in tandem (Grabar 1946).

Corporeal relics could be contained within churches large enough to fulfil the entire range of liturgical functions, as at Kildare (Connolly and Picard 1987, 25–26) and Armagh (Doherty 1984), but such instances were exceptional rather than typical in Early Medieval Ireland. It is conceivable that at places such as Labbamolaga the *memoria* buildings were erected directly above the original burials, without becoming the foci around which great churches later developed. It is also possible that they were built with the intention of translating the sacred remains from another location, a practice well-attested in the Anglo-Saxon world (Biddle 1986, 7–11; Blair 1992, 253). Whichever the case, they were and remained structurally independent of larger churches and they did not later relinquish their relics to larger churches, as is apparent from the discovery in the nineteenth century of Ciarán's relics inside Teampall Chiaráin (Macalister 1909, 155).

The basilicas at Armagh lay side by side with that to the south containing the relics; it is hardly surprising that this arrangement of churches reflects the Early Medieval Italian practise (Lusuardi Siena 1996), given what we know of Armagh (Doherty 1984). Not unrelated was the longitudinal division of the church of the double monastery of Kildare into northern and southern halves. The image-laden screen which Cogitosus describes at its eastern end (Connolly and Picard 1987, 25) certainly recalls Benedict Biscop's *tabulatum* at Wearmouth (Meyvaert 1979; Gem 1990, 2–3) and suggests a Mediterranean pedigree for the Kildare building. If connections with the Roman world explain the configurations of these seventh-century churches, the same sources may explain why church clusters in Ireland invariably follow a north-south arrangement, as at Labbamolaga and Inis Cealtra, and at Liathmore, County Tipperary, and Inisfallen, County Kerry. They may also explain those instances where earlier forms of *memoriae* stand in front of or behind the main church, but not on the same axis, as is notably the case at Teampall Chrónáin. Oughtmama, located in a small valley in the Burren, is a rare Irish example of a group of churches standing in the sort of east-west pattern that is so well-attested in England (Blair 1992, Figs. 10.8; 10.9).

Churches with antae and architraved doorways

Antae, projections of the side walls past the end walls, were in use in churches in the tenth century: they were used on the 'great church' of Clonmacnois, built around the first decade of the century (Manning 1995, 25), and at Tuamgraney, County Clare (Fig. 12.4a), built half a century later (CS *sub anno* 964). The gateway at Glendalough, County Wicklow, also had antae, suggesting there was a chapel above the arched entranceway. Antae are also found on most of the *memoria* buildings, including Teampall Chiaráin with its early radiocarbon date. Given that these *memoriae* may be the earliest mortared stone buildings of an ecclesiastical nature in Ireland, as Harbison points out (1991, 151), it is likely that antae were first used in Ireland in this funerary context. Funerary monuments have long been recognised as central to the evolution of church architecture, with similar architectural conventions being used for various forms of tomb-shrines and for conventional churches (Colvin 1991, 123–36).

The small corpus of excavated timber churches in Ireland does not provide evidence to support the contention (Leask 1955, 55–56) that antae are features inherited from timber architecture, although some timber churches outside Ireland have antae-like features (Ahrens 1979, Fig. 25; Rodwell and Rodwell 1985, Fig. 62 A, C). Whether inherited from timber architecture or not, the case has been made for seeing antae on stone churches as supports for barge-boards (Leask 1955, 56). It does seem rather a lot of trouble, however, to build two pairs of large, engaged piers simply to carry the barge-boards of a roof when projecting corbels at eaves level could fulfil the duty as easily, as is clear from Teampall Chrónáin and from the largest church at Oughtmama, for example. Indeed, not only were corbels as effective as antae, but for some church-builders they were clearly preferable, and one might suggest that many of the churches without antae originally had corbels projecting from their eaves. At Kilmalkedar, County Kerry, and St Macdara's church, County Galway, the former dating to the second quarter of the twelfth century and the latter possibly dating to around 1100, the antae continue up the sides of the gables and are thus integrated with the roofing material. But is it possible that in earlier generations buildings with antae had a particular status or function, and that the antae either communicated this iconographically or provided support for horizontal beams on which crosses or other images were mounted?

Whatever the form of the few documented eighth-century churches (Hamlin 1984, 117–18), we can be confident that from the start of the tenth century when the great church at Clonmacnois was built there had developed the church with upright walls, an angled roof of material other than stone, and antae. The church at Tuamgraney, built in the mid-tenth century, is comparable in form to Clonmacnois but is smaller and also possesses what must surely be regarded as its original doorway (Fig. 12.4a). This is lintelled in form and has an architraved surround. An insubstantial addition to the material of a building perhaps, but such an embellishment of a doorway signalled to the worshipper that a sacred place was about to be entered (O'Keeffe 1995, 268). Among Christian communities accustomed to plain and simple buildings, a cross carved on an architraved lintel – as is found at Clonamery, County Kilkenny, and Fore, County Westmeath – must have made the point even more eloquently. The concept may still have been current in the thirteenth century if one accepts Harbison's suggested date for the cross on the façade of Killinaboy, County Clare (1976, 12).

Antae might not have become a feature of non-funerary buildings in Ireland until around 900, when the great church at Clonmacnois was built, and architraves may well have appeared in the doorways in tandem with them. The fact that we know of no architraved doorways prior to the mid-tenth century (Tuamgraney) tempts us to see this small but significant change in architectural conception as parallel to the appearance of the Round Tower, for which the earliest recorded reference is also mid-tenth century (Slane: *AU sub anno* 949). Indeed, the abbot responsible for the church at Tuamgraney also built a Round Tower at the site (*CS sub anno* 964).

It is with the building of Round Towers that Irish monastic communities first reveal themselves to be more than capable of high quality stone construction. The contact with an overseas architectural tradition, probably the Carolingian one, which resulted in the development of the Round Tower may not only explain the simple embellishment of church doorways with architraves, but may also have paved the way for subtle transformations in the architectural design of churches after the turn of the millennium.

Architectural transformations in the eleventh century

Lintelled church doorways became unfashionable in the twelfth century as highly elaborated round-arched doorways, derived principally from the English Romanesque architectural tradition, became popular, although occasionally a church would be provided with a doorway in which the two traditions were consciously straddled, as at Aghowle, County Wicklow (Leask 1955, Fig. 44). When Ardfert was overlooked as the diocesan centre of Kerry in 1111 the honour went instead to Ratass, near Tralee, and the small church there would have fulfilled the diocesan function. Ratass church began life as a single-cell structure, entered through a lintelled and architraved

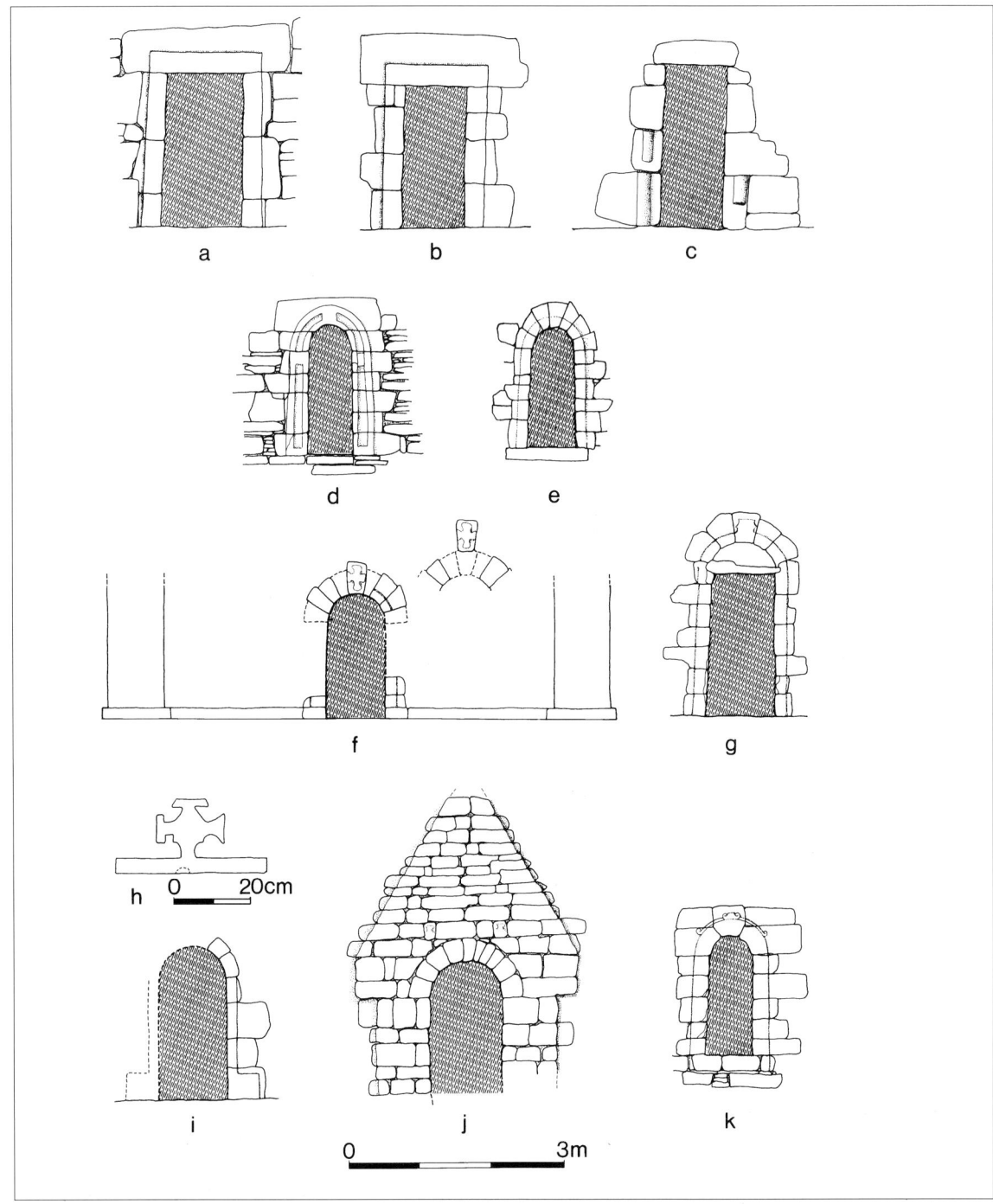

Fig. 12.4 a) Tuamgraney, Co. Clare, doorway; b) Ratass, Co. Kerry, doorway; c) Reefert, Co. Wicklow, doorway; d) Monasterboice, Co. Lough, Round Tower doorway; e) Cashel, Co. Tipperary, Round Tower doorway; f) Killeenemer, Co. Cork, west facade (reconstructed); g) Britway, Co. Cork, doorway; h) Killodiernan, Co. Tipperary, east window; i) Ardskeagh, Co. Cork, west portal (reconstructed); j) Ballyhea, Co. Cork, south doorway; k) Ratoo, Co. Kerry, Round Tower doorway

doorway in a façade flanked by antae (Fig. 12.4b). A chancel was later added to it, probably shortly after 1111 when extra liturgical space might have been needed. Despite having the technology to build a true arch – an arch with voussoirs – over the opening between the nave and chancel, the builders at Ratass retained the original lintelled west door. Exactly the same phenomenon can be observed in two groups of churches in the Dublin region: the churches at Killiney and Palmerstown, both in County Dublin, had chancels added but their original lintelled doors were retained, while at Reefert and Trinity at Glendalough coeval naves and chancels were given lintelled doors. The Reefert west doorway had an architrave with a sunken moulding (Fig. 12.4c) almost identical to that on the round-arched door of the Round Tower of Monasterboice, County Louth (Fig. 12.4d), which was destroyed in 1097 (*AU*). This type of architrave is so distinctive that both constructions must be of about the same, pre-1100 date. The relationship between Reefert and Monasterboice suggests, then, that while lintelled doorways were still in use in churches in the later 1000s, round-arched doorways were in use in contemporary Round Towers. Examples of nave and chancel churches which have lintelled west doorways are so few that they probably belong within a short time-span; if the evidence of Reefert suggests that the association of lintelled entrances with round-arched chancel openings began before 1100, it is possible that the arrival of Romanesque decorated motifs for round-arched church doorways in the second quarter of the twelfth century brought the association to an end.

The round-arched doorway may well, therefore, have first appeared in Ireland in the Round Towers, and its appearance did not precipitate the abandonment in churches of the lintelled doorway form. Given that decorative motifs of overseas Romanesque origin appear on some Round Tower doorways, as at Dysert Oenghusa, County Limerick, for example, it seems reasonable to assume that most, if not all, of the unembellished or plainly architraved round-arched Round Tower doorways predate the arrival of decorative Romanesque architecture around the time Cormac's Chapel at Cashel, County Tipperary, was begun in 1127. Significantly, the Round Tower at Cashel, dated to the later eleventh century by the radiocarbon method (Berger 1995, 172), has a round-arched doorway with an architrave (Fig. 12.4e) identical to those embellishing lintelled church doorways.

Round-arched doorways comparable to those in the Round Towers are very rarely found in churches, which again suggests a limited time-span for their construction, and the meagre comparative evidence continues to suggest a date around 1100. North Cork possesses a small number of doorways of considerable interest. One can be reconstructed at Killeenemer (Fig. 12.4f). The doorway at Britway, which is still complete, has a lintel and a relieving arch (Fig. 12.4g), a configuration with parallels at Confey, County Kildare (O'Keeffe 1987), and at St Kevin's in Glendalough, the latter having a radiocarbon date of AD 1000–1280 (Berger 1995, 172). It may be compared with Killeenemer in having a cross at the top of the architrave. The Britway cross is unusual in shape and is not entirely unlike the motifs on the top of the architraved doorway into the Round Tower at Ratoo, County Kerry, dated by the radiocarbon method to the later eleventh century (Berger 1995, 172), and on the exterior of the lintel of the twelfth-century east window at Killodiernan, County Tipperary (Fig. 12.4h). West of Britway is the much-damaged doorway at Ardskeagh (Fig. 12.4i). The architrave here has a step (in other words, it widens horizontally and then drops vertically again) on the bottom stone on each side. This unusual embellishment seems to be an almost embryonic version of the flat pediment-like feature, enclosing a round-arched doorway, which projects in the manner of a shallow architrave at nearby Ballyhea (Fig. 12.4j). The close proximity of the Ardskeagh and Ballyhea doorways, and the hints of a conceptual link between them, suggests near-contemporaneity.

A tale of two Romanesques?

Churches described in the literature as 'Irish Romanesque' (Leask 1955) or 'Hiberno-Romanesque' (Edwards 1990, 124–26) are essentially those which possess at least some of the sculptural motifs that can be found in Cormac's Chapel in Cashel, begun in 1127 and completed in 1134 (de Paor 1967; O'Keeffe 1994b). Cormac MacCarthaig, the patron of the small chapel at Cashel, may well be the key figure in the creation of this architectural tradition. He is known to have founded churches at Lismore, County Waterford, in 1127, and the survival there of material of the 1120s, allied with the survival of fragments of sculpture of about the same date at two other monasteries, both in the vicinity of Lismore, allows a case to be made for locating the birthplace of the stylistic tradition not on the plains of Tipperary (de Paor 1967) but, as is discussed elsewhere (O'Keeffe 1994b), further south, either in the lower Blackwater valley around Lismore in the 1130s, or indeed at Ardfert in Kerry in the 1120s. While much of the architectural forms and decorative motifs found in Romanesque work in Ireland after the 1130s are English in origin, there are reminders in the corpus of the Munster Romanesque that the province looks towards the Continent rather than England: the five-bay façade used at Ardfert, and possibly copied at Roscrea, County Tipperary, is more readily paralleled in France (Angoulême Cathedral, for example) than in England, while the musician at Church Island, Lough Currane, County Kerry (O'Sullivan and Sheehan 1996, 319) may be akin to those represented in sculptural programmes in Romanesque France (Jullian 1987).

Are we justified in restricting the use of the term Romanesque to those churches of the second quarter of the twelfth century and later which have motifs imported from overseas? Can the round-arched doorways in the Round Towers and in the churches discussed earlier not also be described as Romanesque? The key point here is that the term Romanesque is not a creation of the Middle Ages but was coined only two centuries ago to describe a body of art and architecture which antiquarians of that time thought to be linked to the Antique world (Waldeier Bizzarro 1992, 132–49). Our perception of the relationship between Antiquity and the Middle Ages is now rather more advanced but the term continues to be used with reference to the eleventh and twelfth centuries. If it is correct to assign works such as the chancel arches of Reefert and Ratass, or the round-arched doorways of Cashel Round Tower and Britway church, to the period around 1100, they could indeed be considered Romanesque from a chronological perspective. An overseas Romanesque tradition – the so-called Saxo-Norman 'overlap' in England, for example (Bony 1967) – might have provided the appropriate inspiration if not also a selection of usable architectonic forms.

These fairly modest works might even be seen as an architectural expression of the early phases of the movement to reform the Irish church around 1100. It is particularly interesting to note that Ardfert Cathedral, Cormac's Chapel and other Munster churches of their ilk were not actually built until two decades after the first reforming synod was held in Cashel in 1101, so there is a period during which one might expect churches to have been built, and these monuments might occupy that gap. Significantly, there is also a case to be made for attributing the two-storeyed format employed at Cormac's Chapel to an architectural tradition which is already present in Ireland around the end of the eleventh century and which also has an overseas Romanesque origin (O'Keeffe 1994b, 139).

It is possible, then, to suggest the presence of an early Romanesque architectural tradition in Ireland around 1100, a tradition which is separate from that represented most spectacularly by Cormac's MacCarthaig's masterwork at Cashel. Cormac's Chapel and those many churches which have sculptural links with it did not, however, evolve out of this putative early Romanesque architectural environment. Rather, they reflect a new input from the mature Romanesque traditions of early twelfth-century England and, to a much lesser degree, France. And it is the rapprochement of new decorative ideas taken from these sources with the traditional Irish concern for small buildings, rather plain walls and, in many cases, the inclusion of antae, which gives churches in the period after 1120 such a distinctive personality.

BIBLIOGRAPHY

Ahrens, C. (1981) *Frühe Holzkirchen im Nördlichen Europa*, Hamburg

AU: Annals of Ulster, W.M. Hennessy and B. MacCarthy (eds.) 4 vols., Dublin 1887–1901

Berger, R. (1995) 'Radiocarbon dating of early medieval Irish monuments', *Proc. Roy. Ir. Acad.* 95C, 159–74

Biddle, M. (1986) 'Archaeology, architecture and the cult of saints in Anglo-Saxon England', in L.A.S. Butler and R.K. Morris (eds.), *The Anglo-Saxon Church: Papers on history, architecture and archaeology in honour of Dr H.M. Taylor*, Counc. Brit. Archaeol. Res. Rep. 60, London, 1–31

Blair, J. (1992) 'Anglo-Saxon Minsters: a topographical review', in J. Blair and R. Sharpe (eds.), *Pastoral Care before the Parish*, Leicester, 226–66

Bony, J. (1967) Review of H.M. and J. Taylor, *Anglo-Saxon Architecture* (Cambridge 1965), *J. Soc. Archit. Historians* 26, 74–77

Colvin, H. (1991) *Architecture and the After-Life*, Yale

Connolly, S. and Picard, J.-M. (1987) 'Cogitosus: Life of Saint Brigit', *J. Roy. Soc. Antiq. Ir.* 117, 5–27

CS: Chronicon Scottorum, W.M. Hennessy (ed.), London 1866

De Paor, L. (1967) 'Cormac's Chapel: the beginnings of Irish Romanesque', in E. Rynne (ed.), *North Munster Studies*, Limerick, 133–45

DIL: Dictionary of the Irish Language: Compact Edition, Royal Irish Academy, Dublin 1990

Doherty, C. (1984) 'The basilica in early Ireland', *Peritia* 3, 303–15

Duval, N. (1992) 'Church buildings', in A. di Berardino (ed.), *Encyclopedia of the Early Church*, Cambridge, 168–75

Duval, N. and Picard, J.-Ch. (eds.), (1986) *L'inhumation Privilégiée du IVe au VIIIe siècle*, Paris

Edwards, N. (1990) *The Archaeology of Early Medieval Ireland*, London

Flanagan, M.T. (1989) *Irish Society, Anglo-Norman Settlers, Angevin Kingship: Interactions in Ireland in the Late Twelfth Century*, Oxford

Gem, R. (1990) 'Documentary references to Anglo-Saxon painted architecture', in S. Cather, D. Park and P. Williamson (eds.), *Early Medieval Wall Painting and Painted Sculpture in England*, Brit. Archaeol. Rep. 216, Oxford, 1–16

Grabar, A. (1946) *Martyrium*, 2 vols., Paris

Hamlin, A. (1984) 'The study of early Irish churches', in P. Ní Chatháin and M. Richter (eds.), *Ireland and Europe: The Early Church*, Stuttgart, 117–26

Harbison, P. (1970) 'How old is Gallarus Oratory? A reappraisal of its role in early architecture', *Medieval Archaeol.*, 14, 34–59

Harbison, P. (1976) 'The double-armed cross on the church gable at Killinaboy, Co. Clare', *N. Munster Antiq. J.* 18, 7–12

Harbison, P. (1982) 'Early Irish Churches', in H. Löwe (ed.), *Die Iren und Europa im früheren Mittelalter*, Stuttgart, 618–29

Harbison, P. (1991) *Pilgrimage in Ireland: The Monuments and the People*, London

Henry, F. (1948) 'Early Irish Monasteries, boat-shaped oratories and beehive huts', *Co. Louth Archaeol. Hist. J.* 11, 4, 296–304

Herity, M. (1995) *Studies in the Layout, Buildings and Art in Stone of Early Irish Monasteries*, London

Herren, M. (1974) *Hisperica Famina*, Toronto

Jullian, M. (1987) 'L'image de la musique dans la sculpture romane en France', *Cahiers de Civilisation Médiévale* 30, 33–44

Leask, H.G. (1955) *Irish Churches and Monastic Buildings, I*, Dundalk

Lusuardi Siena, S. (1996) 'Il complesso episcopale di Milano: riconsiderazione della testimonianze Ambrosiana nella Epistola ad sororem', in *Les Église Doubles et les Familles d'Églises, Antiquité Tardive* 1, 121–32

Macalister, R.A.S. (1909) *The Memorial Slabs of Clonmacnois, King's County*, Dublin

Macdonald, A.D.S. (1981) 'Notes on monastic archaeology and the annals of Ulster, 650–1050', in D. Ó Corráin (ed.), *Irish Antiquity*, Cork, 304–19

Manning, C. (1995) *Clonmacnoise*, Dublin

Mertens, J. (1976) 'Tombes mérovingiennes et églises chrétiennes, Arlon, Grobbendonk, Landen, Waha', *Archaeologica Belgica* 187, Bruxelles

Meyvaert. P. (1979) 'Bede and the church paintings in Wearmouth-Jarrow', *Anglo-Saxon Engl.* 8, 63–77

Murray, H. (1979) 'Documentary evidence for domestic buildings in Ireland c. 400–1200 in the light of archaeology', *Medieval Archaeol.* 23, 81–97

O'Keeffe, T. (1987) 'The church and castle at Confey, Co. Kildare', *J. Co. Kildare Archaeol. Soc.* 16, 5, 408–17

O'Keeffe, T. (1994a) 'Omey and the Sands of Time', *Archaeol. Ireland* 8, 2, 22–24

O'Keeffe, T. (1994b) 'Lismore and Cashel: reflections on the beginnings of Romanesque architecture in Munster', *J. Roy. Soc. Antiq. Ir.* 124, 118–52

O'Keeffe, T. (1995) 'The Romanesque portal at Clonfert and its iconography', in C. Bourke (ed.), *From the Isles of the North: Early Medieval Art in Ireland and Britain*, Belfast, 261–69

O'Kelly, M.J. (1958) 'Church Island, near Valentia, Co. Kerry', *Proc. Roy. Ir. Acad.* 59C, 57–136

O'Sullivan, A. and Sheehan, J. (1996) *The Iveragh Peninsula: An Archaeological Survey of South Kerry*, Cork

Oswald, F., Schaefer, L. and Sennhauser, H. (1966) *Vorromanische Kirchenbauten*, Munich

Radford, C.A.R. (1977) 'The earliest Irish churches', *Ulster J. Archaeol.* 3, ser. 40, 1–11

Rodwell, W.J. and Rodwell, K. (1986) *Rivenhall: Investigations on the Roman villa, church and village, 1950–1977*, Counc. Brit. Archaeol. Res. Rep. 55, Oxford

Ryan, J. (1931) *Irish Monasticism: Origins and Early Development*, Dublin

Thomas, C. (1971) *The Early Christian Archaeology of North Britain*, Oxford

Thomas, C.A. (1976) 'Imported late Roman Mediterranean pottery in Ireland and western Britain', *Proc. Roy. Ir. Acad.* 76C, 245–55

Wakeman, W.F. (1893) *A Survey of the Antiquarian Remains on the Island of Inismurray*, Dublin

Waldeier Bizzarro, T. (1992) *Romanesque Architectural Criticism: A Prehistory*, Cambridge

13. Ireland's Earliest 'Celtic' High Crosses: The Ossory and Related Crosses

ETIENNE RYNNE

Conservatism and simplicity sometimes go hand-in-hand, and I am often accused, not only by my wife and family but also by some of my friends and colleagues, of being innately conservative and basically rather simple. I am occasionally inclined to agree with both assessments, feeling sometimes that I am an old-fashioned dinosaur doing his damnedest to survive amongst all these young tigers airing new and oft-times exciting opinions and theories, even if they are sometimes little more than variations on a well-worn theme. But one should beware of throwing out the baby with the bathwater, as Alexander Pope so wisely stated almost three centuries ago in *An Essay on Criticism*: 'Be not the first by whom the New are try'd, / Nor yet the last to lay the Old aside.' With that approach in mind, readers should be warned that what follows will offer little which might be deemed radically new or revolutionary; rather it should be looked on as an outline summary of a line of thought which seems tenable, reasonable, and basically acceptable.

In order to identify Ireland's earliest 'Celtic' High Crosses one must start by listing the prima facie premises which one accepts. Firstly one should explain what one means by 'Celtic' and by which salient features one identifies an early date. Then one must apply these features to a coherent group of crosses, recognising their relationship one with the other and tracing their development from the first to the last of the group.

High Crosses cannot be Celtic in the true sense of the term, even those in Ireland. Although the term can probably legitimately be extended into the Christian period in non-Romanised, non-Germanicised Ireland, it is perhaps preferable to write it in inverted commas at that stage or to use the term Irish. However, for well over a century the characteristic ringed crosses of Early Medieval Ireland have been termed 'Celtic', and they are universally recognisable as such. Although the origin of the 'Celtic' cross has been much disputed, for the present writer it would appear that the theory suggested by Ó Ríordáin is the most reasonable and acceptable. He argued that the stone 'Celtic' crosses are skeuomorphs of wooden prototypes (1947, 110), a theory which a priori makes admirable sense: just as the first churches were wooden oratories, so the first High Crosses would have been of wood.

Accepting that wooden High Crosses were the prototypes for later stone examples, one should next ask oneself what they may have looked like. Assuming that the cross-form, *per se*, was what was primarily important and significant and not any decoration it might have, one must visualise a tall cross, prominent and plainly visible to all, indicating the Christian nature of the place where it was sited. But tall wooden crosses present difficulties of construction and of survival in the

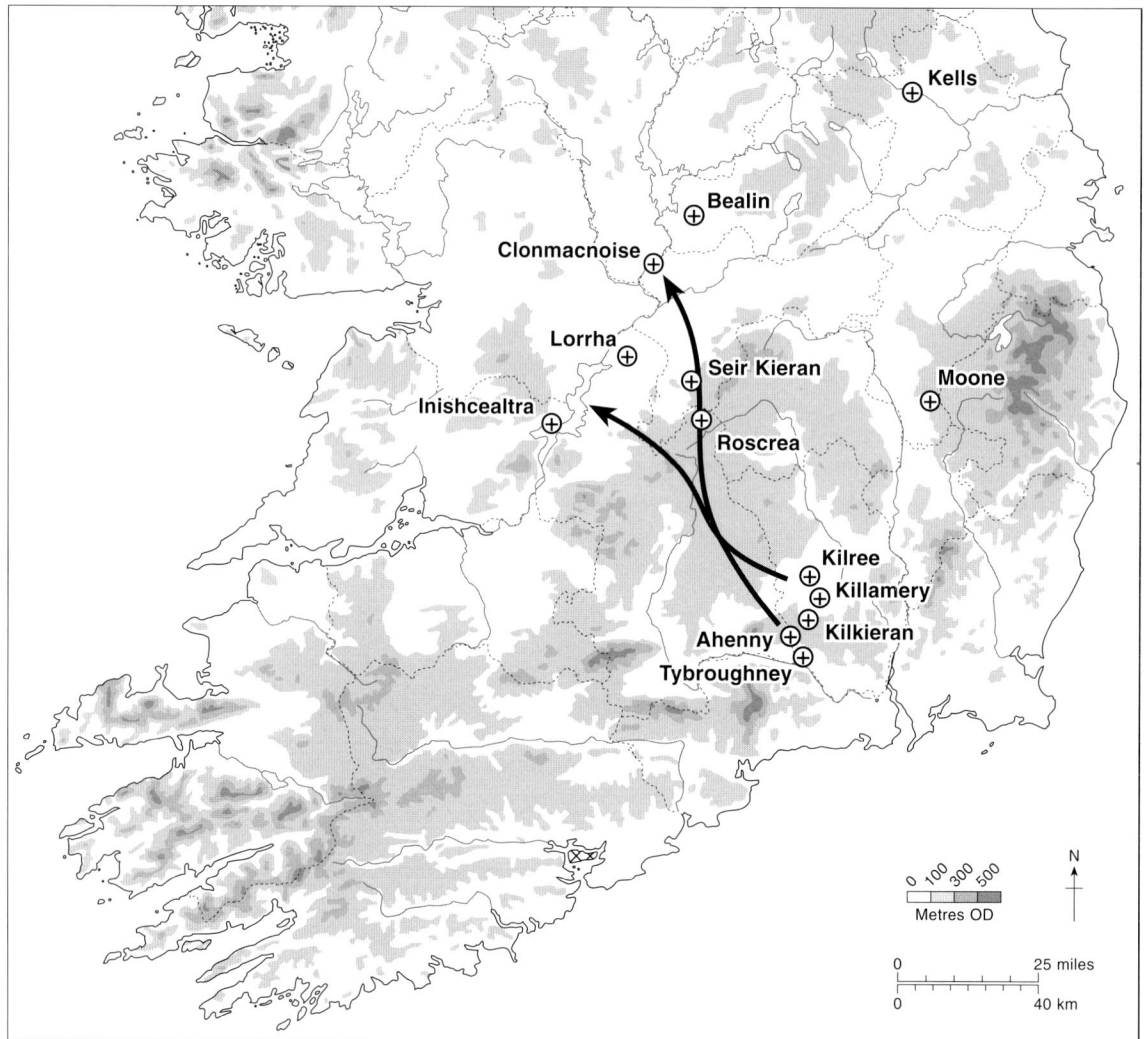

Fig. 13.1   Ireland's earliest High Crosses (from Ahenny to Clonmacnoise)

Irish climate: the best mortice-and-tenon carpentry would not secure the arms and shaft in a steady position for long, and the rain would seep down through the vertical upright above the arms and distort and split it. The problem of securing the arms and upright top extension would readily be solved by placing struts to steady and/or support them, but, as Ó Ríordáin pointed out, for efficiency and for aesthetic reasons these would be curved, making up four segments of a circle. All these pieces of timber, probably seven in total, would need to be carefully dowelled together. The dowels would show and perhaps be artistically unpleasing, and therefore their visible ends would be knobbed or perhaps covered by a wooden boss to disguise them. The topmost member of the cross would be capped so as to throw off the rain.

So much for the basic form of the wooden 'Celtic' cross. The next step probably quickly followed and the crosses would have been decorated with carved ornament. But ornament at this time was primarily applied to metalwork, and we have reason to believe that metal-covered altar and processional wooden 'Celtic' crosses existed. It therefore should not be surprising that the High Crosses might be decorated similarly to these smaller crosses.

If the above evolution of the 'Celtic' High Cross is accepted as reasonable, then the earliest stone-carved examples should most closely resemble those wooden models. Such crosses should be expected to have bosses at the junctions of the shaft and transom and of the ring with the resultant cross, and should be decorated in metalworking style, i.e., superficially covered with abstract decorative motifs (representative art was not in vogue among the Irish of the time) rather than carved in true sculptural style.

There are three main classes of stone-carved Irish High Crosses: (i) those covered with abstract ornament; (ii) those covered mainly with panels of scriptural scenes, including one of the crucifixion; (iii) those which are true crucifixions, i.e., with large high relief figures of Christ suspended on the cross. The generally accepted chronology, based on sound artistic and morphological grounds, is that these three classes follow one another in that order, the first two being of pre-Viking type and the third following, after a break of about two centuries, in post-Viking times (see Cronin, ch. 14).

The first and acceptably the earliest class differs from the others in more ways than one in that its decoration is pretty well confined to abstract ornament, mostly interlace, though scrollwork is also prevalent, not counting the cross-bases which can have figurative art (ranging from a row of small horses to larger not strictly iconographical scenes). These earlier crosses have bosses of varying degrees of rotundity at the junctions of the cross and its ring; they also generally have high mouldings around their edges which are often reminiscent of binding-strips such as would be found on a metal-covered wooden cross. The earlier examples of the class (see below) tend to have a squatter, heavier, less elegant appearance and a very different type of capping compared with all other High Crosses.

Taking all the features and characteristics briefly outlined above, the earliest class of Irish High Crosses can be said to originate with the Ossory Group, as defined by Roe (1958, 7–10), with later extensions up through north Tipperary and east Clare, terminating with the South Cross at Clonmacnoise (see Fig. 13.1). These High Crosses all have features which link them together, some perhaps less obviously than others, though convincingly enough to form what seems to be a reasonably unified grouping.

There are two main lines of development apparent which lead, in three stages, from the earliest High Crosses to the second group comprising those generally termed the Scripture Crosses. One concerns the type of decoration involved, the other the presence of the crucifixion scene and its position on the cross. In both cases only the first two stages concern the first class of crosses; with the third stage one is dealing with the Scripture Crosses. These two lines of development can be listed as follows:

1. All abstract decoration	1. Crucifixion absent
2. Abstract decoration with minimal iconography/figurative art	2. Crucifixion on shaft
3. Iconography with less abstract decoration	3. Crucifixion at centre of cross-head

Without arguing each case individually, on artistic, morphological and distributional grounds and using the two lines of development outlined above, one might propose a rough chronological order for the crosses (and pillars, shafts and bases, where only such survive) as follows: Ahenny Crosses; Kilkieran Crosses; Kilree Cross; Killamery Cross; Tybroughney 'Pillar'; Roscrea Pillar; Lorrha Crosses; Iniscealtra Cross; Seir Kieran cross-base and Clonmacnoise South Cross, Co. Offaly. One might possibly include with this group, though somewhat tenuously, some of the

Fig. 13.2 Ahenny South Cross, East Face

other cross-fragments from Clonmacnoise, the Banagher cross-shaft, and the Bealin Cross, though these might preferably be regarded as a sub-group.

The chronological range generally suggested for the above list is about a century. Though some would prefer a much shorter range, a slightly longer period would seem more reasonable, say from the last quarter of the seventh century to the first quarter of the ninth century, or from *c.* 680 to *c.* 820. Perhaps the best way to justify these dates and the proposed order of development, without quibbling about the correct order of the middle monuments of the series, would be to discuss the first and the last in the list, namely the Ahenny Crosses and the South Cross at Clonmacnoise.

The two Ahenny Crosses (Figs. 13.2–13.5) are so obviously closely related that they can be discussed as a unit. Both crosses bear plenty of highly developed scrollwork of 'trumpet-pattern' or 'Ultimate La Tène' style. Such scrollwork is best exemplified in metalwork (hanging-bowl escutcheons, hand-pins, the silver medallions on the Moylough Belt-Shrine, the back of the Tara Brooch), woodwork (the Brough of Birsay box), manuscript illumination (the 'Page of Spirals' in the Book of Durrow and in the Book of Lindisfarne), and stone sculpture (Slab no. 2, Carrowntemple, Co. Sligo), and is of a type which can most readily be dated to between about 550 and 750, though such dates are not, of course, absolute, even as the outside limits for the style.

Both Ahenny Crosses bear much interlaced decoration, mostly of a fairly simple, closely woven, two-strand type. Such interlace is not, in itself, easily datable. It seems to occur most frequently at an early stage in the general progression of interlace, though not as early as the bordered broad-ribbon types. It appears to be fairly shortlived during these earlier phases, beginning towards the close of the seventh century and, for all practical purposes, disappearing from use after about a century and a quarter, before reappearing a few centuries later. It is found, for instance, on metalwork such as the Athlone (Rinnagan, Co. Roscommon) Plaque and on the back of the Hunterston Brooch, and also in stone sculpture, such as on various Scottish wheeled crosses and Pictish slabs (for example, those at Glamis, St Andrews, Invergowrie, Govan and Whithorn), for all of which a late seventh-century date has often been proposed, though generally one plumps for the safer dating of *c.* 700. Such interlace gives the appearance of being that of beginner's work, insofar as it seems so plain and uninspired as to be little more than 'matting' to cover an area with no attempt at intricacies. Such simplicity and absence of any real development would seem to indicate that interlace had only relatively recently entered the Irish artistic repertoire, which is not surprising as it is generally accepted that a date of *c.* 630–50 is likely for its introduction. There is, however, one minor development to be found in the interlace on the South Cross at Ahenny. This is the manner in which the interlace on the cross-head diverges at its bottom to expand into two animal heads. These heads have curled-up snouts and lower jaws, and recall those found on the back of the Killamery Brooch and to some extent on some of the ring-brooches from the Ninian's Isle hoard. Such parallels suggest a somewhat later date than that proposed for most of the above-mentioned evidence for the double-strand interlace and the scrollwork, but earlier possibilities such as the zoomorphic heads on some of pre-Tara penannular brooches and on the Moylough Belt-Shrine might be invoked, albeit not so convincingly.

On the shaft of the North Cross at Ahenny are some square panels of ornament which are relevant to the dating of the monument. Two of them, in particular, are important in this regard: the panel containing four intertwined human figures on the west face and that on the east face, which is filled with nine squares each consisting of four sunken L-shaped corners framing four small rectangular areas. The former is a version of a well-known design which is found on eighth- and ninth-century metalwork and stone carving,

Fig. 13.3   Ahenny South Cross, West Face

'Celtic' High Crosses 131

Fig. 13.4   Ahenny North Cross, East Face

Fig. 13.5   Ahenny North Cross, West Face

and even in the Book of Kells. However, it has an earlier ancestry, and a related three-person version is to be seen on the seventh- or perhaps early eighth-century disc-brooch from Togherstown, Co. Westmeath (an item which is typologically closely related to Anglo-Saxon saucer-brooches). The L-shaped and rectangular sunken areas on the second panel are clearly versions in stone of the L-shaped, T-shaped and rectangular settings for enamel which are typically found on late seventh- and eighth-century Irish metalwork (the Moylough Belt-Shrine and the Lough Gara belt-buckle for example).

Comment is necessary on the mouldings bordering the corner angles of the crosses. These are not plain, but are striated transversely at right-angles, slantwise or criss-cross, changing from one direction to the other every so often. As is universally agreed, these early crosses appear to be skeuomorphs of metal-covered wooden crosses, probably of much smaller processional or altar crosses. These striated mouldings can be viewed as skeuomorphs of metal binding-strips, and their similarity to the binding-strips of the escutcheons on the Sutton Hoo hanging-bowls, for which a date in the early seventh century is accepted, is striking. These are now generally believed to have been made at or near Ballinderry crannog (no. 2), Co. Offaly, where a fragment of a like binding-strip of apparently similar metal was found. A short fragment from a much larger object (perhaps the ring of an altar cross) was found in Lough Kinale, Co. Longford, where a beautiful eighth-century or maybe late seventh-century book-shrine was discovered in 1986. Two long fragments of a similarly decorated bronze mount, found during drainage of the River Shannon near Athlone, Co. Westmeath, in the middle of the last century, have been dated to the sixth or seventh century. Also to be considered is the well-known penannular zoomorphic brooch from Ballinderry crannog (no. 2), the ring/hoop of which bears closely related striated decoration; it has over the years been assigned various dates, but one in the early seventh-century seems most acceptable. These objects, decorated with such a characteristic design, surely suggest that the most likely metal prototypes for the Ahenny mouldings date to the seventh century.

One hesitates to use the peculiar beehive-shaped capstones of the Ahenny and Kilkieran Crosses to suggest an early date for these monuments, but as they are often regarded as skeuomorphs of the early monastic beehive cells, such as those found on Sceilig Mhichíl, Co. Kerry, and elsewhere (just as the later High Crosses are capped with house- or church-shaped capstones), such an argument might be permissible. Another suggestion, but one which is not really admissible, is Kingsley Porter's (1931, 22) that they might represent an early form of mitre. Finally, while the bosses at the junctions of the rings and crosses proper and at the centre of the cross-heads have been mentioned as deriving from wooden or metal-mounted wooden prototypes which makes them early features, it is perhaps worth pointing out that their prominence and openwork details recall those on some Pictish slabs of relatively early date. Therefore, there are several strong arguments for suggesting a date during the late seventh or early eighth century for the Ahenny Crosses and for the beginning of this series of Ireland's High Crosses.

But when and where does the series end? As suggested above and as indicated in Fig. 13.1, the writer believes that it ends with the South Cross at Clonmacnoise, Co. Offaly (Figs 13.6 and 13.7), sometime shortly before AD 820. There is nothing new in this idea, but recently there seems to be a tendency to remove the South Cross from the series and include it with the Midland Scripture Crosses, consequently assigning it a considerably later date. It has several characteristic features of the series of early High Crosses, such as bosses at the centre of the cross-head and at the junctions of the cross and ring, and the row of small horses high on the base (which parallel those on the base of the West Cross at Lorrha and, to some extent, on the bases of the West Cross at Kilkieran and of the South Cross at Ahenny). The panelling on the base of the South Cross at Clonmacnoise also recalls that

134　*Early Medieval Munster*

Fig. 13.6　Clonmacnoise South Cross, East Face

'Celtic' High Crosses 135

Fig. 13.7   Clonmacnoise South Cross, West Face

on the same Kilkieran High Cross, while the virtually complete covering of the Clonmacnoise South Cross with abstract decoration and the outlining of the cross with herring-bone decorated roll-mouldings likewise indicate a link with the earlier crosses, as does the longitudinal bisecting of the outer faces of the ring. The major difference is the large depiction of a crucifixion scene on the west face of the cross-shaft, the inhabited vine-scroll at the bottom of its east face, and the framing of panels of ornament on the shaft (but not on the head) of the cross. It is these new features which put the South Cross at Clonmacnoise at the end of the series of earlier crosses and which, if their introduction can be explained, might suggest a date for the cross.

It is generally accepted that there is a relationship between the South Cross at Clonmacnoise and the Cross of Patrick and Columba at Kells. Both bear a panel of the inhabited vine-scroll, rare in Ireland, and both have closely related crucifixion scenes on the west face of their cross-shafts. In addition, both show ornament related to the Scottish boss-style. The inhabited vine-scroll is primarily a Northumbrian motif, and its appearance in Ireland is generally thought to have occurred somewhat later – on Muiredach's Cross, Monasterboice, yes – but need it always be much later? The relationship of these crosses with the Scottish boss-style can be readily explained when one realises that the monastery at Kells was founded, or re-founded, in the early ninth century by monks fleeing from Iona.

As stated above, the present writer believes in what Stalley has described as 'a Darwinian insistence that things must evolve in an orderly sequence' (1994, 262), and that, therefore, the placing of the crucifixion on the shaft of a High Cross is an early feature. If the cross itself was the primary feature and its decoration secondary, it seems logical that when a crucifixion scene was to be applied it would be placed at eye-level. Only subsequently, when scriptural scenes became much more important, would such a scene be moved up to a more appropriate place at the centre of the cross-head.

But which cross influenced the other? Clearly the one most closely related to the earlier group but bearing new features must have acquired those features from elsewhere; therefore the South Cross was influenced by the Cross of Patrick and Columba. But is the latter cross early enough to have overlapped with the culmination of the earlier series? It is undoubtedly so if one accepts that it is 'not later than the second half of the 8th century', as stated by Helen Roe (1959, 11). However, this date would seem to be too early and few would accept it nowadays, even as a possibility. Others have suggested much later dates, too late to have influenced the South Cross at Clonmacnoise. Harbison, for instance, suggests that it was carved 'a number of decades' after the Columban *paruchia* of Iona had expanded to Kells (1994, 73), thus apparently indicating a date about the middle of the ninth century for it, while Stalley (1994, 263), hints at a date about two decades after 900. While accepting a date in the eighth century for the South Cross at Clonmacnoise and a date 'very close to the first decade of the ninth century' for the Cross of Patrick and Columba, Kelly (1990) has suggested that the crucifixions on their shafts owe much to metal crucifixion plaques. But, apart from the only early one, that from Rinnagan, Co. Roscommon (already mentioned above), these plaques are all apparently of early twelfth-century date, and it is these later examples which most closely resemble the crucifixions on the crosses.

The Irish monks at Iona suffered the first Viking raid on their island monastery in 795, and within the following decade suffered even more severely when further raids took place. As a consequence they were given Cenannus (Kells) in 803 and are credited with founding or refounding a Columban monastery there between 804 and 807, the buildings of which were completed in 814. The move to Kells was finalised later when the monks travelled to Ireland in 831 and 849 with the reliquaries of St Columcille. The Cross of Patrick and Columba is generally associated with these events, being considered to mark the founding or refounding of the monastery at Kells, and it is perhaps most acceptably dated to within the first couple of decades of the ninth century. This date would allow for monks from Clonmacnoise to see and appreciate it and to borrow ideas from it.

But how much later than the Cross of Patrick and Columba is the South Cross at Clonmacnoise? Probably not much, though Harbison (1994, 42) has recently suggested that the newly revealed fragmentary inscription on the bottom of the west face of its shaft might indicate 'that the cross was erected by the king Maelsechnaill, who reigned from 846 to 862'. This was Maelsechnaill Mac Maelruanaid and it is true that if the reading proposed by Ó Murchadha and Ó Murchú (1988, 62–63) is acceptable, and they were very tentative about it, one might complete the relevant part to read *Maelruanaid*. But the reading, despite the methods used to reveal it, remains very doubtful: it is so abraded that it is virtually invisible to the naked eye. One might usefully quote Harbison's comment (1992) on the much clearer inscriptions on the nearby Cross of the Scriptures at Clonmacnoise as a warning against accepting any reading of the inscription on the South Cross. He states: 'But despite the efforts of Ó Murchadha . . . it must be admitted that the inscriptions on both faces of this cross are so tantalisingly incomplete to the naked eye today that it would be unwise to place too much reliance on them as the basis for dating' (1992, 368).

It should be pointed out that, as Edwards has suggested, there may well have been 'some kind of special relationship between the *paruchiae* of St Columba and St Ciarán' (1986, 31) due to St Columba's visit to Clonmacnoise some time between 586 and his death in 597. Such a relationship could account for a visit to the new monastery at Kells by a monk from Clonmacnoise, or vice versa. And, as Edwards also points out, the first Viking raid on Clonmacnoise was in 834, followed by others during the 840s, events which 'might have tended to preclude major artistic projects and it seems likely that Clonmacnoise South would have been completed before these began' (ibid, 31). It therefore seems most probable that the South Cross at Clonmacnoise was erected in or about AD 820. This date, consequently, marks the end of the series of Ireland's earliest 'Celtic' High Crosses.

BIBLIOGRAPHY

Edwards, N. (1986) 'The South Cross, Clonmacnoise', in J. Higgitt (ed.), *Early Medieval Sculpture in Britain and Ireland*, BAR British Series, 152, 23–47

Harbison, P. (1992) *The High Crosses of Ireland, an Iconographical and Photographic Survey*, 3 vols., Bonn

Harbison, P. (1994) *High Crosses with the Figure Sculptures Explained*, Drogheda

Kelly, D. (1990) 'Cruciform plaques', *The G.P.A. Irish Arts Review, Yearbook 1990–1991*, 204–09

Kingsley Porter, A. (1931) *The Crosses and Culture of Ireland*, New Haven

Ó Murchadha, D. and Ó Murchú, G. (1988) 'Fragmentary inscriptions from the West Cross at Durrow, the South Cross at Clonmacnois, and the Cross of Kinnitty', *J. Roy. Soc. Antiq. Ir.* 119, 53–66

Ó Riordain, S.P. (1947) 'The genesis of the Celtic cross', in S. Pender (ed.) *Féilscríbhinn Torna*, Cork, 108–14

Roe, H.M. (1958) *The High Crosses of Western Ossory*, Kilkenny

Roe, H.M. (1959) *The High Crosses of Kells*, Kells

Stalley, R. (1991) *Irish High Crosses*, Dublin

Stalley, R. (1994) 'Scribe and mason: the Book of Kells and the Irish High Crosses', in F. O'Mahony (ed.), *The Book of Kells: Proceedings of a Conference at Trinity College Dublin, 6–9 September 1992*, Dublin, 257–65

14. Late High Crosses in Munster: Tradition and Novelty in Twelfth-Century Irish Art

RHODA CRONIN

Introduction

The twelfth century witnessed a remarkable renaissance in Irish ecclesiastical art which manifested itself not only in a revival of the erection of High Crosses but also in the production of high quality metalwork, the writing and illumination of manuscripts and the advent of architectural sculpture (Henry 1970). This artistic resurgence had many impetuses, not least among these being the vigorous Church reforms and the growth of patronage among provincial kings eager to demonstrate their wealth and influence.

The twelfth century was also a period when novel artistic styles and techniques were influencing the repertoire of native craftsmen. Particularly distinctive in this respect was the adoption, and indeed adaptation, of late Scandinavian zoomorphic ornament – namely, Ringerike and, more especially, Urnes. Romanesque architecture, whose first appearance in Ireland is generally associated with the building of Cormac's Chapel, Cashel, between 1127 and 1134 (de Paor 1967), also left its mark in other media. In terms of freestanding stone sculpture, likely borrowings from architectural ornament include the use of plant-derived motifs and the development of high relief carving, although the link between the latter and architectural carving as manifested in Ireland is not particularly overt.

In general accounts of twelfth-century High Crosses in Ireland much emphasis is placed on these novel and distinctive developments. It is also frequently noted that scriptural scenes become relatively rare while prominent representations of Christ Crucified, or Christ Triumphant, come to dominate the compositions of some of the most striking crosses of the period. Obvious examples of these include St Patrick's Cross at Cashel and the cross at Dysert O'Dea. It is also often pointed out that on a number of crosses a second prominent figure, that of a high-ranking ecclesiastic, occurs. This figure is variously identified as a local saint, 'Christ as Abbot of the World', or, perhaps, more appropriately in the climate of Church reform, as a bishop or the Pope. Some caution should be exercised, however, in accepting such iconography, decorative style and techniques as being characteristics of twelfth-century High Crosses, as is discussed below.

Henry claims that the remains of only about twenty crosses survive from the late eleventh- to early twelfth-century period (1970, 125). This is a conservative estimate: there are strong arguments, for example, for ascribing a group of crosses in south County Dublin and north County Wicklow to the period (O'Brien 1988, 412–24; Ó hEalaidhe 1958, 109–10) and these, coupled with some new discoveries, would bring

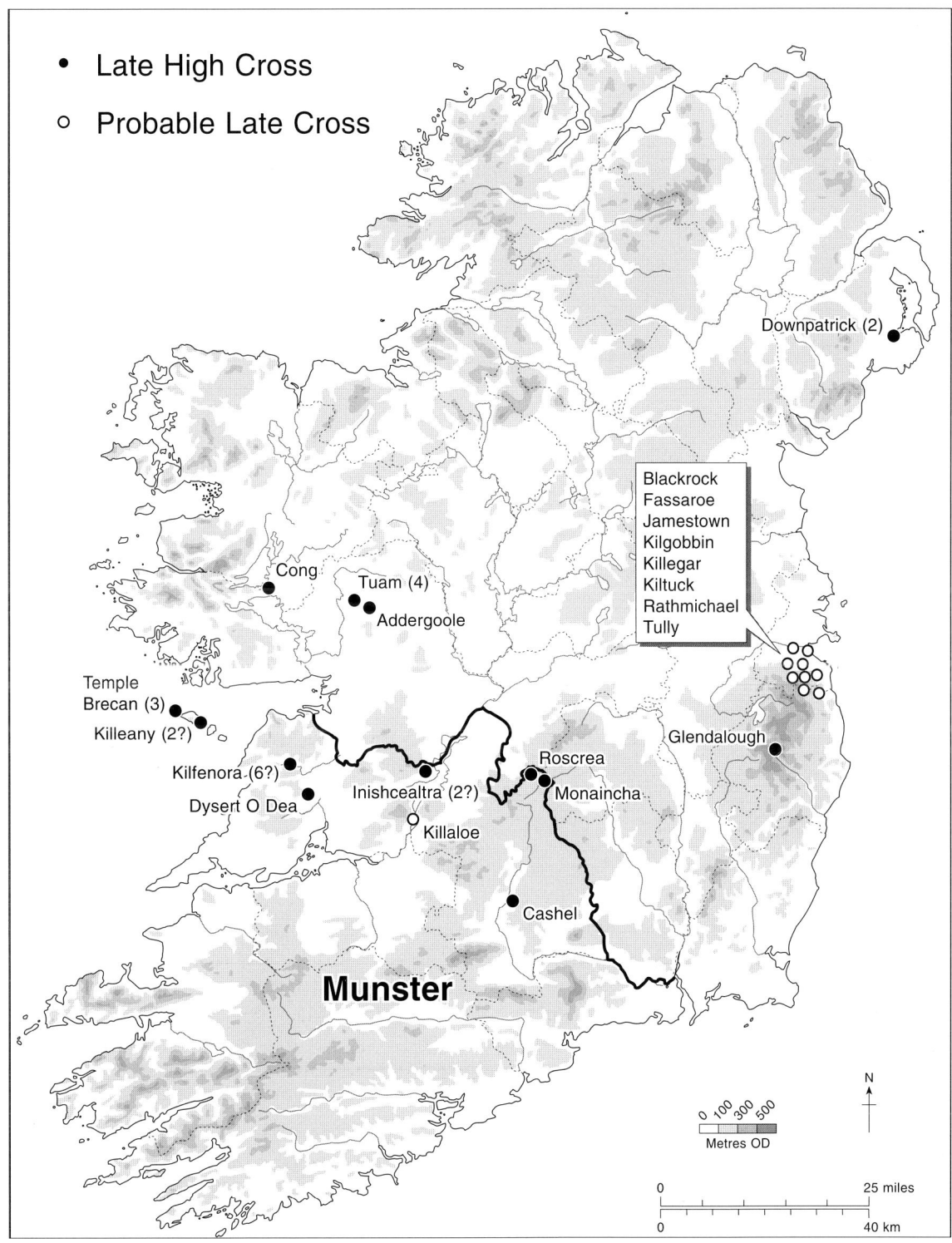

Fig. 14.1 Distribution of late High Crosses in Ireland

the figure to nearly forty. (Fig. 14.1). However, even this is by no means an exhaustive figure as many relatively plain crosses without obvious diagnostic features may well belong to the period also.

In North Munster there is a distinct though somewhat diffuse group of crosses which embraces the more novel elements of twelfth-century art: high relief carving; the distinctive iconography of a Crucified Christ and ecclesiastic; Romanesque-style plant ornament and Urnes-derived animal ornament. The crosses at Dysert O'Dea, Co. Clare, and those at Roscrea, Mona Incha and Cashel, Co. Tipperary, all belong to this group. To these one could also, with reservations, add the 'Doorty' Cross at Kilfenora although, as we shall see, it sits rather uncomfortably in any category. It should be stressed at this point that despite their prominence in the literature such crosses as those listed above represent only about a third of the twelfth-century crosses in Munster. The picture on the ground is one of great variation, even among crosses broadly unified in terms of style or iconography. It could be suggested that there are in fact two broad groupings of crosses representing different artistic currents, one being quite progressive, the other leaning towards a continuation of long-established formulae. The latter is represented by the remains of five or six crosses from Kilfenora and one, or possibly two, from Inishcealtra, Co. Clare.

Group 1

The first identifiable group consists of the crosses at Cashel, Monaincha, Roscrea, Dysert O'Dea and, perhaps, the 'Doorty' cross at Kilfenora. These crosses clearly embrace the whole ambit of twelfth-century innovations. Each one bears a large figure of Christ clothed in a long robe, although the details of the robe vary. At Cashel, it is ankle-length and belted, the ends of the belt extending almost to the hem of the garment. At Dysert O'Dea and Monaincha, Christ is dressed in a robe with a pleated skirt. The form of dress on the Roscrea Christ is indistinct but it appears to be a long robe, possibly belted at the waist. Three out of the four, Monaincha being the exception, also bear the figure of a high-ranking ecclesiastic. Apart from these figures, other figures and figurative scenes do occur but they tend to occupy less prominent positions on the cross and to be smaller in scale. At Roscrea, for instance, a depiction of Adam and Eve occurs at the bottom of the cross's east face.

It is in this respect that the Doorty cross at Kilfenora differs quite radically from the others in this group. Its faces are almost exclusively occupied by large-scale figurative sculpture (Fig. 14.2): on the west face, Christ Crucified (or In Majesty?) and a horse and rider associated with an interlace of beasts; on the east face, two figures in bust being attacked by a large bird, a pair of hooded figures bearing croziers and, above, a high-ranking ecclesiastic. Conversely, non-figurative ornament, namely animal interlace and fretwork, is confined to the sides of the cross. While a detailed discussion of the iconography of the cross is not possible here, the author follows de Paor's suggestion that at least some of its scenes are apocalyptic (de Paor, 1956, 65; Cronin, forthcoming).

In addition to bearing accomplished zoomorphic ornament of Urnes derivation the Group 1 crosses display confident handling of the high relief technique. Despite these shared features, there is enough variation within the group to indicate that it more than likely represents the work of four individual sculptors – Roscrea and Monaincha being probably the work of one.

St Patrick's Cross at Cashel is particularly distinctive in terms of its form. It originally had a support, probably in the form of a slender cross, under each arm. In addition, there is a mortice hole on the top of the surviving arm and presumably one also existed on the other. Leask suggested that these may once have held small figures, perhaps angels (1951, 14–19). If this was indeed the case, one could tentatively suggest that a parallel for the arrangement is to be found in the Clonmacnoise crucifixion plaque which is

Late High Crosses 141

Fig. 14.2 The 'Doorty' cross at Kilfenora, Co. Clare

dated by Harbison to the late eleventh or early twelfth century (Harbison, 1980). It is interesting to note that the west face of the Dysert O'Dea cross, with its panels of stepped ornament and the raised lozenges on the head (Fig. 14.3), prompts comparison with metalwork, suggesting that it was perhaps based on a now lost metal prototype.

The Group 1 crosses are clearly the products of a Hiberno-Romanesque milieu, and a future study encompassing both the crosses and architectural sculpture may prove fruitful. It is the author's opinion that crosses and architectural embellishments were frequently the products of the same workshops, perhaps even of the same hands. For the moment, however, we must confine ourselves to some random observations in this regard. Even a cursory examination of the Dysert O'Dea cross and the portal of the nearby church reveals that there are strong stylistic ties between the two. A striking resemblance may be observed between the head of the ecclesiastic on the cross and a number of the heads forming the outer arch ring of the portal. Common characteristics include the elongated shape of the heads, the large almond-shaped eyes and the slightly protruding, down-turned mouths. Ornamental features such as the flat pellets outlining the east face of the cross head and the multi-petalled flowers on its west face are also to be found on the door portal. The animal ornaments on the cross and portal are closely related, with details such as head lappets and blunt snouts featuring in both.

Some admittedly less striking parallels may be drawn between other crosses in the group and their associated churches. In the case of the Cashel cross, the animal head on which the figure on the west face stands is paralleled among the animal head corbels in the chancel and on the south wall of Cormac's Chapel. Roscrea and Monaincha share similar ornament and have a similar cross head form. The tall pillar-like figure above the portal of St Cronan's, Roscrea, although extremely weathered, can be likened in form and proportion, if not in detail, with the figures occurring on the adjacent cross.

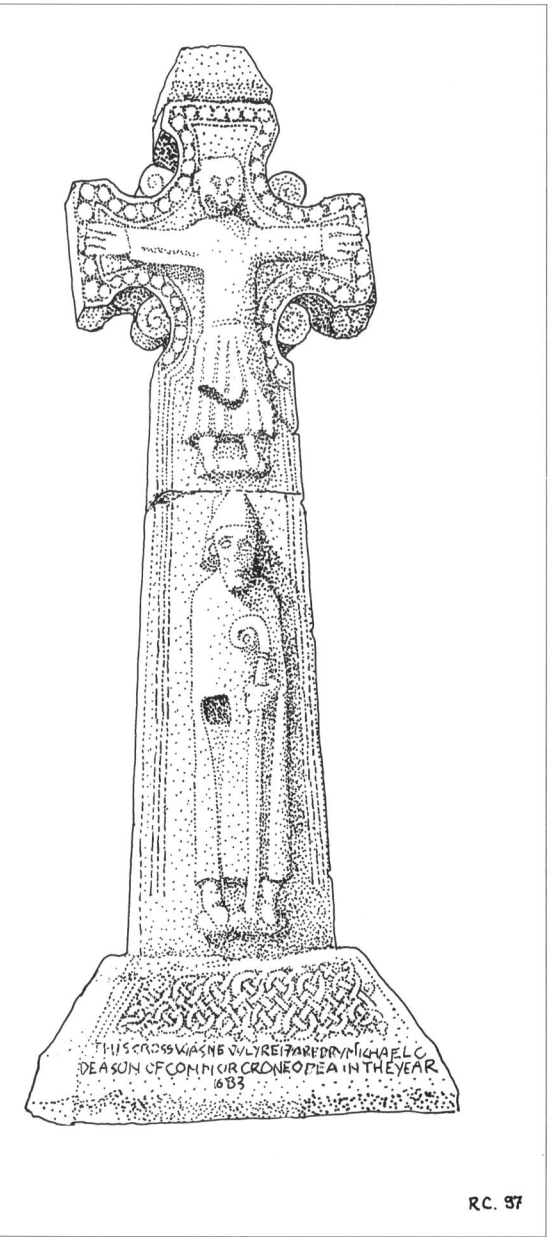

Fig. 14.3   The Dysert O'Dea cross, east face (after Westropp)

Group 2

This group consists of three complete crosses and the fragments of two or perhaps three from Kilfenora and one or perhaps two from Inishcealtra. These crosses are far less overtly twelfth century in style and, in the case of the Kilfenora examples, this has led to some debate as to their date. The problem is that they bear a high proportion of insular ornament, and a rather limited repertoire of such ornament at that. Cathasach's Cross at Inishcealtra is one of only three late crosses which bear a datable inscription (the other two are at Tuam and indicate a date of between 1126 and 1152). The Inishcealtra cross bears an inscription suggesting a late eleventh- or early twelfth-century date. It bears purely insular ornament and, if it were not for the inscription, it and its companion, the West Cross, would undoubtedly be considered to belong to an earlier period. If we accept that the Romanesque was introduced with the building of Cormac's Chapel, these crosses were certainly the products of a pre-Romanesque milieu. Therefore, it is no surprise that they do not display features such as high-relief carving or large format figure sculpture. It would have been convenient if an example of late Scandinavian-derived animal ornament had been included among the decorative motifs, but the sculptor did not oblige. The inscription is almost wasted as it does little to further our knowledge regarding the adoption of twelfth-century innovations. It is, however, of some value since it alerts us to the fact that there was a pre-Romanesque tradition of cross carving in at least this part of Munster in the late eleventh or early twelfth century. (Indeed the Rune-bearing cross fragment in Killaloe Cathedral, Co. Clare, may also belong to this period.) As well, it should serve as a warning about putting too much faith in stylistic criteria for the dating of such monuments. It raises the question as to whether there might be other twelfth-century crosses lurking incognito in the corpus of Irish High Crosses.

The Kilfenora crosses (excluding the 'Doorty' Cross) share a limited repertoire of knotwork, plaitwork and fretwork motifs (Fig. 14.4), suggesting that they are contemporary with each other and perhaps the work of a single sculptor or small group of sculptors. Unlike the Inishcealtra cross, they do not have the benefit of an inscription to aid in their dating. There are, however, several features which point to a twelfth-century date for them. De Paor pointed out that there were several areas of comparison between the Kilfenora crosses and those on Inishmore, Co. Galway, namely the three crosses at Templebrecan and two at Killeany (1956, 71). Having looked at the ornament in detail, the present author found that about 25 per cent of the geometric motifs on the Kilfenora crosses are directly paralleled on the Inishmore crosses and, significantly, that these are frequently the more complex examples (1991, 212–14). In addition, small details such as collared beasts and simple spiral-ended mouldings are to be found on crosses from both locations. There are undoubtedly marked differences between the two groups of crosses also: for example, depictions of a naked Christ occur on the North and West Crosses at Templebrecan but at Kilfenora he is clothed. Nevertheless, there are enough elements in common to sustain the argument that the groups are related and are probably roughly contemporary. This point is supported, to some extent, by the historical evidence which suggests that both areas were linked politically and ecclesiastically in the Early Medieval period (Sheehan 1982, 30; Westropp 1900, 113).

The Aran crosses are generally dated to the late eleventh or early twelfth century, largely on the basis of a panel of interlace on the shaft of the Killeany cross. This interlace has been likened to the Ringerike style current in Ireland during the eleventh century, though it must be said that if this is the case it is a very debased version of the style (Fuglesang 1980, 192). Nevertheless, this dating is supported by the iconography of the cross which includes a depiction of Christ in a long pleated robe and, on the reverse face, an ecclesiastic bearing a crozier. Interestingly, the Kilfenora crosses also share several motifs with the cross shaft housed in Tuam Cathedral (Cronin 1991, 214). This fragment bears an inscription which allows it to be dated to between 1126 and 1152 (Henry 1970, 124).

The figure of Christ on the West Cross at

144 *Early Medieval Munster*

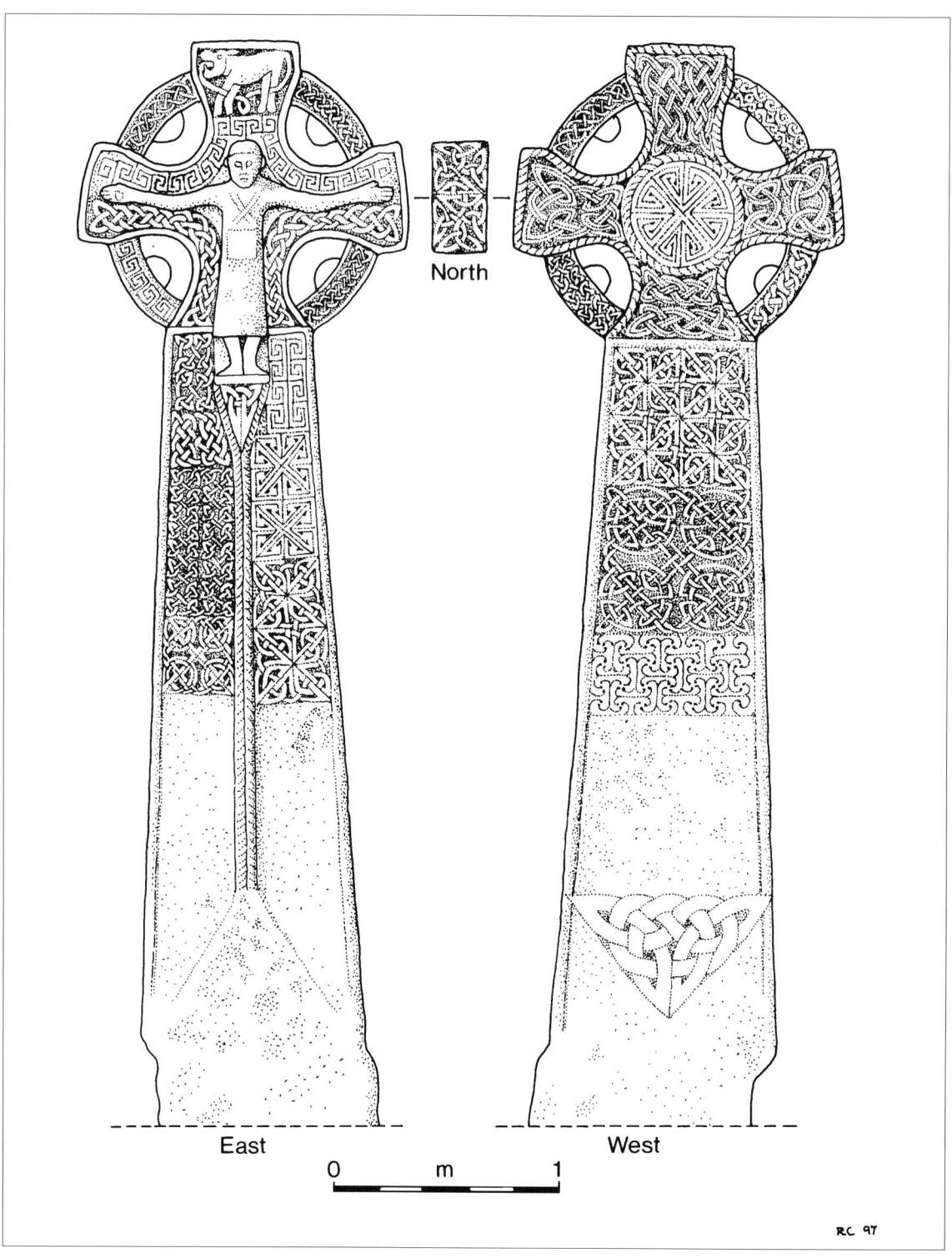

Fig. 14.4   The West cross at Kilfenora

Kilfenora is depicted with a square panel, perhaps a book satchel or reliquary, suspended on crossed straps from his neck. This is quite a distinctive feature: the closest parallel for it is to be found on the lower knop of the Lismore crozier which is dated to the period between 1090 and 1120. It is interesting to note that the Christ on the Cashel cross also seems to have a rectilinear object on his chest and the feature occurs as well on a presumably late cross at Downpatrick, which, with its companion, is strikingly similar to the Kilfenora cross now kept in Killaloe Cathedral.

Conclusions

At this stage it is pertinent to address the question as to what extent the distribution of late High Crosses reflects the Early Medieval political unit of Munster. It appears on the basis of this evidence that rather than Munster emerging as a unit, North Munster emerges as a discrete cultural entity. From a cursory glance at the distribution of late crosses it is immediately obvious that the counties of Cork, Kerry, Waterford and Limerick are devoid of crosses of an obviously twelfth-century date. Indeed, this is an area in which High Crosses of any date are poorly represented, although not entirely absent. There are a number of rather plain and eminently undatable crosses in the area, particularly in west Kerry, where examples include Kilmalkedar and Killiney, and Tonaknock in north Kerry. In addition, the Annals of Inisfallen record that in 1282 the 'holy cross' at Aghadoe was broken by a violent wind (MacAirt 1951, 381): is it safe to assume that this cross was erected to commemorate the twelfth-century establishment of the diocese of Aghadoe? We could attempt to explain the dearth of late crosses in south Munster in terms of uneven survival rates or by suggesting that crosses here were executed in a perishable medium such as timber. However, if the first hypothesis were true we might at least expect the survival of a few diagnostic fragments, and if the latter were true it would still suggest a north-south difference.

The reasons for the largely North Munster distribution of late High Crosses are probably many and complex. One possible factor, a precondition really, is that North Munster, especially the part of it which was once part of the kingdom of Ossory, was an area where there was a strong earlier tradition of monumental cross carving, thus predisposing it to a renaissance in the art form. Secondly, there can be little doubt that much of the impetus for Church reform emanated from North Munster. At the reforming synod held in Cashel in 1101, Muirchertach Ua Briain, who was at this time the undisputed king of all Munster, transferred ownership of the royal site of Cashel to the Church. A decade later the synod of Rathbreasil – for which there are strong arguments in favour of it too being in Tipperary – was held, at which the diocesan decisions taken had a permanent effect on the subsequent history of the Irish Church (Gwynn 1992, 155–92). Such political and ecclesiastical activity is reflective of a dynamic ethos in the Church in North Munster, one which drew support, both moral and material, from its ruling dynasties. The period between the two synods of Rathbreasil and Kells was marked by intense artistic activity as ecclesiastical centres vied to improve or reinforce their status. Roscrea, for example, failed to gain diocesan status in 1111 but sought to elevate its position consequently by investing in a fine Romanesque church, a shrine for the Book of Dimma, a Life of St Crónán and the erection of a High Cross (Ó Floinn 1987, 180). A similar flurry of activity could well explain the erection of the Kilfenora crosses, as has been suggested by Rynne for the 'Doorty' Cross (pers. comm.).

The connection between Church reform and the erection of High Crosses is further emphasised by the fact that within and indeed outside the study area there tends to be a correlation between the location of crosses and diocesan sees. Hence we find crosses at Kilfenora, Cashel, Roscrea, Glendalough, Tuam, Cong and Down. It is tempting to add Aghadoe to this list, although there is no way of being certain that the cross there was of twelfth-century date; however, given the building activity evidenced at the site in this period, it is a possibility.

Another point worthy of mention in relation to the distinctiveness of North Munster concerns Hiberno-Romanesque architecture. De Paor (1967) and more recently O'Keeffe (ch. 12) have identified Cashel as one of the sources of decorated Romanesque architecture in Ireland. It is not surprising, therefore, that a school of High Cross carving would develop in its environs, given that it drew quite heavily on the technical expertise and ornamental style of those engaged in the embellishment of church portals, chancel arches and windows.

ACKNOWLEDGEMENTS

I would like to thank my thesis supervisor, Mr John Sheehan, University College Cork and Professor Etienne Rynne, University College Galway, for their constructive criticism over the years.

BIBLIOGRAPHY

Cronin, R. (1991) 'A Study of the Early Medieval Crosses at Kilfenora, Co. Clare', unpublished MA thesis (NUI), University College, Cork

Cronin, R. (*forthcoming*) 'Apocalypse Now: the iconography of the "Doorty" cross at Kilfenora, Co. Clare', *N. Munster Antiq. J.*

De Paor, L. (1956) 'The limestone crosses of Clare and Aran', *J. Galway Archaeol. Hist. Soc.* 26, 53–71

De Paor, L. (1967) 'Cormac's Chapel: the beginnings of Irish Romanesque', in E. Rynne (ed.), *North Munster Studies: Essays in Commemoration of Mons. Michael Moloney*, 133–45, Limerick

Fuglesang, S.H. (1980) *Some Aspects of the Ringerike Style – A Phase of Eleventh Century Scandinavian Art*, Odense

Gwynn, A. (1992) *The Irish Church in the 11th and 12th Centuries*, Dublin

Harbison, P. (1980) 'A lost crucifixion plaque of Clonmacnoise type found in Co. Mayo', in H. Murtagh (ed.), *Irish Midland Studies: Essays in Commemoration of N.W. English*, 24–38, Athlone

Henry, F. (1970) *Irish Art in the Romanesque Period, 1070–1170 A.D.*, London

Leask, H.G. (1951) 'St. Patrick's Cross, Cashel, Co. Tipperary: an enquiry into its original form', *J. Roy. Soc. Antiq. Ir.* 81, 14–19

Mac Airt, S. (1951) *The Annals of Inisfallen*, Dublin

O'Brien, E. (1988) 'Churches of south-east County Dublin, seventh to twelfth century', in G. Mac Niocaill and P.F. Wallace (eds.), *Keimelia: Studies in Memory of Tom Delaney*, 504–24, Galway

Ó Floinn, R. (1987) 'Schools of metalworking in eleventh- and twelfth-century Ireland' in M. Ryan (ed.), *Ireland and Insular Art A.D. 500–1200*, Dublin, 179–87

Ó hEailidhe, P. (1958) 'Fassaroe and associated crosses', *J. Roy. Soc. Antiq. Ir.* 88, 101–10

Sheehan, J. (1982) 'The early historic church sites of north Clare', *N. Munster Antiq. J.* 24, 29–45

Westropp, T.J. (1900) 'The churches of county Clare, and the origins of the ecclesiastical divisions in that county', *Proc. Roy. Ir. Acad.* 6, 100–80

15. Viking Age Hoards from Munster
A Regional Tradition?

JOHN SHEEHAN

It has long been recognised that the nature of Scandinavian activity in Ireland during the Viking Age was distinctive. This was partly due to the fact that the political, social and economic conditions which the Vikings encountered in Ireland were quite different from those found elsewhere in the North Atlantic and the West. The foundation of towns – unknown, for instance, in Scandinavian Scotland – formed one such response to Irish conditions, while the establishment of a commercially orientated economy constituted another. Given that the principal medium of exchange throughout the Viking world was silver, it is not surprising that a large amount of this prized commodity has been found in Ireland. Indeed, the Viking Age hoards and single-finds of silver from Ireland represent an exceptional concentration of wealth unequalled in the West and the North Atlantic and only rarely surpassed elsewhere in the Viking world. Although only a few are of Munster provenance, this chapter aims to detail these particular hoards and to examine them in the light of what is known about Scandinavian activity and settlement in both Munster and Ireland during the period $c.$ 800 to $c.$ 1100.

Hoards in Ireland
The number of silver hoards of Scandinavian and Hiberno-Viking character on record from Ireland totals over 130 finds. These are composed of coins or a combination of ingots, ornaments and hack-silver (the cut-up fragments of ingots or ornaments), with or without coins. It was only in the late Anglo-Saxon economy of Viking Age England that silver circulated for commercial purposes solely in the form of coin. Elsewhere, as in Ireland, it still circulated by weight and was thus acceptable in alternative forms – such as the range of distinctive ornaments (mostly of armring type) that was produced in the Hiberno-Viking silver-working tradition during the century between $c.$ 850 and $c.$ 950. Thus Ireland's silver hoards, like those of the Scandinavian homelands, may be divided into three categories: coinless hoards, mixed hoards and coin hoards (Sheehan 1998a, 167–71).

Coinless hoards consist exclusively of non-numismatic material and range in composition from complete ornaments and/or ingots to hack-silver, while mixed hoards consist of non-numismatic material combined with coins. Fifty-two of the Irish silver hoards fall into the coinless category and there are a further sixteen mixed examples on record. With one late exception, all of the latter were deposited during the tenth century and most contain ingots or ingot fragments in addition to the coins. A small number, however, also contain ornaments of Hiberno-Viking type (or hack-silver derived from such ornaments) as do a large proportion of the coinless hoards. Ingots are generally neither regionally nor culturally diagnostic and if they are excluded from the coinless hoards it becomes apparent that Hiberno-Viking ornaments constitute the bulk of their diagnostic components. The remainder consists of a small amount of native Irish silver as well as imported objects from Scotland, Scandinavia and the Baltic region.

Hoards comprised exclusively of coins constitute the third category of Ireland's Viking Age silver hoards. Over sixty examples are on record, the vast majority of which were deposited after *c.* 940. The types of coins found in the tenth-century hoards are predominantly Anglo-Saxon, though Arabic issues, as well as those from the Viking Northumbrian and East Anglian rulers, are also represented, while Hiberno-Norse issues dominate the composition of the eleventh-century hoards.

Analysis of the chronology, structure and distribution of the Viking Age silver hoards allows a number of important general conclusions to be drawn (Sheehan 1998, 171–77). Firstly, the range of deposition dates of the coin hoards does not reflect the period during which the Scandinavians began to introduce silver into Ireland. The chronology of the coinless hoards and the existence of a vibrant Hiberno-Viking silver-working tradition indicate that by far the greatest amount of silver – in terms of its bullion weight – was in circulation during the period between *c.* 850 and *c.* 950. Clearly, as a result of Scandinavian activity, large quantities of silver had already been amassed in Ireland before the foundation of the Hiberno-Norse towns during the opening decades of the tenth century. This point serves to focus attention on the nature of earlier Scandinavian settlement and activity in Ireland, especially during the second half of the ninth century. In particular it raises questions about the precise roles and functions of the *longphuirt*, which are too often simply regarded as mere raiding bases.

The second general point concerns the distribution of Ireland's provenanced hoards (Sheehan 1998, Fig. 6.4), which reveals a number of interesting patterns. The coinless hoard distribution is spread fairly evenly throughout the northern and southern parts of the country, with a pronounced concentration in the central midlands, while the distributions of the coin and mixed hoards are focused on the midlands and the east coast. It may be concluded, on the basis that most of the hoards from Ireland were deposited in areas of the country that were not controlled or settled by the Scandinavians, and on other evidence, that a very considerable amount of silver wealth ended up in native Irish ownership during the Viking Age. The means and processes by which the Irish acquired this wealth are unclear, though given the nature and scale of the evidence it is clear that the traditional explanation – that these finds represent an outcome of Irish raids on Scandinavian settlements – is unsatisfactory. It is more likely that they evidence trade between the Scandinavians and the Irish, as well as processes of tribute and mutual gift-exchange.

Finally, as the Viking Age in Ireland progresses, the changing structure of its hoards indicates a steady transformation from the late ninth- and early tenth-century bullion economy, with its coinless hoards, to one in which imported coins began to be conserved and retained – presumably for commercial purposes (Sheehan, forthcoming). This transition is represented by the mixed hoards, with their coins, ingots and hack-silver, and it is tempting to associate it with the foundation of the Scandinavian towns during the opening decades of the tenth century. From the mid-point of this century onwards, however, the coinless and mixed hoards decline markedly in significance while the coin hoards rise to the fore. By the beginning of the eleventh century the transformation from a bullion economy is completed, following the establishment of the Hiberno-Norse mint in Dublin in *c.* 997.

Hoards in Munster

Only twenty out of Ireland's minimum number

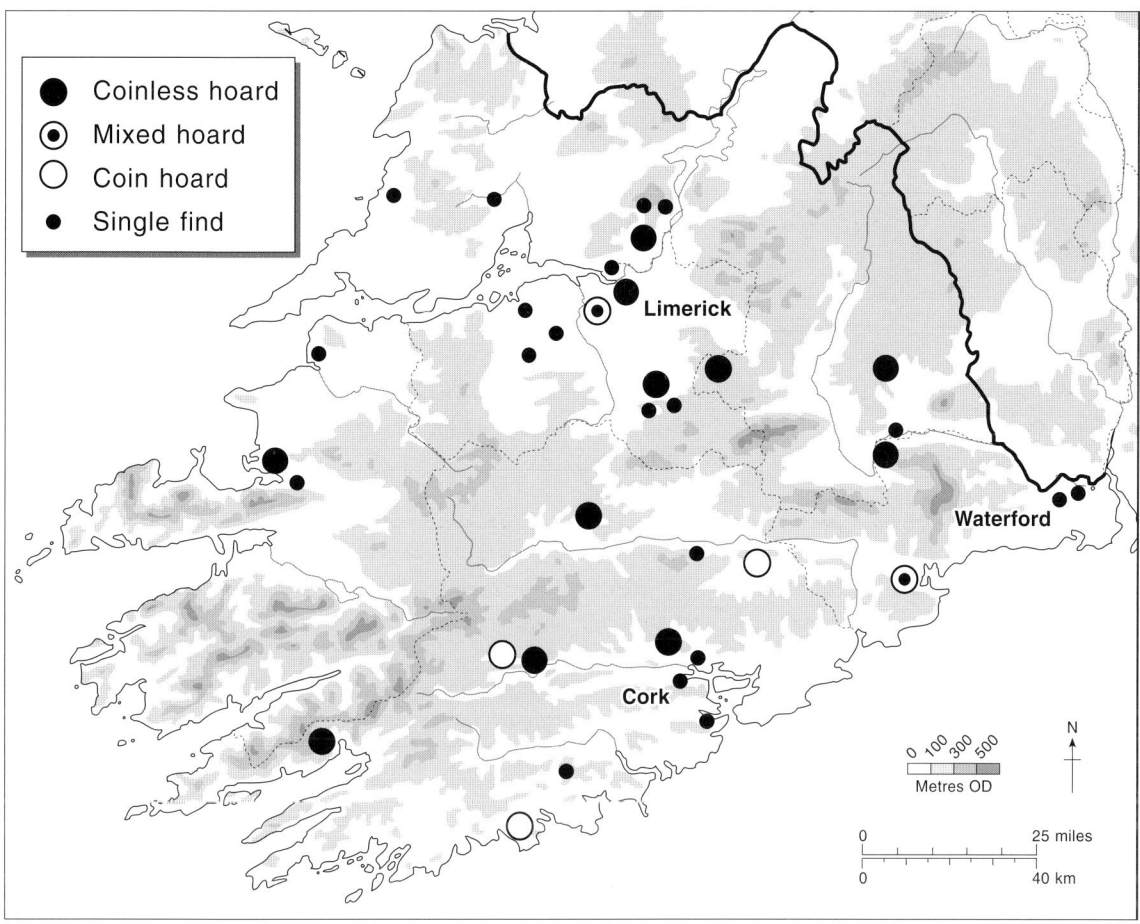

Fig. 15.1   Distribution of gold and silver finds of Scandinavian character in Munster

of 120 provenanced silver hoards of Scandinavian and Hiberno-Viking character are of Munster provenance (Fig. 15.1). These comprise twelve coinless hoards (26 per cent of the total from Ireland) from Kilbarry, Lohort and Macroom, Co. Cork; Fenit, Co. Kerry; Carraig Aille II, Co. Limerick; Rathmooley and Cullen, Co. Tipperary; Kilmacomma, Co. Waterford; and four finds with county provenances only (two from Cork and one each from Limerick and Clare). Two mixed hoards (13 per cent of the total from Ireland) come from Mungret, Co. Limerick, and Knockmaon, Co. Waterford, and six coin hoards (just 8 per cent of the Irish total) from Rathbarry, Macroom and Castlelyons, Co. Cork; Adare, Co. Limerick and two finds provenanced only to counties Tipperary and Limerick. In addition there is one gold hoard, from Glengarriff, which is likely to be of Viking Age date. These hoards are listed together with summary information on their contents in Appendix One, where selected references for them are also cited.[1] (A number of finds are excluded from this list on the grounds of uncertainty as to their character or date.)[2] A total of twenty single-finds of gold or silver of Scandinavian and Hiberno-Viking character is also on record from Munster. These objects are listed in Appendix 2 and comprise seven silver coins, eight non-numismatic silver objects (mostly armrings) and five gold objects; the latter group includes two finger-rings, an armring and an ingot.³

There are many problems associated with the study of the Munster material. Only four out of the total of twenty-one hoards came to light during the twentieth century, with the bulk of the remainder having being unearthed before or during the first half of the nineteenth. With the absence of museums and permanent collections in the region at this time, many of these early discoveries passed into the hands of antiquarian dealers and collectors – such as Neligan, Windele, Crofton Croker and Sainthill – who frequently split them up and traded or sold their individual components. Some items remain lost, possibly forever, but occasionally the tortuous trails of others may be followed by studying the correspondence, notebooks and sale catalogues of these and other collectors, as well as the minute books and proceedings of antiquarian societies and the acquisition registers of museums throughout Britain and Ireland.

The fate of one Munster hoard, that from Lohort, amply illustrates the difficulty of dealing with material of this kind. Discovered in 1848, this silver find comprised six linked rings of a rather rare type. These were separated from one another shortly after discovery and distributed among five local collectors, including Neligan and Windele of Cork and Haines of Mallow. Subsequently, individual rings from the hoard passed through the collections of Crofton Croker, Pitt-Rivers and Bateman. The available documentation, ranging from the Windele MSS, through two sale catalogues, an annotated letter of Sainthill's, an antiquarian publication, an exhibition catalogue and various museum registers and labels, indicates that the Lohort rings had at least ten different owners. At present four of the original six rings are identifiable in museum collections in Dublin, Oxford and Carlisle, but the whereabouts of the remaining two are unknown.⁴

Not all of Munster's hoards survive to the same extent as the Lohort find. Only a single object is known to be extant from an important hoard, which may have comprised up to fifty silver rings, that was discovered in 1844 at Kilbarry, near Cork City,⁵ while little is known about the ultimate fate of the hoards from Macroom, Cullen, Knockmaon, and the Clare side of the Shannon. Out of the absolute minimum of thirty-eight non-numismatic objects on record from the Munster hoards discovered prior to 1880, only eighteen are known to exist today and these are located in museums, both national and local, in Ireland, Britain and the United States. Some of the remainder may have been sold to the jewellery trade and consigned to the melting-pot, though it is clear that other objects entered the auction houses. Some of the latter, perhaps, still lie secure but unprovenanced in museum collections.

Not all aspects of the nineteenth-century antiquarian tradition, however, have negative consequences. Some collectors and antiquarians tended to generate records concerning specific types of finds, particularly those made of intrinsically valuable metals such as gold and silver. As a consequence these finds have a greater likelihood of retaining their provenances, as Woodman has demonstrated in the case of prehistoric goldwork (1993, 13–14). This is equally true in the case of Viking Age hoards from Munster and elsewhere in Ireland, the majority of which have reasonably specific provenances,⁶ and general confidence in the validity of the overall distribution patterns of the material is therefore increased.

Antiquarian records of gold and silver hoards are also more likely to include valuable information on the actual contents and contexts of these finds. Windele, for instance, has provided sketches – sometimes accompanied with measurements and weights – of several 'lost' hoards from Munster, including the silver example from the Clare bank of the Shannon and the important gold find from Glengarriff.⁷ The existence of a body of antiquarian records of this kind has not only facilitated several identification and reprovenancing exercises on Viking Age material from Munster (e.g. Briggs and Graham-Campbell

1986; Sheehan 1990, Cahill and Ó Floinn, forthcoming), but also serves as a reminder that some of the twenty apparent single-finds from the province could well be derived from unrecorded hoards.

Despite the imperfect nature of the evidence, as outlined above, it is both possible and worthwhile to address certain questions concerning Munster's Viking Age hoards. Firstly, there is the question of regional distinctiveness. Are the Munster hoards distinctive, in terms of their form and components, within the overall Irish context? Secondly, is there evidence to indicate that there was a Hiberno-Viking silver-working tradition in Munster to parallel that which seems to have been centred on Dublin? Thirdly, is it possible to date the Munster hoards to within any particular phase of the Viking Age in Ireland? Finally, what does the distribution of Viking Age gold and silver in Munster signify, particularly in terms of the ownership and control of this form of wealth during the period?

The regional question

In order to investigate whether or not the Munster hoards are distinctive within an overall Irish context they may be considered in two separate ways: firstly, with regard to their general form and structure; and, secondly, on the basis of the cultural attribution of their diagnostic components. It has already been noted that Viking Age hoards may be divided into three general categories – coinless, mixed and coin hoards. The form and structure of the first two categories have recently been analysed (Sheehan, forthcoming) and several trends have emerged with which the Munster evidence may be compared.

The coinless hoards, which together form by far the largest category, may be divided into three sub-groups on the basis of their form and structure. The first constitutes the typical Irish Viking Age hoard, accounting for practically half (48 per cent) of the total number. Hoards of this type contain neither ingots nor hack-silver, being composed exclusively of complete ornaments; in many cases these ornaments are of Hiberno-Viking type and vary in number from two to four examples. In Munster eight of the total of twelve coinless hoards belong to this sub-group, with most featuring Hiberno-Viking ornaments of some form. In terms of the number of objects they contain the Munster hoards are also typical; six of the seven hoards which have sufficient recorded details have either two or three components. Examples of such hoards from Munster include the one from Rathmooley, which consists of two armrings, and from Fenit, which comprises an armring and a neckring, as well as the find of two kite-brooches from near Limerick.

There are no recorded examples from Munster of the second sub-group of coinless hoards, those which contain ornaments and/or ingots but no hack-silver. This type is relatively uncommon and represents only 16 per cent of the total number of coinless hoards from Ireland. The third sub-group, accounting for 36 per cent of the total, is characterised by the presence of hack-silver (whether derived from ingots or ornaments) and most examples also contain ingots. The remaining four coinless hoards from Munster are of this type, with three featuring ingots or ingot-derived hack-silver. A classic example is the hoard from Carraig Aille II (Fig. 15.2), which contains one complete ring, three ring fragments, two ingots and an ingot fragment.

Ingots dominate the structure of the second general category of Viking Age hoards, the mixed hoard, occurring in fourteen of the sixteen recorded examples. As well as coins, in just over half of the total number, some ornaments are also represented, usually in hack-silver form. The two mixed hoards from Munster are not at variance with these trends: the one from Mungret consists of coins and ingots and the other, from Knockmaon, comprises coins and ornament-derived hack-silver.

The final general category of Viking Age hoards, the coin hoard, is poorly represented in Munster with only six examples on record. In terms of their size and of the types of coins

Fig. 15.2   Silver hoard from Carrig Aille II, Co. Limerick

represented in them, however, the Munster hoards are quite typical of Irish coin hoards generally (Kenny 1987, 514). Anglo-Saxon and Viking issues comprise the three recorded tenth-century hoards with Hiberno-Norse coins dominating the eleventh- and twelfth-century finds.

In summary, the Viking Age hoards from Munster of the coinless and mixed categories generally conform in terms of their form and structure with such hoards on record from elsewhere in Ireland. The relative proportions of the sub-categories of these hoards also conform with those from Ireland as a whole. However, there is a great scarcity of coin hoards from the province, and this clearly indicates that it is the coinless and, to a lesser extent, the mixed hoards that are characteristic of the Viking Age in Munster. In this sense Munster differs markedly from other relevant areas of Viking Age Ireland, particularly the north Leinster and central midland regions, where coin hoards occur far more commonly and actually outnumber the coinless examples.

The identification of this regional difference forms the backdrop for the second test to which the Munster hoards may be subjected, that is, a consideration of the cultural attributions of their components. A high proportion of the non-numismatic elements of Ireland's Viking Age hoards are diagnostic in form, and consequently it is possible to suggest regional or cultural attributions for these. Most of the material is of Hiberno-Viking origin, though there are also some Scandinavian, Baltic, Scoto-Norse and native Irish elements represented. By comparing the relative proportions of these separate components in the Munster hoards with those from elsewhere in Ireland, it should be possible to judge whether the former are distinctive in terms of their overall composition.

If ingots, which are usually neither regionally nor culturally diagnostic, are excluded from Ireland's coinless and mixed hoards it becomes apparent that Hiberno-Viking ornaments constitute the bulk of their diagnostic components. Most of these ornaments are of armring type and several different classes have been identified. By far the most important in numerical terms is the broad-band type, of which there are over a hundred individual examples on record. They occur in at least twenty-three silver hoards, including five examples from Munster: County Cork (no. 2: Fig. 15.3), Cullen, Fenit, Kilmacomma and Carraig Aille II. There is also a lost hoard from Glengarriff, which appears to have comprised two such rings in gold, and there are three single-finds: one possibly from Limerick, a hack-silver fragment from Inislounaght and a gold example from Edenvale. It appears that these broad-band armrings – the most characteristic of the Hiberno-Viking products – are numerically under-represented both in Munster and in the southern part of Ireland generally. If Munster, with its fourteen coinless and mixed silver hoards, is combined with the adjoining south-eastern counties of Wexford, Carlow, Kilkenny and Laois, with their seven hoards,[8] there is a resulting total of twenty-one such hoards from the southern third of Ireland. Broad-band armrings occur in only 28 per cent of these, while they feature in 42 per cent of the hoards provenanced to the remainder of the country.

Although this is a rather simplistic method of analysing the data, the resulting impression that broad-band armrings are under-represented in Munster and in the south generally is supported by another observation. These rings are represented in hack-silver form in 66 per cent of the southern hoards in which they occur, which is more than double the comparable figure for the

Fig. 15.3   Unlocalised hoard from Co. Cork (No. 2)

remainder of the country. This is of particular relevance because, as a general rule, it appears that the farther Viking Age silver objects are removed from their point of origin, within a particular economic or cultural milieu, the greater the likelihood that they will be reduced to hack-silver form.

Both of these observations suggest that broad-band armrings were not manufactured in Munster and support the evidence which indicates that they were products of the Hiberno-Norse who were centred on Dublin. It is interesting to note that there are no examples on record from Munster of the coiled armring type, Ireland's second most common Hiberno-Viking ornament class (Sheehan 1991), apart from a copper-alloy copy from Edenvale. Again this appears to indicate that, in terms of the under-representation of classic Hiberno-Viking components at any rate, the Munster hoards are distinctive. When one considers that there are more Hiberno-Viking broad-band and coiled armrings known from Norway than from Munster, this distinction is further emphasised.

It has already been noted that Viking Age ingots are not usually regionally or culturally diagnostic. It may be reasonably assumed, nevertheless, that much of the ingot material from Ireland is of Hiberno-Viking manufacture (Sheehan 1998, 183–84). Consequently, if there is a high incidence of ingot occurrence in the Munster hoards this might, to some extent, compensate for the low levels of occurrence of the common Hiberno-Viking ornament types. This is, however, not the case: ingots occur in only four (29 per cent) of the fourteen coinless and mixed hoards from Munster (those from Mungret, Kilmacomma, Carrig Aille II and County Cork (no. 2)), while they are found in twenty-nine (61 per cent) of the forty-eight hoards provenanced to elsewhere in Ireland. Clearly, this pattern further emphasises the distinct composition of the Munster hoards.

The second body of non-numismatic diagnostic material present in the Irish hoards comprises objects of Scandinavian type which are likely therefore to have been imported from Scandinavia. This is not a large group of material and only three items from Munster are to be considered as probable imports. These comprise the twisted-rod neckring from the Fenit hoard, the neckring from Milltown Malbay and the rod armring from the Rathmooley hoard. In addition, it is possible that the lost ring from the Macroom hoard and two single-finds from county Kerry – provenanced to 'near Tralee' and 'near Ballybunion' respectively – were variants of rod armrings. These seem likely to be of Norwegian origin, as is the Rathmooley armring and the Milltown Malbay neckring. Imported material of this general type is also found elsewhere in Ireland. What is not found in Munster, however, is the material of Baltic or southern Scandinavian origin which forms a small but important part of the hoard evidence from north Leinster and the central midlands (Sheehan 1998, 184–89). This negative fact, combined with the total absence from Munster of the Arabic coins of Kufic type which travelled to Ireland by way of the Baltic and which are found in ten hoards here (Sheehan forthcoming, Fig. 5), indicates again the distinctiveness of the Munster hoards within their overall Irish context.

The final category of non-numismatic material present in the Irish hoards comprises material most probably imported from Scandinavian Scotland. Two Munster hoards, those from the Clare side of the Shannon and Knockmaon, are composed of Scoto-Norse 'ring-money' – a simple type of armring which dominates Scotland's hoards between the mid-tenth and mid-eleventh century (Graham-Campbell 1995, 57–59). Elsewhere in Ireland 'ring-money' is known from three hoards.

In summary, two important general points become evident when the components of Munster's coinless and mixed hoards are examined with regard to their regional and cultural origins. Firstly, although a small amount of imported Norwegian silver objects are present, as would be expected, there is an absence of Baltic and southern Scandinavian material. Secondly, there is either an under-representation or an absence in Munster (and in the southern third of Ireland generally) of the most characteristic types of Hiberno-Viking ornaments and, where these are found, they are more than twice as likely to occur in hack-silver form as elsewhere in Ireland. Therefore, while the Munster hoards are not unusual in their form and structure they clearly have different composition patterns. This indicates that there are broad regional trends in the manufacture and circulation of Viking Age silver objects within Ireland and invites discussion on what type of objects fill the void in the composition of Munster's hoards.

A Munster silver-working tradition?
There are two types of object found in Munster's coinless hoards that are relevant to a consideration of whether or not there was a Munster-based Hiberno-Viking silver-working tradition. These are the penannular rod armring and the penannular ingot. The former are manufactured from unornamented rods of circular cross-section; they are penannular in form and sometimes exhibit slightly expanded terminals (Fig. 15.4). Examples are on record from only four provenanced finds in Ireland, all

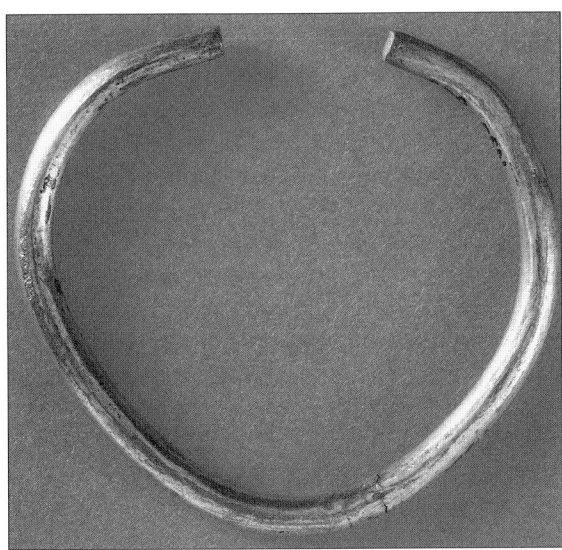

Fig. 15.4 Penannular rod armring from the Kilbarry hoard, Co. Cork

from Munster. Three are coinless hoards – those from Kilbarry, Rathmooley and Macroom – and the fourth is an apparent single-find from Carrigaline. Apart from an unprovenanced example in the National Museum,[9] no other examples of this type of ring are known from Ireland. On present evidence, namely the association of the type with annular rod armrings in the Macroom and Rathmooley hoards, it would appear to be dated to the late ninth or the first half of the tenth century (Sheehan 1992, 214–15).

Although rings similar to these penannular rod armrings are on record from a small number of Scandinavian hoards, such as the Gashagen find from Gotland (Stenberger 1958, 239–41), it seems likely that those from Ireland are of local manufacture. The southerly distribution of the type, with three of the four provenanced findspots located within thirty kilometres of Cork, suggests that a product of the tenth-century Scandinavian settlement there may have been identified. This proposal is reinforced by the nature of the Kilbarry hoard, found on the northern fringes of the modern city. It may have contained as many as fifty rings, though the existence of only nine is unequivocally attested to,[10] making it by far the largest hoard from Munster and among the largest from Ireland. Of greater relevance, however, is the fact that contemporary records of its discovery clearly indicate that these rings were notable for their close relationship in form and probably in weight, indicating that they are likely to be the products of a single silversmith or workshop. The fact that no other ornament types were present in the hoard, and that its hack-silver element appears to have been derived from the same type of ring represented in it in complete form, suggests that it may not have been long in existence before it was buried. Each of these points reinforces the proposal that penannular rod armrings derive from a Munster, and possibly a Cork, milieu.

The second object-type found in the Munster hoards for which a local origin may be proposed is the 'penannular ingot' or 'Irish ring-money' (Graham-Campbell 1995, 30). Examples of this type take the form of small, unornamented, penannular rings made from thick bands of silver; their outer faces are usually concave. They are too small to serve as armrings, yet are generally too large and cumbersome for use as finger-rings, and so may have been – like ingots – manufactured primarily as a convenient method of storing silver. In most of the recorded instances where two or more examples are present in a hoard they are found linked together. A minimum total of twenty-six penannular ingots is on record from Ireland, occuring in five provenanced hoards – Cushalogurt, Co. Mayo, Ballyadams, Co. Laois, Derrynahinch, Co. Kilkenny, and the two Munster finds from Lohort and Carraig Aille – all but one of which are from the southern third of the country. This appears to be a significant distribution pattern, and equally telling is the fact that no objects of this type are known from the many hoards from the midlands, north Leinster or Ulster. On the basis of this evidence it seems probable that penannular ingots were manufactured in a southern Irish milieu, possibly in one of the Hiberno-Norse settlements of Limerick, Cork, Waterford or Wexford. From its hoard associations in the Carraig Aille and Cushalogurt finds it is clear that the type was developed and in circulation within the period from the late ninth to the mid-tenth century.

This proposed date-range for the currency of penannular ingots is supported by the occurrence of at least one example in the Cuerdale find, from Lancashire, the deposition of which is coin-dated to c. 905.[11] This massive hoard is widely accepted as being generally representative of the silver wealth of the Dublin-based Hiberno-Norse (Graham-Campbell 1992, 113–14). The presence of penannular ingots at Cuerdale, along with the lost hoard of three probable objects of this type from the Isle of Skye (Graham-Campbell 1995, 105), demonstrates that these objects gained some circulation outside the Munster area, both in Ireland and the Irish Sea region. This is not the case with the other identifiable product of the Munster-based Hiberno-Norse, the penannular rod armring, which suggests that the penannular ingot was the more common and important type. This conclusion is supported when the hoard associations of the two types are considered – penannular ingots occur with Hiberno-Viking broad-band armrings in a number of finds, namely Carraig Aille, Cushalogurt and Cuerdale, while there are no recorded associations at all between penannular rod armrings and this type of armring. These points may indicate that the penannular rod armring was a relatively short-lived development.

Both of the object types under discussion here may have been developed and manufactured by the Munster Irish, rather than the Hiberno-Norse. It is clear that Scandinavian activity in Ireland resulted in significant quantities of silver becoming available to Irish craftsmen for the first time, particularly between c. 850 and c. 950, which led to the development of silver penannular brooches of the bossed and ball types (Graham-Campbell 1976, 53). While there are instances of such native products entering the Hiberno-Viking pool of silver and occurring as hoard components, these are remarkably few in number. Indeed, native brooches are usually found as single-finds rather than in hoards – the characteristic context of Scandinavian and Hiberno-Viking material. On this basis it seems unlikely that the penannular rod armrings and penannular ingots being discussed here, all of which derive from hoards, are of native Irish origin. It is worth noting, furthermore, that the forms of these object types are without precedent in Early Medieval Ireland, and that when Irish craftsmen did experiment through the medium of silver they tended to produce highly decorative and sophisticated brooches far removed in technical accomplishment and style from the plain and simple rings being considered here.

In summary, therefore, it would appear that two distinct types of ornament – the penannular rod armring and the penannular ingot – may be identified as being the products of a Munster-based Hiberno-Viking silver-working tradition. They differ in form and style from the principal object types being produced by the Hiberno-Norse centred on Dublin, not least because they do not feature the stamped ornament characteristic of the main products of the dominant tradition. The Munster tradition generally appears to have been of only regional importance and compares poorly with that of Dublin in terms of output and innovation. It seems to have been centred, at least in part, on Cork, though it would be unwise to deny the potential roles of Waterford or Limerick. Indeed, if the group of hoards from the river Shannon as far north as Lough Ree was regarded as being connected with Limerick, and if some of the hoards from south-east Leinster were linked with Waterford, the impressions derived solely from the Munster evidence might well be modified.

Chronology

The Viking Age in Ireland is generally considered to have extended from c. 800 to as late as 1169–70, when the towns founded by the Scandinavians were captured by the Anglo-Normans. This is a lengthy time-frame, and consequently it is necessary to examine the Munster hoards from a chronological perspective in order to establish their main period of deposition. The deposition dates of eight out of the total of twenty silver hoards from the province are determinable from their coin-content, with half dating to the 940s and 950s and the remainder scattered throughout the period between 1000 and 1150 (Table 15.1).[12] Four of the seven single-finds of coins also date to the tenth century. On the basis of the coin evidence alone, therefore, it appears that the decades centring on the mid-point of the tenth century constitute an important phase in terms of silver circulation.

One of the mid-tenth-century coin hoards referred to above, that from Mungret, also contains non-numismatic silver in the form of ingots. This find serves as a reminder that, in terms of their bullion value, coins represent only an insignificant proportion of the overall amount of Viking Age silver from Munster. What chronological patterns emerge from a consideration of the dating evidence for the much greater amount of silver represented by the non-numismatic material?

Most of the material of this kind may be dated by association with other objects and/or coins to the later ninth or the first half of the tenth century. It is not possible to detail here the case for each individual hoard, though the dating evidence for those from Kilbarry, Macroom and Rathmooley (with their penannular rod armrings) and Lohort and Carraig Aille (with their penannular ingots) has been referred to above. The case for assigning the hoards from County Cork (no. 2), Fenit, Cullen and Kilmacomma to this period rests on the occurrence in each of them of broad-band armrings, as these were mainly manufactured between *c.* 880 and *c.* 930–40 (Sheehan 1989, 125). Two Munster hoards, namely the finds of kite-shaped brooches from near Limerick and of animal-headed armrings from County Cork (no. 1), may be more firmly dated to the tenth century (Whitfield 1997, 504–05; Sheehan 1990, 51). The only remaining hoards, those from Knockmaon and the Clare bank of the Shannon, are probably

TABLE 15.1
Deposition dates of coin and mixed hoards from Munster

Co. Tipperary	*c.* 942
Rathbarry, Co. Cork	*c.* 945
Macroom, Co. Cork	*c.* 953
Mungret, Co. Limerick	*c.* 953
Knockmaon, Co. Waterford	*c.* 1000
Adare, Co. Limerick	mid-11th C
Co. Limerick	*c.* 1065
Castleyons, Co. Cork	*c.* 1140

temporally distinct from the majority of the non-coin hoards from Munster: both are composed of Scoto-Norse 'ring-money', and the Knockmaon example contains coins which allows its deposition to be assigned to *c.* 1000.

In summary, therefore, both the numismatic and non-numismatic evidence indicate that the majority of Munster's twenty Viking Age silver hoards are assignable to the period between the later ninth and the mid-tenth century. This is also the period during which most of the coinless and mixed hoards from elsewhere in Ireland were deposited, though the relative scarcity of coin hoards from later tenth- and eleventh-century Munster is notable.

Distribution and ownership

The distribution of the provenanced hoards and single-finds of Viking Age gold and silver from Munster is plotted in Fig. 15.1. Two patterns immediately become evident: firstly, there is a noticeable concentration of finds from around Limerick and, to a lesser extent, Cork; and, secondly, there is an equally significant number of finds from areas – such as north Cork, east Limerick and south Tipperary – that are located away from the Hiberno-Norse towns. These distributional trends raise the question of who owned and controlled the wealth that these finds represent.

Bradley has drawn attention to historical and other evidence for the existence and extent of Scandinavian settlement in the rural hinterlands of Waterford, Cork and Limerick (1988, 62–65) and it is possible that the hoards and single-finds on record from these interface zones represent Scandinavian-owned wealth. These include the hoards from Kilbarry and Mungret, from near Cork and Limerick respectively, the two apparent single-finds of tenth-century coins from Cork and the armring from Carrigaline. Finds of this kind from around Waterford are not strongly represented, though there is a gold finger-ring on record from near the city. In addition, the mixed hoard from Knockmaon, near Dungarvan, derives from an area known to have been controlled by the Waterford Norse.

It is, perhaps, predictable that such hoards and single-finds should be found in and around areas of Scandinavian settlement in Munster. However, hoards such as Lohort, Cullen, Kilmacomma, Carraig Aille and Rathmooley, as well as the single-find from Inislounaght, derive from areas that remained under Irish control for all of the Viking Age. The conclusion to be drawn from this distributional pattern, as well as from similar evidence from elsewhere in Ireland, is that a considerable proportion of Hiberno-Norse silver wealth ended up in Irish ownership. Irish control of silver is also evidenced by the fact that a high proportion of those hoards for which detailed find circumstances are on record are known to have been found on native types of settlement sites. For instance, three of the five hoards noted above – Kilmacomma, Carraig Aille and Rathmooley – were found in ringforts, the Rathbarry coin hoard was recovered from a souterrain, and the Inislounaght find derives from an ecclesiastical site. There is no reason to believe that the means and processes by which the Irish acquired significant amounts of silver during the late ninth and tenth centuries, namely trade and tribute (Sheehan 1998, 173–77), operated any differently in Munster than elsewhere in Ireland.

Conclusions

In order to assess the issues that arise from this consideration of Munster's Viking Age hoards it is necessary to compare the region with others, particularly the area comprising north Leinster and the midlands. The reason for this, apart from the fact that it is in the latter area that most Viking Age hoards occur, is simply because it was along the littorals of Munster and Leinster that the Scandinavians eventually chose to found their towns. The Ulster hoards, which are about equal to the Munster ones in number, have little in common with them otherwise but compare quite favourably with those from the midlands and north Leinster.

During the period between *c.* 850 and *c.* 950 coinless hoards predominate in Munster. In terms of their form and structure these are little different from those known from elsewhere in Ireland, but in content they are reasonably distinctive. Silver ornaments of the type produced in the Hiberno-Viking tradition centred on Dublin are under-represented, being replaced by objects manufactured in a local silver-working tradition. This tradition may have been centred, in part, on Cork, though it is possible that Limerick and Waterford also had a role to play. Overall, however, the Munster tradition appears to have been of only regional importance. Its products are rarely found outside the southern half of Ireland, while those of the Dublin-centred tradition have been found in significant numbers in northern England, Scotland and Norway.

It is tempting to associate most of the early coinless hoards with the foundation of the Scandinavian towns in Munster during the early decades of the tenth century and to assign the Munster-based silver-working tradition to the early to mid-tenth century. We know, however, that the Scandinavians were responsible for introducing significant amounts of silver into Ireland before the tenth century. It therefore seems possible that ninth-century *longphort*-type settlements, such as the *Dún* at Cork, which is documented by annalistic references in both 846 and 865,[13] may have been more than simply raiding bases. Whether the wealth represented by the coinless hoards was introduced through mid- to late ninth-century *longphuirt* or early to mid-tenth-century towns, or through both, it is clear from its distribution patterns and find-contexts

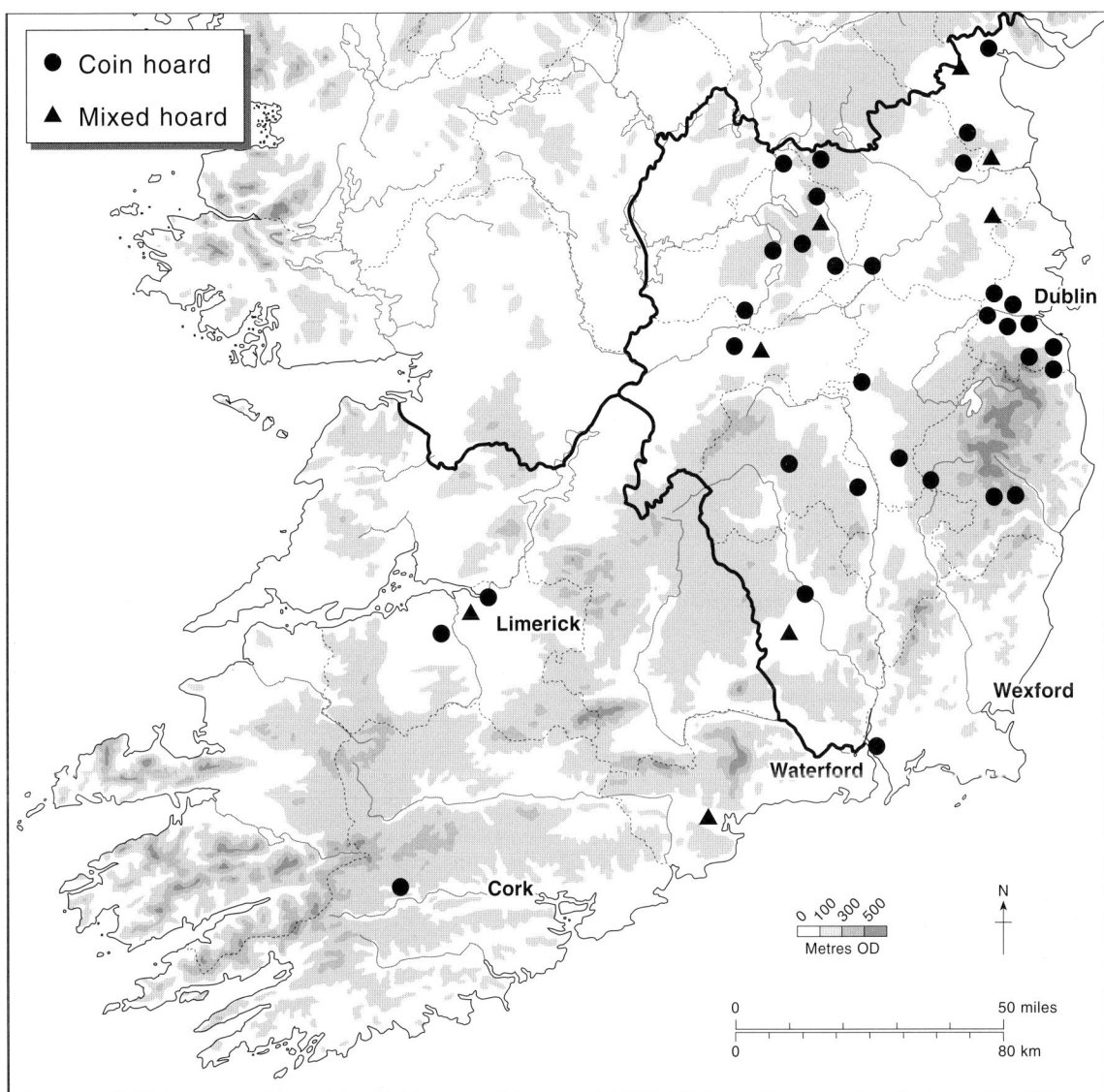

Fig. 15.5 Distribution of coin hoards deposited after *c.* 950 in Munster and Leinster

that a share of this wealth ended up in Irish ownership. This trend is also evidenced strongly elsewhere in Ireland, and suggests the importance of trade and tribute – rather than raiding – as the main factors behind the redistribution.

Until around the mid-point of the tenth century the province of Munster with its Scandinavian towns seems to progress along broadly similar lines, in terms of what is evident from the hoards, to the midlands and north Leinster. Thereafter, this picture changes rather dramatically. The move towards the development of a monetary economy, evidenced by the occurrence of mixed hoards in the latter region, is represented in Munster only by the Mungret hoard. (The presence of hack-silver in one-third of Munster's coinless hoards may represent some move in this direction, however, if hack-silver is regarded as a transitional stage between a bullion and a coin-using economy.) After the mid-point of the century the bullion economy appears to decline markedly in Ireland. In the north Leinster region, as this decline occurs, there is a concomitant and striking increase in the rate of coin-hoarding and, presumably, in coin-use. This process culminates in the establishment of a mint in Dublin around 997. But Munster remains virtually devoid of coins, with only 8 per cent of the total number of Viking Age coin-hoards from Ireland on record from the province (Fig. 15.5).

The evidence seems to indicate that, in terms of economic development as measured by hoarding patterns and coin-use, the Hiberno-Viking towns of Munster faded into relative insignificance after *c.* 950 by comparison with Dublin. Why this should be so is unclear, particularly when up to this point they seem to have been developing steadily. The geographical factor of their location away from the important nexus of the Irish Sea may be of some relevance, though it is also possible that the evidence simply reflects regional differences in the patterns and practices of hoarding.

ACKNOWLEDGEMENT

The author gratefully acknowledges the assistance of Professor J.A. Graham-Campbell, Institute of Archaeology, University College, London, who commented on a draft version of this paper, and Ms Joan Rockley, M.A., Department of Archaeology, University College, Cork, for discussing Cork's antiquarian tradition with him.

NOTES

1. The dates given in Appendix 1 and Table 1 for the deposition of Munster's mixed and coin hoards are those proposed by Blackburn and Pagan (1986). (It should be noted, however, that the Knockmaon find (ibid., no. 195) is a mixed, not a coin, hoard.)
2. These doubtful finds include: Adare, Co. Limerick [A tenth-century silver ringed-pin, in five pieces, which was suggested by Fanning to be a hack-silver hoard (1994, 30). The form of fragmentation of the pin is not, however, typical of Viking Age hack-silver and it is uncertain if the breaks are ancient or modern. It seems prudent to regard the pin as a single-find.]; Rathcormac, Co. Cork [A late nineteenth-century 'find' of up to eight silver rings, which are most probably contemporary forgeries; see Macalister (1928, 70) and Graham-Campbell (1976, 70).]; 'Barrykovin', Co. Cork [The minutes of the Cork Cuvierian Society meeting held on June 6th, 1849, record that Rev. Dr C. Neligan displayed 'two specimens of silver ring money, and a stone celt battle axe of siliceous slate like the bronze, found in a fort at Barrykovin.' It is not clear from this record, unfortunately, whether it was the silver rings or the stone object or both that were found at 'Barrykovin' or whether the silver rings were found together. 'Barrykovin' may be Ballycrovane, in West Cork (OS 6" Sheet No. 102). The author is grateful to Ms Joan Rockley for bringing the evidence for this material to his attention.]; the 1852 find of 'torques' from a rath in Co. Limerick, included in Sheehan 1998 (167, fn. 5) as a possible Viking Age find, is now known to be a Bronze Age hoard (see Cahill 1993, 13–14).
3. Again, several doubtful finds are omitted from this list, as are finds of native Irish manufacture such as silver penannular brooches.
4. The history of the find is published by Briggs and Graham-Campbell (1986, 310–11). The Lohort ring in Tullie House Museum, Carlisle, will shortly be published by Prof. J.A. Graham-Campbell.
5. Antiquarian accounts differ as to the size of this find, with the records of the Cuvierian Society, 1 May 1844, stating: 'Mr Denis Murray produced 5 pieces of silver ring money, found at Kilbarry, the property of Mr Wise in the N. Liberties. There were between 40 and 50 of them found in a wooden box. These exhibited are the property of Counsellor Reeves of Vosterberg.' A local newspaper's account of this meeting (*Southern Reporter*, 25 May 1844) states: 'They found a portion of a hoard of between forty and fifty in a wooden box in the progress of farming operations on lands of Kilbarry, in the North Liberties of Cork – the property of Mr Wise. They were all of a similar plain pattern, destitute of the broad bowl like extremities, and nearly all alike in weight, one of them weighing 14 dwts. 16 grains.' See Rockley 1995, 101–02.
6. Only six out of Ireland's recorded total of over a hundred and thirty Viking Age silver hoards do not have at least a county provenance.
7. Both of the instanced hoards are recorded in the Windele MSS – a large number of volumes of miscellaneous notes, sketches and letters preserved in the Royal Irish Academy.
8. These are Ballyadams, Co. Laois, Blackcastle, Co. Wexford, and Derrynahinch, Dunmore Cave, Dysart, Kilkenny (west) and an unlocalised hoard, all from Co. Kilkenny.
9. National Museum of Ireland, registration number W.39.
10. See footnote 5 above.
11. This is British Museum registration number 1841, 7–11, 359. It is also likely that 1841, 7–11, 361 and 699 – two hack-silver fragments – also derive from penannular ingots.
12. See footnote 1 above.
13. Annals of the Four Masters.

BIBLIOGRAPHY

Blackburn, M. and Pagan, J. (1986) 'A revised check-list of coin-hoards from the British Isles, *c.* 500–1100', in M.A.S. Blackburn (ed.), *Anglo-Saxon Monetary History: essays in memory of Michael Dolley*, 291–313, Leicester

Bøe, J. (1940) 'Norse antiquities in Ireland', in H. Shetelig (ed.), *Viking Antiquities in Britain and Ireland*, III, Oslo

Bradley, J. (1988) 'The interpretation of Scandinavian settlement in Ireland', in J. Bradley (ed.), *Settlement and Society in Medieval Ireland: Studies Presented to F.X. Martin, o.s.a.*, 49–78, Kilkenny

Cahill, M. (1993) 'Some unrecorded Bronze Age gold ornaments from county Limerick', *N. Munster Antiq. J.* 35, 5–23

Cahill, M. (forthcoming) 'John Windele's Treasury: late Bronze Age gold from Co. Cork', *Proc. Roy. Ir. Acad.*

Cahill, M. and Ó Floinn, R. (forthcoming) 'Two silver kite-shaped brooches from Co. Limerick', *N. Munster Antiq. J.*

Cuvierian Society *Minutes of the Cork Cuvierian Society (1835–1878)*, MSS in University College, Cork (U221)

Day Collection (1913) *Catalogue of the Day Collection, Sothebys*, London

Dolley, R.H.M. (1960) 'Some new light on the Viking-age silver hoard from Mungret', *N. Munster Antiq. J.* 8 (3), 116–33

Dolley, R.H.M. (1962a) 'The 1843 find of Viking-age silver coins from county Tipperary', *J. Cork Hist. Archaeol. Soc.* 57, 41–47

Dolley, R.H.M. (1962b) 'The coins from Beal Boru', 18–27 in M.J. O'Kelly, 'Beal Boru, Co. Clare', *J. Cork Hist. Archaeol. Soc.* 67, 1–27

Dolley, R.H.M. (1966) *The Hiberno-Norse Coins in the British Museum*, London

Dolley R.H.M. and Ingold, J. (1961) 'Viking-age coin-hoards from Ireland and their relevance to Anglo-Saxon studies', in R.H.M. Dolley (ed.), *Anglo-Saxon Coins: Studies Presented to F.M. Stenton*, 241–65, London

Fanning, T. (1994) *Viking Age Ringed Pins from Dublin*, Medieval Dublin Excavations 1962–81, Ser. B, vol. 4, Dublin

Garside, A. (1980) *Jewelry: Ancient and Modern*, New York

Graham-Campbell, J.A. (1976) 'The Viking-age silver hoards of Ireland', in B. Almquist and D. Greene (eds.), *Proc. Seventh Viking Congress, Dublin 1973*, 31–74, Dublin

Graham-Campbell, J.A. (1992) 'The Cuerdale hoard: comparisons and context', in J.A. Graham-Campbell (ed.), *Viking Treasure from the North-West: The Cuerdale Hoard in its Context*, 107–15 Liverpool

Graham-Campbell, J.A. (1995) *The Viking-age Gold and Silver of Scotland (AD 850–1100)*, Edinburgh

Graham-Campbell, J.A. and Briggs, C.S. (1986) 'Some neglected Viking-age silver hoards from near Athlone and Co. Cork', *Peritia* 5, 309–16

Hall, R. (1973) 'A check list of Viking-age coin finds from Ireland', *Ulster J. Archaeol.* 36, 71–86

Jennings, J.R.B. (1912) 'On some ancient coins found in west Waterford', *J. Waterford & South-East Ir. Archaeol. Soc.* 15, 162–67

Kenny, M. (1987) 'The geographical distribution of Irish Viking Age coin hoards', *Proc. Roy. Ir. Acad.* 87C, 507–25

Macalister, R.A.S. (1928) *The Archaeology of Ireland*, London

McCarthy, J.P. and Dolley, M. (1977) 'The Castle Freke (Rathbarry, Co. Cork) find of tenth-century Anglo-Saxon coins', *Numismatic Circ.* 85 (11), 488–90

Ó Floinn, R. (1983) 'A gold band found near Rathkeale, Co. Limerick', *N. Munster Antiq. J.* 25, 3–8

Ó Ríordáin, S.P. (1949) 'Lough Gur excavations: Carraig Aille and "the Spectacles"', *Proc. Roy. Ir. Acad.* 52C, 39–111

Ó Ríordáin, S.P. (1954) 'Lough Gur excavations: Neolithic and Bronze Age houses on Knockadoon', *Proc. Roy. Ir. Acad.* 56C, 297–459

Rockley, J. (1995) 'Antiquarian activity in Cork 1803-1881', unpublished MA thesis (NUI), University College, Cork

Scharff, R.F. et al. (1906) 'The exploration of the caves of county Clare', *Trans. Roy. Ir. Acad.* 33B, 42–75

Sheehan, J. (1982) 'A Viking Age silver hoard from the River Shannon, Co. Clare', *N. Munster Antiq. J.* 24, 89–91

Sheehan, J. (1989) 'A Viking-age silver armring from Portumna, Co. Galway', *J. Galway Arch. Hist. Soc.* 42, 125–30

Sheehan, J. (1990) 'A pair of Viking-age animal-headed armrings from Co. Cork', *J. Cork Hist. Archaeol. Soc.* 95, 41–54

Sheehan, J. (1991) 'Coiled armrings: an Hiberno-Viking silver armring type', *J. Ir. Archaeol.* 6, 41–53

Sheehan, J. (1992) 'The Rathmooley hoard and other finds of Viking Age silver from county Tipperary', *Tipperary Hist. J.*, 210–16

Sheehan, J. (1998) 'Early Viking-age silver hoards from Ireland and their Scandinavian elements', in H. Clarke et al. (eds.), *Scandinavia and Ireland in the Early Viking Age*, 166–202, Dublin

Sheehan, J. (forthcoming) 'Ireland's Early Viking-age silver hoards: components, structure and classification', in K. Randsborg and S. Stummann-Hansen (eds.), *Vikings in the West*, Acta Archaeologica (Sonderband), Copenhagen

Whitfield, N. (1997) 'The Waterford kite-brooch and its place in Irish metalwork', in M.F. Hurley and O.M.B. Scully, *Late Viking Age and Medieval Waterford: Excavations 1986–1992*, 490–517, Waterford

Woodman, P.C. (1993) 'The prehistory of south-west Ireland – an archaeological region or a state of mind?', in E. Shee-Twohig and M. Ronayne (eds.), *Past Perceptions: The Prehistoric Archaeology of South-West Ireland*, 6–15, Cork

APPENDIX ONE
Viking Age Hoards of Scandinavian or Hiberno-Viking Character from Munster

Provenance	Contents	Deposition Date	Discovery Date	Reference
Co. Clare				
River Shannon	3 armrings	—	<1865	Sheehan 1982
Co. Cork				
Kilbarry	At least 7 armrings, 2 armring fragments	—	1844	Cuvierian Society 1/6/1884; Briggs and Graham-Campbell 1986, 312–13
Lohort	6 rings	—	1848	Ibid., 310–11
Macroom	2 armrings	—	<1850	Ibid., 311–12
Unlocalised, no. 1	2 armrings	—	<1836	Sheehan 1990
Unlocalised, no. 2	2 armring fragments, 1 ingot	—	<1850	Graham-Campbell and Briggs 1986, 311–12
Glengarriff	2 gold armrings	—	1860	Cahill, *forthcoming*
Rathbarry	Anglo-Saxon coins	*c.* 945	<1799	McCarthy and Dolley 1977
Macroom	Anglo-Saxon coins	*c.* 953	*c.* 1840 (?)	Dolley and Ingold 1961, 242
Castleyons	Hiberno-Norse bracteates	*c.* 1140	1837	Dolley 1966, 86–90
Co. Kerry				
Fenit	2 armrings	—	<1880	Graham-Campbell 1976, 67; Garside 1980, no. 413
Co. Limerick				
Carraig Aille II	Ring, 3 armring fragments, 2 ingots, ingot fragment	—	1948	Ó Ríordáin 1949, 62–64
Mungret	7(+) ingots, Anglo-Saxon and Viking coins	*c.* 953	1840	Dolley 1960
near Limerick	2 kite-brooches	—	1845	Cahill and Ó Floinn, *forthcoming*
Adare	Anglo-Saxon and Hiberno-Norse coins	mid-11th C	1834	Dolley 1966, 69
Unlocalised	Hiberno-Norse coins	*c.* 1065	1833	Dolley 1966, 70
Co. Tipperary				
Bog of Cullen	Armrings (unknown quantity)	—	1770s	Sheehan 1992, 211

APPENDIX ONE (Continued)

Provenance	Contents	Deposition Date	Discovery Date	Reference
Rathmooley	2 armrings	—	1925	Ibid., 211–15
Unlocalised	Anglo Saxon and Viking coins	c. 942	1843	Dolley 1962a
Co. Waterford				
Kilmacomma	Armring fragment, 10 ingot fragments, rod fragment	—	1981	Unpublished
Knockmaon	3 armring fragments, Anglo-Saxon, Hiberno-Norse and Continental coins	c. 1000	1912	Jennings 1912; Dolley 1966, 57

APPENDIX TWO
Viking Age Single-Finds of Scandinavian or Hiberno-Viking Character from Munster

Provenance	Object	Discovery Date	Reference
Co. Clare			
Miltown Malbay	Neckring	<1840	Bøe 1940, 122–23
Edenvale	Gold armring	c. 1903	Scharff et al. 1906, 68
Beal Boru	Hiberno-Norse coin	1961	Dolley 1962b, 19–24
Beal Boru	Hiberno-Norse coin	1961	Ibid., 24–27
Co. Cork			
Carrigaline	Armring	<1913	*Day Collection*, no. 455
Bandon (?)	Gold finger-ring	<1848	Graham-Campbell 1976, 71
Cork	Viking coin (Northumbria)	1833	Hall 1973, 82
near Cork	Viking coin (Northumbria)	<1850 (?)	Ibid., 82
near Fermoy	Hiberno-Norse bracteate	c. 1820	Ibid., 83
Co. Kerry			
near Tralee	Armring	<1913	*Day Collection*, no. 457
near Ballybunion	Armring	1863	*Cuvierian Society*, 11/10/1864
Co. Limerick			
Adare	Ringed-pin	1860	Fanning 1994, 30
Limerick (?)	Armring	<1866	Sheehan 1989, 129
Askeaton	Gold ingot	<1905	Cahill 1993, 10–11
near Rathkeale	Gold band	1855	Ó Floinn 1983
Lough Gur	Anglo-Saxon coin	1940	Ó Ríordáin 1954, 359
Lough Gur	Anglo-Saxon coin	1940	Ibid., 35
Co. Tipperary			
Inislounaght	Armring fragment	1984	Sheehan 1992, 11
Co. Waterford			
near Waterford	Gold finger-ring	<1848	Bøe 1940, 105
Waterford	Kite-brooch	1988	Whitfield 1997

16. Viking Age Towns: Archaeological Evidence from Waterford and Cork

MAURICE F. HURLEY

Introduction

Tangible evidence of the Viking raids on Ireland can be extremely elusive to archaeologists. The presence of the Vikings is primarily documented in the historical record (Ó Corráin 1972, 80–110; Sawyer 1982), though the occasional chance discovery of a Viking sword (Walsh, A. 1998) or a hoard of their coveted silver (Graham-Campbell 1976; Sheehan 1998) may sometimes be seen as proof of their transitory presence here. The recovery in the Scandinavian homelands of foreign booty is indicative of their safe return (Wamers 1985) – their passports marked, as it were, with the stamps of foreign lands. Evidence in the Irish material culture suggesting more than a fleeting visit is rare and is usually indicated by the introduction of Scandinavian art styles or by the influence of these on native artistic traditions (Graham-Campbell 1987, 150–51).

Viking Age houses have not been positively identified in Ireland except in the cities.[1] Only one potential ship-harbour or *longphort* has been investigated,[2] although a number of other possible sites have been suggested (Kelly 1995). Viking graves have been identified with greater certainty, but with one possible exception these have not been found in recent years (Edwards 1990, 189–91)[3] and so this valuable source of information has largely evaded modern archaeological investigation. In short, our archaeological knowledge of the Vikings is not what it might be.

The term 'Viking Period' or 'Viking Age' is, strictly speaking, applicable only to the period between the ninth and mid-eleventh century. The mid-eleventh to later twelfth-century period is also described as 'Viking Age' in Ireland (sometimes qualified as 'late Viking Age') but it could perhaps more correctly be termed the 'Hiberno-Norse' period because of the 'marked fusion of native Irish and Viking elements' evident in the culture of that time (Simms 1990, 42). The Viking towns are one product of this fusion and interaction, with tenth-century Dublin being the earliest urban development thus far excavated. The slightly later but parallel growth of the Munster towns – Waterford, Cork and Limerick – is indicative of this critical formative process, a process which in turn shaped the contemporary patterns of modern Ireland and is reflected in the latter day prominence of the Munster cities.

The archaeological evidence for Viking Age towns in Munster is not spectacular when compared with the evidence from Dublin. Dublin's pre-eminence in this regard is attributable to two basic factors: firstly, it was 'the principal town of Ireland' in the Viking Age (Wallace 1988, 123) and, secondly, its archaeological discoveries have been the more impressive. The nineteenth-century discovery of what appear to be two separate Viking cemeteries at Islandbridge and Kilmainham (O'Brien 1998) may be regarded as a mixed blessing. Although a treasure trove of artefacts was unearthed, the undoubted loss of others and the unfortunate lack of scientifically recorded detail compromise the value of the discovery. The city excavations, on the other hand, have established Dublin as one of the foremost cities for stratified evidence of Viking Age archaeology in western Europe. These strata have yielded uniquely preserved organic remains providing a comprehensive record of Dublin's domestic architecture (Wallace 1992a) and defensive systems (Wallace 1988), replete with a splendid array of artefacts dating from the tenth to the twelfth century (e.g. Lang 1988). It is against this background of fortuitous discoveries and extensive excavation in Dublin that we must set the comparatively meagre archaeological assemblages from Waterford and Cork. Viking Age cemeteries have not been recognised in Munster and consequently they have no role in any comparative assessment.

Waterford, where more than six thousand square metres were excavated (Hurley and Scully 1997), is the principal source of information on Munster's Viking Age towns and it provides a broad perspective wherein, for the first time, the Dublin evidence can be seen in wider context. Much of the discussion of Cork is based on inference, and a recent reassessment of the archaeological evidence is largely based on comparison with the Waterford discoveries (Hurley 1997a). Thus the pivotal importance of Waterford cannot be overestimated providing, as it does, a counterpoint for the theme set by Dublin and a framework within which the more fragmentary evidence from Cork can be broadly interpreted. Limerick is referred to only briefly in this chapter as the synthesis of many of the recent excavations there is envisaged as a long-term project (O'Rahilly, pers. comm.). Like Cork, however, Limerick has produced little identifiable evidence for pre-Norman occupation (O'Rahilly 1995).

The archaeological excavations in Waterford, undertaken between 1986 and 1992, produced a wealth of information on the late Viking Age and early Norman period. There was no evidence for the early Viking Age settlement and material remains dating to the early to mid-eleventh century were poorly represented. The later eleventh- and twelfth-century levels were the most comprehensively represented. In Cork, the earliest urban development excavated to date has come from the area of South Main Street, formerly the South Island. The excavations here took place between 1974 and 1976 and the earliest excavated strata were dated to the late twelfth and thirteenth centuries by the excavator, the late Dermot Twohig (1975; 1978; 1985). This led to the supposition that the Viking town lay elsewhere. A number of suggestions based on the historical evidence were put forward, one of the most plausible and well argued being made by Jeffries (1985), who proposed that the greater part of the settlement was located on the south bank of the river Lee. The recent excavations in Waterford promoted a reassessment of the archaeological evidence from Cork. This review has led to the conclusion that, firstly, material remains of earlier date may have been present at South Main Street but remained unrecognised within the conventional framework of dating,[4] and secondly, that a more rigorous approach to excavation in the notoriously difficult tidal conditions of Cork is required.

Late Viking Age Waterford: location, development and defences

The earliest excavated levels in Waterford can be reliably dated to the mid-eleventh century. These were preceded by some insubstantial and fragmentary strata for which it was not possible to give a *terminus post quem*; however, they probably dated to the early eleventh century. The excavation covered about one-fifth of the total area likely to have been settled prior to the Norman invasion of 1170, centring on the western side of the triangular Hiberno-Norse town, in an area probably settled in the

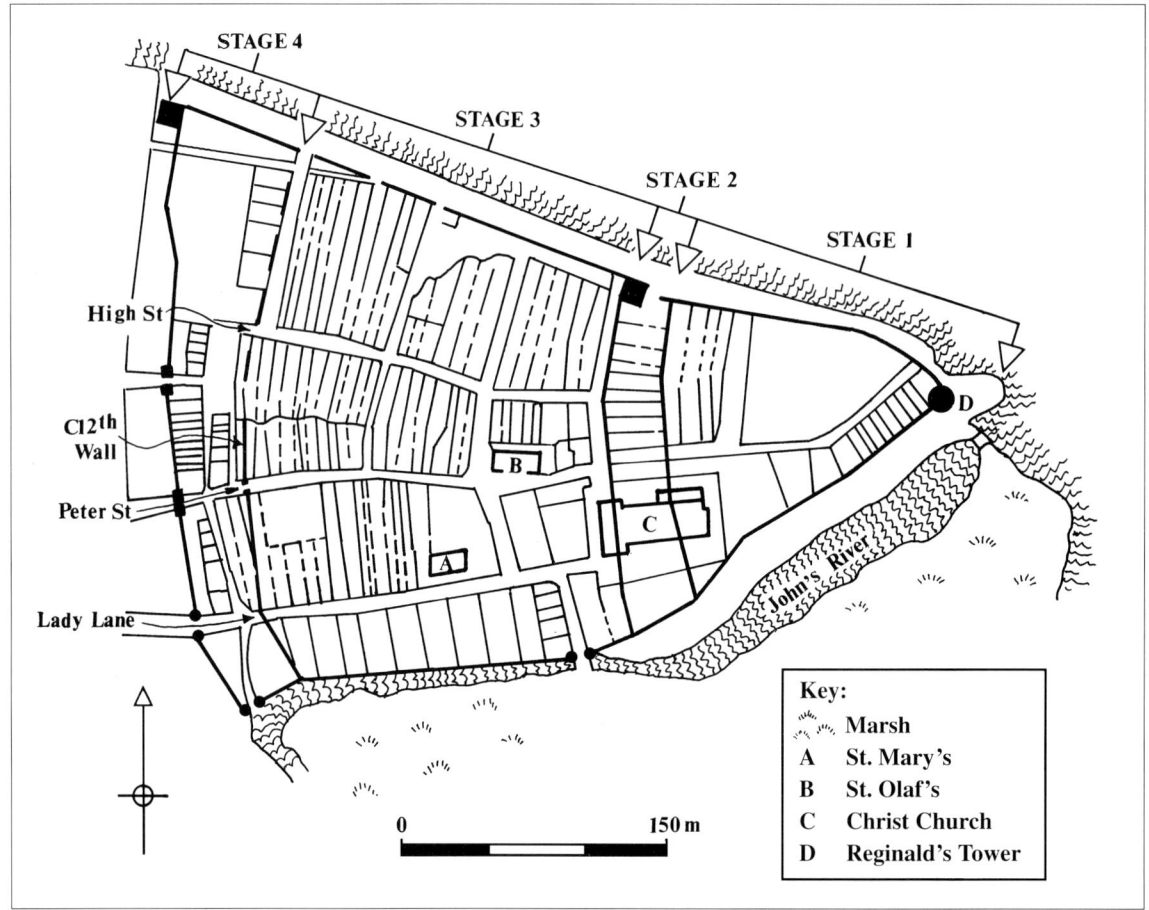

Fig. 16.1 Proposed sequence of development of Hiberno-Norse Waterford

penultimate of several expansions of the town. This triangular promontory was formed by the crest of a ridge that attained a maximum height of 6 m above the banks of the River Suir and the marsh of St John's river, which flank it on the north and south respectively. The eastern point of the triangle, close to the confluence of the rivers, forms a naturally defensive site and it is here that the largely thirteenth-century structure of Reginald's Tower still stands. From here the ground rises gradually to the site of the Cathedral of the Blessed Trinity (Christ Church), while to the north and south there is an increasingly sharp fall of ground. Further west, the crest of the ridge is broader with the break in slope occurring to the north of High Street and to the south of Lady Lane.

The enclosure of this triangular area is unlikely to have taken place as a single episode, and a model of sustained westward development taking place in three or four stages has been suggested (Fig. 16.1; Hurley, 1997b and c). The initial *longphort* of c. 912–14 was probably established at the eastern end of the promontory (Bradley and Halpin 1992, 106). From this primary nucleus the initial westward expansion enclosed an area of c. 1.3 hectares (3.2 acres). That the second extension was an intermediary stage is suggested on the basis of the cartographic evidence of later property boundaries (Hurley

1997b). Stage three was the single largest expansion of the town: two main streets, Peter Street and High Street, extended westwards from the stage two enclosure. It was in this area, probably developing as an unenclosed 'suburb' throughout the eleventh century, that the archaeological excavations took place.

In Waterford, therefore, there is evidence for a well-developed town layout from the mid-eleventh century onwards, with a progressive increase in the density of occupation. Security may have been provided by the adjacent fortified citadel where the inhabitants could take refuge during an attack. This proposed model may explain apparent contradictions in a number of historical documents: for example, the town was attacked and burned in 1088 but the annalistic sources differ regarding the outcome of this event. The contradiction may be reconciled by the suggestion that only the unenclosed part of the town was burnt, while the fortress or citadel held out (Bradley and Halpin 1992, 107–08). The very existence of unenclosed suburbs implies that a perception of safety existed for the inhabitants. This is anathema to a school of thought (e.g. Wilson 1980, 17) that saw the Irish Viking cities as constantly beleaguered garrisons, shut up in fortified seaports, waiting to snap out like a cobra at a vulnerable target. Security for Waterford was clearly provided by the Hiberno-Norse dominance of its immediate hinterland, within which the agricultural community was also of mixed ancestry (Bradley 1988), as well as by the flexible political and military alliances it developed with other towns and with the native Irish kingdoms (de Paor 1976, 32). The eleventh century saw unprecedented expansion of Hiberno-Norse towns elsewhere in Ireland (Simms 1990, 46; Bradley 1992, 47). Regarding Limerick, a similar pattern of development is suggested by an entry in *Chronicum Scotorum* which describes the burning in 1015 of the 'fortress and all the houses that were from the fortress outwards'.

By the late eleventh century the number and wealth of the inhabitants of Waterford had increased sufficiently to warrant further defence. This was provided by fortifying the vulnerable western side of the triangular promontory with earthen ramparts (Hurley 1997c). This greater emphasis on defence was probably a necessary response to the increased hostilities of the later eleventh century (Bradley and Halpin 1992, 107), as by that time the control of the Hiberno-Norse ports was a necessary prerequisite to the establishment of regional, and ultimately national, supremacy.

The late eleventh-century defences of Waterford, located adjacent to Bakehouse Lane, comprised a ditch, 8.5 m wide and 2 m deep, with a bank on its inner side which was mainly raised from its upcast. The bank appears to have been further strengthened by a wooden palisade and was surmounted by a wooden walkway. The construction of these defences is reliably assigned to the 1080s by dendrochronological dating of timbers, some of which were found *in situ* (Hurley 1992, 52). The ramparts were augmented by a stone wall in the second quarter of the twelfth century. This sequence of events is closely paralleled by the development of the Dublin defences (Wallace 1988, 130–35). The Dublin city wall of *c.* 1100 is very similar in construction and appearance to that at Waterford, which in turn is strikingly similar in appearance to a twelfth-century defensive wall at Limerick (Wiggins 1991, 43). The Limerick wall, however, is understood to date to later in the century and postdates the capture of Limerick by the Anglo-Normans (O'Rahilly 1995, 169). Such comparisons have little value for dating purposes, as the wall in Dublin is also said to be similar in appearance (Barry 1987, 128) to a wall excavated by Moore at Lady Lane, Waterford (Fig. 16.1; Moore 1983). The dating of Moore's wall, however, remains contentious. It would, if projected, lie *c.* 30 m to the west of the early to mid-eleventh-century wall excavated at Bakehouse Lane. This brings us to the fourth stage of the westward expansion of the Hiberno-Norse town. Houses were built in the Hiberno-Norse structural tradition (McCutcheon 1997) above the backfilled ditch immediately to the west of the city wall. These are likely to have been built prior to 1170, indicating extra-mural development to the west of the stage three enclosure. This area was defended by a further ditch lying c. 20m to the west (Moore 1983; 1984), but whether or not it was enclosed by another wall remains unclear. Was the wall excavated by Moore the ultimate achievement of the Hiberno-Norse defence of Waterford or the first major contribution by the Anglo-Normans to the defence of their newly captured city? There is no definitive answer to this question. The evidence appears to place the structure in a similarly ambiguous position to the twelfth-century city wall at Limerick.

Town layout and houses
The two streets, High Street and Peter Street, probably developed along the lines of pathways leading from gateways in the primary nucleus of the city. Peter Street was paved with rough cobbles and gravel in the mid-eleventh century. With the exception of a small number of houses in the centre of the blocks, there is unambiguous evidence for a regular sub-division of property fronting the streets from the earliest levels. A street frontage was evidently a basic requirement in property ownership, hence the arrangement of long narrow plots at right angles to the streets. Although the properties were aligned to the street frontages, the houses were not always contiguous with the streets and each plot was not continuously occupied by a house. These inconsistencies and discontinuities of occupation are not easily explained.

Much of the evidence for domestic architecture in Waterford was fragmentary by comparison with that from Dublin. In particular, the frequent absence of evidence for structural timbers and walls meant that the floor surfaces provided the principal indication of the size and shape of the structures (Fig. 16.2; Plate 1). The excavations produced evidence for over ninety houses of eleventh- and twelfth-century date. The underlying boulder clay and the impermeability of the clay floors created conditions favourable to the preservation of organic material. As each layer was laid down the process was compounded, resulting in the accumulation of increasingly more substantial layers as the twelfth century progressed. It can be seen, therefore, that the evidence cannot be interpreted solely as indicative of population density since factors relating to preservation and survival are also relevant.

The similarity between the Hiberno-Norse houses of Waterford and Dublin is strong. With one notable exception, the street-fronting houses were all rectangular, wattle-walled structures, divided into three longitudinally, with a central hearth and two doorways, one in each of the end-walls; these are what Wallace (1992a) defines as type 1 houses in Dublin. Allowing for the scarcity of evidence for roof supports in Waterford and acknowledging the intrinsic importance of these in Wallace's typology, it can only be said of the Waterford houses that where evidence for roof supports existed these were frequently arranged in opposing pairs on the aisle divisions (ibid., vol. 2, 59, Figs. 46, 48). In other instances it seems likely that one pair of posts located in the floor area may have supported the roof in conjunction with structural timbers in the end walls (ibid., Fig. 49). The internal layout and most other features of the Waterford houses are paralleled in one way or another by the Dublin type 1 houses.

Type 1 houses are interpreted as the principal residences, providing accommodation for all domestic activities as well as space for storage, crafts and trade. Smaller square houses with rounded corners, type 2 (after Wallace 1992a), were generally located to the rear of the type 1 street-fronting houses. Only three type 2 houses were street-fronting. This type is seen as subsidiary, perhaps providing additional domestic or sleeping accommodation for the occupants of the main house. There was usually only one type 2 house associated with each type 1 house, and this was frequently located to one side of a pathway leading from the back door of the latter. In contrast to the Dublin examples hearths were normally present, although these were smaller

Fig. 16.2 Late eleventh-century houses fronting Peter Street: type 1 with pathway leading from 'back-door'; type 2 house to left of pathway and another in upper left

and less elaborately defined than those in type 1 houses. In all other respects the morphology, proportions and internal layout of the Waterford type 2 houses paralleled their Dublin counterparts, but evidence for wattle mats – a characteristic Dublin feature – was rarely present.

Type 3 houses are not present in Waterford, indicating that this 'slimmed-down and shortened version of type 1' (ibid., vol. 1, 16) is not in fact a distinct type but a response to the particular physical limitations of part of the Fishamble Street site. In Waterford one group of houses, built outside the early to mid-twelfth-century city wall, may also be interpreted as a similar compromise dictated by their location. Similar to Type 1 houses in many respects, these structures had their doorways in the long side-walls and displayed other unique features in their internal layout.

There was evidence in Waterford for six type 4 houses, otherwise known as 'sunken buildings' (Walsh, C. 1997). Houses of this type have a distinct morphology and date range. They were constructed in the mid to late eleventh century and had gone out of use and been backfilled by the mid-twelfth century. The buildings are interpreted as cellars with elaborate entrances leading from their backyards to the sunken floors. They probably had an upper floor, which was in most instances entered from the street. For this reason they are, perhaps, more accurately described as cellared buildings.

Type 4 houses are comparatively rare in Dublin (Wallace 1992a), although a further example has recently been discovered (Hayden and Walsh, pers. comm.). Houses of similar type are known from tenth-century contexts in Denmark and from the second half of the tenth and early eleventh centuries in England (Richards 1991, 61). They may be a Scandinavian introduction to England or may be 'simply part of a general north-west European development' (ibid.). Walsh (1997) has suggested that their presence in Waterford may provide evidence for 'an influx of people' from England, and while this is a debatable point their occurrence certainly highlights the significance of foreign trade and contacts in late eleventh-century Waterford. The cellars would have provided cool and secure storage space and elsewhere 'appear to be associated with tenth-century revival of trade and growth of trading towns' (Richards 1991, 61). Although the Waterford sequence is somewhat later than the known English examples, the occurrence of three comparable houses in Limerick shows the widespread popularity of this type of house in late eleventh- and twelfth-century urban contexts in Ireland. The Limerick houses are said to be even later in date than the Waterford examples, as 'the backfilled deposits . . . produced quantities of 12th/13th century pottery, implying that they may have been in use up to the time the castle was constructed' (Wiggins 1991, 43).

It is likely that the houses were constructed by owner occupiers. The fusion of native Irish and foreign influences apparent in the buildings (Wallace 1992a) is almost certainly a result of the diverse strands and influences which made up the cultural milieu of eleventh- and twelfth-century Irish ports. The skills required for house construction were unlikely to be beyond the capabilities of most citizens, and the uniformity apparent in house styles and building traditions may be interpreted as resulting from communal effort in such undertakings (Hurley 1997d). Trade and foreign contacts produced an awareness of and an adaptability to new methods of construction, even before the arrival of the Anglo-Normans in 1170. The wattle house-building traditions of the eleventh and early twelfth century had already been replaced by new methods of construction, and hence a new type – houses of sill-beam construction – appeared. The plot layout, internal proportions and ground plans of the houses did not change, but the form of the walls and location of the structural timbers were very different. The roof was supported by large, earth-fast oak beams arranged in opposing pairs on the side-walls. The walls were probably made of staves set vertically in grooved sill-beams. Although the early sequence of sill-beam houses of mid-twelfth-century date were still tripartite in plan, it is possible that the massive uprights facilitated the introduction of a second floor and that the inspiration for this was originally the type 4 cellared buildings.

Christianity and churches
Christianity had become well established in the Hiberno-Norse towns by the eleventh century and it is likely that Christianisation 'was under way before the close of the 10th century' (Bradley and Halpin 1992, 111). By the end of the eleventh century the role of the Hiberno-Norse towns in the ecclesiastical affairs of Ireland was as critical as their role in its political sphere, and both were inextricably intertwined. The people of Waterford City established their own diocese and chose Malchus, who had studied as a Benedictine monk at Winchester, as their bishop. He was consecrated at Canterbury in 1096 (Gwynn and Hadcock 1970, 100). Close ecclesiastical links were also fostered between Dublin and Canterbury in the twelfth century (ibid., 70–71). The development of the involvement between the Hiberno-Norse towns and the powerful English ecclesiastical centres, rather than with monastic centres in Ireland, is indicative of the singular status possessed by Dublin and Waterford in the late eleventh and twelfth century. The dedication of the principal church in both cities to the Blessed Trinity (Christ Church), and the subsequent elevation of both to cathedral status, underscores their unique and powerful position. A similar dedication of the main parish church in the Hiberno-Norse area of Cork is significant, but the failure of the latter church to achieve cathedral status undoubtedly relates to the continuing power of St Finbarr's monastery. This situation

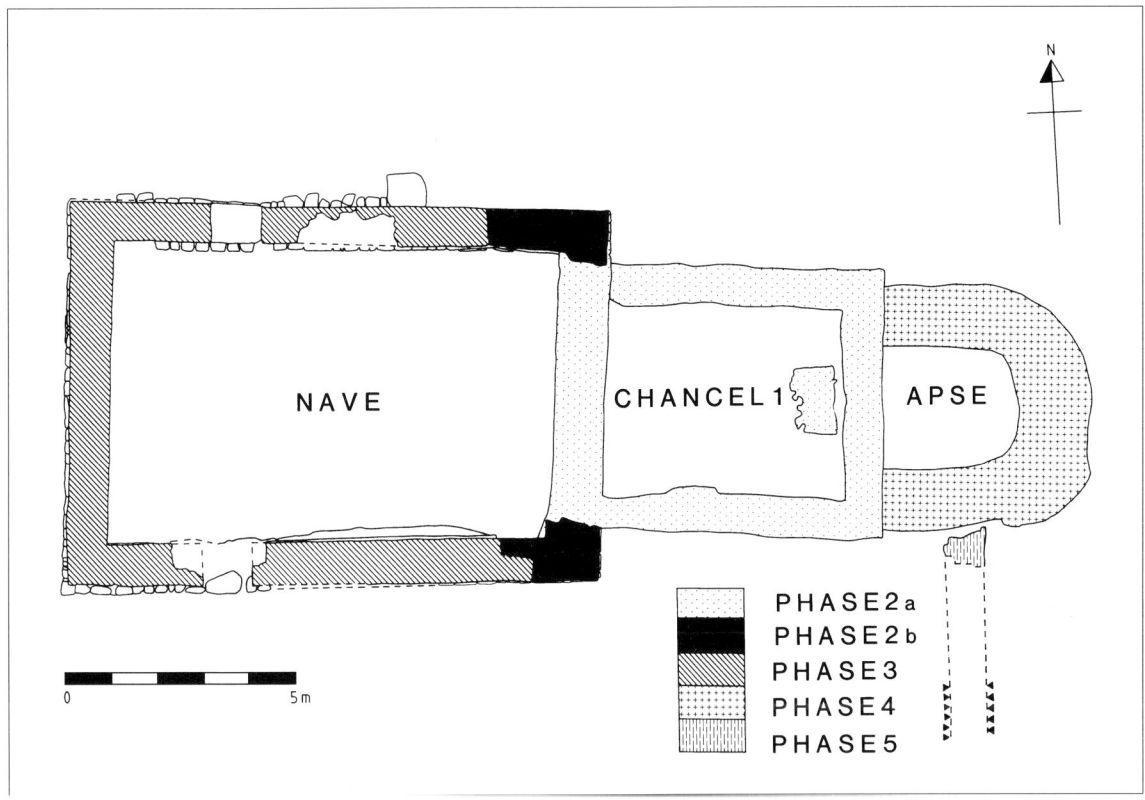

Fig. 16.3   St Peter's Church, Waterford: plan of twelfth-century three-cell church

may also reflect the smaller size and less prominent role played by Hiberno-Norse Cork according to Jeffries (1985, 15, 21); a picture apparently contradicted by the twelfth-century historical references (Bradley and Halpin 1993, 19).

At least two parish churches were built in twelfth-century Waterford, St Olaf's and St Mary's (Fig. 16.1), and the latter was the subject of a lengthy archaeological excavation. Although a wooden church may have preceded the construction of the first stone church, there was insufficient evidence to confirm this beyond doubt. Possibly as many as sixty burials were interred prior to the construction of the stone church; timbers were preserved in twelve of these and two interments were surrounded by charcoal, reflecting 'a practice current [in England] around the mid-eleventh century but not common for a long period before or after that date' (Gilmour and Stocker 1986, 20). In the early twelfth century the first stone church was built, with construction taking place in three stages (Fig. 16.3; Hurley and McCutcheon 1997). The chancel was built first together with the east end of the nave, all constructed of rough ashlar masonry (Murtagh 1997). At this stage the remainder of the nave may have been of wooden construction. The stone nave was completed in the early to mid-twelfth century. A contemporary or slightly later apse was added to the east end, thus creating a three-cell church. This apse is, to date, a unique feature in the general context of Irish churches of this period, although it is possible and indeed likely that other churches in the Hiberno-Norse ports were provided with such features. The influence of Bishop Malchus in this instance has already been suggested (Hurley 1992, 55), although the balance of the archaeological evidence places its construction at a later date.⁵ In this regard, however, it must be emphasised that Malchus was one of the leaders of the twelfth-century reform of the Irish Church and the role played by the Hiberno-Norse towns in this movement was very significant (de Paor 1976, 32–33). The apse, even if post-dating Malchus, may owe much to his zealous reforms and concurs with Harbison's suggestion that he was responsible for the church at Lismore 'which reflected the architectural developments which he would have seen during his stay in England at the end of the 11th century' (1978, 8).

Late Viking Age Cork

Archaeological evidence for an early Viking Age presence in Cork is scant and material available from other sources is 'negligible' (Jeffries 1985, 14). Historical references for the later Viking Age – the twelfth century in particular – are more informative and these are augmented by archaeological evidence (Cleary et al. 1997).

Viking raids on Cork are recorded from the early ninth century onwards, specifically the years 826 (AFM) and 838 (AU). These raids were focused on the wealth of St Finbarr's monastery. Sources referring to Viking Cork in the later ninth century refer to a *dún* or *caisteol* there, and this is indicative of the foundation of a permanent settlement. An entry in the *Annals of the Four Masters* for the year 846, for example, refers to an attack by Ólchobhar mac Cinóida, king of Cashel, on the *dún Corcaighe* (fort/fortress of Cork). This settlement may have been short lived (Jeffries 1985, 15) and Cork, like Dublin and Waterford, appears to have been re-established as a Viking stronghold early in the tenth century (Wallace 1992b, 36–37).

The accommodation eventually worked out between the monastic centre at Cork and the earliest settled Vikings is unclear. It has been suggested that the absence of references in the annals to the eleventh-century Hiberno-Norse town implies that the ecclesiastical chroniclers were 'not much interested in those who settled or traded' (Jeffries 1985, 14).⁶ Perhaps this silence should not be interpreted as a lack of interest but rather a lack of 'newsworthy events' in the growth and development of the town. Some form of symbiotic relationship clearly developed, presumably one whereby the Hiberno-Norse traders procured otherwise unobtainable foreign goods for the monastery and, perhaps, also provided military aid to assist in the monastery's territorial ambitions (ibid., 16; Bradley and Halpin 1993, 19).

Location and layout
Hiberno-Norse Cork may have developed directly from the ninth century *dún* or *longphort* or it may have been re-established in the early tenth century on a different site. In either case it is clear that the town which existed at the time of the Norman conquest of 1177 was located on the South Island (Fig. 16.4). By reference to other Hiberno-Norse towns, such as Dublin, Wexford, Waterford and probably Limerick, I suggest that twelfth-century Cork developed on the site of its tenth- to eleventh-century predecessor and that its genesis lay in the ninth-century *dún*. The major problem arising in the verification of this hypothesis is the scarcity of archaeological evidence and a belief that the Vikings shunned low-lying sites in favour of the strategic advantages offered by higher ground (Jeffries 1985, 17). Both of these issues need to be examined separately, for neither is as clear-cut as it may initially seem.

First and foremost, the archaeological evidence must be addressed. Archaeologists are wont to be suspicious of evidence summed up too neatly, and in the case of the urban strata in Cork this has been the case, for many pockets of human occupation debris are interspersed with flood-borne alluvial silts in the lower levels. Excavations on the islands of Cork city have rarely reached 'the bottom',⁷ for these levels currently lie below sea-level and are constantly awash (Hurley 1986, 19, 21; 1995, 69). This situation is a result of the compaction of the underlying clay strata by the weight of the modern city (Beese and Nyhan 1995, 86–87), and consequently the earliest

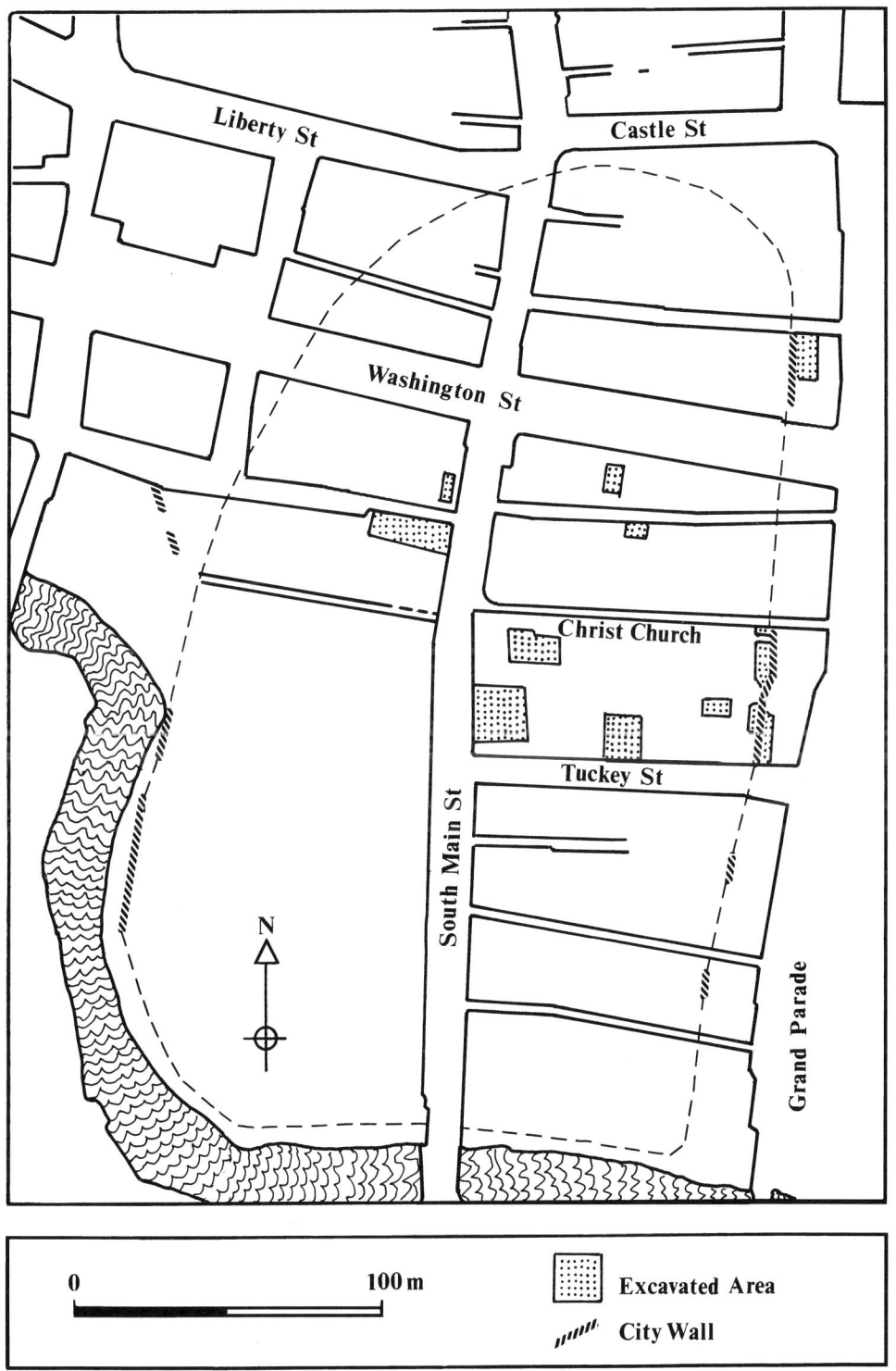

Fig. 16.4 Plan showing suggested location of Hiberno-Norse Cork and location of archaeological excavations

levels are now lower than they were at the time they were occupied.

With the exception of Twohig's excavations at South Main Street (College of Holy Trinity, Christ Church) in the mid-1970s, large-scale excavations have not taken place in the area likely to have been within the confines of the Hiberno-Norse town. The absence of archaeological evidence for Hiberno-Norse Cork in the South Main Street area is explained, to some extent, by the conventional dating framework for imported pottery current until the late 1980s.[8] The lack of material of pre-thirteenth century-date from sites adjacent to the city wall at the Grand Parade (Hurley and Power 1981; Hurley 1985; 1989; 1990) is understandable, as this was on the periphery of the island that evidently sloped downwards from its central crest at South Main Street. The infilling of the outlying areas was gradual. The sites excavated at Tobin Street (Papazian 1985) and Washington Street (McCutcheon, forthcoming) may also lie outside the nucleus of the settlement. From this it can be seen that any opportunity to undertake archaeological excavation in the vicinity of South Main Street should not be missed;[9] perhaps the ghosts of Cork's missing Vikings may at last be put to rest, or, more aptly, may take on a tangible substance.

Regarding the nature of the South Main Street site and the 'unattractive nature' (Jeffries 1985, 17) of marshes *vis-à-vis* high ground, it is important to bear in mind that defence was the primary motivation influencing the choice of site. 'Locating towns at estuarine river mouths near tributaries and capitalising on natural defences may have been the most original physical contribution of the Vikings to Irish colonisation' (Wallace 1992b, 39). In these terms the South Island of Cork is a classic site, for it was surrounded by deep river channels and marshy islands, making it largely unassailable until the development of artillery. Even in the well-documented siege of 1690 the Williamite soldiers were 'up to their armpits in water' when crossing the South Channel at low tide (Ó Murchadha 1990, 11).

The suggested location of Viking Cork on the south bank of the River Lee proposed by Jeffries (1985, 18–21) is largely based on a number of early Anglo-Norman charters. These clearly refer to Hiberno-Norse settlement but not necessarily to settlement located in the core of the city. It is likely that by the later twelfth century extra-mural settlement had developed on the main thoroughfare leading to the south from the South Gate bridge – the principal entrance to the island city. Two archaeological excavations in this area (O'Brien 1993, 27–49; Cleary 1996), as well as numerous trial excavations in the Barrack Street, Cove Street, Douglas Street and Sullivan's Quay areas,[10] have failed to reveal evidence for occupation predating the late twelfth century. More importantly, perhaps, the topography of a steadily rising slope to the south offered little by way of defence at this location, and there is no documentary evidence for the founding of a new city on the South Island in the twelfth century. There is, however, every indication that the South Island was in fact an existing fortification at the time of the Anglo-Norman invasion (Bradley and Halpin 1993, 20). The gradual development of the Hiberno-Norse town from an indefensible site on the south bank to a defensive site on the South Island is illogical, while the reverse is supported by the model of sustained development in the Anglo-Norman period (Candon 1985) and is certainly not contradicted by the current state of archaeological evidence. Such a development is paralleled by the evidence from Waterford and, perhaps, by Limerick also. The suburban nature of the settlement on the south bank of the river Lee can easily be reconciled with the historical references. It was referred to as the *vill* and was apparently unenclosed by defences, hence the boundary was referred to as the 'curtilages of the burgesses' (ibid., 19). The term *civitas* was used to describe the south island (Bradley and Halpin 1993, 20) – the heart of the city as it existed at the time of the conquest. The expulsion of the Hiberno-Norse (Ostmen) to an area outside the city walls, and the resultant development of the suburb of *Fayth* (suggestion by K.W. Nicholls, in Jeffries 1985, 22), is also paralleled at Waterford (Barry 1977).

The genesis of the Munster cities in the *longphuirt* of the tenth century remains speculative. The later eleventh century was, however, the critical formative period and the developments that took place at that time are reflected in the contemporary population centres of Munster. The shadows of the early towns are also strong in the present-day streetscapes of Cork and Waterford. In the past ten years extensive archaeological excavations, particularly in Waterford, have become the principal source of information for these developments.

NOTES

1. Bradley (1995, 12) has suggested that Feltrim Hill (Hartnett and Eogan 1964) and Brownsbarn (Sleeman and Hurley 1987) – where part of a settlement was excavated and where the finds included a bone comb of ninth- to tenth-century date and a lignite bracelet – may both represent Hiberno-Scandinavian rural settlements. It has also been proposed that House 1 at Beginish Island, Co. Kerry, may have formed part of a Scandinavian settlement there (O'Kelly 1956, 191).
2. This is Lonehort Harbour, Bere Island, Co. Cork, investigated in 1995 by Colin Breen and John Sheehan.
3. An inhumation excavated at Mayfield/Rocketscastle, Portlaw, Co. Waterford, is probably of ninth- to tenth-century date and may be a Viking burial. The grave appears to be associated with a contemporary settlement (Gowen 1988, 166–69).
4. The early thirteenth century was the accepted date for the first introduction of Ham Green pottery from Bristol (Twohig 1985). The occurrence of fragmentary strata predating the occurrence of Ham Green ware led Twohig to date these layers to the late twelfth century. Ham Green ware is now generally accepted as dating to the mid-twelfth century or earlier (Ponsford 1991, 81–103). In Waterford, it occurs in layers dating to the second quarter of the twelfth century and it was in widespread use there by the mid-twelfth century (Gahan and McCutcheon 1997). Large quantities of Ham Green ware, with a general absence of later imported pottery (Saintonge ware, Redcliffe ware, etc.), were recovered from Twohig's excavations at the College of Holy Trinity (Christ Church) site at South Main Street (Gahan et al. 1997). It now seems likely that the lowest layers excavated at Christ Church were of early to mid-twelfth-century date, and some fragmentary evidence for earlier occupation may also have been present.
5. Malchus translated to Lismore in 1110 and later to Cashel (Gwynn and Hadcock 1970, 100).
6. For similar see Sawyer 1962, 31–32.
7. Recent excavations at Tuckey Street, Cork, by Ms M.G. O'Donnell, have uncovered the remains of a revetment at a depth of *c.* 4 m below the street level and 2 m below the upper level of the estuarine silts. This is dendrochronologically dated to the twelfth century.
8. See footnote 4 above.
9. Excavation at the junction of Hanover Street and South Main Street in 1996, by Ms R.M. Cleary, showed that houses of sill-beam construction, with earthfast roof-supports on the side-walls, were built from the mid-twelfth century onwards. The underlying strata at this site were not available for excavation.
10. Excavation reports on file in the Planning Department, Cork Corporation.

BIBLIOGRAPHY

AFM *Annals of the Four Masters* (1848–51), O'Donovan, J. (ed.), Dublin

AU *Annals of Ulster* (1893), Hennessey, W. (ed.), Dublin

Barry, T.B. (1987) *The Archaeology of Medieval Ireland*, Cambridge

Barry, T.B. (1997) 'Waterford: an historical introduction', in M.F. Hurley and O.M.B. Scully, *Late Viking Age and Medieval Waterford: Excavations 1986–1992*, Waterford

Beese, A.P. and Nyhan, M.V. (1995) 'An investigation of three geological features', in M.F. Hurley, 'Excavations in Cork City: Kyrl's Quay/North Main Street and at Grand Parade (Part 1)', *J. Cork Hist. Archaeol. Soc.* 100, 86–87

Bradley, J. (1988) 'The interpretation of Scandinavian settlement in Ireland', in J. Bradley (ed.), *Settlement and Society in Medieval Ireland*, 49–78, Kilkenny

Bradley, J. (1992) 'The topographical development of Dublin', in F.H.A. Aalen and K. Whelan (eds.), *Dublin: History and Society*, 43–56, Dublin

Bradley, J. (1995) 'Scandinavian rural settlement in Ireland', *Archaeology Ireland* 9.3, 10–12

Bradley, J. and Halpin, A. (1992) 'The topographical development of Scandinavian and Anglo-Norman Waterford', in W. Nolan and T.P. Power (eds.), *Waterford: History and Society*, 105–30, Dublin

Bradley, J. and Halpin, A. (1993) 'The topographical development of Scandinavian and Anglo-Norman Cork', in P. O'Flanagan and C.G. Buttimer (eds.), *Cork: History and Society*, 15–44, Dublin

Candon, A. (1985) 'The Cork suburb of Dungarvan,' *J. Cork Hist. Archaeol. Soc.* 90, 91–103

Chronicum Scotorum (1866), Hennessey, W. (ed.) Dublin

Cleary, R.M. (1996) 'Excavations at Cove Street, Cork', *J. Cork Hist. Archaeol. Soc.* 101, 94–111

Cleary, R.M., Hurley, M.F. and Shee Twohig, E. (eds.) (1997), *Excavations by D.C. Twohig at Skiddy's Castle and Christ Church, Cork, 1974–77*, Cork

De Paor, L. (1976) 'The Viking towns of Ireland', in B. Almquist and D. Green (eds.), *Proceedings of the Seventh Viking Congress 1973*, 29–37, Dublin

Edwards, N. (1990) *The Archaeology of Early Medieval Ireland*, London
Gahan, A. and McCutcheon, C. (1997) 'The medieval pottery', in M.F. Hurley and O.M.B. Scully, *Viking Age and Medieval Waterford: Excavations 1986–1992*, Waterford
Gahan, A., McCutcheon, C. and Twohig, D.C. (1997) 'The medieval pottery assemblages from Skiddy's Castle and Christ Church', in R.M. Cleary, M.F. Hurley and E. Shee Twohig (eds.), *Excavations by D.C. Twohig at Skiddy's Castle and Christ Church, Cork, 1974–77*, Cork
Gilmour, B.J.J. and Stocker, D.A. (1986) *St Mark's Church and Cemetery*, The Archaeology of Lincoln 13/1
Gowen, M. (1988) *Three Irish Gas Pipelines: New Archaeological Evidence in Munster*, Dublin
Graham-Campbell, J. (1976) 'The Viking-age silver hoards of Ireland', in B. Almqvist and D. Greene (eds.), *Proceedings of the Seventh Viking Congress, Dublin 1973*, 39–55, Dublin
Graham-Campbell, J. (1987) 'From Scandinavia to the Irish Sea: Viking art reviewed', in M. Ryan (ed.), *Ireland and Insular Art A.D. 500–1200*, Dublin
Gwynn, A. and Hadcock, R.N. (1970) *Medieval Religious Houses: Ireland*, Dublin
Harbison, P. (1978) *Irish Art and Architecture*, London
Hartnett, P.J. and Eogan, G. (1964) 'Feltrim Hill, Co. Dublin, a Neolithic and Early Christian site', *J. Roy. Soc. Antiq. Ir.* 94, 1–38
Hurley, M.F. (1985) 'Excavations of part of the medieval city wall at Grand Parade', *J. Cork. Hist. Archaeol. Soc.* 90, 65–90
Hurley, M.F. (1986) 'Excavations in Medieval Cork: St Peter's market', *J. Cork. Hist. Archaeol. Soc.* 91, 1–25
Hurley, M.F. (1989) 'Excavations at Grand Parade, Cork II (Part 1)', *J. Cork. Hist. Archaeol. Soc.* 94, 27–45
Hurley, M.F. (1990) 'Excavations at Grand Parade, Cork II (Part 2)', *J. Cork. Hist. Archaeol. Soc.* 95, 64–87
Hurley, M.F. (1992) 'Late Viking age settlement in Waterford city', in W. Nolan and T.P. Power, (eds.), *Waterford: History and Society*, 49–72, Dublin
Hurley, M.F. (1995) 'Excavations in Cork city: Kyrl's Quay/North Main Street and at Grand Parade (Part 1)', *J. Cork. Hist. Archaeol. Soc.* 100, 47–90
Hurley, M.F. and Power, D. (1981) 'The Medieval town wall of Cork', *J. Cork Hist. Archaeol. Soc.* 86, 1–20
Hurley, M.F. (1997a) 'Domestic architecture', in R.M. Cleary, M.F. Hurley and E. Shee Twohig (eds.), *Excavations by D.C. Twohig at Skiddy's Castle and Christ Church, Cork, 1974–77*, Cork
Hurley, M.F. (1997b) 'Topography and development', in M.F. Hurley and O.M.B. Scully, *Late Viking Age and Medieval Waterford: 1986–1992*, Waterford
Hurley, M.F. (1997c) 'Defences', in M.F. Hurley and O.M.B. Scully, *Late Viking Age and Medieval Waterford: Excavations 1986–1992*, Waterford
Hurley, M.F. (1997d) 'Wood as a structural raw material', *Late Viking Age and Medieval Waterford: Excavations 1986–1992*, Waterford
Hurley, M.F. and McCutcheon, S.W.J. (1997) 'St Peter's church and graveyard', in M.F. Hurley and O.M.B. Scully, *Late Viking Age and Medieval Waterford: Excavations 1986–1992*, Waterford
Hurley, M.F and Scully, O.M.B. (1997) *Late Viking Age and Medieval Waterford: Excavations 1986–1992*, Waterford
Jeffries, H. (1985) 'The history and topography of Viking Cork', *J. Cork. Hist. Archaeol. Soc.* 90, 14–25
Kelly, E.P. (1995) 'Vikings on the Barrow – Dunrally Fort', *Archaeology Ireland* 9.3, 30–32
Lang, J. (1988) *Viking Age Decorated Wood*, Dublin
McCutcheon, S.W.J. (1997) 'Catalogue of houses: Bakehouse Lane' in M.F. Hurley and O.M.B. Scully, *Late Viking Age and Medieval Waterford: Excavations 1986–1992*, Waterford
McCutcheon, S.W.J. (forthcoming) *Excavations at 11–13 Washington Street, Cork*
Moore, M.J. (1983) 'City walls and gateway at site of St Martin's castle', *Decies* 23, 50–61
Murtagh, B. (1997) 'The architecture of St Peter's church', in M.F. Hurley and O.M.B. Scully, *Late Viking Age and Medieval Waterford: Excavations 1986–1992*, Waterford
O'Brien, E. (1998) 'The location and context of Viking burials at Kilmainham and Islandbridge', in H.B. Clarke, R. Ó Floinn and M. Ní Mhaonaigh (eds.), *Ireland and Scandinavia in the Early Viking Age*, Dublin
O'Brien, M. (1993) 'Excavations at Barrack Street/French's Quay, Cork', *J. Cork. Hist. Archaeol. Soc.* 98, 27–49
Ó Corráin, D. (1972) *Ireland before the Normans*, Dublin
O'Kelly, M.J. (1956) 'An island settlement at Beginish, Co. Kerry', *Proc. Roy. Ir. Acad.* 57C, 57–136
Ó Murchadha, D. (1990) 'The siege of Cork in 1690', *J. Cork Hist. Archaeol. Soc.* 95, 1–19
O'Rahilly, C. (1995) 'Medieval Limerick: the growth of two towns', in H. Clarke (ed.), *Irish Cities*, 163–76, Cork
Papazian, C. (1985) 'Excavations at Tobin St., Cork', *Medieval Archaeol.* 29, 213
Ponsford, M. (1991) 'Dendrochronological dates from Dundas Wharf, Bristol and the dating of Ham Green and other medieval pottery', in E. Lewis (ed.), *Custom and Ceramics*, 81–103, Wickham
Richards, J.D. (1991) *Viking Age England*, London
Sawyer, P. (1962) *The Age of the Vikings*, London
Sawyer, P. (1982) 'The Vikings and Ireland', in D. Whitelock, R. McKitterick and D. Dumville (eds.), *Ireland in Early Medieval Europe: Studies in memory of Kathleen Hughes*, 345–61, Cambridge
Sheehan, J. (1998) 'Early Viking-Age silver hoards from Ireland and their Scandinavian elements', in H.B. Clarke, R. Ó Floinn and M. Ní Mhaonaigh (eds.),

Ireland and Scandinavia in the Early Viking Age, Dublin

Simms, A. (1990) 'Medieval Dublin in a European context: from proto-town to chartered town', in H. Clarke (ed.), *Medieval Dublin: the making of a metropolis*, 37–51, Dublin

Sleeman, M.J. and Hurley, M.F. (1987) 'Brownsbarn, Co. Dublin', in R.M. Cleary, M.F. Hurley and E. Shee Twohig (eds.), *Archaeological Excavations on the Cork–Dublin gas pipeline (1981–82)*, 71–73, Cork

Twohig, D.C. (1975) 'Cork City excavations', in T. Delaney (ed.), *Excavations 1974: Summary Account of Archaeological Work in Ireland*, 11–12, Belfast

Twohig, D.C. (1978) 'Cork City excavations 1974–1977', *Bulletin of the Group for the Study of Irish Historic Settlement* 5, 19–22

Twohig, D.C. (1985) 'Archaeological heritage', *The Cork Examiner*, April 7th

Wallace, P.F. (1988) 'Archaeology and the emergence of Dublin as the principal town of Ireland', in J. Bradley (ed.), *Settlement and Society in Medieval Ireland, 123–60*, Kilkenny

Wallace, P.F. (1992a) *The Viking Age Buildings of Dublin*, 2 vols., Dublin

Wallace, P.F. (1992b) 'The archaeological identity of the Hiberno-Norse town', *J. Roy. Soc. Antiq. Ir.* 122, 35–66

Walsh, A. (1998) 'Viking Age swords from Ireland' in H.B. Clarke, R. Ó Floinn and M. Ní Mhaonaigh (eds.), *Ireland and Scandinavia in the Early Viking Age*, Dublin

Walsh, C. (1997) 'Sunken buildings', in M.F. Hurley and O.M.B. Scully, *Late Viking Age and Medieval Waterford: Excavations 1986–1992*, Waterford

Wamers, E. (1985) *Insularer Metallschmuck in Wikingerzeitlichen Gräbern Nordeuropas*, Neumünster

Wiggins, K. (1991) 'King John's Castle' in I. Bennett (ed.), *Excavations 1990: Summary Accounts of Archaeological Work in Ireland*, 43–44 and cover illustration

Wilson, D.M. (1980) *Economic aspects of the Vikings in the West: the archaeological basis*, Gothenburg

17. Nationalists, Archaeologists and the Myth of the Golden Age

JERRY O'SULLIVAN

Origin myths

The chapters in this volume offer a review of the Early Medieval period in Munster. Some are forward-looking and identify opportunities for further inquiry, while others attempt to summarise what is already known. This chapter aims to provide a general retrospective on Early Medieval Irish archaeology and seeks to identify the sources of mainstream thinking about this period. Irish archaeology has a long memory, but this may be more subtle and diffuse than is sometimes realised. Not all of its content is archaeologically derived, and some of its major themes stem from the popular and political nationalism which, in the last century, flowered into a full-blown 'Gaelic revival'.

This is not a novel proposal. As a whole, the archaeological discipline has come to terms with the idea that modern states have sometimes looked to the subject to supply the narrative of a heroic age from which they can derive validation, unity and a sense of purpose. This is especially characteristic of the smaller nation states which gained their sovereignty in the modern period. As a general proposal, this idea was first set out in a short paper by Trigger (1984) and since then the relationship between politics and archaeology, or more specifically national identity and archaeology, has been explored by means of numerous individual case studies (see Kohl and Fawcett 1995; Diaz-Andreu and Champion 1996; Atkinson et al. 1996).

In Ireland, popular interest in a pre-Norman 'Golden Age' was part of a cultural movement which gathered momentum throughout the later nineteenth century and overflowed into the politics of independence during the early decades of the present one. Thus, in figurative terms, this Gaelic revival forms a kind of unconscious reservoir of ideas for Irish archaeologists. This may not be specifically articulated in contemporary writing on the Early Medieval period, but there are salient themes – including the archetype of dispersed farm settlements and the monumental landscape of the early Church – which have an endurance and resonance beyond their purely archaeological content. Indeed, it may be argued that, from an early date, the archaeology of secular settlements and ecclesiastical monuments became reified or fixed within limited parameters; the prevailing ideas might subsequently be enlarged or refined by additional data, but would not be challenged by the development of alternative models or new lines of inquiry (but see Monk, ch. 5).

The Gaelic revival

From the 1840s – but more particularly from the 1870s – a full-blown, popular, romantic nationalism began to find expression in Ireland in a range of artistic, literary and athletic organisations. A common theme was the authority they derived from a remote Celtic or Gaelic past. A spate of associations for the promotion of Gaelic culture were founded from the 1860s onwards (amongst others, the Shamrock in 1867, the Society for the Protection of the Irish Language and its splinter organisaton, the Gaelic Union, in 1867, the Gaelic Athletic Association in 1884, the Gaelic League (Conradh na Gaeilge) in 1893 and the Young Ireland League in 1891). From the 1850s the Ancient Order of Hibernians aimed to promote not only a Gaelic national culture but a specifically Catholic one. In an earlier decade, there is something both pointed and poignant in Daniel O'Connell's organisation of mass rallies for Catholic emancipation at locations – like Tara and Clontarf – which could stir a romantic identification with pre-Norman Irish kings.

Literature was a motive force as much as an ideological vehicle. The importance of *The Nation* newspaper as a forum for nationalist ideas is well known. Its founders – Thomas Davis and others – also initiated a publication series, called the *Library of Ireland*, to promote Gaelic values and folk literature and projected a programme of work which included the preservation of ancient monuments and tombs and the revival of Gaelic placenames and personal names. Jeremiah O'Donovan Rossa's National and Literary Society was founded in 1856 and John O'Leary founded the National Literary Society in 1892. Standish O'Grady's *History of Ireland* (1878–80) mixed scholarship with prose rhapsody and offered the first glimpses in the English language of the heroic world of the Ulster Cycle. Various 'penny journals' began to feature stories from Irish folklife, but also carried illustrations and descriptions of church ruins, High Crosses and other antiquities. Much of the popular literature of the day – like A.M. Sullivan's *Story of Ireland* (1867) – focused on the conflict of *Gael* and *Gall*, or on the struggles of an indigenous Gaelic people against the incursions of Normans, Tudors and later planters. Henry Giles published his *Penny Readings for the Irish People* in the 1880s, with the elegiac introductory reflection that 'the meanest man lingers under the shadows of piles [ruins] that tell him that his fathers were not slaves . . . He toils in the fields with structures before him through which echoes the voice of centuries – the voice of soldiers, of scholars and of saints.'

Early scholars and learned societies

Academic effort in the period of the Gaelic revival was driven by neither public demand nor political motive. A school of antiquarian writers had already begun to establish a considerable pedigree before the Gaelic revival added popular interest to their researches. Publications on the artefacts and monuments of the Early Medieval period appeared at a rate which would provoke envy today, including works by Petrie (1845, 1872, 1878), Wakeman (1848), O'Neill (1857), Wood Martin (1886), Stokes (1878, 1894), Coffey (1909) and Champneys (1910). This litany is by no means exhaustive, but it serves to attest to the importance of the Early Medieval era as a core period in antiquarian studies. Some later figures, like Eoin MacNeill, were overtly engaged in political nationalism: as Professor of Early Irish History at University College, Dublin, and President of the Irish Volunteers, he asserted the antiquity of Irish nationhood via the national extent of early Irish law and kingship (Boyce 1995, 26). It would be wrong, however, to exaggerate the contribution of early scholarship to this end. The antiquarian tradition was certainly an ingredient in the milieu from which a sense of Celtic/Gaelic national identity emerged in Ireland, but it was not the conscious author of this identity.

This conclusion is borne out by recent commentaries on the learned societies of the day. Woodman concludes that these societies were generally not politicised, whatever the beliefs of individual members, and made no deliberate contribution to the popular fervour for cultural/ethnic nationalism (1995, 282). This is probably true of all of the more venerable societies, whose transactions are still important currents in the archaeological mainstream – such as the *Proceedings of the Royal Irish Academy* from 1836 (formerly *Transactions*, from 1786), the *Journal of the Royal Society of Antiquaries of Ireland* from 1890 (formerly the 'Kilkenny Society', from 1846), the *Ulster Journal of Archaeology* from 1853 and, of course, the *Journal of the Cork Historical and Archaeological Society* from 1885 – but it would be interesting to discover more about the aims of the minor societies, since defunct, whose names at least suggest a more explicit concern with cultural/ethnic scholarship, such as the Gaelic Society of Dublin (1806), the Hiberno-Celtic Society (1818) and the Celtic Society (1843). Borland has examined the records of some of these smaller groups and has observed a conscious determination to eliminate sectarian and political differences from their affairs. The Dublin-based Ossianic Society provides an explicit example of this with its ruling that 'all matters pertaining to the Religious and Political differences in this country be strictly excluded from the meetings and publications of the Society' (vol. 3, 1855, 8; quoted in Borland 1995). This repudiation of sectarianism is a sign that scholars were seeking to maintain their independence and objectivity, but the self-policing by the societies also discloses that there was an uneasy awareness that their activities were of direct interest to the political factions of the day. Images and tokens quarried from the past could be translated into a politicised vocabulary of potent symbols.

Celtic idylls/political ideals
Inevitably, the idylls of literary editors became the rhetoric of political ideologues. Images of Ireland's golden age became a source of validation for Irish independence in the early twentieth century and are to be found everywhere in the political rhetoric of the day. Michael Collins saw the establishment of the Free State as the opportunity 'to fill our minds with Gaelic ideas and our lives with Gaelic customs until there is no room for any other', while Arthur Griffith declared the racial supremacy of the Celts over their Saxon neighbours and proposed that the rapid industrialisation of Ireland would be the 'unavoidable acid test of such Celtic pre-eminence'. Even James Connolly, though he warned against a morbid idealising of the past, succumbed to the image of early Irish society as a utopia of primitive Celtic communism (Boyce 1995, 296, 302, 354). The utopian theme was sometimes juxtaposed with the theme of exodus: Patrick Pearse evoked the image of the Gaels as Children of Israel, internally exiled in the desert of colonialism. It is easy to envisage the ecclesiastical ruins in this lost homeland as sacred places and milestones in the desert, not merely monuments to an idealised past but the ubiquitous tokens of a utopian future. It is this vision of the landscape that Eamon de Valéra would later evoke when he mourned in the partition of Ireland the loss of 'some of our holiest and most sacred places' (Coogan 1995, 521).

After independence, the Gaelic/Celtic myth continued to supply a political vocabulary which bolstered the sense of national unity and purpose. Although Government was exchanged in the 1920s, 30s and 40s between several single-party and coalition governments, the political ethos in these decades was dominated by de Valéra. He was at least as well versed in the myth of the golden age as any of his contemporaries. After a private meeting between him and Sir James Craig in 1921, the Ulster Unionist leader complained that 'after half an hour he had reached the era of Brian Boru and after another half an hour had advanced to the period of some king a century or two later. By this time I was getting tired' (Coogan 1995, 215). De Valera went on to lead successive governments as head of the Fianna Fáil party he had founded on leaving Sinn Féin in 1926. The party's original manifesto included the advancement of the Irish language and culture as well as the promotion of family life, rooted in the soil. Land issues were to the fore in the 1930s especially, when de Valera refused to continue paying land annuities to Britain; the resulting 'economic war' (1932–38) created an even sharper focus on the issue of self-sufficiency. Against a background of 'real politik', which involved employment, housing, industrial development and education reform, de Valéra's appeals to unity and purpose in national life repeatedly emphasised rural, frugal self-sufficiency. He would often idealise his personal recollections of farm life. The general ethos he espoused is popularly remembered in terms of the St Patrick's Day radio broadcast in 1943, which envisioned strong lads and comely maidens dancing at the crossroads, but its conservative nature is expressed at greater length – and in less idyllic terms – by the Constitution of 1937 with its explicit endorsements of patriarchy, the home, the nuclear family and Catholic supremacy. A Gaelic education system and way of life were the stated aspirations of Government. In election campaigns de Valéra appealed to his constituents as 'worthy descendants of Clare men who fought under Brian Boru' or – on the election trail in the 1930s – made dramatic entries to town squares, mounted on a white horse, draped in a flowing black cape and surrounded by the torch-bearers of the volunteer cavalry (Coogan 1995, 432). These powerful images owe as much to the popularisation of Irish medieval heroic tales as they do to Mussolini and the public theatre of European fascism. In the terms of Lee's (1989, 183) wry observation: 'Fianna Fáil extended its emotional sway over past as well as present, establishing a virtual monopoly in the historical mythology market'.

The first generation of modern field archaeologists

What has all of this to do with archaeology? At the very least, a retrospective view of modern Irish history affords some idea of the sense of identity imparted to the first generation of Irish field archaeologists. Through their experience, the Gaelic revival was as formative for Irish archaeology as it was for the identity of the new state. Although there was no state-sponsored programme of 'validation by excavation', the core theme of a pre-Norman/Celtic golden age certainly supplied a degree of momentum to the emerging archaeological discipline during the first decades of independence. It should not be surprising then that Early Medieval sites were favoured, in particular those which exhibited high status or royal associations.

The earlier, nineteenth-century works on art and architecture were being supplanted in the 1930s, 40s and 50s with new works by Adolph Mahr (1932), Joseph Raftery (1941, 1944), François Henry (1933, 1936) and Harold Leask (1955). But fieldwork proper was to make a relatively slow start. In the late 1920s R.A.S. Macalister complained of a paucity of published accounts of reliable excavations (1928, 168). Only ten years later, Adolph Mahr's presidential address to the Prehistoric Society (1937), in London, could cite dozens of excavations on both sides of the border. The influential Harvard Expedition, led by Movius and O'Neill Hencken in the 1930s, contributed to the adoption of systematic excavation techniques by Irish archaeologists, and advances of lasting impact were made in the archaeology of the Early Medieval period. O'Neill Hencken targeted high status Early Medieval sites and, where possible, ones which could be interpreted by reference to early documentary sources, including Lagore (1950), Cahercommaun (1938) and Ballinderry I and II (1936; 1942). In Munster, classic sites were excavated and published by Seán P. Ó Ríordáin, including settlement sites at Leacanabuaile (Ó Ríordáin and Foy 1943), Ballycatteen (Ó Ríordáin and Hartnett 1943), Carraig Aille (1949a), Cush (1940) and Garranes (1942). This last was also a site with purportedly royal associations, as was the settlement and cemetery at Knockea, excavated by M.J. O'Kelly in the 1960s (1967). François Henry's (1957) survey work on Early Medieval sites on the Iveragh peninsula set an early standard in deriving general conclusions from the observations of systematic survey but, oddly enough, few ecclesiastical sites were actually excavated. North of the border, Lawlor's (1925) excavation of a large ecclesiastical enclosure at Nendrum was an ambitious beginning, but in Munster, O'Kelly's (1958) much later excavation of Church Island and Fanning's (1981) still later investigation of Reask remain the only other published examples of total excavaton on early ecclesiastical sites.

These early decades were energetic and formative. Classic sites were excavated which even today are used as touchstones in the interpretation of excavation results. The pursuit of high status buildings and artefacts proved to be disappointing but, nevertheless, central themes were put in place which have continued to shape archaeological writing on the Early Medieval period. It would be interesting to test the validity of this proposal over the full spectrum of relevant themes. These might include: the perceived unity of material culture throughout the island; the perceived significance of Early Medieval contacts with Britain and Europe; art historical accounts of 'valorised' objects as national treasures (brooches, church vessels and reliquaries); the locus of artisan/industrial output within a landscape of dispersed rural settlements; and the direct application of documentary-source explanations to archaeological data (indeed, this last deserves the attention of a full volume in its own right). Within the short scope of this chapter, however, it is only possible to argue the general proposal with particular reference to two themes: firstly, the representation of secular settlements as archetypal farmsteads and, secondly, the representation of ecclesiastical sites as enduring monuments (see also discussion Monk, ch. 5).

Secular settlements/archetypal farmsteads

The archetypal representation of Early Medieval secular settlement depicts ringforts as typical examples of dispersed, rural settlements, supporting self-sufficient family units subsisting on a mixed farming economy. Even today, despite attrition by modern agriculture, ringforts are by far the most numerous and conspicuous early field monuments in the Irish landscape. The sheer number and density of these sites contribute to the perception that they are somehow 'already explained', occupying a natural niche within a predominantly pastoral landscape. In the earlier decades of this century, the appeal of this archetype can easily be imagined against the background of a modern Irish demography where successive land reform bills by British and Irish governments revolutionised land-ownership, almost within a single lifetime. The inequalities of the landed estates and their tenantry were largely eliminated and replaced by an economy founded on small farms owned in freehold by former tenants. In the 1930s, de Valéra's election promises of further land reforms to create 'happy homesteads . . . each with its herdsman's house' are strikingly consonant with then current archaeological motifs. Thus, for example, in the late 1920s, Macalister could still quote no reliable or systematic excavation of a ringfort in *Irish Archaeology* (1928) but – with a guarded confidence in the evidence of the laws of status set out in the *Críth Gabhlach* – he could conjecturally describe the dwelling house and outbuildings which characterised the ringfort as family farmstead. Eventually, this representation would be more solidly founded on concrete archaeological evidence. Proudfoot's paper on 'The Economy of the Irish Rath' (1961) is the classic example of such a representation; though here again, one feels that empirical evidence is cited to expand upon a conclusion which was already widely accepted. The archetypal narrative of the dispersed rural family settlement was given its fullest expression by Evans in his *Prehistoric and Early Christan Ireland* (1966). His evocative description of the ringfort as a motif of the Irish pastoral idyll is worth quoting at length (1966, 192):

> Their geographical distribution, thickly scattered throughout the fattest grazing lowlands, suggests the general findings of excavations that the majority were the homes of farmers . . . The enclosed space in the average rath is from 60 ft to 110 ft across, and in it was a dwelling house, and perhaps animal shelters and other

outhouses, built of timber and mud. It was a single farm. The isolated farm is a characteristic feature of the Irish cultural landscape today; it is adapted to a predominantly pastoral economy, the farmers and their livestock living in close proximity, and so it has been for centuries.

The long continuities of rural life form a pervasive theme in the writings of Evans, but he was not alone in applying this perception to ringforts. Indeed, the terms chosen by O'Kelly were even more specific in this regard (1970, 53):

> The Irish ringfort may be an indigenous invention of late Neolithic times. Once invented, the type continued to be built down to the 17th century AD, there being numerous variations in the details of construction. The ditch and bank of the *rath* and the dry-built wall of the *caiseal* or *cathair* were little more than stack-yard enclosures around the house and animal shelters of a farming family. This pattern of isolated dwellings persists to the present day.

According to Lee, the promise of such long continuities was a magnet which drew numerous researchers to Ireland in the middle decades of the twentieth century, attracted by the misguided hope that they would 'excavate communities frozen in time' (1989, 70).

These days, the identification between ancient settlement patterns and the modern farm landscape rarely appears in academic writing (though it can still be found in the less self-conscious pages of popular publications). On the other hand, the mass of excavated archaeological evidence now available has largely justified the early interpretation of ringforts as family farmsteads dependent on a mixed regime of agriculture and livestock husbandry. The ongoing engagement of field archaeologists with documentary sources appears to bear out Macalister's (1928) confidence in the *Críth Gabhlach* as a source for actual rather than normative details of economy, architecture and social hierarchy (e.g. McCormick 1983, 1995; Lynn 1994; Stout 1997). There is danger, however, as well as reward in the seductive explanatory power of documentary sources. Stout's *The Irish Ringfort* (1997) is without doubt an important, ground-breaking book with a core of valuable observations based on detailed distribution studies, but there is something alarming about the assertion that 'if no ringforts had survived in Ireland it would still be possible to reconstruct this settlement form from contemporary sources, and more importantly, the society that built them' (ibid., 110). The engagement of fieldworkers with documentary sources somehow deepens the perception of ringforts as being familiar and 'already explained', and the satisfying sense of closure and repletion this offers may exclude some alternative lines of inquiry.

Historically, much of the archaeological literature on secular settlement – responsive to documentary suggestions – has focused on the evidence for high or low status sites, or for their use as defensive and livestock enclosures; these inquiries have been supplemented by chronological boundary skirmishes, with papers relating to early or late dates for individual sites or for the type as a whole (e.g. Rynne 1964; O'Kelly 1970; Proudfoot 1970; Barrett and Graham 1975; Lynn 1975a, 1975b, 1983). Within this framework of inquiry, it has generally been considered acceptable for fieldworkers to treat excavated sites in isolation rather than as elements in a settled landscape defined by boundaries, routeways and relationships (see Monk, ch. 5). Corresponding field strategies were directed towards evidence for the construction and date of the enclosures, and the continuity and duration of occupation of their interiors. As entire sites are rarely excavated (more often because of practical constraints rather than strategic thinking), sample excavations have been directed towards earthwork sections, entrance features and, frequently, a central area over the likely main house site. This is not a strategy which considers the whole of the site's interior as a theatre of work and social relations, with specialised areas set aside for gendered or industrial activities. In more practical terms, it is a strategy which largely overlooks the potential of the earthworks themselves (social implication of earthworks discussed by Monk 1995, 113-16; ch. 5). After all, the fills of a ringfort ditch are likely to comprise the deepest repository of undisturbed and sometimes waterlogged stratigraphy on these sites; and the areas beneath upstanding banks offer the potential to examine buried Early Medieval or later prehistoric land surfaces and their associated soil horizons. In addition, this strategy assumes that the whole of the settlement is circumscribed by its main enclosing element. There have been hundreds of excavations on ringfort sites, but on none of these was an extended attempt to locate and characterise associated extra-mural settlement carried out, even in the immediate vicinity of the enclosure. In the wider landscape, beyond secular settlement enclosures, archaeologists have made few efforts to discover and investigate other forms of Early Medieval settlement. A small corpus of excavations on unenclosed settlement sites has explored house sites with souterrains, nucleated settlement clusters and unenclosed workshops or industrial sites (e.g. Ó Ríordáin 1949; Henry 1952; O'Kelly 1956; Waterman 1956; Ó Ríordáin and Rynne 1961; Hamlin and Lynn 1988), but the potential to map and excavate similar sites on a much larger scale has largely been ignored. This neglect is strikingly underlined by the potential offered by the sites of unenclosed souterrains (which comprise up to 40 per cent of all known souterrains in some counties). Even the small number of unenclosed structures of possible Early Medieval date which are actually upstanding and well preserved – the so-called *clocháns* of the western uplands – remain largely ignored by excavators, although the excavation of an example at Glin North, Co. Kerry, has attempted to break this particular mould (Bennett 1993, 44–5).

The monumental church

The treatment of early ecclesiastical sites has evolved in a different way, but again it owes much to the fact that they are perceived as enduring monuments rather than as elements within a complex landscape of settlements and associated relationships (see Monk, ch. 5). Archaeological interest has chiefly been directed towards the buildings themselves, reflecting Cooney's observation (1995, 265) that state-sponsored archaeology in Ireland has tended to regard field monuments in terms of the management problems they present rather than of the investigative opportunities they represent. (A supplementary theme has focused on topographical detail gleaned from documentary sources; e.g. MacDonald 1984). Several models have been advanced to explain the siting and purpose of Early Medieval ecclesiastical sites in these islands. They have seen the church as centrepiece in the monastic or episcopal settlement, as an elaboration of a founder's tomb, as a stage in the development of an earlier cemetery; the sites themselves as proprietorial or proto-parochial institutions and as territorial boundary markers. In Ireland, however, the perception of early ecclesiastical sites as monuments has generated a corpus of archaeological writing which is dominated by architectural studies in typology and chronology. Hence Edwards's cautionary advice that 'the visible remains of the early Irish Church are impressive, but we should not allow them to lure us into creating an oversimplified and static image' (1990, 130). Even sustained attempts to animate the landscape of ecclesiastical buildings by applying a single broad interpretative theme are prone to capture by this perception of churches as monuments. Thus, Harbison could preface his *Pilgrimage in Ireland* with the hope that it would 'encourage fresh discussion about the religious atmosphere of Early Christian Ireland, a period which can only be seen as the zenith of achievement in the country's long cultural history' (1991, 8).

Certainly, the insular development of a distinctive pre-twelfth-century church architecture deserves a substantial literature, and publications by later commentators (e.g. de Paor 1967; Harbison 1970 and 1982; Hamlin 1984; Hare and Hamlin 1986; Berger 1992; Manning 1995) have built on the tradition established by Petrie, Stokes, Champneys, Leask and others. But it is time to expand the field of inquiry and accept, at last, Rahtz's longstanding challenge to consider 'monasteries as settlements' (1973). An estimated two thousand early ecclesiastical sites can already be identified in the Irish landscape (Swan 1994) and the ongoing publication of inventories and surveys will probably increase this number. The practical problem of coastal erosion, combined with the romance of the eremitic church, has attracted attention to the maritime sites of the Atlantic fringe (e.g. O'Kelly 1973). Otherwise, scarcely a dozen early ecclesiastical sites have been the subject of any sort of extensive fieldwork, and this has almost invariably been in the form of rescue excavations. The current excavations at Clonmacnoise (O'Sullivan 1996; King 1997) have only begun to produce the physical evidence to support the theory that urban living may have been an indigenous development in Early Medieval Ireland (although many early monastic enclosures rival the scale of Anglo-Norman planned towns of the twelfth century, or their Hiberno-Norse predecessors, and further fieldwork may yet discover that some of these were not monastic or ecclesiastical centres at all). Further initiatives of this kind are required if we are to explore the full range of early ecclesiastical archaeology as it was recently defined by Morris (1996, xv): 'Having outgrown old assumptions . . . we can place the study of churches where it properly belongs – in the realm of socio-economic (as well as socio-religious) historical change. Church archaeology is not simply, or even mainly, about churches, but about human motivations, mentalities, communities, and power.'

Heterogeneous burial practices
The perceived familiarity with the landscape of Early Medieval monuments – the sense that they are remembered, relate to present practices and are somehow, therefore, already understood – can be extended to include the burial record. New evidence has only now begun to challenge the longstanding assumption that cemeteries in the Early Medieval period normally represent the whole population, in congregational burial-grounds extending around a main church.

Amongst the small corpus of excavated Early Medieval cemeteries, burial assemblages of mixed age and sex are usually identified. Where a sex bias occurs, it appears to represent the burials of clergy (e.g. Kendrick 1939; O'Kelly et al. 1975; White Marshall et al. ch. 9). These are the expected norms. But recent excavations at some sites offer glimpses of a more heterogeneous scene than previously suspected, with some strands drawn from beyond the Christian tradition. Studies by Raftery (1981) and O'Brien (1992) attest to the existence of residual pre-Christian or pagan burial practices until perhaps as late as the seventh century. In particular, documentary research by O'Brien indicates that kindred burial-grounds may have survived in use – in defiance of the Church – until the seventh or even the eighth century (ibid.). The early cemetery enclosure at Knockea (O'Kelly 1967) may have been one of these. Results from sites like Dooey (Ó Ríordáin and Rynne 1961), Millockstown (Manning 1986) and Boolies Little (Sweetman 1983) are puzzling: settlement features and burials coincide on sites which are not obviously ecclesiastical settlements and which may represent some complex form of tenure and burial practice. The women's cemetery on Iona (O'Sullivan 1994) is the first excavated example of segregated burial on a site with early Irish ecclesiastical origins; Hamlin and Foley (1983) suggested that this phenomenon might have been widespread, and also speculated about other kinds of segregation, based on social status and even circumstances of death.

Wendy Davies was concerned with a Welsh context when she wrote 'give careful consideration to burials, as the largest untapped source of new information on the period which is now available to us' (1988, 21). Evidently this advice can be applied in Ireland too. Any Irish excavator approaching the interpretation of an Early Medieval cemetery should now be armed with a healthy uncertainty, but should also be furnished with a corresponding degree of interpretative latitude, and must be allowed to look beyond the previously assumed hegemony of Christian rite and congregational, churchyard burial.

A moral conclusion: the tale of three books
The de Paors' *Early Christian Ireland* (1958) was the first general synthesis of current knowledge of the archaeology of the period in Ireland. It was set out in a recognisably modern hierarchy of thematic chapters which dealt with art, settlement, economy and so forth. It remained a standard reference work for many years and, surprisingly, the de Paors had no successors in offering specifically Irish syntheses – setting aside more general works by the Laings on the Early Medieval archaeology of Britain and Ireland (1975; 1990) – until the task was taken up more or less simultaneously by both Edwards and Mytum.

Nancy Edwards's *Archaeology of Early Medieval Ireland* (1990) is an excellent reference work and was very well received by its reviewers. Like the de Paors' earlier book, it marshals the evidence in thematic chapters on settlement and economy, the Church, craft and exchange etc. Each chapter identifies grey areas or blanks in the data, rather than offering an overall analysis. In contrast, Mytum's *Origins of Early Christian Ireland* (1992) declares from the outset his intention to offer a sustained analysis of Early Medieval Irish society from a processualist viewpoint; according to this analysis, the origins of Early Medieval Ireland lay in a change in the belief system. The adoption of Christianity from sub-Roman Britain broke the mould of late Iron Age society. Individuals were released from a moribund economic base – land-use organised around communal ownership by the kin-group – and began to pursue individual free enterprise and greater social mobility. Mytum's book is a lively and stimulating read, but the response of the reviewers was largely negative and flaws were identified in his application of documentary sources to field data. This much was fair; but the vilification of his overall theoretical approach was intemperate and sometimes even plainly Anglophobic. Ó Cróinín objected to the application of any theoretical model at all (1992, 25): The book is a catalogue of half-baked and often downright bizarre, unproven and even untested theories, vitiated from start to finish by *a priori* assumptions and half-digested 'theory', most of it taken from the jargon-riddled ramblings of American 'psychoarchaeology.'

But Ó Cróinín's real objections seem to revolve around the fact that the cultural zenith of Irish society was being ascribed, not to indigenous Celtic genius, whistling its native woodnotes wild, but to the introduction from post-Roman Britain of some kind of conspicuously Thatcherite free-enterprise ideology, and even the Great Famine of the 1840s was brought down in execration upon the head of Mytum before the reviewer had vented his indignation.

Ó Cróinín's own book on the Early Medieval period (1995) is also a lively read and offers an authoritative survey of the documentary sources. Perhaps predictably, it climaxes in a chapter on the 'Golden Age'. An earlier chapter on 'Land, settlement and economy' is almost entirely devoid of references to the archaeological evidence. In a cameo appearance in an archaeological publication – a contribution to Ryan's *Illustrated Irish Archaeology* (1994, 132-33) – he describes the beauties of illuminated manuscripts and the success of Irish missionary activity in Dark Age Europe. One suspects that his reaction to Mytum's *Origins of Early Christian Ireland* represents, to some extent, the view that our present responsibility is to curate the legacy of Early Medieval Ireland, not stain its exquisite pages with heterogeneous ideas and novel lines of inquiry.

I suggest that somewhere in the space between these three publications – Edwards' thorough collation of the facts generated by excavation and survey work but deliberately limited in its interpretative content; Mytum's daring but unsuccessful effort to shake the edifice with a theoretical assault; and Ó Cróinín's authoritative survey of the documentary sources, blithely untroubled by archaeological data – lies a healthy programme for further archaeological work in the Irish Early Medieval period. This would be a captive of neither documentary sources nor archaeological theory for theory's sake; it would generate new research proposals based both on archaeological data and a largely archaeological epistemology.

However, before a leap forward comes a look behind. Cooney has observed a 'marked lack of concern with the theoretical basis of archaeological practice in Ireland' (1995, 263). To redress this, a good starting point would be a greater awareness of the historiography of archaeological writing on the Early Medieval period, across a range of themes. The freedom to adapt a more expansive approach in our interpretations will be facilitated by understanding the ethos in which our received ideas were generated. We should know more about the personality and politics of the first generation of fieldworkers in Ireland and we should explore in much greater depth the sensibility of Gaelic revivalism in which they were schooled. (Stout's study (1996) of the career of Evans has set an excellent example here.) A wealth of archival material also begs attention: studies of the parliamentary records relating to archaeological acts, newspaper coverage of archaeological events in the pre-War period and the early transactions, minutes and correspondence of learned societies would allow us to read the archaeological data both of that time and of our own in a stronger light.

BIBLIOGRAPHY

Atkinson, J., Banks, I. and O'Sullivan, J. (eds.) (1996) *Nationalism and Archaeology*, Glasgow

Barrett, G. and Graham, B. (1975) 'Some considerations concerning the dating and distribution of ringforts in Ireland', *Ulster J. Archaeol.* 4 (3), 39–51

Bennett, I. (1993) 'Glin North', *Excavations 1992: Summary Accounts of Excavations in Ireland*, 44–45, Dublin

Berger, R. (1992) '14C dating mortar in Ireland', *Radiocarbon* 34, 880–89

Borland, D. (1995) 'Nineteenth-century antiquarians in Ireland', unpublished paper read to the seventeenth annual conference of the Theoretical Archaeology Group (TAG 1995, University of Reading)

Boyce, D. G. (1995, 3rd edn) *Nationalism in Ireland*, London and New York

Champneys, A. (1910) *Irish Ecclesiastical Architecture*, London

Coffey, G. (1909) *Guide to the Celtic Antiquities of the Christian Period*, Dublin

Coogan, T.P. (1995) *De Valera: Long Fellow, Long Shadow*, London

Cooney, G. (1995) 'Theory and practice in Irish archaeology', in P. Ucko (ed.), *Theory in Archaeology: A World Perspective*, 263-77, London and New York

Davies, W. (1988) 'The myth of the Celtic Church', in N. Edwards and A. Lane (eds.), *The Archaeology of the Early Church in Wales and the West*, 12–21, Oxford

de Paor, L. (1967) 'Cormac's Chapel: the beginnings of Irish Romanesque', in E. Rynne (ed.), *North Munster Studies*, Limerick

de Paor, M. and de Paor, L. (1958) *Early Christian Ireland*, London

Diaz-Andreu, M. and Champion, T. (eds.) (1996) *Nationalism and Archaeology in Europe*, London

Edwards, N. (1990) *The Archaeology of Early Medieval Ireland*, London

Evans, E. E. (1966) *Prehistoric and Early Christian Ireland*, New York

Fanning, T. (1981) 'Excavation of an Early Christian cemetery and settlement at Reask, Co. Kerry', *Proc. Roy. Ir. Acad.* 81, 67–172

Hamlin, A. (1984) 'The study of early Irish churches,' in P. Ní Chathain and M. Richter (eds.), *Irland und Europa: Die Kirch im Furhmittelalter*, 117–26, Stuttgart

Hamlin, A. and Foley, C. (1983) 'A women's graveyard at Carrickmore, Co. Tyrone, and the separate burial of women', *Ulster J. Archaeol.* 46, 41–46

Hamlin, A. and Lynn, C. (1988) ' "Ballywee" a thousand-year-old farm', in *Pieces of the Past*, 32–33, Belfast

Harbison, P. (1970) 'How old is Gallarus Oratory? A reappraisal of its role in early Irish Architecture', *Medieval Archaeol.*, 14, 34-59

Harbison, P. (1982) 'Early Irish churches', in H. Lowe (ed.), *Die Iren und Europa im fruheren mittelalter*, 618–29, Stuttgart

Harbison, P. (1991) *Pilgrimage in Ireland*, London

Hare, M. and Hamlin, A. (1986) 'The study of early church architecture in Ireland: an Anglo-Saxon viewpoint', in L.A.S. Butler and R.K. Morris (eds.), *The Anglo-Saxon Church: Papers on History, Architecture and Archaeology in Honour of Dr H.M. Taylor*, 131–45, London

Hencken, O'Neill H. (1936) 'Ballinderry Crannóg No I', *Proc. Roy. Ir. Acad.* 43C, 103–239

Hencken, O'Neill H. (1938) 'Cahercommaun: a stone fort in Co. Clare', *J. Roy. Soc. Antiq. Ir.* (special vol.)

Hencken, O'Neill H. (1942) 'Ballinderry Crannóg No II', *Proc. Roy. Ir. Acad.* 47C, 1–76

Hencken, O'Neill H. (1950) 'Lagore crannóg: an Irish royal residence of the seventh to tenth century AD', *Proc. Roy. Ir. Acad.* 53C, 1–248

Henry, F. (1933) *Les sculptures irlandaises pendant les douze premiers siècles de l'ère Chrétienne*, Paris

Henry, F. (1936) 'Hanging bowls', *J. Roy. Soc. Antiq. Ir.* 66, 209–46

Henry, F. (1952) 'A wooden hut on Iniskea North, Co. Mayo', *J. Roy. Soc. Antiq. Ir.* 82, 163–78

Henry, F. (1957) 'Early monasteries, beehive huts and drystone houses in the neighbourhood of Caherciveen and Waterville (Co. Kerry)', *Proc. Roy. Ir. Acad.* 58C, 45–166

Kendrick, T.D. (1939) 'Gallen Priory excavations 1934–35', *J. Roy. Soc. Antiq. Ir.* 69, 1

King, H. (1997) 'New Graveyard, Clonmacnoise Early Christian settlement', in I. Bennett, *Excavations 1996: Summary Accounts of Archaeological Excavations in Ireland 1992–1993*, Dublin

Kohl, P. and Fawcett, C. (eds.) (1995) *Nationalism, Politics and the Practice of Archaeology*, Cambridge

Laing, L. (1975) *The Archaeology of Late Celtic Britain and Ireland*, London

Laing, L. and Laing, J. (1990) *Celtic Britain and Ireland, AD 200–800*, Dublin

Lawlor, H. C. (1925) *The Monastery of Saint Mochaoi of Nendrum*, Belfast

Leask, H. G. (1955) *Irish Churches and Monastic Buildings*, 3 vols., Dundalk

Lee, J. J. (1989) 'Ireland 1912–1985', *Politics and Society*, Cambridge

Lynn, C. (1975a) 'The dating of raths: an orthodox view', *Ulster J. Archaeol.* 38, 45–47

Lynn, C. (1975b) 'The medieval ring-fort – an archaeological chimera?', *Ir. Archaeol. Res. Forum* 2, 29–36

Lynn, C. (1983) 'Some "early" ringforts and crannogs', *J. of Ir. Archaeol.* I, 47–58

Lynn, C. (1994) 'Houses in Rural Ireland, A.D. 500–1000', *Ulster J. of Archaeol.* 57, 81–94

Macalister, R.A.S. (1928) *The Archaeology of Ireland*, London

McCormick, F. (1983) 'Dairying and beef production in Early Christian Ireland: the faunal evidence', in T. Reeves-Smyth and F. Hamond (eds.), *Landscape Archaeology in Ireland*, 253–67, Oxford

McCormick, F. (1995) 'Cows, ringforts and the origins of Early Christian Ireland', *Emania* 13, 33–37

MacDonald, A.D.S. (1984) 'Major early monasteries: some procedural problems for field archaeologists', in D. Breeze (ed.), *Studies in Scottish Antiquity*, 69–86, Edinburgh

Mahr, A. (1937) 'New aspects and problems in Irish prehistory: Presidential address', *Proc. Prehist. Soc.* 3, 261–436

Mahr, A. (1932) *Christian Art in Ancient Ireland*, vol. 1, Dublin

Manning, C. (1986) 'Archaeological excavation of a succession of enclosures at Millockstown, Co. Louth', *Proc. Roy. Ir. Acad.* 86C, 135–81

Manning, C. (1995) 'Clonmacnoise Cathedral – the oldest church in Ireland?', *Archaeology Ireland* 9.4, 30–33

Monk, M. (1995) 'A Tale of Two Ringforts: Lisleagh I and II', *J. Cork Hist. Archaeol. Soc.* 100, 105–16

Morris, R. (1996) 'Introduction', in J. Blair and C. Pyrah (eds.), *Church Archaeology: Research Directions for the Future*, xv-xvi, York

Mytum, H. (1992) *The Origins of Early Christian Ireland*, London

O'Brien, E. (1992) 'Pagan and Christian burial in Ireland in the first millennium AD: continuity and change', in N. Edwards and A. Lane (eds.), *The Archaeology of the Early Church in Wales and the West*, 130–37, Oxford

Ó Cróinín, D. (1992) Review of H. Mytum, *The Origins of Early Christian Ireland*, *Linen Hall Review* 9.1, 23–25

Ó Cróinín, D. (1995) *Early Medieval Ireland 400–1200*, London and New York

O'Grady, S. (1878–80) *History of Ireland*, Dublin

O'Kelly, M.J. (1956) 'An island settlement at Beginish, Co. Kerry', *Proc. Roy. Ir. Acad.* 57C, 159–94

O'Kelly, M.J. (1958) 'Church Island, near Valencia, Co. Kerry', *Proc. Roy. Ir. Acad.* 59C, 57–136

O'Kelly, M.J. (1967) 'Knockea, Co. Limerick', in E. Rynne (ed.), *North Munster Studies: Essays in Commemoration of Monsignor Michael Moloney*, 72–101, Limerick

O'Kelly, M.J. (1970) 'Problems of Irish ringforts', in D. Moore (ed.), *The Irish Sea Province in Archaeology and History*, 50–4, Cardiff

O'Kelly, M.J. (1973) 'Monastic Sites in the West of Ireland', *Scot. Archaeol. Forum* 5, 1–16

O'Kelly, M.J., Lynch, A. and Cahill, M. (1975) *Archaeological Survey and Excavation of St Vogue's Church, Enclosure and Other Monuments at Carnsore Co. Wexford*, Dublin

O'Neill, H. (1857) *Sculptured High Crosses of Ancient Ireland*

Ó Ríordáin, B. and Rynne, E. (1961) 'A settlement in the sandhills at Dooey, Co. Donegal', *J. Roy. Soc. Antiq. Ir.* 91, 58–64

Ó Ríordáin, S.P. (1940) 'Excavations at Cush, Co. Limerick', *Proc. Roy. Ir. Acad.* 45C, 83–181

Ó Ríordáin, S.P. (1942) 'Excavation of a large earthen ringfort at Garranes, Co. Cork', *Proc. Roy. Ir. Acad.* 47C, 77–150

Ó Ríordáin, S.P. (1949) 'Lough Gur excavations: Carraig Aille and the "Spectacles"', *Proc. Roy. Ir. Acad.* 52C, 39–111

Ó Ríordáin, S.P. and Foy, J.B. (1943) 'The excavation of Leacanabuaile fort, Co. Kerry', *J. Cork Hist. Archaeol. Soc.* 46, 85–99

Ó Ríordáin, S.P. and Hartnett, P.J. (1943) 'Excavation at Ballycatteen fort, Co. Cork', *Proc. Roy. Ir. Acad.* 49C, 1–43

O'Sullivan, A. (1996) 'Ireland's oldest bridge', *Archaeology Ireland* 10.4, 24–27

O'Sullivan, J. (1994) 'Excavation of a women's cemetery and early church at St Ronan's medieval parish church, Iona', *Proc. Soc. Antiq. Scot.* 124, 327–65

Petrie, G. (1845) *The Ecclesiastical Architecture of Ireland Anterior to the Norman Invasion*, Dublin

Petrie, G. (1872, 1878) *Christian Inscriptions in the Irish Language*, 2 vols. M. Stokes (ed.)

Proudfoot, B. (1961) 'The economy of the Irish rath', *Medieval Archaeol.* 5, 94–122

Proudfoot, B. (1970) 'Irish raths and cashels: some notes on origin, chronology and survivals', *Ulster J. Archaeol.* 33, 37–48

Raftery, B. (1981) 'Iron Age burials in Ireland', in D. Ó Corráin (ed.), *Irish Antiquity: Essays and Studies Presented to Professor M.J. O'Kelly*, Cork

Raftery, J. (1941) *Christian Art in Ancient Ireland*, vol. 2, Dublin

Raftery, J. (1944) 'The Turoe Stone and the Rath of Feerwore', *J. Roy. Soc. Antiq. Ir.* 74, 23–52

Rahtz, P. (1973) 'Monasteries as Settlements', *Scott. Archaeol. Forum* 5, 125–35

Ryan, M. (1994) *Illustrated Irish Archaeology*, Dublin

Rynne, E. (1964) 'Some destroyed sites at Shannon Airport, Co. Clare'. *Proc. Roy. Ir. Acad.* 63C, 245–77

Stokes, M. (1878) *Early Christian Architecture*, Dublin

Stokes, M. (1894) *Early Christian Art in Ireland*, Dublin

Stout, M. (1996) 'Emyr Estyn Evans and Northern Ireland: the archaeology and geography of a new state', in J. Atkinson, I. Banks, and J. O'Sullivan (eds.), *Nationalism and Archaeology*, 111–27, Glasgow

Stout, M. (1997) *The Irish Ringfort*, Dublin

Sullivan, A.M. (1867) *The Story of Ireland*, Dublin

Swan, L. (1994) 'Early monastic sites', in M. Ryan (ed.), *Illustrated Irish Archaeology*, 137. Dublin

Sweetman, D. (1983) 'Souterrain and burials at Boolies Little, Co. Meath', *Ríocht na Midhe* 7 (2), 42–57

Trigger, B. (1984) 'Alternative archaeologies: nationalist, colonialist, imperialist', *Man* 19, 355–70

Wakeman, W.F. (1848) *Archaeologica Hibernica*, 2 vols., Dublin

Waterman, D. (1956) 'An excavation of a house and souterrain at Craig Hill, Co. Antrim', *Ulster J. Archaeol.* 19, 87-91

Woodman, P. (1995) 'Who possesses Tara', in D. Ucko (ed.), *Theory in Archaeology: a World Perspective*, 278–97, London

Wood Martin, W.G. (1886) *The Lake Dwellings of Ireland*, Dublin

18. Theory and Politics in Early Medieval Irish Archaeology

MICHAEL TIERNEY

Introduction

This chapter offers a critique of Early Medieval archaeology in Ireland and its approach is informed by theoretical and political considerations; aspects of the development of Irish archaeology are referred to in an attempt to understand the particular shape the discipline has taken. Most Irish archaeologists feel that the virtue of being knowledgeable practitioners is sufficient to contribute to the discipline and they consider that a primary concern with the theoretical approach does not equate with doing 'real' archaeology. Some theoretically informed archaeologists, including this author, therefore feel the need to justify their stance. The justification of the approach taken here will become evident below but, first of all, it is necessary to enlarge upon the concept of critique.

The particular sense in which the concept is used in this chapter contains within it the basic meaning of criticism of ideas, opinions and points of view. However, critical or radical archaeologists have extended this meaning in order to 'subject everything to rational scrutiny, unveiling, debunking and reflecting on the constraints to which people succumb in the historical process of their self-formation' and have described critique 'not as a methodology but more an attitude which focuses on the social construction of knowledge' (Hodder and Shanks 1995, 234). It is a form of negative thinking which 'includes ideology critique as the scrutiny of sedimented meanings within cultural works which serve particular social interests' (ibid., 234).

In recent years the focus of radical archaeologists' interests have been on power, identity, the human agency and, most crucially, the relationship between the past and the present and how the former is used in the latter. In the context of Early Medieval studies in Ireland (and indeed in historical and archaeological studies generally) such approaches are frequently scoffed at. The implications of such sceptical attitudes to what is often cynically called 'theory' form another strand to this paper.

Critical engagement with the work of others and an appreciation of the wider contexts of the discipline have always been present in Irish archaeology. This is why the use of a specific form of critique, which is qualitatively different to criticism, can be so instructive. It directly touches on and engages with a different level of self-reflexivity and awareness to that usually found in the discipline. A critique-centred approach can be found in some recent work by Irish prehistorians (Woodman 1992; Cooney 1995; Stanley 1996), historical geographers (Graham and Proudfoot 1993) and cultural historians (Brett 1996).

A common thread running through these works is the identification of empiricism as the dominant framework of scholarship within Irish archaeology. Within critical circles in archaeology it is commonplace to hold that certain traditions are empiricist, to agree that this is philosophically unacceptable and to then offer alternative approaches. However, it is necessary to extend the parameters of these discussions about and against empiricism (e.g. Hodges 1982; Collier 1994) to demonstrate that there are more than esoteric philosophical questions at stake in the consideration of the underlying ideas which structure approaches to the past. This extension is applied here on the basis of the acceptance of Trigger's proposition that the dominance of an empiricist worldview within archaeology is intimately linked with middle-class values and the bourgeois nature of the discipline (1989, 14). The majority of national, regional and local traditions are united by the dominance of empiricist epistemologies at the core of the discipline, and some of the effects empiricist hegemony has on Early Medieval studies in Ireland are considered below. Towards the end of the discussion an attempt is made to show how archaeologists' work is shaped by political and philosophical factors of which they are often totally unaware, and this is explored by reference to a case-study of Early Medieval metallurgical studies in Ireland.

A further point of clarification is necessary. The level of abstraction (Ollman 1993, 24–27) referred to below may seem a bit rarefied in relation to the general experience of the production and consumption of archaeological knowledge. At least three basic steps must be taken if archaeologists are to free ourselves from the constraints imposed by the traditions within which we work. These steps are, firstly, the analysis of the political philosophies which seem to inform the discipline (Gramsci 1986, 324), secondly, the study of the political economy and the everyday manifestations of these philosophies and, finally, the development of alternative narratives and ways of working which challenge the more dominant understandings of the past. The purpose of this difficult process is to construct archaeologies of liberation and to move towards better representations of people's lives in the past, two goals that are intimately related.

The despotism of fact

Empiricism in the context of this chapter refers to that philosophy which states that one gains knowledge of the world by observing and describing what one sees and experiences. The relationship between the individual and the world is simple and straightforward. Doyal and Harris define empiricism as the epistemology that is most generally accepted by people without philosophical training; it embodies the most common beliefs about successful scientists and is reflected in the images employed in the media to depict them (1986, 7). Crude empiricism assumes that the scientist is a sort of spectator of the object of enquiry. In other words, reality is presumed to exist absolutely externally and its

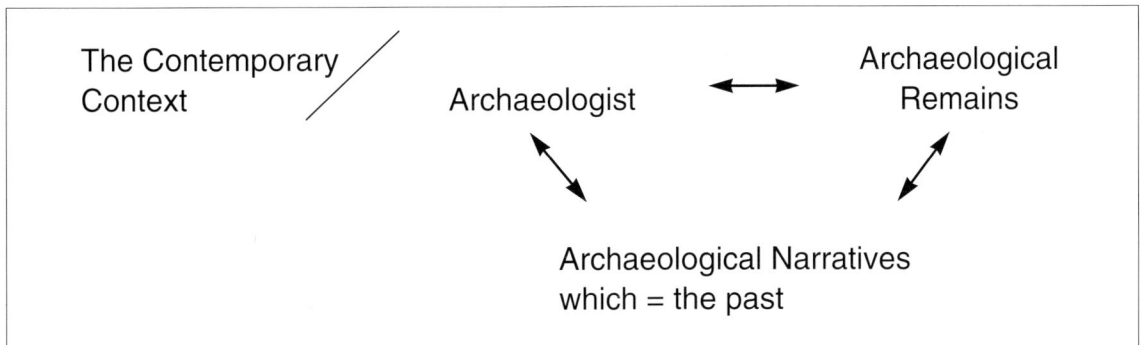

Fig. 18.1   A simplified view of empiricist methodology in archaeology

structure and content are seen to be independent of the observer's beliefs and desires (Fig. 18.1).

The focus of intellectual activity is the discovery and presentation of facts which are understood to directly equate with reality and are supposedly devoid of the clutter of human opinion or prejudice. All efforts to understand the world are accompanied by attempts to be objective and neutral in order to avoid the pitfalls and biases of ideology and subjectivity. However, it can be suggested that such attempts are themselves ideological, subjective and biased. They have a history, they originated somewhere and, ultimately, they are in some social group's interest (Eagleton 1991, 10; Jenkins 1991, 18). It needs to be stated that most archaeologists are well aware of their involvement in a whole series of social negotiations. They deal with various questions: 'What should we do?', 'Why should we do it?' and 'Who should we do it for?' While most archaeologists live their working lives in the manner indicated in Fig. 18.2, they continue to pretend otherwise. The empiricist imperative at the heart of archaeology allows this disciplinary blindness to continue.

It is quite difficult to come across explicit statements of empiricist intent in Irish archaeology. There is obviously no need to be explicit about one's own common sense. The preference for 'Fact' over 'Fancy' comes through quite clearly in Giot's review of one of M.J. O'Kelly's major publications (1983, 150):

'O'Kelly was a man of the field, an expert excavator, an experimental archaeologist, not at all involved in pseudo-Marxist, pseudo-Freudian or pseudo-Structuralist interpretation. He was an archaeologist, not an ethno-archaeologist.' This particular form of anti-intellectualism is rarely expressed in such an explicit manner, at least not in print. In terms of this publication this empiricist position is advocated by several contributors (e.g. Monk and Sheehan ch. 1; Monk, Tierney and Hannon ch. 8; Rynne, C. ch. 10; Thomas ch. 2) in their calls for the collection of more data to fill various gaps in our knowledge. Woodman has put forward a related critique of this attitude and the way it stunts the development of a more relevant and exciting archaeology (1992). An archaeology of fact is a relatively straightforward endeavour. Most archaeologists are educated in a tradition of archaeology which centres around the results of excavation and field-survey. More and more data is gathered in order to refine ideas about the past and to reassess existing theories in relation to this evidence. If, however, the relationship between archaeological facts and the past is not one of simple equivalence then there is a problem.

This chapter deals with the nature of Irish archaeology rather than simply rehearsing the ongoing critique of the kind of one-dimensional empiricist archaeology that is manifested in Early Medieval studies (see Moreland 1991). It should, however, be stated that such points of critique

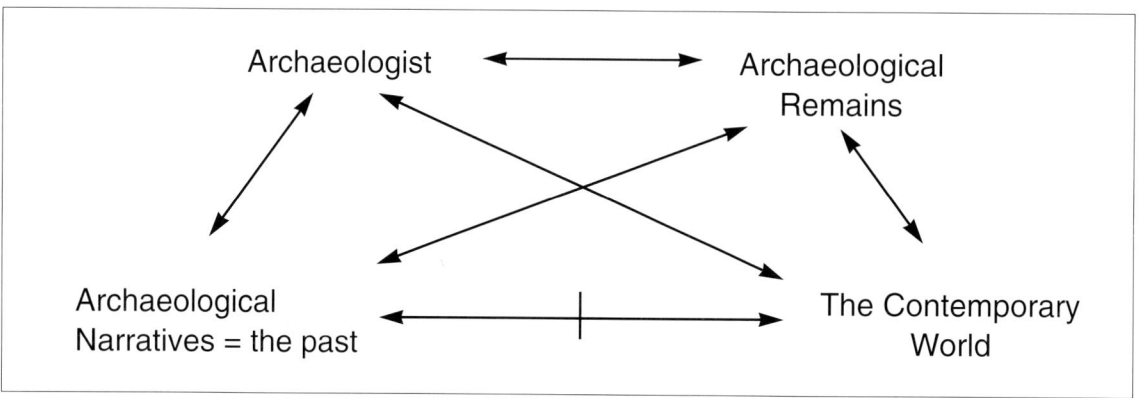

Fig. 18.2   A view of how archaeologists 'know' they work but pretend otherwise

need to be made over and over again given the dominance of the empiricist tradition. Indeed, it is almost amusing to note the slightly bewildered comments of some radicals when their devastating critiques are ignored (e.g. Moreland 1995, 235).

The most effective way to explain why it is necessary to reconsider the empiricist approach involves delving into the realms of intellectual and cultural history. It is necessary to historicise and contextualise the discipline in order to understand it (Daniel 1981; Jameson 1981). In his attempt to do this, Trigger claimed that archaeology is a discipline of and for the middle-classes. He suggests that while the influences that societies exert on archaeological interpretations are potentially very diverse, the development of the subject has corresponded temporally with the rise to power of the middle classes in Western society (1989, 14–15). Furthermore, he points out that:

> archaeologists have been predominantly members of the middle-classes: civil servants, clergymen, merchants, country squires, and, with increasing professionalization, university teachers. In addition, much of the public interest in archaeological findings has been found among the educated middle classes, including sometimes political leaders [witness Charles J. Haughey's patronage of the Discovery Programme in Ireland]. The relevance of archaeology and history for current political, economic, and social issues makes relations between archaeology and society especially complex and important. It therefore seems reasonable to examine archaeology as an expression of the ideology of the middle-classes and to try to discover to what extent changes in archaeological interpretation reflect the altering fortunes of that group.

Such claims about the value-laden, as opposed to the value-free, nature of the work done by archaeologists (Shanks and Tilley 1993, 9) are central to the argument here.

Intellectual closure and Irish society

A useful statement concerning matters empiricist was made Mr Gradgrind in one of the opening scenes in Charles Dickens's *Hard Times*:

> Fact, Fact, Fact said the gentleman. And Fact, Fact, Fact! repeated Thomas Gradgrind. You are to be in all things regulated and governed, said the gentleman, by Fact. We hope to have, before long, a Board of Fact, composed of Commissioners of Fact, who will force the people to be a People of Fact, and nothing but Fact. You must discard the word Fancy altogether. You have nothing to do with it.

Gradgrind is very much the archetypal Englishman (of a particular kind anyway). The gentleman is a prominent local businessman visiting Mr Gradgrind's school to ensure that the children are getting a proper education. The quoted passage highlights a number of issues relating to empiricism. It shows that it is a social construct coming from a particular time and place, an attitude which – like all other points of view, theories and ideologies – serves particular social and political interests (Gero 1983, 1–4).

The dominant philosophical position in nineteenth-century England was empiricist (Stedman Jones 1972, 96–119). It was a philosophy of the world of industrial interests. To this extent it is the dominant international philosophy, given the incorporation of virtually the whole globe in the world of late capitalism. Thus, we find educationalists like Mr Gradgrind and their business allies everywhere. Given that the focus of this publication is on a province of Ireland it is necessary, because of the legacy of colonialism, to consider England as the source of empiricism in Irish intellectual life (see Said 1992, 273–88; Kiberd 1995). The claim that England is the source of this empiricism (rather than Germany and Adolph Mahr – see Cooney 1995,

268) should be placed in the context of colonial and post-colonial relationships between England and Ireland, the construction of national identity in Ireland and the ideological struggle for the soul of the Irish nation. Most importantly, it should be placed in the context of the conflict between various factions of labour and capital regarding the form which the new political institutions should take in the Free State. Arkins's critique of Irish intellectual culture has relevance in this context (1994).

Arkins offers a 'history of modern times in which culture and identity are seen as emerging out of struggles centring on issues of class, gender and nation'. This is somewhat at odds with empiricist and psychologistic accounts of this period, in particular the well-known work by Lee (1989). Therefore, the descriptive categories that Arkins uses, like 'bourgeoisie', may initially jar with the modern reader. This jarring experience need not be a negative one, however, as it can force one to confront and rethink the categories used to make sense of the world.

It can be argued that the Irish Rebellion of 1916 led to particular social interests taking control. The faction which assumed power mainly represented commercial and mercantile interests, a classic *comprador bourgeoisie* whose main concern was the re-establishment of stable conditions for the resumption of trading relations with Britain. Representing the dominant economic interests of the new state, the government placed emphasis on agricultural development and made only token gestures towards Sinn Féin's policies of industrialisation via protectionism (Breathnach 1988, 131). In effect what occurred in Ireland was the establishment of a native bourgeois hegemony from 1922 onwards (see Ó Giolláin 1989 for a similar account dealing with folklore studies). It is this hegemony which Arkins describes as being responsible for what he calls 'the closing of the Irish mind'. He argues that:

> Those remaining bourgeois men and women sought to preserve the social status quo at all costs and to resist any efforts to ameliorate the economic position of the less fortunate in society. As part of that highly successful policy, they ensured that anything that might disturb the status quo, general ideas, sexuality, the Left, women and writers, were kept in check (1994, 50).

Arkins uses the term 'the dominant', which comes from art criticism, in a manner similar to the use of the term 'hegemony' here (after Gramsci, see Joll 1977). The dominant is defined as 'the focusing component of the work of art: it rules, determines, and transforms the remaining components'. This idea is transformed by Arkins who suggests that 'the dominant that pervades Irish society is the refusal of general ideas' (1994, 51). In making a statement about the nature of philosophy in Ireland, he says:

> the general principles of any major area of human activity are systematically ignored in favour of analysis of the particular form those activities take at a particular time. Thus [in Ireland] the central issue of the rival claims of left and right yields to detail about how the ideologically indistinguishable Fianna Fáil and Fine Gael differ, and the central issue of decentralisation to details about the workings of the central government. In economies, the vital question of what economic theory might serve to alleviate poverty, unemployment, and emigration yields to discussion about the technicalities of the capitalist system. In religion, the crucial question of the status of the sacred in our time yields to discussion about the sexually related matters of contraception, divorce, and abortion, or, more recently, about economic justice (specific ethics is substituted for general metaphysics). In art, discussion of the nature of poetry or music or painting in a postmodernist world yields to debate about the merits or failings of individual artists. And so on. And so on.

Archaeology can be placed in the context of the above 'And so on' in this way: the central issues in Irish archaeology revolve around methodological concerns and the collection of more and more data, with little or no regard to questions about the relationship of the past to the present, the role of archaeology in society or any form of fundamental epistemological and ontological questioning. It is no wonder that this should be the case, given the wider social context in which the discipline developed (Cooney, 1995).

It can be seen that the hold of empiricist philosophy over Irish archaeology may be of greater import than has previously been considered. Archaeology and archaeologists may be complicit in social processes which are more significant than merely adding to the pool of general knowledge or the dilettantist pursuits of personal interests. It can be concluded that Irish archaeologists have been active in the construction of a national identity which is reactionary, conservative and serving the interests of a particular social class at the expense of other types of representations of the past (Rowlands 1994, 135). This conclusion is inevitable if it is accepted that the dominant philosophy in Irish archaeology, as in Irish life, is empiricism, be it explicitly stated or not. This means that the representations of the past contained in archaeological writings and other work will always support, in the end, what Ó Giolláin has called 'the official world-view's' notion of history (1989; 1990, 173). He describes academic historians in a manner which is equally applicable to many archaeologists as 'cultural functionaries in the same sense as priests, policemen, army officers, judges, journalists and doctors, all working against the unofficial phenomena of folk history, popular religion, traditional codes of right and wrong, folk-medicine, rural and working-class and regional dialect and so forth'.

In effect, under the guise of empiricist common sense, most archaeologists in Ireland and around the world police the past in the interests of dominant social groups. This may be a controversial claim, and it is necessary to expand on it somewhat by examining some of the key archaeological texts that deal with the Early Medieval period. The period itself has an importance that extends beyond these texts, being firmly lodged in the national psyche as the Golden Age to which the Nationalist movement and the Irish Republic turned in the early years of nation building (see also O'Sullivan, ch. 17).

The writing of Early Medieval Ireland

Writing the past is part of what archaeologists do for each other and for the public. This process has a cultural significance which is not confined to the past itself. It should be expected that these writings reflect socio-political and economic factors found in contemporary society, specifically those relating to bourgeois social interests. We represent the past in many different ways, sometimes producing what can be called 'literary artefacts' (Dunne 1987, 4). The form and content of such artefacts are also the proper concern of archaeologists, but it is vital that this form of 'artefactual analysis' extends beyond plundering them for facts about, or photographs of, nice objects. More finely nuanced and contextually sensitive analysis is demanded if the empiricist grip on the discipline is to be loosened. The work of synthesis, as defined by Shanks and Tilley (1993, 18), is one type of archaeological writing which is now well represented in Irish Early Medieval studies. Three case studies have been selected for critique here – Edwards 1990, Mytum 1992 and Patterson 1994 – though only in a necessarily perfunctory way (see Ryan 1996 for a similar kind of appraisal from a more traditional perspective).

Edwards's book is the most sophisticated and widely available example of an empiricist, cultural-historical approach to Early Medieval Ireland. It provides a good vehicle for the process of critique, not because of anything directly stated in the text but rather because of what is absent (Bhaskar, 1993). The book is structured in such a way as to give the impression that the text is a simple exposition of facts. And this is true in one sense, but what of the author herself? By and large she appears to be absent from the text. Aside from the general empiricist assumptions underlying the book, however, it is in fact possible to work out something about her or rather about the broader political and intellectual context from which she writes.

Her British background slips into the text through odd but consistent snippets of information relating to the explanation of social changes within Ireland. External causes and agents for these are almost invariably called upon from within a subtle but ever-present narration of the old colonial tale of Ireland (as a place without historical agency because of some presumed innate primitiveness). Reading the book and looking for what gives it its narrative coherence – what ties the facts together – makes for interesting discoveries. This colonial hangover is present throughout, from the period of stunted Romanisation up until the Viking Age, but one example will have to suffice.

This example concerns Edwards's treatment of what she describes as 'The Roman Impact', in which she concludes: 'at the beginning of our period we are dealing with an Iron Age society which was being transformed as a result of contact with the Roman world' (1990, 5). Given the critique of a fact-centred approach discussed earlier, the present writer's argument against this statement may seem odd. However, there is little *evidence* in her book to sustain such a claim. The odd bits and pieces which are brought together do not on their own make the case that the transition to a different kind of Irish society in the fifth and sixth centuries was caused by the regional presence of the Roman empire. Practically the only thing sustaining the claim is the claim itself and its presumption that causes for social change in Ireland are likely to be external. Ultimately, this is a political statement. Within empiricist frameworks little can be done to avoid being unconsciously influenced by inherited conditioning because empiricists deny being subjective. Edwards's flawed conclusion is compounded by a fundamental error common to archaeologists, which is to allow archaeology to play second fiddle to history (Driscoll 1988, 163–68; Austin 1990, 11–14): she creates the impression that the importance of archaeological evidence lies in those areas where it can be made sense of by documentary sources (1990, 1). These comments are not intended to dismiss casually what is in many ways a considerable enterprise of scholarly achievement, but rather to point the way to other possibilities by showing the necessity of critique.

Mytum's work is a very different kind of book. It is the first explicitly theoretical book for the period in Ireland and for this reason is to be welcomed. Unfortunately, if one prefers one's archaeology to be politically progressive, Mytum's extension of neo-liberal assumptions on human nature, society, competition and entrepreneurship into fifth-century Ireland is a cause of some concern. Once again the origins of dynamic change in Ireland are sought outside the country. In this case individualist attitudes and behaviour are allegedly caused by the introduction of Christian salvationist beliefs. However, Mytum's championing of processual archaeology needs to be supported even though one may disagree with this particular theoretical stance. The fact that he is so explicit about much of his background agenda adds a level of sophistication and openness to discussion on the period previously lacking.

If Edwards's book represents an approach to the past in which archaeology plays a supporting role to the dominant discipline of history and Mytum's work demonstrates what happens if the wrong kind of social theory is applied, then how should scholars choose and apply relevant theoretical approaches that can withstand critical appraisal? Patterson shows one way out of this dilemma. Her book focuses on people and social relations, leaving aside the artefactual fetishism of empiricist archaeology and the reification of documents in history (with the attendant consequence of producing élite-centred narratives) for a social anthropological approach to Early Medieval Ireland. The significance of her work should not be taken as the triumph of one discipline over another. It may be best to think of it not as that of an anthropologist, but rather as an example of the science of studying social relations.

It must be significant that all three works are produced by non-Irish academics. Generalised works of synthesis in Ireland still tend to be very much in the 'Saints and Scholars' mould. The twentieth-century partition of the country has left a colonial legacy which is evident in Early Medieval studies and which has kept the subject firmly within the state-centred camp. Given the particular importance of this period to Irish national identity this is hardly surprising, especially when the social background of most practising scholars of the period is considered. Irish archaeologists need to recognise the political consequences of this state of affairs and the effect it has on our work.

Archaeologies of iron-smithing and myth-making

The wealth of metalworking known from Early Medieval Ireland has meant that this area has long been of interest. In recent years knowledge of the period has been greatly augmented by metallurgical studies, particularly through the important work of Scott (1990). This is to be welcomed because of the way it has contributed towards a shift from the study of élite goods to more mundane artefacts (see Monk and Sheehan, ch. 1).

A look at Scott's work reveals that his appliance of science is not without its drawbacks, the main one being his ultimate reliance on empiricist epistemology. This 'factology' has taken on a particular form in this case, where the description of artefacts is supported by the results of metallurgical analysis and research on historical sources. The uncritical application of scientific techniques can cause blindness in a number of areas; particularly acute forms of myopia associated with political assumptions are generally found in cases of chronic empiricism. There are two consequences to this approach in Scott's work. In the first place there is the social framework into which Scott places part of his analyses and, secondly, there is the resultant narrative which consistently falls into a techno-fetishism dominating what could have been a more exciting consideration of the social roles of different kinds of metalworking in the Early Medieval period (but see Monk and Sheehan, ch. 1, for an alternative view).

A few examples from Scott's work are offered here to justify the above criticisms. When looking at the rise in the number of iron artefacts throughout the Early Medieval period he says that 'this rise in capacity was market driven' (1990, 99). When writing about the Lagore collar he comments that those producing such products 'may be seen as serving ... the upper-end of the market'. He also writes of a 'do-it-yourself segment of the market', 'the market for iron' and 'servicing the top consumers' (ibid., 100–01). Scott's statements about Early Medieval Ireland are centred on this phraseology, which has no relevance to the period as it is applicable only to a capitalist society. Any attempt to import it into the past has ideological implications and involves, in the end, the past being used as a justification and means of naturalising contemporary social relations (Conkey and Spector 1984, 1). An empiricist philosophy allows such slippage to occur uncritically. This has other consequences for his work. While Scott confidently uses historical sources he does so for a curious reason, or at least for a purpose which is more limited than it need be. He draws on the law tracts for information on different ironworking techniques and technological terms but relegates social insights to a secondary position. A technology-centred approach brings little to the study of past society if it is so focused as to exclude almost all other understandings. This may tell us as much about the discipline's preoccupation with technological considerations as about the ostensible focus of academic attention.

These two elements also effect the kinds of archaeological narratives produced. An archaeologist researching within the domain of the empiricist imperative often asks stupid questions. The way Scott's substantive chapters, outlining specific metallurgical analysis of 'the rise in technological standards', are used to investigate whether swords became progressively better at chopping off heads is a case in point.

Conclusion

Alternative histories and archaeologies are not only possible but desirable (Schmidt and Patterson 1996). A significant global shift is required in how material culture is viewed. In Ireland as elsewhere the history of the discipline of archaeology needs further critical analysis, particularly with regard to the complicity of archaeologists in the construction of state-centred narratives in which the past is mobilised in the interests of dominant social groups in the present (Stanley 1996, 28). This is particularly relevant for Early Medieval studies given the special hold that the 'Saints and Scholars' metanarrative continues to have over the discipline, at least in its popular manifestations. Archaeologists working on Irish material need to confront and exorcise the ghosts of colonialism and neo-colonialism in their work. One way of achieving this is by evaluating the role empiricist philosophies have played in ensuring that only one kind of archaeology is possible in this country.

Consideration of how this approach may work out in practice is necessary. What is the political economy of archaeological practice (Wylie 1996, 267)? How does the structure of the discipline exclude so-called minority interests by the very nature of archaeologists' daily interactions among themselves and with the traces of the past? Archaeologists need to shift away from a fetishised focus on material culture to include anthropological understandings combined with explicit theorisation, brought together in a complex interaction with contemporary political considerations and the traces of the past themselves.

ACKNOWLEDGEMENTS

Many thanks to David Austin, Mary Baker and John Tierney for reading and commenting on various drafts of the chapter, and special thanks to Joanna Davies. Mick Monk and John Sheehan must be thanked for allowing space for this kind of critical thinking by inviting me to contribute to this volume (and for being such patient and diligent editors). Nancy Edwards's comments at the conference about engendering archaeology were particularly welcome in opening up the realms of the possible in the discipline.

BIBLIOGRAPHY

Arkins, B. (1994) 'The closing of the Irish mind: Ireland since 1922', *The Welsh Internationalist* 103, 48–64

Austin, D. (1990) 'The "proper study" of medieval archaeology', in D. Austin and L. Alcock (eds.) *From the Baltic to the Black Sea*, 9–35, London

Bhaskar, R. (1993) *Dialectic: The Pulse of Freedom*, London

Breathnach, P. (1988) 'Uneven development and capitalist peripheralization: the case of Ireland', *Antipode* 20 (2), 1–141

Brett, D. (1996) *The Construction of Heritage*, Cork

Collier, A. (1994) *Critical Realism: An Introduction to Roy Bhaskars's Philosophy*, London

Conkey, M.W. and Spector, J.D. (1984) 'Archaeology and the study of gender', in M. Schiffer (ed.), *Advances in Archaeological Method and Theory*, 1-37, London

Cooney, G. (1995) 'Theory and practice in Irish archaeology', in P.J. Ucko (ed.), *Theory in Archaeology: A World Perspective*, 263–73, London

Daniel, G. (1981) *Towards a History of Archaeology*, London

Doyal, L. and Harris, R. (1986) *Empiricism, Explanation and Rationality*, London

Driscoll, S.T. (1988) 'The relationship between history and archaeology: artefacts, documents and power', in S.T. Driscoll and M.R. Nieke (eds.), *Power and Politics in Early Medieval Britain and Ireland*, 162–87, Edinburgh

Dunne, T. (1985) 'A polemical introduction: literature, literacy theory and the historian', in T. Dunne (ed.), *The Writer as Witness: Literature as Historical Evidence*, 1–9, Cork

Eagleton, T. (1991) *Ideology: An Introduction*, London

Edwards, N. (1990) *The Archaeology of Early Medieval Ireland*, London

Gero, J.M. (1983) 'Introduction', in J.M. Gero et al. (eds.), *The Socio-Politics of Archaeology*, 1–4, Amherst

Giot, P.R. (1983) Review of *Newgrange: Archaeology, Art and Legend*, *Antiquity*, 57, 150

Graham, B.J. and Proudfoot, L.J. (1993) *An Historical Geography of Ireland*, London

Gramsci, A. (1986) *Selections from Political Notebooks*, London

Hedges, R. (1982) 'Method and theory in medieval archaeology', *Archaeologia Medievale* 8, 7–37

Hodder, I. et al. (1995) *Interpreting Archaeology: Finding Meaning in the Past*, London

Jameson, F. (1981) *The Political Unconscious: Narrative as A Socially Symbolic Act*, London

Jenkins, K. (1991) *Re-thinking History*, London

Joll, J. (1977) *Gramsci*, London

Kiberd, D. (1995) *Inventing Ireland: The Literature of the Modern Nation*, London

Lee, J.J. (1989) *Ireland 1912–1985: Politics and Society*, Cambridge

Moreland, J. (1991) 'Method and theory in medieval archaeology in the 1990s', *Archeaologia Medievale* 18, 7–42

Moreland, J. (1995) 'Medieval archaeology from east to west', *Scot. Archaeol. Rev.* 9–10, 228–41

Mytum, H. (1992) *The Origins of Early Medieval Ireland*, London

Ó Giolláin, D. (1989) 'An bealoideas agus an Stat', *Bealoideas* 57, 151–63

Ó Giolláin, D. (1990) 'Folklore, history and the State', *ARV* 46, 169–73

Ollman, B. (1993) *Dialectical Investigations*, London

Patterson, N. (1994) *Cattle Lords and Clansmen: The Social Structure of Early Ireland*, London

Rowlands, M. (1994) 'The politics of identity in archaeology', in C.L. Bond, and A. Gilliam (eds.), *Social Construction of the Past: Representation as Power*, London, 128–43

Ryan, M. (1996) 'Early medieval Ireland: some archaeological issues', in K. McCone and K. Simms (eds.), *Progress in Medieval Irish Studies*, Maynooth, 155–63

Said, E. (1992) *Culture and Imperialism*, London

Schmidt, P.R. and Patterson, T.C. (eds.) (1996) *Making Alternative Histories: The Practice of Archaeology and History in Non-Western Settings*, Santa Fe

Scott, B.G. (1990) *Early Irish Ironworking*, Belfast

Shanks, M. and Tilley, C. (1992) *Re-Constructing Archaeology: Theory and Practice*, London

Shanks, M. and Tilley, C. (1993) *Social Theory and Archaeology*, Oxford

Stanley, M. (1996) 'Politics and the past', *Trowel* 7, 23–31

Stedman Jones, G. (1972) *Ideology in Social Science: Readings in Critical Social Theory*, London

Trigger, B. (1989) *A History of Archaeological Thought*, Cambridge

Woodman, P.C. (1992) 'Irish archaeology today: a poverty among riches?', *The Irish Review* 12, 34–39

Wylie, A. (1996) 'Alternative histories: epistemic disunity and political integrity', in P. Schmidt and T.C. Patterson (eds.), *Making Alternative Histories*

19. Early Medieval Munster: Summary and Prospect

NANCY EDWARDS

In this closing chapter it is intended to examine some of the more general issues that have been raised in this volume or in the questions and discussions at the Early Medieval Munster conference itself. I have chosen to concentrate primarily on areas for future research, though I will also touch upon some of the methods that should be used to conduct such research and upon some of the problems which continue to beset us. I should say that nearly all my comments apply not only to Early Medieval Munster but also to the rest of Ireland in this period.

The importance of interdisciplinary studies
The publicity material for University College Cork's Early Medieval Munster conference stated that its aim was to bring together 'archaeologists, linguists and historians in order to examine the province of Munster in the Early Medieval period'. Charles Thomas's paper demonstrated the importance of interdisciplinary studies. He is almost equally at ease with archaeology, history, Latin and the Celtic languages. It is becoming increasingly difficult for the majority of us to be polymaths in this way, but Thomas's paper, amongst others, has pointed up the vital importance of archaeologists, historians, art historians, linguists, place-name specialists, ecologists, geographers and ethnographers not just communicating with each other and being cognisant of each other's research on the Early Medieval period, but also *working together* in order to understand the evidence more fully. I would go so far as to say that in the future multidisciplinary studies will prove crucial for much of the research on this period, and this is echoed in Monk and Sheehan's opening chapter in this volume. After all, our ultimate aims, whatever our particular discipline, are not only to reconstruct as much as we can of every aspect of Early Medieval life but also to try and understand *how* society evolved and changed and *why*. In pursuit of these aims the Early Medieval archaeologist has a tremendous advantage over the prehistorian in that documentary sources can provide some kind of chronological, social and political frameworks, information about how society was ordered, religious beliefs – in this case primarily Christianity – and so forth.

It is incumbent upon archaeologists to try to set their excavations or surveys or artefactual studies in the wider context, including the historical background wherever this is possible. Indeed, an awareness of the historical context can lead them to a broader understanding of the material evidence, as, for example, in the case of the functions of ogham stones. At the same time historic archaeology has, thankfully, thrown off the last shackles of its image as the 'handmaiden of history' and is now free to develop its own identity. It is equally important for historians, linguists and others studying this period to be aware that, increasingly, archaeological evidence can illuminate their work. The discovery of archaeological material may sometimes provide a key to the explanation of difficult terminology in the law texts, as Colin Rynne's research on the physical evidence for Early Medieval mills has demonstrated. Equally, as indicated by Michael Monk, John Tierney and Martha Hannon, environmental evidence for crop processing may be able to shed light on food preparation, as discussed by Regina Sexton, who has combined a study of the early Irish texts with practical cookery.

Data gathering versus theory
A perceived, but in my view false, conflict between data gathering and archaeological theory was raised by a number of speakers at the conference and was also the subject of hot debate in ensuing discussions. I hope it is agreed by all that data gathering and its dissemination, whether the research excavation and subsequent analysis of a ringfort, such as Lisleagh I and II, of an ecclesiastical site such as Illaunloughan, large-scale rescue excavations such as those in Waterford city, or the detailed compilation of a corpus of Viking Age silver hoards, have a value in themselves, especially for a period where we still know so comparatively little. Indeed, the rapid expansion of research on all aspects of environmental archaeology over the last twenty years is vital to our understanding of many previously hidden areas of daily life and the economy, and its importance should not be underestimated.

A lack of factual information has also been highlighted many times in this volume. Some authors, such as Margaret McCarthy in her examination of the archaeozoological material, have had no option but to admit to considerable *lacunae* in our knowledge of Early Medieval Munster and have instead been forced to look at Ireland as an apparently homogeneous whole.

Nevertheless we must try and interpret our evidence in whatever way we can. Here I think that, in addition to multidisciplinary and interdisciplinary studies, archaeologists must continue to set their own agendas. What light can archaeological evidence shed upon the organisation of past societies, as, for example, in the study of ringforts and unenclosed homesteads, which is *not* suggested by a reading of the documentary sources? What can the variety, distribution, organisation and chronology of early eccesiastical sites tell us about ritual and religion? Arising from this we need to ask a more general question. To what extent should archaeologists studying this period in Ireland be making use of the theoretical methods which are now commonplace elsewhere and which are beginning to have an impact on Early Medieval archaeology?

Theory has yet to play a major role in Irish archaeology of any period, though some recent publications have definitely raised the temperature in this regard (Mytum 1992; Cooney and Grogan 1994; Aitchison 1994). In my own view there is emphatically a role for theoretical archaeological methodologies, and these are certainly not in conflict with the more traditional data-gathering approaches: they should complement each other. As both Jerry O'Sullivan and Michael Tierney have shown, there has been an increasing realisation in recent years that archaeologists, their agendas and the ways in which they interpret the material evidence are very much the (often unconscious) products of their own backgrounds and of the broader cultural forces at work in their contemporary societies. It is also worth mentioning that, although data gathering in the field has continued unabated, the comparative lack of academic interest amongst archaeologists in the Early Medieval period in Ireland over the last thirty years or so and the concentration of the majority of research on the prehistoric era have resulted in a curtailment of advances in our understanding. In the future we must try to guard against the false imposition of our own contemporary outlooks, philosophies and mentalities on the Early Medieval evidence.

But it is also clear that other theoretical approaches can aid us in interpreting the ever increasing amount of data more critically and in setting out frameworks for future research. However, in order for this to happen the use of archaeological theory needs to be more widely accepted. To achieve this the explanation of theory needs to be aimed not just at the initiated, and jargon should never be used as a substitute for clear analysis.

Regionalism and diversity

This volume is concerned, very broadly speaking, with the province of Munster. In some instances it is possible to point to a regional identity for the province. Using the evidence of the ogham stones, Charles Thomas and Fionnbarr Moore have suggested that their distribution might indicate this region as the area where literacy first took hold. Dagmar Ó Riain-Raedel has discussed the origins of Christianity and the important role of early Munster saints, such as Declan of Ardmore. (Incidently, sites with any evidence of very early Christianity deserve more detailed archaeological investigation if we are to increase our understanding of the conversion period.) Rhoda Cronin has emphasised the great variation in the late High Crosses and has identified two broad groups in Munster, one conservative and one innovative, and local trends are also apparent in the emergence of distinctive ornamental metalworking styles in the eleventh and twelfth centuries (Ó Floinn 1987, 183–85). John Sheehan considers the distinctions between Viking Age silver hoards from Munster and elsewhere. But inevitably, because of the continuing paucity of evidence in many areas, we are often still forced to view Ireland as a homogeneous entity, with the result that various geographical and cultural regions and political units are regarded as evolving in the same way and at the same pace throughout the Early Medieval period. This is clearly nonsense, and for this reason I want to emphasise the importance of regional studies in the future. Different parts of Ireland must have developed at a different pace and consequently had different identities – just as they do today. For example, at a provincial level the perceived lack of sixth- and seventh-century ornamental metalwork in Munster contrasts with other areas further north; indeed, a number of authorities have remarked upon the apparent poverty of Munster in the Early Middle Ages compared with some other areas. The Hiberno-Norse towns (with their hinterlands), discussed in this volume by Maurice Hurley, provide a more obvious regional and cultural identity when compared with the rest of Ireland. Furthermore, potentially interesting distinctions have been suggested by both Sheehan and Hurley between the Munster Hiberno-Norse towns and Dublin.

There is also a need to emphasise regional studies at a more local level. As Michael Monk has suggested, by sampling and/or excavating several ringforts in a small area it may be possible to determine a settlement history for that kind of monument and to determine how that settlement history differs, for example, from similar sites in Ulster. We need to know how ringforts related to unenclosed Early Medieval settlements in local areas, which are sometimes shown up by souterrains in Cork and by *clocháns* in the stony Kerry landscape. How do such settlements relate to their environment and how did the people who occupied them exploit their surroundings? John Tierney's contribution clearly demonstrates the importance of woodland and Colin Rynne's hints at the vital role of water, not just for milling, but, as Margaret McCarthy shows, for the broader exploitation of riverine, lacustrine and marine environments for food and other resources. There is also the relationship of such settlements to arable land and grazing, and the role of transhumance which Monk refers to. It is increasingly clear that the exploitation of metals, notably as a result of the ongoing excavations at Ross Island, Co. Kerry (O'Brien 1995), was of some importance during the Early Medieval period and we need to try and study this on a regional level. As Monk has indicated we need to know how secular settlements related spatially and functionally to the wide range of ecclesiastical sites, from major monasteries, with their many religious and other activities, to smaller sites, which provided pastoral care for particular communities, and to hermitages, apparently separate from the secular world. How does Illaunloughan, for example, fit into this picture and into the broader landscape of Valencia Island and the Iveragh peninsula? It is only when we begin to examine sites in their contexts, and not just as dots on a map, that we will be able to begin to build up an Early Medieval landscape and to discern how it evolved over time.

The beginning and end of the period

The contributions of Charles Thomas, Dagmar Ó Riain-Raedel and Fionnbarr Moore concentrate on the beginning of the period and, obliquely, they address the vital question of why the Early Medieval period evolved when and how it did. To what extent did it depend upon the impact of Roman culture and the introduction of literacy and Christianity? To what extent was it driven by other, less obvious, factors, such as expanding agriculture (hinted at in the pollen evidence) suggesting the impact of technology exemplified by horizontal and vertical mills, or by political and social change as indicated in the widespread migrations to western Britain at the end of the Roman period? At the end of the Early Medieval period (the eleventh and twelfth centuries are generally far more neglected in terms of research than the earlier part), John Sheehan has examined the Viking Age hoards, Maurice Hurley the Hiberno-Norse towns, Tadhg O'Keeffe the Romanesque architecture, and Rhoda Cronin the importance of the late High Crosses.

It seems to me that we should also begin to address the issues of change and continuity at the beginning and end of the Early Medieval period through small-scale regional studies. We should be trying to understand the evolution of a landscape over time. On the one hand we need to try and reach back into the Iron Age in order to understand the changes which took place in the early centuries of the first millenium. On the other, at the end of our period, we should attempt to understand not only the impact of the Vikings and to what extent, as Hurley and Sheehan have suggested, the native Irish influenced the development of Hiberno-Norse towns and artefacts, but also the impact of the Anglo-Norman conquest and when and to what extent native settlement types such as ringforts died out, lingered or evolved, especially in the parts of Munster, such as those held by the O'Briens and the McCarthys, that remained entirely in native control for centuries after 1169.

Problems of dating and context

Continuing problems with dating and chronology were the subject of a lively discussion during the Cork conference and are also considered by Monk and Sheehan in the opening chapter. My own response is that our understanding of the chronology of the Early Medieval period in Ireland is considerably better than it was even fifteen years ago. Radiocarbon dating is being steadily refined. Dendrochronological dating of wood from such sites as Moynagh Lough crannog, Co. Meath (Bradley 1993), and the raised rath at Deer Park Farms, Co. Antrim (Lynn 1989), has revolutionised our ability to date artefacts in such contexts and then to use these to provide an indication of date for similar artefacts elsewhere. For example, the metalworking evidence at Moynagh Lough has important implications for the work of art historians and archaeologists on the relative chronology of ornamental metalworking. Similarly, the late Tom Fanning's research (1994) on the ringed pins from Hiberno-Norse Dublin, where they were found in well-stratified contexts securely dated by coins, is also of great importance. There will doubtless be other examples of this kind of research in the future. I think, however, that in the case of illuminated manuscripts in particular we have become rather obsessive about dating. Although a few examples, such as the Book of Armagh (Alexander 1978, 76–77), may be dated precisely by colophon, the dating of the majority depends entirely upon palaeographical and art-historical criteria which cannot provide more than a broad chronological framework. Dating aside, it is perhaps more important to try to determine the roles and functions of such art-historical objects, their audience, who produced them and why. Artefacts should be seen in their context rather than in isolation, and Rhoda Cronin has emphasised the importance of examining the late High Crosses in conjunction with Romanesque architectural sculpture.

Technology
Technology is an important subject and is therefore worth addressing here, however briefly. It has been mentioned in various chapters in this volume and an interest in how things were made was one of the guiding forces behind all of the late Professor O'Kelly's research. For example, forest management, woodworking and carpentry of various kinds must have played an important role in the lives of the Early Medieval Irish. What was the impact of the introduction of horizontal and vertical mills or the heavy plough on grain production? Equally, during the eighth century and earlier, ornamental metal- and glass-working technologies were continually developing and being experimented with in order to produce such objects as the Derrynaflan paten. Is it possible to define more closely the role of the Church and secular authorities in the fostering and dissemination of technological innovations? In the future, studies of technology will continue to play an important part in increasing our understanding of economic and other developments in Early Medieval Ireland.

Women in Early Medieval Ireland
During the Cork conference somebody remarked, during a discussion of the economy, that women appear to be invisible in Early Medieval Ireland. In this volume Regina Sexton has indicated that baking was a female-dominated activity and she also referred to the association of particular types of food with particular social groupings, for example porridge with children. Clearly a lot more work needs to be done to try to recognise the role of women in Early Medieval Irish society and to reconstruct their lives. We face a problem, however, in attempting to identify their role through the archaeological evidence. Spindle whorls, weaving equipment and sewing are always associated with women, as is raising children, but what else? It is likely that women were looking after the farm animals around the settlement, as well as making butter, cheese and other food products (and pottery where it occurs), but at present little more can be said. Unlike pagan Anglo-Saxon England, there are few burials with gravegoods to help in this regard. However, one area which has proved rewarding in England (Gilchrist 1994, esp. 25–36) and which should undoubtedly be investigated archaeologically in Ireland is the ecclesiastical sites that are known to have been nunneries. I do not know whether any such sites are mentioned in the documentary sources for Munster, but Killevy, Co. Armagh (DOENI 1983, 81–82), which is associated with St Moninne and, unlike Kildare, has not been disturbed by modern settlement, is a prime candidate for investigation. Excavation of cemeteries with well-preserved skeletal material also offers the opportunity to study the health and diet of women and it is worth remembering that, in some instances at least, women were buried separately from men (Hamlin and Foley 1983). Clearly the documentary sources also need to be studied more closely for what they might reveal about the role of women, children and other social groupings in Early Medieval Irish society. The results of this approach might, in turn, throw light on the material evidence.

Conclusion
I would like to think that the Cork conference and its publication come at a turning-point in the study of Early Medieval Munster. The survey of potential Early Medieval sites in counties Cork and Kerry is now well advanced (Cuppage 1986; Power et al. 1992, 1994, 1997; Toal 1995; O'Sullivan and Sheehan 1996) and, on a smaller scale, there is also the survey of the barony of

Ikerrin in County Tipperary (Stout 1984). It is to be hoped that similar surveys for the rest of Munster will be completed in the near future. The systematic recording of sites in this way will not only aid their preservation and management, but will also enable the formulation of research strategies which will include the meaningful archaeological investigation of sites under threat. But, above all, we need to concentrate upon regional studies, interdisciplinary research and the innovative analysis of data in order to learn more about Early Medieval society, not just in Munster, but also in other areas of Ireland to determine how and why they differed from each other.

ACKNOWLEDGEMENTS

In preparing this chapter, which I hope continues to impart a flavour of the concerns and debates of the original conference, I would like to thank all those who brought material to my attention. I also want to thank Michael Monk and John Sheehan, for their kind invitation to provide the summing up and for the opportunity to write and think about some of the broader issues raised in the contemporary study of Early Medieval Ireland.

BIBLIOGRAPHY

Aitchison, N.B. (1994) *Armagh and the Royal Centres of Early Medieval Ireland: Monuments, Cosmology and the Past*, Woodbridge

Alexander, J.J.G. (1978) *Insular Manuscripts 6th to the 9th Century*, London

Bradley, J. (1993) 'Moynagh Lough: an insular workshop of the second quarter of the 8th century', in R.M. Spearman and J. Higgitt (eds.), *The Age of Migrating Ideas*, 74–81, Edinburgh

Cooney, G. and Grogan, E. (1994) *Irish Prehistory: a Social Perspective*, Dublin

Cuppage, J. et al. (1986) *Archaeological survey of the Dingle Peninsula*, Ballyferriter

DOENI (1983, 6th ed.) *Historic Monuments of Northern Ireland*, Belfast

Fanning, T. (1994) *Viking Age Ringed Pins from Dublin*, Medieval Dublin Excavations 1962–81, Ser. B, vol. 4, Dublin

Gilchrist, R. (1994) *Gender and Material Culture: The Archaeology of Religious Women*, London, New York

Hamlin, A. and Foley, C. (1983) 'A women's graveyard at Carrickmore, Co. Tyrone, and the separate burial of women', *Ulster J. Archaeol.* 3 ser. 46, 41–46

Lynn, C.J. (1989) 'Deer Park Farms', *Current Archaeol.* 113, 193–98

Mytum, H. (1992) *The Origins of Early Christian Ireland*, London, New York

O'Brien, W. (1995) 'Ross Island', in I. Bennett (ed.) *Excavations 1995: Summary Accounts of Archaeological Excavations in Ireland*, 42, Bray

Ó Floinn, R. (1987) 'Schools of metalworking in eleventh- and twelfth-century Ireland', in M. Ryan (ed.), *Ireland and Insular Art A.D. 500–1200*, 179–87, Dublin

O'Sullivan, A. and Sheehan, J. (1996) *The Iveragh Peninsula: an Archaeological Survey of South Kerry*, Cork

Power, D. et al. (1992, 1994, 1997) *Archaeological Inventory of County Cork*, Vols 1–3, Dublin

Stout, G.T. (1984) *Archaeological Survey of the Barony of Ikerrin*, Roscrea

Toal, C. (1995) *The North Kerry Archaeological Survey*, Dingle

ILLUSTRATIONS

		page
	Munster, showing counties, centres of population and principal natural features	ii
	Early Medieval figure from cross inscribed slab at Ballyvourney, Co. Cork	v
Fig. 2.1	Ogham memorials with Roman personal names: 1. single Roman names; 2. Irish-named sons of Roman-named fathers	11
Fig. 2.2	Density-distribution map of ogham-inscribed memorial stones (totals per county adjusted to median area of all counties)	12
Fig. 2.3	Density-distribution map of ecclesiastical place-names of the type 'Donagh-', etc. (OIr *domnach*); totals per county adjusted to median area of all counties (Source: selectively from maps in Flanagan, 1984)	13
Fig. 2.4	Density-distribution map of ecclesiastical place-names with prefix Kil-, Kill- (OIr *cell*); totals per county adjusted to median area of all counties (Source: lists in Goblet, 1931)	13
Fig. 4.1	Distribution and contexts of ogham stones in Ireland (by Sharyn MacMenamin, courtesy Dúchas, The Heritage Service)	24
Fig. 4.2	Cross inscribed ogham stone from Ballynahunt, Dingle, Co. Kerry. The inscription reads: DUGENNGG ... MAQI RODDOS	26
Fig. 4.3	Cross inscribed ogham stone from souterrain at Coolmagort, Co. Kerry. Drawing by Kevin O'Brien, based on original by F. Moore	28
Fig. 4.4	Cross inscribed ogham stone from Kinard Td., Dingle, Co. Kerry. The inscription reads: MARIANI. Drawing by Kevin O'Brien based on original by F. Moore	29
Fig. 4.5	Ogham stone in the Promontory Fort on Dunmore Head, Coumeenole North Td., Dingle, Co. Kerry. The inscription reads: ERC MAQI MAQI-ERCIAS MU DOVINIA	30
Fig. 5.1	Caherlehillan and other sites of probable Early Medieval date in the Ferta valley, Co. Kerry	36
Fig. 5.2	Distribution of sites of probable Early Medieval date in the Lisleagh meso study area, Co. Cork	38
Fig. 5.3	Distribution of sites of probable Early Medieval date in the Lisleagh micro study area, Co. Cork	39
Fig. 5.4	Reconstruction of the penultimate phase of activity at Lisleagh II, Co. Cork	41
Fig. 5.5	Aerial view of Curraheen I and II, Co. Cork	42
Fig. 5.6	Distribution of known and recently discovered probable ringforts in the north-west Blackwater area, Co. Cork (OS 6" sheet no. 24)	43
Fig. 5.7	Aerial view of Killeenemer ecclesiastical site, Co. Cork	45
Fig. 6.1	Seventeenth-century woodlands in Muskerry, Co. Cork (Source: Civil Survey)	54
Fig. 8.1	Location map of sites discussed in chapter 8	67
Fig. 8.2	Pie charts showing the relative proportion of different plant species at Lisleagh I and II, Co. Cork	69
Fig. 8.3	Pie charts showing the relative proportion of different plant species at Loher and Ballyegan, Co. Kerry	69
Fig. 8.4	Pie charts showing the relative proportion of plant species at Kilanully and Lisnagun, Co. Cork	70
Fig. 10.1	Conjectural reconstruction of twin-flume horizontal-wheeled mill at Little Island, Co. Cork (c. AD 630)	88
Fig. 10.2	Conjectural reconstruction of vertical-wheeled mill at Little Island, Co. Cork (c. AD 630)	89

Fig. 10.3	Horizontal waterwheels from a) Mashanaglass, Co. Cork (Early Medieval); b) Cloontycarthy, Co. Cork (c. AD 833); c) Moycraig, Co. Antrim (ninth century AD)	93
Fig. 10.4	Waterwheel paddles from a) Mashanaglass; b) Moycraig; c) Cloontycarthy	94
Fig. 10.5	Regional variations of horizontal waterwheel paddles in Portugal (after J. Galhano, *Moinhos e Azenhas de Portugal*, Lisbon, 1978)	95
Fig. 11.1	Location map of south-west Kerry, showing Illaunloughan	102
Fig. 11.2	Plan of Illaunloughan, Co. Kerry, showing excavated areas	103
Fig. 11.3	Plan of oratory area, Illaunloughan, Co. Kerry	104
Fig. 11.4	Plan and section of the gable-shrine and terraced mound, Illaunloughan, Co. Kerry	107
Fig. 11.5	Plan of excavated huts, Illaunloughan, Co. Kerry	109
Fig. 12.1	Location map of sites mentioned in chapter 12	113
Fig. 12.2	a) Church Island (Valencia), Co. Kerry; b) Gallarus Oratory, Co. Kerry; c) Sceilig Mhichíl, Co. Kerry	115
Fig. 12.3	a) South 'church' at Labbamolaga, Co. Cork; b) St Declan's 'house' at Ardmore, Co. Waterford	117
Fig. 12.4	a) Tuamgraney, Co. Clare, doorway; b) Ratass, Co. Kerry, doorway; c) Reefert, Co. Wicklow, doorway; d) Monasterboice, Co. Louth, Round Tower doorway; e) Cashel, Co. Tipperary, Round Tower doorway; f) Killeenemer, Co. Cork, west facade (reconstructed); g) Britway, Co. Cork, doorway; h) Killodiernan, Co. Tipperary, east window; i) Ardskeagh, Co. Cork, west portal (reconstructed); j) Ballyhea, Co. Cork, south doorway; k) Ratoo, Co. Kerry, Round Tower doorway	120
Fig. 13.1	Distribution of earliest High Crosses in Ireland (from Ahenny to Clonmacnoise)	126
Fig. 13.2	Ahenny South Cross, east face (Dúchas, The Heritage Service)	128
Fig. 13.3	Ahenny South Cross, west face (Dúchas, The Heritage Service)	130
Fig. 13.4	Ahenny North Cross, east face (Dúchas, The Heritage Service)	131
Fig. 13.5	Ahenny North Cross, west face (Dúchas, The Heritage Service)	132
Fig. 13.6	Clonmacnoise South Cross, east face (Dúchas, The Heritage Service)	134
Fig. 13.7	Clonmacnoise South Cross, west face (Dúchas, The Heritage Service)	135
Fig. 14.1	Distribution of Late High Crosses in Ireland	139
Fig. 14.2	The 'Doorty' cross, Kilfenora, Co. Clare	141
Fig. 14.3	The Dysert O'Dea cross, east face (after Westropp)	142
Fig. 14.4	The West Cross at Kilfenora	144
Fig. 15.1	Distribution of gold and silver finds of Scandinavian character in Munster	149
Fig. 15.2	Silver hoard from Carraig Aille II, Co. Limerick (National Museum of Ireland)	152
Fig. 15.3	Unlocalised hoard from Co. Cork (No. 2) (British Museum)	153
Fig. 15.4	Penannular rod armring from the Kilbarry hoard, Co. Cork (Ashmolean Museum, Oxford)	155
Fig. 15.5	Distribution of coin hoards deposited after c. 950 in Munster and Leinster	159
Fig. 16.1	Proposed sequence of development of Hiberno-Norse Waterford	166
Fig. 16.2	Late eleventh-century houses fronting Peter Street: type 1 with pathway leading from 'back door'; type 2 house to left of pathway and another in upper left	169
Fig. 16.3	St Peter's Church: plan of twelfth-century three-cell church	171
Fig. 16.4	Plan showing suggested location of Hiberno-Norse Cork and location of archaeological excavations	173
Fig. 18.1	A simplified view of empiricist methodology in archaeology	191
Fig. 18.2	A view of how archaeologists 'know' they work but pretend otherwise	192

Contributors

Rhoda Cronin is a graduate of the Department of Archaeology, University College, Cork, and lives in Switzerland.

Nancy Edwards is a lecturer in the Department of History, University College of North Wales, Bangor.

Martha Hannon is a tutor in the Department of Archaeology, University College, Cork.

Maurice F. Hurley is Cork City archaeologist.

Margaret McCarthy is a member of the Archaeological Services Unit, University College, Cork.

Michael A. Monk is a lecturer in the Department of Archaeology, University College, Cork.

Fionnbarr Moore is an archaeologist with the National Monuments Service, Department of Arts, Heritage, Gaeltacht and the Islands.

Tadhg O'Keeffe is a lecturer in the Department of Archaeology, University College, Dublin.

Dagmar Ó Riain-Raedel is a lecturer in the Department of History, University College, Cork.

Jerry O'Sullivan is an editor with the Society of Antiquaries of Scotland.

Colin Rynne is curator of the Cork Butter Museum.

Etienne Rynne is Professor of Archaeology, University College, Galway.

Regina Sexton is a food historian and a graduate of the Department of History, University College, Cork.

John Sheehan is a lecturer in the Department of Archaeology, University College, Cork.

Charles Thomas is Emeritus Professor of Cornish Studies, University of Exeter.

John Tierney is a consultant archaeologist.

Michael Tierney is a doctoral student at the University of Wales, Lampeter.

Claire Walsh is a consultant archaeologist.

Jenny White Marshall is a researcher in University College, Los Angeles.

INDEX

Abban, St, 19
Adalhard, abbot, 91
Adare, Co. Limerick, 149
aerial photography, 34, 40, 42–3
Aghabullogue, Co. Cork, 28
Aghadoe, Co. Kerry, 145
Aghowle, Co. Wicklow, 119
agriculture
   animal husbandry, 59–64
      dairying, 60
      developments in, 46–7
      farm size, 55
      intensive, 48
      pastoralism, 65
      ringforts, 40, 182–4
      and woodlands, 56–7
Ahaliskey, Co. Cork, 28, 31
Ahenny Crosses, 127–33
Ailbe, St, 19–20, 21
Aislinge meic Conglinne, 76, 79, 83
Albert, St, archbishop of Cashel, 21
Albinus, bishop of Ferns, 20
Aldwincle bridge, 94
Ancient Order of Hibernians, 179
Anglo-Normans, 6, 56, 74, 170, 203
   Cork charters, 174
   Limerick, 167–8
Anglouleme Cathedral, 122
Annals of Inisfallen, 145
Annals of the Four Masters, 172
anthropology, 57, 196–7
antiquarianism, 179–80
   Viking hoards, 150–1
Apicius, 81
Araglen, Co. Kerry, 29
Aran Islands, 73, 143
archaeobotanical studies, 65–74, 201
    contamination, 81
    sites and contexts, 66
Archaeological Services Unit, 66
archaeological surveys, 5–6, 7
archaeology
   contract archaeology, 2–4, 7
   data gathering *versus* theory, 201–2
   first Irish generation, 181–2
   'Golden Age' myth, 178–87
   and historical evidence, 6–7, 196
   historiography of, 187
   influence of colonialism, 195–8
   interdisciplinary studies, 200–1
   mitigation policy, 3
   myth-making, 197–8
   publication of results, 3, 4
   theoretical, 5
   theory and politics in, 190–8
      despotism of fact, 191–3
      intellectual closure, 193–5
archaeozoological studies, 59–64, 201
   data and problems, 59–63
architecture. *see* church building
Ardfert, Co. Kerry, 119, 122
Ardmore, Co. Waterford, 19–20, 21, 116, 117
Ardskeagh, Co. Cork
   doorway, 120, 121
Arkins, B., 194
Arklow, Co. Wicklow, 18
Armagh, 12, 118
   Patrician cult, 17–19, 18–19
Arraglen, Co. Kerry, 26
   artefacts, 5, 110
   ringforts, 35
   traded, 40
Athlone, Co. Westmeath, 133
Athlone Plaque, 129, 136
Auxerre, 17, 18
Auxilius, 12, 18

Baillie, M.G.L., 48
bairgen banfuine, 79–80
bairgen ferfuine, 80
Ballinderry, Co. Offaly, 133
Ballinderry I, 181
Ballineesteenig, Co. Kerry, 28
Ballingarry, Co. Limerick, 28
Ballintaggart, Co. Kerry, 28, 29
Ballintermon, Co. Kerry, 31
Ballinvoher, Co. Kerry, 28
Ballyadams, Co. Laois, 155
Ballycarty, Co. Kerry, 74
Ballyegan, Co. Kerry, 60, 66, 68, 74
   palaeobotany
      spreads and layers, 72
      structural features, 71
   souterrain fills, 68, 70
Ballyhank, Co. Cork, 28, 31

Ballyhea, Co. Cork
   doorway, 120, 121
Ballykilleen, Co. Offaly, 92, 94–5
Ballyknock, Co. Cork, 28, 29, 31
Ballymoreragh, Co. Kerry, 28
Ballynahunt, Co. Kerry
   ogham stone, 26, 27
Ballynavenouragh, Co. Kerry, 57
Ballypalady, Co. Antrim, 33
Ballyquin, Co. Waterford, 29
Banagher cross-shaft, 129
Bann river, 57
Bantry Bay, 9
Barrett, G.F. and Graham, B.J., 33
Barrett, G.F., 34
Barrow river, 9, 11, 53
Bateman (collector), 150
Bealin Cross, 129
Bede, the Venerable, 108, 112
Beginish Island, 36
Benedict Biscop, 118
Benedictine Order, 20
Bennett, I., 36
Berger, R., 5, 116
Berrad Airechta, 25
Betha Colmáin maic Lúacháin, 83
birds, evidence for, 62, 63
Blackwater river, 11, 42
   survey area, 43
   woodlands, 53, 54, 55
Book of Armagh, 203
Book of Dimma, 145
Book of Durrow, 129
Book of Kells, 133
Book of Lindisfarne, 129
booleying, 36, 37
Boolies Little, 185
Borland, D., 180
Bray Head, Valencia, 44, 105, 110
breads, 79–83, 84–5
   condiments and relishes, 83
   ingredients, 80–1
   monastic and penitential, 82–3
   utensils and preparation, 81–2
Bretha Comaithchesa, 80
Bretha Crolige, 77
Bretha Déin Chécht, 73
Bretha im Fhuillema Gell, 81
Bride river, 55
Brigid, St, 91
Britannia, 9–10, 11
British language, 14
Britway, Co. Cork
   doorway, 120, 121, 122
   brothchan, 77–8
Brough of Birsay box, 129
Buckley, V., 34

bullaun stones, 44
burials. *see* grave-sites
Burnfort, Co. Cork, 28
Bushe, Paddy, 4

Caheravart, Co. Cork, 34
Cahercommaun, 181
Caherlehillan, Co. Kerry, 35–7, 61, 74
Cahirvagliair, Co. Cork, 114
Cáin Adamnáin, 78
Cáin Aicillne, 79–80, 81
Cáin Íarraith, 76, 79, 82
Camp, Co. Kerry, 29
Canones Hibernenses, 82
Canterbury, 170
Cappoquin, Co. Cork, 54
carbonisation
   palaeobotanical studies, 66–8, 72–3
Carhoovauler, Co. Cork, 29
Carlow, County, 11, 153
Carraig Aille, Co. Limerick, 181
Carraig Aille II, 149, 154–8
   hoard, 151, 152, 153
Carrigaline, Co. Cork, 155, 157–8
Carrowntemple, Co. Sligo, 129
Cashel, Co. Tipperary, 18, 121, 122, 143
   doorway, 120
   ecclesiastical status of, 19–21
   high cross, 138, 140, 142
Cashel, synod of, 1101, 122, 145
Cashen river, Co. Kerry, 94
Castlelyons, Co. Cork, 149
Cath Maige Tuired, 76
Cathasach's Cross, Inishcealtra, 143
Cato, 81
Caulfield, S., 33
ceallúnach, 106
Celestine, Pope, 17
cell/kill, 12–14
'Celtic' high crosses, 125–37
Celtic Society, 180
Celtic Studies, Dublin School of, 8
cereal foods, 76–85
   breads, 79–83
   porridges and gruels, 76–9
   use of mills, 96
Chad, St, 108
Champneys, A., 179, 185
charcoal studies, 56, 57
Chrichad an Chaoilli, 44
Christianity. *see also* church building
   arrival of, 9, 11–15
   Hiberno-Norse Waterford, 170–2
   in Munster, 17–21
   12th c., 20–1
Chronicum Scotorum, 167

church building, 105, 112–23, 184–5
   antae and architraved doorways, 118–19
   architecture of the Memoria, 116–18
   Gallarus Oratory, 114, 115
   Hiberno-Norse Waterford, 170–2
   mos Scottorum, 112, 114
   Romanesque, 122–3, 138, 143
   11th c. changes, 119–21
   wooden, 118–19
Church Island, Co. Kerry, 14, 29, 34, 45, 102, 103–4, 182
   architecture, 112, 114, 115, 116, 118
   burials, 106
   fishing, 62
   oratory, 105
Church Island, Lough Currane, 122
Ciarán of Clonmacnois, St, 137
Ciarán of Saighir, St, 19–20, 83
Cill Chais, 57
Civil Survey, 1654-56, 53–4, 56
Clare, County, 5, 56, 127
clientship, 40, 47, 48
climate, 48
clocháns, 36–7, 114, 184, 202
Clonamery, Co. Kilkenny, 119
Clonlonan, Co. Westmeath, 96
Clonmacnois, Co. Offaly, 116, 118
   church architecture, 118, 119
   Cross of the Scriptures, 137
   cross-fragments, 129
   crucifixion plaque, 140, 142
   excavations, 185
   South Cross, 127, 133–7
Clontarf, Co. Dublin, 179
Cloontycarthy, Co. Cork, 91, 92, 94, 98, 99
Coarhabeg, Valencia Island, 36–7
coastal erosion, 185
Codex Salmanticensis, 19, 20
Coffey, G., 179
Cogitosus, 91, 118
Coibnes Uisci Thairidne, 90, 91
coins, 106, 108, 148
   Arabic, 154
   Viking hoards, 147–8, 151–2, 157
Collins, Michael, 180
colonialism, influence of, 195–8
Columba, St, 137
Columella, 81
Compostela, Spain, 108
Confessio (Patrick), 12
Confey, Co. Kildare, 121
Cong, Co. Mayo, 145
Connaught, 13, 63, 97
Connolly, James, 180
Connolly, Michael, 74
Consuetudines Corbinienses, 91
contextual problems, 203–4

contract archaeology, 2–4, 7
Coolineagh, Co. Cork, 28
Coolmagort, Co. Kerry, 27, 28, 31
Coolowen, Co. Cork, 33
Coomeenole, Co. Kerry, 28
   ogham stone, 30
Cooney, G., 184, 187
coppicing, 55
Corbie monastery, 91
Corcannon, Co. Wexford, 96
Corcu Loegde, 19
Cork, County, 121, 145
   archaeological survey, 5–6
   hoards, 153, 154, 157
   ogham stones, 23, 27
Cork, Earl of, 54
Cork Archaeological Survey, 42, 43
Cork city, 1, 3, 155, 156
   Hiberno-Norse, 170–1, 172–5
   settlement, 155, 157–8, 164, 165
Cork diocese, 21
Cork Harbour, 9
Cork Survey, 34
Corkaboy, Co. Kerry, 28
Cormac MacAirt, 87
Cormac's Chapel, Cashel, 121, 122, 138, 142, 143
Cornhill, 42
Cornwall, 11
Cosmographia (Ptolemy), 9
Coumcille, St, 136
crafts, 46
Crag, Co. Kerry, 26, 29, 31
Craig, Sir James, 180
Cresen/Christianus, 13–14
Crith Gabhlach, 80, 83, 182, 183
Croker, Crofton, 150
Cromglaise, Co. Cork, 44
Cronan, St, 145
Crónán, Rhoda, 202, 203, 204
Cross of Patrick and Columba, Kells, 136–7
cross-slabs, 114
Crushyriree, Co. Cork, 90
Cuerdale, Lancashire, 156
Cullen, Co. Tipperary, 149, 150, 153, 157, 158
Curraghmore West, Co. Kerry, 28–9
Curraheen, 42
Cush, Co. Limerick, 181
Cushalogurt, Co. Mayo, 155, 156
Cuthbert, St, 106–7

dating problems, 203–4
Davies, Wendy, 25–6, 185–6
Davis, Thomas, 179
Davys, Sir John, 57
De Ceithri Slichtaib Athgábala, 88, 90, 96, 97
de Paor, Liam, 6, 18, 37, 140, 143, 146, 186
de Paor, Máire, 37, 186

de Valera, Eamon, 180–1, 182
Déclán, St, 19–20, 202
Deelish, Co. Cork, 28
Deer Park Farms, Co. Antrim, 55, 57, 203
Deer Parks Farms, Co. Antrim, 92
deforestation, 53, 97, 99
Déisi, 6, 11, 18, 19, 21
dendrochronology, 46, 53, 203
Denmark, 169
Derry, County, 12
Derrycunnihy Wood, Co. Kerry, 58
Derrygarrane South, Co. Kerry, 29
Derrynaflan, Co. Tipperary, 18, 204
Derrynahinch, Co. Kilkenny, 155
Derrynasaggart mountains, 32
Desert Fathers, 14
Desmond, 20
development archaeology, 2–4, 35
Devon, 11
Di Chetharshlicht Athgabála, 81
Dickens, Charles, 193
Din Techtugad, 82
Dingle Peninsula, 34, 102, 114, 115
Discovery Programme, 1–2, 56, 193
documentary sources
    animal remains, 63
    millwrights, 87
    palaeobotany, 73–4
Doherty, C., 48
doimliacc, 114
Domesday survey, 91
dominica/domnach, 12–14
Dooey, 185
'Doorty' Cross, Kilfenora, 140, 141, 143, 145
Down, County, 145
Down Survey, 53
Downpatrick, Co. Down, 145
Doyal, and Harris, R., 191–3
Dromkeare, Co. Kerry, 29
Dromlusk, Co. Kerry, 29
Dromore, Co. Waterford, 28
Drumard, Co. Derry, 92
Drumcliffe, Co. Sligo, 62
Drung Hill, Co. Kerry, 31
Dublin, 74, 202
    defences, 167
    diocese, 21, 170
    faunal remains, 60, 61–2
    Hiberno-Norse, 164–5, 172, 203
    houses, 55, 168–9
    mint, 148, 160
    silver-working, 156, 158
    watermill, 99
Dublin, County, 138
Dublin, Louth, 11
Dúchas, 2–3, 4
Dumville, C., 17

Dungarvan, Co. Waterford, 158
Dunshaughlin, Co. Meath, 18
Dunsilly Rath, Co. Antrim, 105
Dysert O'Dea, Co. Clare, 138, 140, 142
Dysert Oenghusa, Co. Limerick, 121

Early Medieval studies, 2
    archaeological texts, 195–7
    need for institute, 8
    radiocarbon dating, 4–5
East Anglia, 148
Easter Rebellion, 1916, 194
ecclesiastical settlements, 6, 34, 43–5. *see also* monasticism
    burial practices, 185–6
    changes in status, 44–5
excavations, 181–2
    field surveys, 34–5
    hoards, 158
    local centres, 46
    as monuments, 178, 184–5
    nunneries, 204
    ogham stones, 27, 28–9, 31
    wealth of, 47
'economic war,' 180–1
Edenvale, 153
Edwards, Nancy, 6, 137, 184, 186–7, 195–7
Emlagh East, Co. Kerry, 28, 29
Emly, Co. Tipperary, 19, 21
empiricism, 190–1
    despotism of fact, 191–3
    intellectual closure and Irish society, 193–5
    myth-making, 197–8
England, 12, 17, 55, 180–1, 196
    archaeobotany, 65
    church architecture, 112, 118, 119, 122, 172
    coins, 148
    ecclesiastical sites, 204
    empiricism, 193–4
    grave types, 106
    house-types, 170
    Irish settlements, 32
    mills, 94–5
    ogham stones, 25–6, 27
    Roman, 9–10, 11, 18
    shrines, 108
    silver, 133, 147, 158
environmental specialists, 4
Eoganachta, 19, 40
Erhard, archbishop of Armagh, 21
ethnoarchaeology, 57
Evans, E.E., 83, 182–3, 187

Fahamore, Co. Kerry, 62
Fahy, E., 34, 40
Fanning, T., 43–4, 182, 203
Farne Island, 106

Faunkill, Co. Cork, 29, 31
Fechin of Fore, St, 90, 91
Fenit, Co. Kerry, 149, 151, 153, 154, 157
Ferta Valley, Co. Kerry, 36
feudalism, 35, 48
Fianna Fáil, 180–1
field surveys, 34–5
field-boundaries, 23, 25, 31, 37
Finnian, St, 83
fish, evidence for, 61–2, 63
Flanagan, Deirdre, 12
Fled Briciu, 88, 97
folklore, 57–8
food studies, 201, 204
    cereal foods, 76–85
Fore, Co. Westmeath, 119
France, 122, 123
frumenty, 76–7
fulachta fiadh, 37
Funshion river, 37, 43

gable-shrines, 106–7
Gaelic Athletic Association, 179
Gaelic League, 179
Gaelic revival, 178–81
    and archaeology, 181–6
Gaelic Society, 180
Gaelic Union, 179
Gallarus Oratory, 114, 115
Galway, County, 11
Garranes, Co. Cork, 18, 40, 181
Garryduff, Co. Cork, 33
Gashagen, Gotland, 155
Gaul, 10, 14
    maritime traffic, 9–10
    ogham stones, 27, 31
    Patrick in, 18
    trade, 18, 32
Gearagh, Co. Cork, 57
gender studies, 6–7
geochemical surveys, 44
geophysical surveys, 44
Geraghty, S., 55
Germanus, bishop of Auxerre, 17
Germany, 20, 193–4
Giles, Henry, 179
Giot, P.R., 192
Giraldus Cambrensis, 98
Glamis, Scotland, 129
Glastonbury, England, 81
Gleensk, Co. Kerry, 31
Glenawillin, Co. Cork, 28
Glendalough, Co. Wicklow, 118, 121, 145
Glengarriff, Co. Cork, 149, 150–1, 153
Glin, Co. Kerry, 36
Glin North, 184

Goblet's Index of Parishes and Townlands of Ireland, 13
Gortnagullinagh, Co. Kerry, 28
Göttweig, Austria, 20
Govan, Scotland, 129
Grabar, A., 118
Graham, B.J., 35, 48
grave-sites, 44
    burial practices, 185–6
    Hiberno-Norse Waterford, 171
    Illaunloughan, 103, 106
    memoria buildings, 116, 118
    Viking, 164, 165
    women's cemeteries, 185, 204
Greek, 14
Greenhill, Co. Cork, 28
Griffith, Arthur, 180
gruels, 76–9, 84–5
Gubretha Caratniad, 25

hack-silver, 147, 148, 151, 154, 159
Haines, C.Y., 150
Hamlin, A. and Foley, C., 185
Hamlin, A., 27, 44
Hannon, Martha, 201
Harbison, P., 118, 119, 136, 172, 184
Harvard Expedition, 181
Haughey, Charles J., 1, 2, 193
hazel, 55, 97–8
Henry, Francoise, 34, 103, 138, 181
Henry II, King, 112
Herity, Michael, 114
Hiberno-Celtic Society, 180
high crosses, 202, 203, 204
    Ahenny Crosses, 127–33
    distribution maps, 126, 139
    early, 125–37
        chronology, 127, 129
    later, 138–46
        Group 1, 140–2
        Group 2, 142–5
    Ossory Group, 127
    Scripture Crosses, 127, 129
    wooden, 125–7, 133, 145
High Island, Co. Galway, 90, 99
Hisperica Famina, 112, 114
hoards, Viking, 147–60, 201, 202, 203
    chronology, 156–7
    distribution, 149, 157–8, 159
    ingots, 147–8, 151, 153–4
    in Ireland, 147–8
    in Munster, 148–51
    Munster silver-working, 154–6
    pennanular ingots, 154, 155–6
    regional question, 151–4
    'ring-money,' 154, 155–6, 157
honey, 80–1
horizontal-wheeled mills, 87–9, 94–5, 96–7

housing
    building techniques, 55
    Viking Waterford, 168–70
Hunterston Brooch, 129
Hurley, Maurice, 34, 44, 55, 202, 203
hut sites, 35, 36–7, 109–10

Ibar, St, 19–20
Ickham, Kent, 94, 95
Ikerrin, Co. Tipperary, 204–5
Illaunloughan, Co. Kerry, 4, 34, 74, 102–10, 201, 203
    domestic quarters, 109–10
    gable-shrine, 106–9
    oratory area, 104–6
Immram Maele Dúin, 91
Indarda Mochuda a rRaithin, 84
industrial archaeology, 1
Iniscealtra, Co. Clare, 18, 118, 140
    high cross, 127, 142–3
Inisfallen, Co. Kerry, 118
Inishmore, Co. Galway, 143
Inislounaght, 153, 158
Inismurray, Co. Sligo, 116
interdisciplinary studies, 6–8, 200–1
interlaced decoration, 129
inventory surveys, 34, 40
Invergowrie, Scotland, 129
Iona, 136–7
    women's cemetery, 185
Irish Archaeological Wetland Unit, 58
Irish Free State, 180, 194
Irish Penitential, An, 77, 78, 82
Irish Volunteers, 179
Iron Age, 203
iron-working, 46
    and myth-making, 197–8
Iserninus, 12, 18
Islandbridge cemetery, Dublin, 165
Isle of Skye, 156
Italy, 91, 92, 97, 118
Iveragh Peninsula, 102, 106, 181, 203

James, St, 108
Jeffries, H., 165, 170, 174
John Cassianus, 82
Journal of the Cork Historical and Archaeological Society, 180
Journal of the Royal Society of Antiquaries of Ireland, 180
Joyce, P.W., 80

Kealvaugh More, Co. Cork, 28, 31
Kedrah, Co. Tipperary, 6
Keenrath, Co. Cork, 28
Kells, Co. Meath, 116
    Cross of Patrick and Columba, 136–7
Kells, synod of, 1152, 21

Kelly, F., 73, 74, 136
Kenney, J.F., 19
Kerry, County, 23, 145
    archaeological survey, 5–6
    church building, 114, 115
    hoards, 154
    settlement sites, 34
Ketch, C., 55
Kilbarry, Co. Cork, 149, 150, 155, 157, 158
Kilbeg, Co. Waterford, 29
Kilcoolaght, Co. Kerry, 28
Kildare, 118, 204
    monastery, 91
Kildee, Co. Cork, 34
Kildreelig, 105
Kilfenora, Co. Clare, 140
    high crosses, 142–5
Kilfinnane, Co. Limerick, 6
Kilkenny, County, 153
Kilkieran Cross, 133, 136
Killabuonia, Iveragh, 106, 108
Killaloe Cathedral, Co. Clare, 143, 145
Killaloe diocese, 21
Killamery Cross, 127
Killanully, Co. Cork, 66, 68, 74
    large fill contexts, 71
    souterrain fills, 68, 70
Killarney, Co. Kerry, 58
kill/cell, 12–14
Killeagh, Co. Cork, 37, 44
Killeany, Inishmore, 143
Killederdadrum, Co. Tipperary, 44
killeen burial-grounds, 44
Killeen Cormac, Co. Kildare, 27
Killeenemer, Co. Cork, 44, 45
    facade, 120, 121
Killeshin, 18
Killevy, Co. Armagh, 204
Killinaboy, Co. Clare, 119
Killiney, Co. Dublin, 121
Killiney, Co. Kerry, 145
Killodiernan, Co. Tipperary
    window, 120, 121
Killoluaig, Iveragh, 106
Killoughan, Iveragh, 102
Kilmacomma, Co. Waterford, 149, 153, 154, 157, 158
Kilmaculla, Co. Cork, 44
Kilmainham cemetery, Dublin, 165
Kilmalkedar, Co. Kerry, 29, 119, 145
Kilnaughtin, Co. Kerry, 28
Kilpeacan, Iveragh, 106
Kilree Cross, 127
Kiltiernan, Co. Galway, 60
Kinard, Co. Kerry, 28
    ogham stone, 29
Knockdrum, Co. Cork, 44
Knockea, 181, 185

Knockmaon, Co. Waterford, 149, 150, 151, 154, 157, 158
Knockrour, Co. Cork, 92
Knockshanwee, Co. Cork, 29
Knowth, Co. Meath, 60, 62

Labbamolaga, Co. Cork, 44, 116, 117, 118
lacustrine settlement, 2
Lagin, 19
Lagore, Co. Meath, 59–60, 110, 181, 197
Laing, L. and J., 186
land ownership, 25, 180–1, 182
Landnamabok, 78
landscape interpretation, 42–3
Laois, County, 153
Latin
   loanwords, 12–14, 74
   and ogham, 10
Law of Ailbe, 19
Law of Patrick, 19
law tracts, 25, 197
   codification of, 46–7
   palaeobotany, 73
Lawlor, H.C., 181–2
Leacanabuaile, 181
leachta, 105–6, 114, 116
learned societies, 179–80
Leask, H., 112, 140, 181, 185
Lee, J.J., 181, 183, 194
Lee river, 32, 53, 74, 174
Leinster
   faunal remains, 59, 60, 62
   Latin literacy, 10, 14
   ogham, 11
   Palladius, 14, 18
   Ptolemy's placenames, 10
   urban development, 47
   Vikings, 152, 158, 159, 160
Letter, Co. Kerry, 29
Liathmore, Co. Tipperary, 118
Library of Ireland, 179
Life of Abban, 20
Life of Ailbe, 19
Life of Déclán, 19–20
Life of Patrick (fragment), 20
Life of St Albert, 21
Life of St Ciarán of Saigir, 19
Life of St Patrick (Tírechán), 19
Limbert, D., 33, 34
Limerick, County, 63, 145, 149, 153
   archaeological survey, 5, 6
Limerick city, 151, 155, 156, 157
   city wall, 167
   established, 157–8, 164, 165
   Hiberno-Norse, 167, 170, 172
Lindisfarne, 106
lintelled graves, 106

Lisduggan, Co. Cork, 33
Lisleagh, Co. Cork, 37–9, 40–1, 201
   charcoal studies, Lisleagh I, 57
   enclosing elements, 41–2
   faunal remains, 61
Lisleagh I
   large fill contexts, 70–1
   palaeobotany, 72
   stratigraphy, 74
   structural features, 71
Lisleagh II
   large fill contexts II, 70–1
   palaeobotany, 72
   souterrain fills, 68, 70
   structural features, 71
   palaeobotanical studies, 66–8
   palaeobotany, 73
Lismore, Co. Waterford, 21, 122, 172
Lismore Crozier, 145
Lisnagun, Co. Cork, 55, 66, 67
   large fill contexts, 70–1
   palaeobotany, 73
      hearth deposits, 72
      spreads and layers, 72
      structural features, 71
   souterrain fills, 68, 70
   stratigraphy, 74
Lissue, Co. Down, 42
literacy, 9
   Latin, 14–15
   in ogham, 10–11
littiu, 76, 84
Little Island, Co. Cork
   mills, 88, 89, 90, 94–5, 98
locational studies, 34–5
Loher, Co. Kerry, 66, 68
   large fill contexts, 70–1
   palaeobotany, 71
Lohort, Co. Cork, 149, 150, 155, 157, 158
Loichsi genealogies, 44–5
Lomanagh, Co. Cork, 29
long cists, 106
longphuirt, 148, 158–9, 164, 172, 175
Lorrha Crosses, 127, 133
Lough Gara belt-buckle, 133
Lough Gur, Co. Limerick, 33
Lough Kinale, Co. Longford, 133
Louth, County, 11
Lucas, A.T., 47, 76–85, 80, 84
Lugnagappul, Co. Kerry, 26, 28
Lynn, C.J., 33

Ma be rí ro-fesser, 25
Mac an Bhaird, Alan, 9
Macalister, R.A.S., 27, 181, 182, 183
MacCarthaig, Cormac, 122
McCarthy, Margaret, 201

McCarthys, 203
McCormick, F., 59–60, 62
McCracken, E., 53–4
McManus, D., 10, 25, 27–8, 29, 31
    ogham chronology, 31–2
MacNeill, Eoin, 179
Macroom, Co. Cork, 149, 150, 155, 157
Maedoc, St, 83
Mael Ruain, St, 77, 82–3
Maelsechnaill Mac Maelruanaid, 137
Magnum Legendarium Austriacum, 20
Mahon, B., 81
Mahr, Adolph, 181, 193–4
Maigue river, 53
Malchus, bishop of Waterford, 170, 171–2
Mallory, J.P. and McNeill, T.E., 37
Mallow, Co. Cork, 54
Manning, C., 28, 44
Manning, Co. Cork, 40–1, 44
Mansuetus, bishop of Toul, 20
manuscripts, illuminated, 203–4
Marshall, Jenny White, 103
Marsh's Library, 19
martyrdom, 116
martyrium buildings, 116–18
Martyrology of Óengus, 19, 102
Mashanaglass, Co. Cork, 90, 91, 92, 99
Meascán Maraíocht, 57
Meath, County, 12
memoria buildings, 116–18
menadach, 78–9
metal-working, 110, 133
myth-making, 197–8
    12th c., 138
Millockstown, 185
mills, 201
Milltown Malbay, Co. Clare, 154
millwright, craft of, 87–99, 202
    buildings and mechanism, 91–3
    declining craft, 96–9
    site layout, 89–91
    vertical-wheeled mills, 94–5
    woodworking technology, 93–4
Milverton, Co. Dublin, 90
Molaise of Devenish, St, 83
Moling, St, 91
Monaincha, Co. Tipperary, 140, 142
Monasterboice, Co. Louth
    doorway, 120, 121
    Muiredach's Cross, 136
Monastery of Tallaght, The, 78
monasticism, 12–13, 14, 15
    eremitical, 34
    Germany, 20
    penitential bread, 82–3
    proto-towns, 47, 48, 185
Monataggart, Co. Cork, 28, 29, 31

Moninne, St, 204
Monk, M. and Sheehan, J., 200, 203
Monk, M., 201, 202
Moore, F., 167–8, 202
morphology
    ringforts, 35, 41–2, 42–3
Morris, R., 185
Movius, 181
Moycraig, Co. Antrim, 92
Moylough Belt-Shrine, 129, 133
Moynagh Lough, Co. Meath, 60, 62, 203
muesli, 77
Muirchú, 17, 18
Muiredach's Cross, Monasterboice, 136
Mungret, Co. Limerick, 149, 151, 154, 157, 158, 159
Munster, 10, 21
Muskerry barony, Co. Cork, 54–5
Mytum, H., 41, 97, 186–7, 195–7

Nation, The, 179
National and Literary Society, 179
National Folklore Archive, 57
National Literary Society, 179
National Monuments Acts, 2
National Monuments and Historic Properties Division, Dúchas, 2–3
National Museum of Ireland, 57, 155
nationalism
    Gaelic revival, 178–81
    'Golden Age' myth, 178–87
    influence on archaeology, 181–6
Neligan (collector), 150
Nendrum, Co. Down, 181–2
Ninian's Isle hoard, 129
Nore river, 53
Northumbria, 148
Norway, 158

Ó Corráin, D., 36, 44, 45, 47, 48
Ó Cróinín, D., 6, 65, 186–7
Ó Giolláin, D., 195
Ó Murchadha, D. and Ó Murchu, G., 137
Ó Riain, P., 27
Ó Riain-Raedel, Dagmar, 202, 203
Ó Ríordáin, Seán P., 33, 40, 125–6, 181
Ó Sé, M., 81
oak
    decline, 96, 97–8
    regeneration, 48
O'Brien, E., 185
O'Briens, 21, 203
O'Connell, Daniel, 179
O'Connell, M., 48
O'Curry, E., 78
O'Donovan Rossa, Jeremiah, 179
O'Duggans, 40, 44
Oengus mac Nadfroich, King, 19

O'Flaherty, B.D., 34
ogham stones, 200, 202
    chronology, 27–8
    distribution, 11, 18, 24
    forfeda, 25
    functions, 23, 25, 31–2
    in Munster, 14–15, 23–32
    pagan or Christian?, 26–7
    script, 10–11, 25–6
    wood oghams, 25, 31
O'Grady, Standish, 179
O'Keeffe, T., 146, 203
O'Keeffes, 40
O'Kelly, Professor M.J., 1, 15, 33, 181, 183
    Church Island, 14, 34, 45, 112
    Giot on, 192
Ólchobhar mac Cinóida, king of Cashel, 172
Old Irish, 12–14
Old Island, Co. Waterford, 28
Old Kilcullen, Co. Meath, 18
Old Windsor mill, 95
O'Leary, John, 179
O'Loan, J., 79
O'Meara, T.J., 39
Omey Island, Co. Galway, 106, 116
O'Neill, H., 179
O'Neill Hencken, H., 181
O'Rahilly, T.F., 9
origin myths, 178
Ossianic Society, 180
Ossory/Osraige, 19, 145
O'Sullivan, A. and Sheehan, J., 103
O'Sullivan, Jerry, 201
Oughtmama, Co. Clare, 118, 119

palaeobotanical studies
    comparison of selected evidence, 66–8
    comparison with documentary sources, 73–4
    contextual comparisons, 68–72
    preservation sampling, 66
Palladius, 9–10, 11–12, 14, 15, 20, 21
    and Patrick, 18–19
    role of, 17–18
Palmerstown, Co. Dublin, 121
palynology, 53, 56–7
Patrick, St, 9, 11–12, 19–20, 21, 105
    conversion of King Oengus, 19
    cult of, 17–19
Patterson, N., 195–7
Pearse, Patrick, 180
Pelagius, 17
Pembrokeshire, 11
Penitential of Finnian, 80
Peter, St, 20
Petrie, George, 179, 185
Pictish slabs, 129, 133
pilgrims, 108–9

Pitt-Rivers, 150
placenames, 44
platform ringforts, 48
Pliny, 78, 81
Plummer, C., 25
pollen analysis, 46, 48
    woodlands, 56–7
Pope, Alexander, 125
population, 46–7
porridges, 76–9, 84–5
Porter, Kingsley, 133
Portugal, 92, 95
pottery, 18, 32, 114
Praeger, Lloyd, 27
Prehistoric Society, 181
Proceedings of the Royal Irish Academy, 180
processual archaeology, 186, 196
Prosper of Aquitaine, 12, 17
Proudfoot, B., 33, 40, 182
Ptolemy, map of, 9

qremiter, 13–14
querns, 65, 81

Rackham, O., 53–4
radiocarbon dating, 4–5, 203
    Illaunloughan, 104, 106, 108
    mortar, 116, 121
    settlement sites, 36–7
    shell midden, 62
    Skellig Michael, 114
Raftery, Barry, 185
Raftery, Joseph, 181
Raheens, Co. Cork, 60, 62
Rahtz, P., 185
raised raths, 63
Rasharkin, Co. Antrim, 92
Ratass, Co. Kerry, 29, 119–21
    doorway, 122
rath mounds, 48
Rathbarry, Co. Cork, 149
Rathbreasail, Synod of, 145
Rathmooley, Co. Tipperary, 149, 151, 154, 155, 157, 158
Rathmullen, Co. Sligo, 62
Ratoo, Co. Kerry
    doorway, 120, 121
Reask, Co. Kerry, 18, 34, 43–4, 103–4, 106, 182
Reefert, Co. Wicklow
    doorway, 120, 121, 122
Regensburg, 20, 21
regionalism, 202–3
Regula Sancti Benedicti, 82
Reid, Clement, 81
rescue archaeology, 2–4, 35
Ringerike ornament, 138, 143

ringforts, 202
   archetypal farmsteads, 182–4
   clusters, 37, 40–1
   dating of, 35
   defensive ability, 48
   definitions of, 35
   and ecclesiastical sites, 44–5
   faunal remains, 60
   field surveys, 34–5
   hoards, 158
   in isolation, 40
   palaeobotany, 74
   in retrospect, 33–4
   socio-cultural context, 40–1
Rinnagan, Co. Roscommon, 129, 136
Rockfield, Co. Kerry, 29, 31
Roe, Helen, 127, 136
Roman empire
   mills, 93–5
   names in ogham, 11
Roman world, 118, 196
   influence of, 9–15, 186, 203
   pottery, 114
Romanesque architecture, 121, 122–3, 138, 203, 204
   ornament, 140, 142, 143
Rome, 17, 18
Roscrea, Co. Tipperary, 122, 145
   high cross, 140, 142
   Pillar, 127
Ross Island, Co. Kerry, 202
Rossach, Co. Cork, 44
Rosscarbery, Co. Cork, 21
round towers, 119
   doorways, 120, 121, 122
Rourke, Grellan D., 103
routeways, 37, 39, 44
Royal Irish Academy, 1
royal sites, 44
Rule of Ailbe of Emly, 79, 80, 81, 82
Rule of Tallaght, 77
Rule of the Céli Dé, 77
runes, 143
Ryan, Michael, 186, 195
Rynne, Colin, 201, 202
Rynne, Etienne, 33, 145

St Andrews, Scotland, 129
St Columba's 'House,' Kells, 116
St Crónán's, Roscrea, 142
St Declan's 'House,' Ardmore, 116, 117
St Finbarr's monastery, Cork, 170, 172
St John's river, Waterford, 166
St Kevin's Church, Glendalough, 121
St Macdara's church, Co. Galway, 119
St Malo pump house, 94
St Mary's church, Waterford, 171–2

St Michael's Church, Skellig Michael, 114, 115, 116
St Olaf's church, Waterford, 171–2
St Patrick's Cross, Cashel, 138, 140, 142
St Peter's Cathedral, Lichfield, 108
Sainthill, 150
saints, pre-Patrician, 6, 17–21
sally gardens, 55
salt, 80
scallop shells, 108
Schottenklöster, 20, 21
Scoti, 12
Scotland, 129, 136, 147, 148
   hoards, 154, 158
Scott, B.G., 197–8
Secundinus, 18
Seemochuda, Co. Waterford, 28
Segetius, 12
Seir Kieran cross-base, 127
Senchas Már, 81
settlement sites, 7, 33–49, 202–3
   archetypal farmsteads, 178, 182–4
   Caherlehillan project, 35–7
   ecclesiastical, 34, 43–5
   field surveys, 34–5
   Lisleagh project, 37–9
   population expansion, 46–9
   ringforts, 40–3
   secular, 33–4
   socio-political developments, 46–9
   unenclosed, 6, 35, 37, 48, 184
Sexton, R., 73, 201, 204
Shamrock, the, 179
Shanks, M. and Tilley, C., 195–7
Shannon river, 9, 133, 150, 154, 156, 157
Sharpe, 19–20
Sheehan, J., 47, 202, 203
shell middens, 62, 108
shrines, 116, 118
silver, 47, 48
   bullion economy, 159–60
   Viking hoards, 147–60
silver-working, 154–6, 158
Sinn Féin, 180, 194
Skellig Michael, Co. Kerry, 102, 114, 115, 116, 133
   oratory, 105, 106
Skibbereen, Co. Cork, 34, 40
slaves, 48
Sligh Dála, Co. Laois, 39
Society for the Protection of the Irish Language, 179
soil analysis, 61
souterrains, 48, 184, 202
   hoards, 158
   and hut sites, 37
   infill deposits, 66, 68, 70
   ogham stones, 26, 27, 28, 29, 31
South Cross, Clonmacnois, 127, 133–7
Spain, 92, 97, 108

Stalley, R., 136
Stokes, M., 179, 185
Stout, M., 33–4, 39, 46–7, 183, 187
Suir river, 53, 55, 166
Sullivan, A.M., 179
Sutton Hoo bowls, 133
Sweetman, D., 34
Swift, C., 27

Tannahill, R., 78
taphonomy, 59, 65, 66
Tara, Co. Meath, 179
Tara Brooch, 129
taxation, units of, 56
Teach Molaise, Inismurray, 116
Teaching of Mael Ruain, The, 82–3
Teampall Chiaráin, Clonmacnois, 116, 118
Teampall Chrónáin, 118, 119
technology, role of, 204
Teermoyle, Co. Kerry, 28–9
Temple MacDuagh, Co. Clare, 116
Temple Martin, Co. Kerry, 114
Templebrecan, Inishmore, 143
theoretical archaeology, 5
Thomas, Charles, 2, 6, 8, 103, 200, 202, 203
    ecclesiastical sites, 34, 43
    ogham stones, 26, 27
Thomond, 20
Thurneysen, R., 83
tide mills, 87
Tierney, John, 201, 202
Tinnahally, Co. Cork, 29
Tinnahally, Co. Kerry, 29
Tipperary, County, 56, 63, 122, 149, 157
    archaeological survey, 5, 6
    high crosses, 127
Tirechan, 17, 18, 19, 105
tiuglagin, 78
Togail Bruidne Da Derga, 97
Togherstown, Co. Westmeath, 133
tomb-shrines, 106–7, 116
Tonaknock, Co. Kerry, 145
Townland Index, 1871, 13
trade, 18, 32, 40
    role of towns, 47–8
    Vikings, 148, 170, 172
Triad 106, 87
Triad 184, 83
Trigger, B., 178–87, 191, 193
Trinity College Library, 19
Tuam, Co. Galway, 21, 143
    Cathedral, 143
Tuamgraney, Co. Clare, 118, 119
tuath, unit of, 56
Tullyallen, Co. Armagh, 33
Twohig, Dermot, 165, 174

Tybroughney 'Pillar', 127
type-sites, 5, 7

Ua Briain, Muirchertach, 145
Ua Lothcáin, Cuán, 87
Uí Liatháin, 18
Ulster, 12, 13, 59, 97, 158
Ulster Journal of Archaeology, 180
University College, Cork, 1, 6, 200
    archaeobotany, 66
    Caherlehillan project, 35–7
Uraicecht Becc, 87
urban archaeology, 3–4, 58
urban development, 47, 48
    'Hiberno-Norse,' 164
    and monasticism, 185
    Vikings, 147, 148, 157–8, 164–75, 203
Urnes ornament, 138, 140

Valencia, Co. Cork, 44, 105, 110, 203
vallum, 34, 44
vertical-wheeled mills, 87, 94–5, 96
Vikings, 47, 48, 62, 127, 136, 137. *see also* hoards
    houses, 55, 57
    ornament, 138
    settlements, 157–8
    towns, 164–75

Wakeman, D.F., 179
Wales, 10, 11, 14, 185–6
    Déisi in, 18
    ogham stones, 25
warfare, 48
Warner, Richard, 9
Waterford, County, 23, 55, 145
    archaeological survey, 5, 6
Waterford city, 3, 6, 9, 21, 74, 155, 156, 201
    Hiberno-Norse, 172, 175
    Viking, 157, 158, 164, 165–72
        Christianity and churches, 170–2
        town layout and houses, 57, 168–70
water-mills, 46
Wearmouth, 118
Wexford, County, 153
Wexford town, 61–2, 155, 172
Whitefield, Co. Kerry, 28
Whithorn, 106, 129
Wicklow, County, 138
Windele, J., 150
wine trade, 18
women, role of, 204
Wood Martin, W.G., 179
woodlands, 53–8, 202
    charcoal studies, 56, 57
    clearances, 46

distribution and extent, 53–5
   mill construction, 97–8
   oak, 48
   pollen analysis, 56–7
   resource management, 55–6
   and society, 57–8
Woodman, P.C., 150–1, 179, 192
woodmanship, 55–6
Woods, the, Co. Cork, 29

woodworking
   millwrights, 91–4
   technology, 93–4
wool production, 60

yew wood, 98
Youghal, Co. Cork, 54
Young, Arthur, 57–8
Young Ireland League, 179